For the Next Generation

AF767082

For the Next Generation

Mental Health in Asian American/Pacific Islander Youth

Edited by Nancy H. Liu

*University of California,
Berkeley*

WILEY

Copyright © 2026 by John Wiley and Sons. All rights reserved, including rights for text and data mining and training of artificial intelligence technologies or similar technologies.

Published by John Wiley & Sons, Inc., Hoboken, New Jersey.

No part of this publication may be reproduced, stored in a retrieval system, or transmitted in any form or by any means, electronic, mechanical, photocopying, recording, scanning, or otherwise, except as permitted under Section 107 or 108 of the 1976 United States Copyright Act, without either the prior written permission of the Publisher, or authorization through payment of the appropriate per-copy fee to the Copyright Clearance Center, Inc., 222 Rosewood Drive, Danvers, MA 01923, (978) 750-8400, fax (978) 750-4470, or on the web at www.copyright.com. Requests to the Publisher for permission should be addressed to the Permissions Department, John Wiley & Sons, Inc., 111 River Street, Hoboken, NJ 07030, (201) 748-6011, fax (201) 748-6008, or online at http://www.wiley.com/go/permission.

The manufacturer's authorized representative according to the EU General Product Safety Regulation is Wiley-VCH GmbH, Boschstr. 12, 69469 Weinheim, Germany, e-mail: Product_Safety@wiley.com.

Trademarks: Wiley and the Wiley logo are trademarks or registered trademarks of John Wiley & Sons, Inc. and/or its affiliates in the United States and other countries and may not be used without written permission. All other trademarks are the property of their respective owners. John Wiley & Sons, Inc. is not associated with any product or vendor mentioned in this book.

Limit of Liability/Disclaimer of Warranty: While the publisher and the authors have used their best efforts in preparing this work, including a review of the content of the work, neither the publisher nor the authors make any representations or warranties with respect to the accuracy or completeness of the contents of this work and specifically disclaim all warranties, including without limitation any implied warranties of merchantability or fitness for a particular purpose. No warranty may be created or extended by sales representatives, written sales materials or promotional statements for this work. The fact that an organization, website, or product is referred to in this work as a citation and/or potential source of further information does not mean that the publisher and authors endorse the information or services the organization, website, or product may provide or recommendations it may make. This work is sold with the understanding that the publisher is not engaged in rendering professional services. The advice and strategies contained herein may not be suitable for your situation. You should consult with a specialist where appropriate. Further, readers should be aware that websites listed in this work may have changed or disappeared between when this work was written and when it is read. Neither the publisher nor authors shall be liable for any loss of profit or any other commercial damages, including but not limited to special, incidental, consequential, or other damages.

For general information on our other products and services or for technical support, please contact our Customer Care Department within the United States at (800) 762-2974, outside the United States at (317) 572-3993 or fax (317) 572-4002.

Wiley also publishes its books in a variety of electronic formats. Some content that appears in print may not be available in electronic formats. For more information about Wiley products, visit our web site at www.wiley.com.

Library of Congress Cataloging-in-Publication Data has been applied for:

Paperback: 9781394299782
ePDF: 9781394299805
epub: 9781394299799
obook: 9781394299812

Cover Design: Wiley
Cover Images: © Nancy H. Liu, © anand purohit/Getty Images,
© alzajac/Getty Images

Printed and bound by CPI Group (UK) Ltd, Croydon, CR0 4YY

C9781394299782_150726

For 爸爸, who always within him the next generation.

For Ethan & Lucas, who are the next generation.

Table of Contents

List of Contributors

David Abramson
New York University School of Global Public Health
New York
NY
USA

Savannah Badt
Tulane University Celia Scott Weatherhead School of Public Health and Tropical Medicine
New Orleans
LA
USA

Annie Bae
UC Angeles, UCLA School of Education and Information Studies
Los Angeles
CA
USA

Surina Bothra
PAU-Stanford PsyD Consortium
Palo Alto
CA
USA

Stephen H. Chen
Department of Psychology
Wellesley College
Wellesley
MA
USA

Belinda C. Chen
Department of Psychology
University of California
Los Angeles
CA
USA

Eileen J. Cheng
Department of Asian Languages and Literatures
Pomona College
Claremont
CA
USA

Danielle L. Carreira Ching
The Baker Center for Children and Families
Boston
MA
USA

Hawai'i Pacific University
Honolulu
HI
USA

Joyce Chu
Palo Alto University
Palo Alto
CA
USA

Sara Chung
University of California
San Francisco
CA
USA

Sheri-Ann Daniels
Papa Ola Lokahi
Honolulu
HI
USA

Jannette Diep
BPSOS/Houston
Houston
TX
USA

Mai P. Do
Tulane University Celia Scott Weatherhead School of Public Health and Tropical Medicine
New Orleans
LA
USA

Jillian M.N. Freitas
University of Hawai'i at Manoa
Honolulu
HI
USA

Deborah Goebert
University of Hawai'i at Manoa
Honolulu
HI
USA

Emily Goldmann
Boston University School of Public Health
Boston
MA
USA

Janie J. Hong
Stanford University School of Medicine and Redwood Center for CBT and Research
Stanford
CA
USA

Caleb Hui
Berkeley, Political Economy
Berkeley
CA
USA

Fatima Z. Hussain
Palo Alto University
Palo Alto
CA
USA

Russell Jeung
SF State, Asian American Studies
San Francisco
CA
USA

Melissa Kahili-Heede
Papa Ola Lokahi
Honolulu
HI
USA

Samantha Keaulana
Papa Ola Lokahi
Honolulu
HI
USA

Julie Heejung Kim
California Pacific Medical Center, Psychiatry
San Francisco
CA
USA

Anna S. Lau
Department of Psychology
University of California
Los Angeles
CA
USA

PhuongThao D. Le
Boston University School of Public Health
Boston
MA
USA

Yutian Li
Harvard College
Cambridge
MA
USA

Anne Li
Boston University Chobanian and Avedisian School of Medicine
Boston
MA
USA

Cindy Liu
Brigham and Women's Hospital/Harvard Medical School
Boston
MA
USA

Richard T. Liu
Massachusetts General Hospital
Boston
MA
USA

Felix Lou
Vanderbilt University
Nashville
TN
USA

Hang Ngo
New York University School of Global Public Health
New York
NY
USA

Kelsie H. Okamura
The Baker Center for Children and Families
Boston
MA
USA

University of Pennsylvania
Philadelphia
PA
USA

Teya Ozgen
Staples High School
Westport
CT
USA

Summer Pascual
Department of Psychology
University of California
Los Angeles
CA
USA

Tessa Palafu
The Baker Center for Children and Families
Boston
MA
USA

Ami Patel
Department of Counseling
Higher Education, & Special Education
University of Maryland
College Park
MD
USA

Davis Rehuher
University of Hawai'i at Manoa
Honolulu
HI
USA

Lorinda Riley
University of Hawai'i at Manoa
Honolulu
HI
USA

Rainer Schmitz
Dwight Schools
New York
NY
USA

Abigail Sedlar-Yamada
SF State, Asian American Studies
San Francisco
CA
USA

John W. Seipp
Department of Counseling
Higher Education, & Special Education
University of Maryland
College Park
MD
USA

Anamalia Anusaga Su'esu'e
University of Hawai'i at Manoa
Honolulu
HI
USA

Sione Tafune
Kahuku Medical Center
Kahuku
HI
USA

Boaz Tang
SF State, Asian American Studies
San Francisco
CA
USA

Jeanne L. Tsai
Department of Psychology
Stanford University
Stanford
CA
USA

Christy Wang
Department of Psychological & Brain Sciences
Washington University in St. Louis
St. Louis
MO
USA

Cixin Wang
Department of Counseling
Higher Education, & Special Education
University of Maryland
College Park
MD
USA

Aya Inamori Williams
Santa Clara University
Santa Clara
CA
USA

Jiawei Wu
Fordham University
Bronx
NY
USA

Angela M. Yang
Lynch School of Education and Human Development
Boston College
Chestnut Hill
MA
USA

Lawrence H. Yang
Duke School of Nursing
Duke University
Durham
NC
USA

Alyssa Yeh
SF State, Asian American Studies
San Francisco
CA
USA

Tiffany Yip
Fordham University
Bronx
NY
USA

Nadia Yoshizumi-Kim
The Baker Center for Children and Families
Boston
MA
USA

Stephanie H. Yu
Department of Psychiatry and Behavioral Sciences
University of California
San Francisco
CA
USA

Maria Zhang
Pomona College
Pomona
CA
USA

Qing Zhou
University of California
Berkeley
CA
USA

Acknowledgments

The community of scholars and expertise gathered in this book was built through a grant funded by the Asian American Research Center at the University of California, Berkeley. Those initial conversational sparks led to more connections and collaborations, many ongoing; all of which we hope will continue to yield good things for the next generation.

Introduction

Creating a New Narrative, Creating a New Conversation

In effective mental health treatments for individuals, couples, and families, there is always a shifting of narratives: those stories repeated within an individual and with close others. From that narrative shift comes new ways of being, feeling, interacting, engaging. The status quo is disrupted until a new normal arises, settling into a healthier equilibrium. This is the goal of our book—to intentionally shift the narratives about Asian American, Native Hawaiian, and Pacific Islander (AANHPI) youth mental health; and from that, to shift the dialogue to our available solutions, strengths, hopes.

Although the topic is not new, the conversation about mental health requires a shift: from a one about underutilization, stigma, and limited access and expanded to creative community-building solutions, interdisciplinary integration, and drawing from that deep reservoir of cultural wealth, our generational inheritance. It also changes those involved in the conversation. Once it was only limited to mental health professionals and now it is expanded and contextualized, to bring into the fold community leaders, educators, social activists, advocates, families, and peers. We cannot do this alone.

This conversational shift is more important than ever. There is currently, as popular media and scientific journals alike highlight, a youth mental health crisis (Center for Disease Control, 2025). The kids, as they say, are not alright. Current events and published research continue to proffer grim foreboding about the doom and gloom of our next generation, from elementary-school age children to the mental health crisis on college campuses (Patel & Lewis, 2023). Meanwhile, growing concerns about AANHPI mental health are ever present. Between 2000 and 2019, Asian Americans and Pacific Islanders (AAPIs) grew by 81%, making them the fastest growing ethnic-racial group in the United States (Pew Research Center, 2021). Suicide looms as the leading cause of death among AANHPI youth (Reyes et al., 2024). Frequently cited statistics emphasize low utilization and high stigma rates (Takeuchi et al., 2007; Sue et al., 2012; Lee et al., 2020). Few however, distill what has been learned from those on the frontline tackling and addressing these issues in recent decades and improving upon what we already do.

With this edited book, several narrative shifts are emphasized. The first builds upon the long lineage of AANHPI mental health expertise—and integrates what is already known about biases extant treatment models, from ethnocentrism (Sue et al., 2024) to hyperindividualism, (Wendt et al., 2015). For this reason, chapter content is inherently communal and contextual, written by our foremost experts on emotion socialization processes in immigrant families and family-based interventions (Chapter 2), culturally responsive treatments (Chapter 5), and culturally-adapted suicide risk frameworks (Chapter 7). In addition, important constructs from the empirical literature—often stuck in the ivory tower—are brought forward for direct integration into clinical practice, including ethnic-racial socialization (Chapter 1) and ideal affect (Chapter 3).

The second shift ensures that the conversation is contemporary and relevant to the youth of *our* time. We include mixed-race individuals, too often unaddressed in the literature, who are a growing part of our AANHPI youth community (Chapter 1). We integrate anti-Asian hate which, with the Stop AAPI Hate movement (Chapter 11), opened the door to new conversations by making visible what was previously invisible and too long silenced in our communities. Interdisciplinary perspectives are intentionally enfolded into this work—from ethnic studies, sociology, public health, and literature. In addition, we directly address rather than simply acknowledge the problem of the "monolith." For too long, East Asian American perspectives have been centered, despite heterogeneity within the AANHPI umbrella. Recent Pew Research Center (2021) results suggest that most Asian Americans do not consider themselves "Asian American" and instead identify more with their subgroup. As disaggregation becomes the norm, we intentionally center and give voice to underrepresented groups, with specific chapters dedicated to Pacific Islanders (Chapter 9) and Native Hawaiians (Chapter 10) and refugee populations (Chapter 12). Beyond this, contemporary issues of neurodiversity (Chapter 7) and engaging in social activism (Chapter 11) have necessitated specificity in our solutions. Last but not least, AANHPIs endorse significant religiosity and spirituality and this has implications for mental health. Yet religion and spirituality are rarely discussed in diversity training for mental health professionals (Vieten & Lukoff, 2022), which warranted a focus (Chapter 5).

The third shift expands the settings where services are delivered and the individuals delivering them. Youth mental health need not be limited to clinics and hospitals. After all, professional need not have the corner on mental health. Community-based work emphasizes meeting people where they are at rather than requiring them to come to us, a barrier for most AANHPIs. Global mental health has many creative options on offer with technology and task-shifting (Velez-Grau & Alvarez, 2024). Task-shifting focuses on training nonspecialists to do the work specialized expert and has broadened—beyond simply the clinicians—who can address youth mental health: educators, parents, peers, and even the role of self-help, through technology. Thus, we spotlight school-based interventions, especially related to bullying (Chapter 6), digital mental health for AANHPIs in natural disaster-prone areas (Chapter 12), and the "accidental therapy" that can happen in college courses (Chapter 13), as students gain deepened perspectives and about themselves and others through understanding literature, history, and popular media, to name just a few.

Overall, these shifts are intertwined, creating threads woven across chapters. For example, ideal affect is important for understanding bullying when affective mismatches abound. Additionally, strengths-based ethnic-racial socialization messages can be enhanced through education in both caregiver-child conversations and teachers who promote this within school curricula. Another throughline is identifying sources of resilience and empowerment, which can include family and community, enhanced models of well-being, and the riches of cultural heritage. In this book, we do not want to repeat the same old story; we instead wanted to flex AANHPI strengths. Every chapter aims at practical applications, including a clinical case illustration and key take-home points—the current crisis necessitates solutions.

From its incipience, this book was created within community, acknowledging that what will get us to our goal requires collective effort. Through another research project on AANHPI mental health, a group of interdisciplinary experts was tasked with identifying the limitations of our current efforts and steps for paving paths forward (Liu & Chen, 2026). And, as with the most meaningful efforts, this gathering was immensely fruitful: meetings led to more meetings, sparked new ideas for projects, led to familiar faces at conferences, and enfolded in more collaborators. This edited book, one of its results, was similar to hosting a large banquet feast where extended family and friends gathered to share insights, gossip (of the constructive, interdependent kind), and actively problem-solve our shared concerns. It was a counternarrative to the prevailing storyline of silos, individualism, and the lone genius of academia. Instead, we know that good community is characterized by mutuality and reciprocity, with a bountiful impact. And, as with any family gathering, we extend our banquet table to invite an even wider community—you, our reader.

References

Center for Disease Control (2025). Youth mental health: The numbers. Last accessed on November 3, 2025, available at https://www.cdc.gov/healthy-youth/mental-health/mental-health-numbers.html

Lee, M., Bhimla, A., Lu, W., & Ma, G. X. (2020). Correlates of mental health treatment receipt among Asian Americans who perceived mental health problems. *J. Behav. Health Serv. Res.*, *48*, 199–212. https://doi.org/10.1007/s11414-020-09704-6.

Liu, N. H., & Chen, S. (2026). Expanding psychotherapeutic intervention frameworks for Asian American & Pacific Islander mental health: qualitative synthesis of multidisciplinary perspectives. *Clin. Psychol. Sci.* https://journals.sagepub.com/doi/10.1177/21677026251392853.

Patel, B. P., & Lewis, B. (2023). Responding to the crisis in college mental health: a call to action. *J. Pediatr.*, *257*. https://doi.org/10.1016/j.jpeds.2023.02.036.

Pew Research Center (2021). Key facts about Asian Americans, a diverse and growing population. Last accessed on August 8, 2024 at: https://www.pewresearch.org/short-reads/2021/04/29/key-facts-about-asian-americans/

Reyes, M.P., Song, I., & Bhatt, A. (2024). Breaking the silence: An epidemiological report onAsian American and Pacific Islander youth mental health and suicide (1999–2021). *Child and Adolesc. Ment. Health, 29*, 136–144. https://doi.org/10.1111/camh.12708.

Sue, S., Cheng, J. K. Y., Saad, C. S., & Chu, J. P. (2012). Asian American mental health: a call to action. *Am. Psychol.*, *67*, 532–544. https://doi.org/10.1037/a0028900.

Sue, D. W., Neville, H. A., & Smith, L. (2024). Racism in counseling and psychotherapy: illuminate and disarm. *Am. Psychol.*, *79*, 593–605. https://doi.org/10.1037/amp0001231.

Takeuchi, D. T., Zane, N., Hong, S., Chae, D. H., Gong, F., Gee, G. C. ... Alegria, M. (2007). Immigration-related factors and mental disorders among Asian Americans. *Am. J. Public Health, 97*, 84–90. https://doi.org/10.2105/AJPH.2006.088401.

Velez-Grau, C., & Alvarez, K. (2024). Looking at global mental health models to prevent youth suicide in the United States. *J. Adolesc. Health*, *75*, 700–702. https://doi.org/10.1016/j.jadohealth.2024.07.022.

Vieten, C., & Lukoff, D. (2022). Spiritual and religious competencies in psychology. *Am. Psychol.*, *77*, 26–38. https://doi.org/10.1037/amp0000821.

Wendt, D. C., Gone, J. P., & Nagata, D. K. (2015). Potentially harmful therapy and multicultural counseling: Bridging two disciplinary discourses. *Couns. Psychol.*, *43*, 334–358. https://doi.org/10.1177/0011000014548280.

1

Ethnic and Racial Identity Development and Mental Health Among AANHPI Youth

Tiffany Yip[1], Jiawei Wu[1], Felix Lou[2], Teya Ozgen[3], Yutian Li[4], and Cindy Liu[5]

[1]*Fordham University, Bronx, NY, USA*
[2]*Vanderbilt University, Nashville, TN, USA*
[3]*Staples High School, Westport, CT, USA*
[4]*Harvard College, Cambridge, MA, USA*
[5]*Brigham and Women's Hospital/Harvard Medical School, Boston, MA, USA*

What Is Ethnic-racial Identity?

Ethnic-racial identity (ERI) refers to a person's connection to a specific cultural group, shaped by shared language, traditions, and ancestry, and the process of having agency to explore and connect with heritage (Phinney, 1990; Umaña-Taylor et al., 2004). More than just ancestry, aspects of ERI drive how people internalize and express their cultural heritage. An important feature of ethnic identity is that it is fluid and evolving. People engage in a process of developing an ethnic identity, which involves exploration (i.e., searching for the meaning of one's ethnicity and race) and commitment (i.e., a clear understanding of the role of ethnicity and race in one's life and identity). This developmental process is influenced by lived experiences within family, peers, and broader society. ERI also includes how society assigns significance to physical differences, such as skin color, facial features, and hair texture. When considering race in identity development, we consider societal structures and historical contexts that influence how people of different racial groups are treated (Helms, 1995). As a social construct, race is not considered an inherent, biological characteristic, but a construct shaped by society. Here, the racial aspects of identity development affect how people are perceived and treated in terms of power, privilege, and discrimination. These influences inform the context of one's ethnic and racial identity including dimensions such as centrality (i.e., the relative importance of ethnicity and race in one's overall self-concept), private regard (i.e., how positively one feels about their ethnic and racial group membership), and public regard (i.e., how positively one thinks that others view their ethnic and racial group; Sellers et al., 1997).

As we describe later in this chapter, experiences that take place in schools and social media shape this development further. A meaningful and integrated sense of self rooted in positive engagement with their ethnic and racial background (Phinney, 1990; Umaña-Taylor et al., 2004) serves as a foundation for optimal mental health. Asian American, Native Hawaiians, and Pacific Islanders (AANHPIs) may or may not make a distinction, and ethnic vs. racial (or vice versa) aspects of identity may be more prominent for particular individuals based on their experience. Research on ERI development among AANHPIs remains less extensive than research on other racial and ethnic groups. Much of the literature on ERI in the United States has focused on the Black–White binary (i.e., Black individuals are racialized in the context of Whiteness). However, scholars have increasingly examined AANHPI ERI, particularly with population growth among Asians within the United States. Much of the ERI research has focused on how AANHPI youth navigate the complexities of bicultural or hybrid identity development as they balance their ethnic cultural heritage with mainstream American culture. For instance, cultural values such as family expectations shape ethnic identity. Increased research on ERI development among AANHPIs focuses on the unique experiences of racial discrimination and microaggression. As we describe later, these include stereotypes disproportionately faced by Asian Americans (e.g., model minority myth).

Overall, the ERI development of AANHPI youth is a dynamic, multifaceted process shaped by different unique factors like cultural socialization, bicultural stress, racial discrimination, and family context. AANHPI adolescents often negotiate continuously, balancing heritage and mainstream cultures while navigating unique social challenges. Understanding these complexities is essential for developing culturally informed frameworks that support positive identity formation and well-being among AANHPI populations.

ERI Development

Although adolescence is a focal period for identity development, ERI development can be a lifelong process that shapes individuals' self-concept, social interactions, and well-being (Williams et al., 2020). ERI development is a complex and challenging process; 20% AANHPI young people reported wanting to be of a different ethnicity (TAAF, 2024). One of the most widely used theories and measures of ERI was developed by Phinney (Phinney, 1990). Phinney's model outlines ERI development across three stages: (1) Unexamined: passively accepting societal norms without critically engaging with their ethnic and racial background; (2) Search: triggered by experiences of discrimination or cultural exposure, prompts individuals to explore their heritage; (3) Achieved: individuals develop a secure, integrated sense of ethnic and racial self-concept after active exploration. Phinney's model assumes a linear progression in ERI development, supported by cognitive developmental foundations. As an example, Piaget's cognitive development theory (Piaget, 1971) charts key socio-cognitive milestones that intersect with contextual exposures (e.g., racism, discrimination) and societal influences (e.g., stereotypes) to lay the foundation for ERI development from childhood to adulthood (Figure 1.1).

While models of ERI development provide a broad understanding of how children construct their ERIs over time, the experience of the AANHPI population presents unique considerations. AANHPI youth navigate their identity by balancing their heritage culture with the mainstream American culture.

Juggling Multiples: Multicultural, Multiracial, and Multiethnic Considerations. A defining feature of AANHPI youth ERI development in the United States is the need to navigate more than one cultural experience (e.g., Asian American home and the broader, mainstream US society). Often, this requires balancing AANHPI cultural influences in predominantly White spaces, even if the family lives in an ethnically and racially diverse neighborhood. In part, this is because "American" is still associated with Whiteness (Cheryan & Monin, 2005).

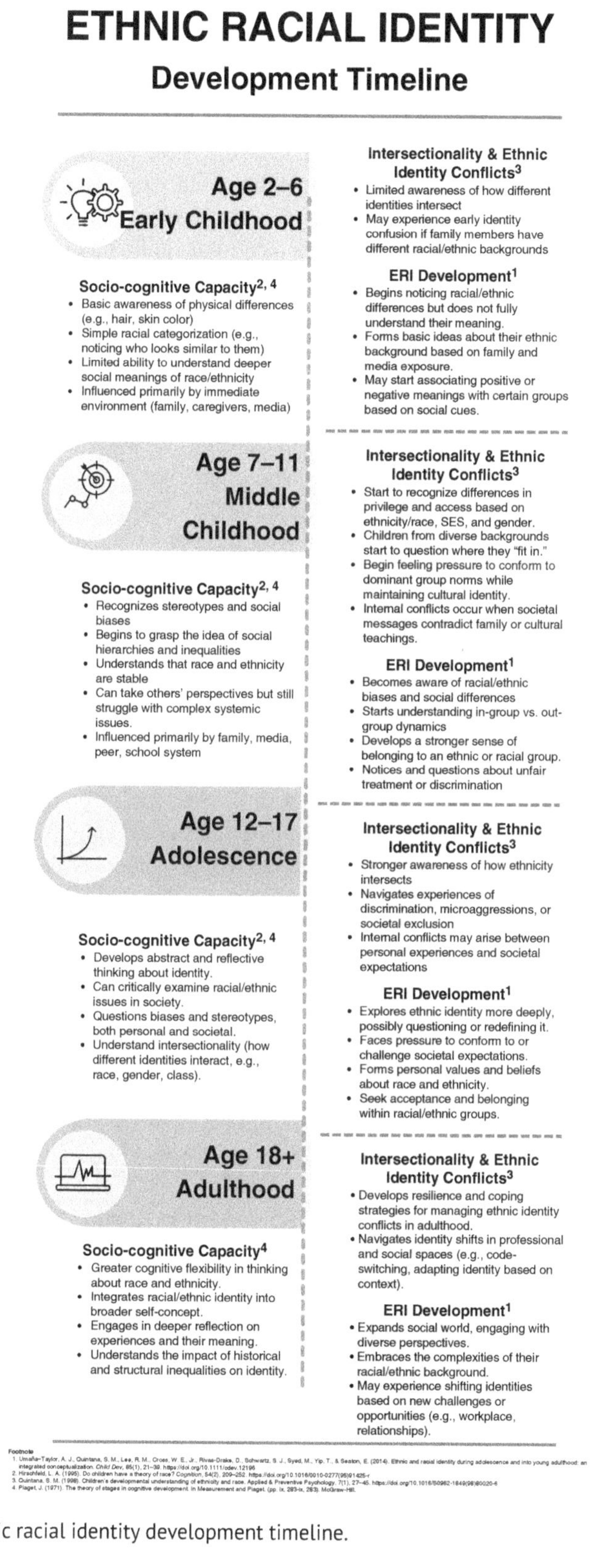

Figure 1.1 Ethnic racial identity development timeline.

Particularly for AANHPI youth with parents born outside of the United States (i.e., first-generation immigrants), their home lives may include an immersion in their heritage culture, including speaking a language other than English, adhering to collectivist values, and following traditional customs. In contrast, their school lives are often in more mainstream spaces that include different cultural values such as individualism, peer norms, and dominant societal expectations. Young people who are able to integrate both cultural spaces develop bicultural competence (Suzuki-Crumly & Hyers, 2004). Adolescents who are less able to find a common ground between the two cultures may experience cultural conflict and feeling marginalized in one or both spaces (Benet-Martínez & Haritatos, 2005).

Multiracial/Multiethnic AANHPIs. In 2021, Asians comprised 14% of the non-Hispanic multiracial population (approximately 3 million individuals). Asian-White biracial adolescents constitute the majority (70%) of Asian multiracial individuals, and this population continues to grow (Budiman & Ruiz, 2021). The challenge of juggling multiple cultures is more pronounced for AANHPI youth who are multiracial (i.e., biological parents who are of different racial backgrounds). Unlike monoracial individuals who often engage in bicultural navigation between their heritage and mainstream cultures, multiracial AANHPI youth must also navigate how they are perceived within each racial community (Lou et al., 2011), as well as how they are perceived within the multiracial community (Chen et al., 2019). According to Root (Root, 1997), ERI development among multiracial individuals includes: 1) accepting a single racial identity: identifying exclusively as one race, 2) identifying with both or all racial heritages; that is, embracing a multiracial ERI, 3) situational identity shift: dynamically adapting ERI depending on social context, or 4) identity confusion: not fitting into any existing ERI categories. Those who identify as Asian and White make up a large majority (70%) of non-Hispanic multiracial Asians. ERI development is further shaped by phenotypic appearance, societal validation, and cultural exposure (Chong & Kuo, 2015). Those with lighter skin or prototypically "White" features may be perceived as White and may struggle with not feeling fully accepted in Asian communities. Conversely, those who are perceived as more phenotypically "Asian" may face racialization and pressure to conform to Asian cultural expectations despite being raised in a bicultural or multiracial household. Therefore, racial ambiguity (Lou et al., 2011) can make ERI development even more complex, as multiracial AANHPI young people must navigate the broader cultural split between home and society and identity validation within their racial communities. For the subset of AANHPI young people who are multiethnic (i.e., biological parents who are both AANHPI, but of different ethnic backgrounds, e.g., Chinese-Indian), ERI concerns may be less about being "Asian" and more about how to juggle potentially different cultural practices of the parents' ethnic backgrounds. Similar to multiracial youth, they likely occupy a liminal space between the ethnic backgrounds of their parents and need to negotiate a sense of belonging in a third space.

Acculturation, the Family Context, and Generational Status. With over 90% of the AANHPIs having immigrant parents or being immigrants themselves, intergenerational conflict may be a common experience among this group (Center, 2013). Grappling with cultural differences appears to be a predominant challenge for youth; 69% of AANHPI teens (14–17 years) report that balancing different cultural expectations had a negative mental or emotional impact (TAAF, 2024). Specifically, acculturation (i.e., the process in which individuals/groups adopt cultural traits, practices, and norms that are different from their home culture; APA Dictionary of Psychology, 2007) plays a key role in ERI development. Immigrants who move to a new country interact with the dominant culture and encounter changes in language use, behavior, and values. According to Rumbaut (1994), personal experiences and social contexts shape acculturation and differences in ERI development (e.g., some may embrace more heritage culture, some might distance away) among young people (Chung, 2001).

Perhaps, the most salient arena where differences in acculturation emerge is the family context. A young person's generational status, place of birth, own/parents' age at immigration, and citizenship status play a key role in their ERI development. First-generation young people (i.e., those who are born outside the United States) often maintain strong ties to their countries of origin, preserving native languages and cultural practices (Kiang, 2006). Their ERI is closely linked to their ethnic heritage, and they may face challenges acculturating to US society. Among first-generation immigrants, considering the age of immigration is critical in understanding ERI development. The term 1.5 generation has been used to describe individuals who immigrate to the United States as children and adolescents, although there is some debate over the appropriate "cut-off" age for this designation.[1] Children who immigrate at a young age develop ERIs similar to those of their US-born peers (Kim et al., 2003; Rumbaut, 1994). Youth adapt more readily to US culture. For example, children who immigrate to the United States at a younger age (i.e., ages 15–19 years) may acculturate faster than their parents (e.g., acquiring language skills and cultural norms of the mainstream culture). In this case, children experience "adultification" where they are forced to assume "adult roles" as children, effectively serving as a conduit between the family and the broader society (Higuera, 2024). On the other hand, first-generation immigrants who come to the United States as adults may be less likely to develop a strong sense of ERI having spent their formative years in a different context.

Second-generation immigrants (i.e., children of immigrants who themselves are born in the United States) may feel more conflict navigating their parents' cultural heritage and mainstream US culture (Center, 2013). Similar to the 1.5-generation immigrants, ERI development occurs more quickly for these youth than for their parents, leading to intergenerational stressors related to English language brokering and cultural brokering more broadly (Higuera, 2024; Vaghela & Ueno, 2017). Second-generation youth are sometimes also referred to as having a third culture—a unique third space for individuals that grew up outside their parent's culture (Useem et al., 1963; Zhang, 2024). It is important to note that the usage of "third culture" differs from the classic definition of Third Culture Kids (TCKs), which traditionally refers to children of expatriate, missionary, military, or diplomatic parents who are raised outside both their parents' passport culture and the host culture. Third culture kids generally identify more strongly with the culture of their birthplace than their parents' native culture (de Waal & Born, 2021).

ERI Development and Culture

ERI development occurs in a cultural context. For AANHPI young people in the United States, these cultural contexts include stereotypes such as the model minority myth and cultural values such as collectivism and filial piety.

Model Minority Myth. The model minority myth (MMM) labels Asian Americans as successful, especially in comparison to other racial minorities, and ascribes academic success to superior cultural values and work ethic (Lee & Zhou, 2014; Wong & Halgin, 2006). MMM in Asian

1 Past research has used different definitions for 1.5-generation immigrants: Rumbaut and Ima (1988) include individuals who are only 12 and below; Park's (1999) definition of 1.5 generation is more based on self-identification

Americans can increase stress to succeed academically, decrease help-seeking behaviors, and worsen mental health (Gupta et al., 2011; Yoo et al., 2015). The MMM is difficult to dismantle in part because many, including AANHPIs, see the myth as a positive stereotype aligned with cultural values around achievement (Oyserman & Sakamoto, 1997). AANHPI parents, teachers, and students adopt this myth at high rates causing AANHPIs students to feel invisible and insignificant (Lee & Zhou, 2014; Li, 2005; Wing, 2007; Wong & Halgin, 2006). When teachers embrace MMM, they pay little attention to Asian students' academic needs, contributing to conduct issues and poorer mental health (Gerard & Booth, 2015; Wing, 2007). The MMM masks interethnic, socioeconomic, and cultural differences and educational disparities within the AANHPI community (Lee & Zhou, 2014; Li, 2005).

ERI and culture affect MMM perception, with students who endorsed collectivism and a strong ERI having more positive views on MMM (Oyserman & Sakamoto, 1997). The unique development of ERI among AANHPI youth necessitates a culturally/ethnic-specific solution to separating AANHPI ERI with the MMM. East Asian American youth with high awareness of discrimination were more likely to internalize the MMM as a response to discrimination (Kim et al., 2023). Although the internalization of MMM is linked to psychological distress and poorer physical health, youth may be using the myth as a coping mechanism to discrimination (Kim et al., 2023; Rajagopal & Durkee, 2024). Model minority stereotyping was found to increase over time throughout high school, consistent with findings that AANHPI youth both better recognize and receive more discrimination throughout adolescence (Greene et al., 2006; Thompson et al., 2016). Importantly, AANHPI adolescents need opportunities such as affinity groups or communities to explore their ethnic identity when stereotyped. A strong ERI may reduce the negative mental health impacts caused by the model minority myth (Xie et al., 2021). Importantly, the effect of ERI on mental health may differ between different Asian American subgroups, highlighting the importance of an individualized and multifaceted approach to promoting ERI (Ai et al., 2015). Although MMM stereotyping predicts ERI exploration, there are nonharmful means of promoting ERI, such as social bonding (Thompson et al., 2016). Conversely, feelings about MMM inversely predict ERI exploration and belonging, demonstrating that ERI exploration may be a coping strategy (Thompson et al., 2016). Given that nearly a fifth of AANHPI youth (17%) feel negatively about their ethnicity, having resources and support to explore identity is essential to mitigate MMM harms (TAAF, 2024).

Collectivism and Filial Piety. The values of independence and self-expression often conflict with Confucian values of collectivism and obligation to family. The premature "adultification" of youth from immigrant families leads to intergenerational tensions, household stress, and conflict (e.g., dating, education, career choices, and general expectations) between the parents and the "adultified" child. Over a third of Asian American youth (36%) report negative mental or emotional impacts from pressure from parents or caregivers and even more (39%) from a sense of duty toward their family (TAAF, 2024). Filial piety describes the Confucian-influenced value of respecting elders (Spielman, 2012). The Dual Filial Piety Model defines the two factors of filial piety as reciprocal and authoritarian (Yeh & Bedford, 2003). Whereas authoritarian filial piety (AFP) describes obedience to hierarchy, reciprocal filial piety (RFP) describes gratitude and care to one's elders, especially parents (Yeh & Bedford, 2003). Filial piety is related to the MMM and academic expectations because students may see academic success as satisfying their role as students/children or to avoid worrying their parents (Chen & Wu, 2021; Tan & Yates, 2011). Endorsement of collectivism rather than ethnicity predicts AFP (Lim et al., 2021). Although filial piety and collectivism are generally seen as Confucian-influenced, similar cultural values exist in South Asia (Ahmed & Lemkau, 2000; Ibrahim et al., 1997).

Collectivist philosophy may encourage AANHPI youth to "save face," exhibiting self-reliance to avoid worrying family members, avoid potential criticism, and adhere to a culture of emotional restraint (Ting-Toomey et al., 2000). Thus, parents and clinicians should proactively reach out to AANHPI youth as they are less likely to rely on social support as a coping mechanism (Ting & Hwang, 2009). Additionally, parents of AANHPI youth especially should avoid judgment or minimizing concerns when AANHPI youth share their challenges or stressors. AANHPI youth must navigate the conflicts between Eastern and Western cultural values, such as the dichotomy of South Asian and American dating and socialization culture (Ahmed & Lemkau, 2000). Religious values may also conflict with Western culture; Hinduism and Islam emphasize achieving oneness of the spiritual, not material, self, whereas in American culture, materialism and aestheticism are prominent (Ibrahim et al., 1997). This conflict between cultures can cause AANHPIs to feel stuck between two cultures, potentially extending periods of ERI exploration, thereby increasing vulnerabilities associated with identity confusion. Importantly though, AANHPI youth are not held to the binary of collectivist or individualistic culture. Parents and clinicians should recognize that AANHPI youth have cultural values that are neither entirely "Asian" nor "American." More likely, their values are situated on a continuum occupying spaces where youth are both Asian and American to varying degrees. Moreover, while AANHPI youth will have general tendencies to identify with being Asian and American, the salience of these identities may also vary according to the specifics of different contexts. For example, Asian values may be more salient in family contexts, and American values may be more prominent in school settings (Yip & Fuligni, 2002).

Promoting ERI Development

Ethnic and Racial Socialization. Ethnic and racial socialization (ERS) refers to "the mechanism through which parents transmit information, values and perspectives about ethnicity and race to their children" (p. 747, Hughes et al., 2006). Please see Box 1.1 for a description of our BOBA Project, investigating ERS among Chinese and Taiwanese American adolescents and parents.

Parents. Parents and caregivers are the primary agents of ERS (Hughes et al., 2006). Parents are the first to shape their children's ideas of the world, including perceptions about race and ethnicity. How important parents think race is and their beliefs about the importance of ERS is the leading predictor of related behaviors (Hughes et al., 2017). Parents' personal beliefs and attitudes about ERS and discrimination are informed by their own experiences and their perceptions about how society is shaping their children's development (Bronfenbrenner, 1979). If a parent presents dislike or ambivalence about their ethnicity or race, AANHPI youth may also distance themselves from their own ERI. Parents' experiences with racial discrimination will also indirectly shape their children's ERIs (Cox & Paley, 2003). A study with 444 Chinese American families showed that parents' discrimination predicted more ERS practices. It also influenced their teenagers' ethnicity-related stressors like cultural misfit, discrimination, and attitudes toward education (Benner et al., 2018). At the same time, adolescent's discrimination experiences can also drive their parents' socialization practices. For example, a study of ninth graders (10% of which were AAs) used daily diary methods where they repeated asked about ERS and child discrimination on a daily basis. They concluded that adolescent ethnic and racial discrimination predicted greater parental ERS the next day (Wang et al., 2023).

Based on research, ERS is commonly defined by dimensions. Parental <u>preparation for discrimination</u> includes parents telling their children about racism and discrimination, with this practice often informed by parents' own experiences of discrimination. The practice of preparing for bias is intended to help youth prepare to handle these negative interactions; messages related to preparation for discrimination and bias are strongly associated with a more secure child ERI. Research suggests that preparation for mistrust may vary by ethnic groups; studies on Indian American immigrant families suggest that parents typically refrain from providing preparation for discrimination messages. Despite reporting personal experiences, a majority of Indian American parents promoted "avoiding" or "ignoring" discriminatory events as opposed to recognizing them as racist. Consequently, children found themselves ill-prepared to face the reality of ethnic-racial discrimination. (Patel et al., 2023; TAAF, 2024). Promotion of mistrust, or parents' efforts to warn their children of negative interracial interactions, aims to protect children from negative interactions with outgroup members (Hughes et al., 2006). Promotion of mistrust generally hinders youth ERI development and leads to lower levels of association with American identity. In a study on Asian American college students, 61% reported parental preparation for bias, and 53% reported parental promotion of mistrust (Tran & Lee, 2010). In instances of both preparation for bias and promotion of mistrust, the child may develop even stronger ERIs. Cultural socialization involves teaching children about ethnic traditions, heritage, and cultural behaviors (Knight et al., 1993). Cultural socialization is generally seen to have a positive influence on ERI development because it fosters a sense of pride in one's group. In a recent review of ERS among AANHPIs, when asked if their parents have ever engaged in cultural socialization, Asian American young adults relayed that their parents "sometimes" or "often" passed on cultural heritage (Juang et al., 2016). Another study on Asian American college students found that 62% reported that their parents had engaged in cultural socialization–pluralism (i.e., encouraging messages about one's own racial group and appreciating others) (Tran & Lee, 2010). AANHPI young adults who received high messaging of maintenance of both cultural heritage and American acculturation and cultural pluralism had the strongest ERI and social connectedness (Atkin & Yoo, 2021). Conversely, emerging adults who received messaging on maintenance of cultural heritage but not American culture or cultural pluralism had lower ERI and social connectedness (Atkin & Yoo, 2021). Finally, socialization related to egalitarianism (i.e., de-emphasizing the role of race) is often referred to as silence about, or even adopting a color-blind approach. When asked if their parents have ever espoused egalitarian messages, AANHPI parents have been reported to promote the idea that all races and ethnicities are equal "sometimes" or "often" (Juang et al., 2017). Overall, parents with lower levels of color-blind ethnic-racial attitudes are more likely to engage in socialization behaviors and conversations about racism and discrimination with their children (Lee et al., 2006). Research also shows that White families (as opposed to families of color) are the most likely to engage in this method.

Peers. While parents help their children manage their ERI, youth ERI development is also formed by social interactions, discrimination and stratification with peers (García Coll et al., 1996). As children become adolescents, peers become influential in the life of adolescents and may pose as socializing agents that shape ERI (Graham & Echols, 2018). Those growing up in environments that are racially diverse experience issues regarding race frequently. These peers help shape how adolescents approach racial issues. Research shows peers engage in common socialization practices as parents, including preparation for bias, promotion of mistrust, and egalitarianism. Although ERS practices are similar for parents and peers, they have different associations with adolescent ERI development. For example, a study conducted with 10% Asian American participants showed that peer cultural socialization was found to promote ERI development, while parental cultural socialization did not (Wang et al., 2023).

Research shows that peer ERS happens quite frequently throughout everyday life, around one to three days per week (Wang, 2021). Peer ERS benefits academic performance, psychosocial functioning, and ERI (Wang, 2021). In particular, peer support related to discrimination and discussing other racial issues was found to have a positive effect on adolescents (Phinney et al., 2001; Syed & Juan, 2012). One study showed that things like discussing racial issues, eating ethnic food, and engaging in cultural activities with peers further promotes ERI; however, a lot of this research is qualitative, and not much quantitative research has been conducted (Sladek et al., 2022). Other research finds that peer ERS takes the form of affiliating with peers from same or diverse ethnicities, learning about peers' ethnic identities, and interacting with said peers on social media all affect one's ethnic socialization (Brown et al., 2008). Researchers have identified five mechanisms through which peers socialize adolescents about their ethnicity and race: behavioral display, peer pressure, behavioral reinforcement, antagonistic behaviors, and structural opportunities (Brown et al., 2008). Because some of these behaviors differ between peers and parents (e.g., peer pressure), they are also highly likely to exude effects on different outcomes. For example, friendships between peers of the same ethnicity foster a more positive ERI.

There is limited data on the roles that peers play when it comes to the association between ERI and adolescent mental health. However, AANHPI youth overwhelmingly (61%) rely on friends for emotional or mental health support, more than double the rate for a mental health professional (TAAF, 2024); among AANHPI peers, there may be a shared understanding about ERI developmental experiences due in part to similarities in racial or cultural experiences. The extent to which peers might present as supports in the effect of ERI, discrimination, and cultural stress on mental health is yet to be further understood through research.

Society and Media. Representation of Asians in the US media also influences youth's ERI development. Asians and Asian Americans are often cast as antagonists to White characters, with AANHPI actors and characters shown as untrustworthy, law breakers, and sexual deviants. At the same time, they have also been cast as model minorities. Such "positive" portrayal of AANHPIs, which began to take place in 1980s (Chou & Feagin, 2015), portrayed Asians as academically gifted. Stereotypes of Asians as foreigners have reinforced the image of a foreign threat to the "American" way of life (Deo et al., 2008). Stereotypical or tokenized Asian characters have continued to be prevalent, increasing internalization of the perpetual foreigner or model minority stereotypes (DuCros et al., 2018). Aside from being cast in ways that reflect such stereotypes, AANHPI are often represented as outsiders, considered the same despite being distinct in their ethnicity, combined into one group, and as side characters receiving little screen time.

Despite AANHPI media representation growing, AAs and especially NHPIs are underrepresented on television even when accounting for relative population size. Overall, such low representation in mainstream media (e.g., television) fosters low cultural belonging in Asian Americans (DuCros et al., 2018). In recent years, there is a rise in Asian American media representation, exemplified by the 2018 release of *Crazy Rich Asians*, the first movie with an all-Asian cast in 25 years, or Michelle Yeoh's 2023 win as the first openly Asian actress to win an Oscar (Lopez, 2021; Academy of Motion Picture Arts and Sciences, 2023). Despite increasing representation, studios and artist are susceptible to perpetuating stereotypes such as the MMM even when designed by or for AANHPI audiences, highlighting the urgent need for more diverse AANHPI narratives (Lopez, 2021).

Critical Historical Context. Perhaps, the most notable societal portrayal of AANHPIs was during the COVID-19 pandemic. During this time, the news framed Asians as guilty, dirty, and diseased. This representation spiked anti-Asian racism and hate crimes. The pandemic exacerbated racism toward Chinese people. Sinophobia, the fear and hatred of China, increased significantly on social media (Schild et al., 2020). The use of racial slurs spiked, and more than 50% of Chinese American parents and youth experienced direct racism in 2020 (Cheah et al., 2020, 2021). One constant is that Asians and Asian Americans are depicted as "foreigner," "outsiders," and not "real Americans." No matter what stereotype, this alienating portrayal makes AANHPIs feel like they can never fully embrace a truly "American" identity. Direct racial discrimination and negative media portrayals exacerbate Chinese Americans' mental health struggles like anxiety and depression (Cheah et al., 2020, 2021). Sinophobia and stress caused by racism influence Chinese Americans' ERI leading to feeling unwelcome and hated. Social media also contributes to stereotypical messaging, with an analysis of thousands of tweets highlighting that AANHPIs are exoticized, emasculated, and sexualized (Azhar et al., 2021). Increasing AANHPI media representation with characters that highlight the diversity of the AANHPI community is crucial to reversing negative media portrayal.

Why Does ERI Matter?

Benefits of ERI. Why should we care about the ERI in AANHPI youth? Because ERI matters for how AA youth move through the world, how they feel about themselves, how they perform in school, how they relate to other people, and their mental and physical health. There is evidence that ERI directly benefits youth. For example, those with higher levels of ERI are likely to have better mental health and grades. In particular, those who have positive regard for their ethnic-racial group experience better mental health including fewer depressive symptoms, higher levels of self-esteem, better psychological well-being, lower levels of internalizing symptoms (e.g., anxiety), and lower levels of externalizing symptoms (e.g., aggression) (Nelson et al., 2018; Rivas-Drake et al., 2014; Smith & Silva, 2011). In addition to mental health benefits, positive ERI regard has also been linked to better social functioning, perspective-taking, academic outcomes, and fewer risky health behaviors (e.g., substance use) (Jorgensen et al., 2025; Rivas-Drake et al., 2014). Of note, while the benefits of ERI are robust, current studies do not have a sufficient sample of AANHPI youth to be able to make meaningful conclusions about how ERI is related to outcomes for AANHPIs specifically (Miller-Cotto & Byrnes, 2016).

Racism, Discrimination, and Microaggressions. Ethnic and racially minoritized young people experience discrimination—unfair or differential treatment due to one's racial or ethnic group membership (Benner et al., 2018; Priest et al., 2021; Williams et al., 2020). The vast majority of AANHPI youth (93%) experienced discrimination in the past year (TAAF, 2024). Although discrimination is not an everyday occurrence (Torres & Ong, 2010; Xie et al., 2021), research has consistently shown an association between discrimination and negative mental health outcomes in adolescence and later in life (Benner et al., 2018; Priest et al., 2021). A study of over 1,500 Asian American families found that repeated exposure to racial discrimination was associated with weaker American identity in youth, as AANHPI teens might feel excluded and alienated from mainstream American society (Woo et al., 2020). Moreover, problematic microaggressive exposures are prevalent, with 62% of AANHPI youth (14–17 years) reporting that microaggressions cause negative mental or emotional impact (TAAF, 2024). Microaggressions are everyday racial slights that demean, tease, or invalidate the victim and are often unintentional or unconsciously driven (Sue et al., 2007). Asian Americans frequently experience microaggressions, with common examples including having one's race confused or being assumed one is not American, and being the target of racial jokes (TAAF, 2024; Wong-Padoongpatt et al., 2020).

While theorists have tried to tease apart the directionality of the association between discrimination and ERI development (i.e., does discrimination precede ERI development, or does ERI development precede experiences of discrimination?), the evidence supports reciprocal dynamics (Yip, 2018). The Rejection-Identification Model (Branscombe et al., 1999) suggests that when individuals experience discrimination and marginalization, they become more aware of their ethnic and racial group membership, which in turn strengthens their ERI. Indeed, stereotyping experiences are associated with higher levels of ethnic identity exploration, suggesting that discrimination may increase awareness and salience of one's ERI (Thompson et al., 2016). On the other hand, the Identification-Attribution Model (Gonzales-Backen et al., 2018) suggests that as individuals develop more advanced ERIs, they become more aware of ethnic-racial discrimination. Past research has support for both models suggesting a bidirectional effect between discrimination and ERI development.

How ERI Protects Against Discrimination. While discrimination and microaggressions predict depressive symptoms in Asian Americans, having strong ERI may be protective against these effects (Choi et al., 2017). That is, the level of one's ERI can modify the effects of discrimination exposures on developmental outcomes. In a meta-analysis of over 18,000 young people, ERI appeared to protect young people from the effects of discrimination, particularly for academic and physical health outcomes (Yip et al., 2019). A study of Asian American college students showed that those with stronger ERIs are more likely to use social support strategies (e.g., support from friends and family) during a stressful encounter of racial or ethnic discrimination (Yoo & Lee, 2005). AANHPIs with stronger ERIs are more likely to ask for social support, more capable of attributing negative responses to discrimination, and have stronger problem-solving skills to deal with discrimination. With low exposures to racial and ethnic discrimination, Asian American youths with stronger ERIs report better well-being (Yoo & Lee, 2005). Critically, the protective effects of ERI extend into adulthood (Yip et al., 2008).

How ERI Is Associated with Vulnerabilities to Discrimination. One caveat is that for youth to establish a strong ERI, they must first explore what their ERI means to them. ERI exploration precedes and predicts all other aspects of ERI, including ERI commitment as well as public and private regard (how others regard their identity and how one regards their own identity, respectively) (Hughes et al., 2017). If a teen has taken the time to understand their AANHPI identity, they are more likely to think positively of and feel like they belong to their ethnic and racial group. When encountering discrimination, high levels of ERI exploration can pose vulnerabilities. Discrimination exposure was associated with worse mental health outcomes for young people who reported high levels of ERI exploration. The exacerbating influence of identity exploration is strongest at 24 years old (Yip et al., 2019). While it is natural and encouraged for AANHPI teens to explore their identity during adolescence, continuous identity exploration post adulthood increases susceptibility to negative mental health outcomes and risky health behaviors. Confusion and high levels of ERI exploration increase vulnerability to internalized discrimination and heighten the risk of self-doubt, depression, and disengagement (Nelson et al., 2018).

Clinical Case Study 1

Kevin is a 16-year-old Chinese American boy raised in a predominantly White suburban community, where he often feels isolated given that his family is one among the few Asian American families in his community. His peers, mostly non-Asian, frequently stereotype him as being "good at math," and although he is indeed skilled at math, Kevin resents being pigeonholed as a "model minority." Kevin is an only child and his parents rely on him to navigate situations that require English knowledge (e.g., medical appointments); as a "broker" between American and Chinese settings, he not only serves as an English translator but helps his parents understand the situation. At home, Kevin's parents, both immigrants from China, uphold traditional Chinese values, emphasizing academic achievement. This pressure creates a tension between upholding high expectations, and not wanting to be reduced to being a "stereotypical Asian," as Kevin wishes to fit in with his predominantly non-Asian peers. Kevin also feels insecure about his physical appearance, feeling he wouldn't be seen as attractive given his Chinese features. Kevin values many aspects of being Chinese, but there are many moments when he wishes he were more "American." He struggles with loneliness, as he does not feel like there is anyone he can connect with.

Given his feelings of being overwhelmed and helpless and the pressures of being Chinese American, Kevin has developed symptoms of depression and has entertained thoughts of what it would be like if he gave up on life. Despite these feelings, Kevin is not inclined to consider professional help, believing that his issues are "not worthy" for treatment, but also knowing that getting such help would be frowned upon by his parents, who hold stigmatizing views around mental health.

Reflection Questions

- What are common challenges that a teenager like Kevin might face in a predominantly White community that affect mental health?
- Within the communities you practice, how does Kevin's experience as a Chinese American fit in or differ from your observations of other Chinese or Asian Americans?
- What are some ways in which family, peer, and community levels of socialization shape Kevin's sense of self? How might theoretical perspectives on identity development help us understand these socialization effects?
- How does the model minority stereotype affect how Kevin thinks about himself and how others perceive him?
- How might Kevin's role as a language broker and expectations to uphold academic achievement affect his cultural identity and mental health?
- In what ways might tensions arise from Kevin's parents' values and expectations and his desire to fit in with peers?
- What are some systemic or cultural barriers that prevent Kevin from seeking help for mental health?
- There are many different Chinese American youth experiences. What similarities and differences does this case study have with youth you have interacted with?
- In what ways does this case vignette reflect characteristics that may also be considered stereotypes? How can educators and mental health professionals avoid reinforcing stereotypes while recognizing real challenges?

Recommendations

It is important for significant adults in Kevin's life to acknowledge the pressures that he faces at home and school and the balance between these domains.

- School: Teachers and school counselors could recognize Kevin's additional demands as a cultural broker for his parents. At the same time, to avoid being pigeonholed as a model minority, school personnel could also encourage Kevin to experiment with strengths outside of math (e.g., sports, drama, debate, student council). Also, school personnel could actively counter the model minority stereotype letting Kevin know that it is ok to voice his struggles with trusted adults and seek help from school counselors.
- Home: As immigrants from China, Kevin's parents are going through their own acculturation processes. Their reflections on this adjustment may inform insights into Kevin's adjustment and his unique role as the family cultural broker. They are likely interested in retaining Chinese cultural values, but it is equally important that they recognize and support Kevin's need to balance American values.
- Community spaces: Kevin may also be involved in third spaces such as places of worship, community centers, sports teams, and other extracurriculars. The adults in these settings should also be on alert for signs of distress and be able to direct Kevin to the appropriate resources.
- Clinical spaces: Ideally Kevin would have access to a clinician with knowledge or experience with Asian (or even Chinese) youth, especially those who come from immigrant families. If this is not possible, it would be valuable for the clinician to try and understand how Kevin's immigrant background and need to juggle both Chinese and American culture is a unique aspect of this mental health and overall adjustment.

Clinical Case Study 2

Danny is a 14-year-old biracial nonbinary Asian teen. Their mom is Hawaiian with part Asian and part Pacific Islander ancestry, and their father is Black. From a young age, Danny's parents have engaged in conversations about racial identity, leading Danny to embrace their heritage. Danny has referred to themselves as "Blasian" and will sometimes tell others they are "100% Asian, 100% Black." While confident about their racial identity at home, Danny is sometimes the subject of racial jokes at school. Comments about their skin color particularly affect Danny. For instance, Danny has been told that they are "too dark" to be Asian or "not Black enough." During the COVID-19 pandemic, Danny watched the news that described anti-Asian sentiments and Black Lives Matter protests.

Danny has many friends; however, they struggle to find a friend group they feel they belong with. Danny recently started attending the Asian Pacific Islander club meetings at school. While the faculty leader has been very welcoming, Danny worries that the students may question why Danny is there. Danny also joined the math team but has continually worried about whether involvement has made them "too Asian." Depending on who Danny is with, they will change their behaviors and speech to better fit in with a group. As someone who identifies as non-binary, Danny worries about openly talking about their gender identity in any group. Danny wishes for a group that openly embraces their various identities.

(Continued)

Clinical Case Study 2 (Continued)

Reflection Questions

Despite Danny's parents' supportive parenting and exposure to their racial identity at a young age, Danny still sometimes struggles with belonging.

- What other people or influences in Danny's life may have shaped their racial belonging?
- In what ways might Danny experience discrimination differently compared to a monoracial Asian or Black peer?
- How do Danny's experiences illustrate the complexities of navigating multiple identities? In what ways does intersectionality theory inform an understanding of Danny's lived experience?
- What are some examples in which Danny's racial identities are questioned or invalidated? How might this impact their self-esteem and mental health?
- Mixed-race individuals sometimes report imposter syndrome. What situations might they encounter that would lead them to feel like an imposter? What psychological effects might arise from not feeling like they truly belong?
- How can educators and mental health professionals address racial jokes, microaggression, and assumptions that take place in schools?
- How can educators and mental health professionals foster a sense of pride for students with multiple identities while addressing challenges?
- What would make a space that would ensure inclusivity for mixed-race and nonbinary students? What organizations or groups could Danny's school host that would help them meet other biracial kids?

Recommendations

It is important for significant adults in Danny's life to acknowledge the pressures that come from being Asian and Black biracial and nonbinary.

- <u>School:</u> Teachers and school counselors are instrumental in creating safe spaces where Danny can be authentic and not feel the need to hide aspects of their identity. Danny seems to be seeking belonging in a variety of spaces (i.e., math club, Asian club), and it is important for adults in these spaces to convey acceptance.
- <u>Home:</u> Danny seems comfortable with their biracial identity at home, and their parents have already done a wonderful job of scaffolding their identity development and engaging in ethnic and racial socialization. At the same time, it is important for their parents to be aware of their struggles at school and engage with school personnel to have an open line of communication about issues they may encounter with feelings of belonging at school. Together, Danny's parents can partner with the school to foster a welcoming space at school for Danny by bridging the gap between home and school contexts.
- <u>Community spaces:</u> Either in person or online, it may be likely that Danny is seeking gender diverse communities where they are able to talk about their gender identity openly. To the extent that these spaces also include youth of color, or even biracial youth, Danny may be more likely to identify similar others with whom they can create a shared community.
- <u>Clinical spaces:</u> Ideally, Danny would have access to a clinician with knowledge or experience with biracial, gender diverse youth. If this is not possible in person, they may need to seek support from knowledgeable therapists via telehealth which may provide access to

a more diverse range of therapists. Kevin's identity includes being biracial and nonbinary, and all of the dimensions, and their unique intersection, are critical aspects of understanding their lived experiences.

Box 1.1 BOBA project.

Research on AA ERI Development: What Is the BOBA Project?

The BOBA Project, which stands for Building Our Bonds Authentically, is a research study we launched in 2022. Our goal is to encourage Asian American parents, teens, and peers to reflect on their identities as Asian Americans. This project emerged during the heightened awareness of anti-Asian hate during the COVID-19 pandemic. As researchers (Cindy and Tiffany), we wondered how parents were discussing these incidents with their teens. We also questioned whether these conversations could foster perspective-taking about what it means to be Asian American in the United States and encourage open discussions about identity among family members and friends.

To explore these questions, we designed a study where parents and teens—as well as teens and their peers—engaged in conversations about hypothetical scenarios related to Asian American identity. By observing these discussions, we aimed to understand how such conversations unfold and what impact they might have on identity development and family communication.

What Were Those Conversations Like?

Our team has analyzed hundreds of video recordings of these discussions. According to their report, many families approached the conversations thoughtfully, with parents and teens engaging in ways they had not previously experienced. Teens shared their perspectives on how they might respond to race-based scenarios, while parents listened and gained insight into the experiences of Asian American teenagers.

Not all families reached a consensus on how to respond to these situations, but they consistently expressed support for the thought process behind any action—or inaction—that was considered. We are conducting formal analyses to determine whether these conversations contribute to stronger relationships and greater well-being among the teens involved.

Has the BOBA Project Shed Light on Asian American Ethnic or Racial Identity?

While our study currently focuses on Chinese Americans and therefore cannot be generalized to all Asian American groups, we have observed a consistent pattern. Participants found it easier to discuss ethnic identity—including cultural heritage, norms, language, and food—than racial identity. When invited to participate in the study, many families expressed unfamiliarity or discomfort with conversations about racial identity and race relations. This hesitation may stem from the dominant Black-White racial framework in the United States. However, through guided discussions facilitated by trained researchers, we hope to foster greater comfort in addressing both ethnic and racial identity experiences among Asian Americans.

Future Directions for AANHPI ERI Research and Application

There is a deep interest in understanding and supporting the ERI development of young people, in large part because there is a recognition that ERI matters for how young people see themselves, how they grow and develop, and how they navigate the world around them. Several key challenges continue to limit our understanding of the full scope of how ERI is related to youth outcomes groups (Rogers et al., 2020). First, there is still debate about when ERI development begins. Although infants are able to distinguish between faces from different racial (Kelly et al., 2005; Quinn et al., 2008; Sangrigoli & De Schonen, 2004; Wheeler et al., 2011), whether this constitutes ERI is unclear. Developmental theories place identity and ERI development squarely within adolescence (Crocetti, 2017; Erikson, 1968; Marcia, 1980); however, it is clear that young people show pride and knowledge of ERI well before this age (Desmarais et al., 2024). As such, for adults who are hoping to support the positive development of ERI among the young people they engage with, it is unclear when we should begin talking to AANHPI youth about their ERI. Another practical consideration relates to whether there is an ideal or aspirational ERI to best support AANHPI youth (Rogers et al., 2020). While there is strong evidence that ERI is good for young people, there is an assumption that "more is better"; however, there are no recommended levels of specific ERI dimensions. Nor are there guidelines regarding the age at which youth should have achieved a certain level of ERI for optimal outcomes. In addition, and for AANHPI youth in particular, there is very little research on ERI development among multiracial/multiethnic young people. One in five AANHPIs report an identity that includes more than one racial group (Monte & Shin, 2022), yet we know little about multiracial identity development (e.g., Asian White) (Charmaraman & Grossman, 2010; Herman, 2004; Root, 1997) and even less about multiethnic identity development (e.g., Indian Chinese) (Gonzales-Backen, 2013; Lee et al., 2018; Oikawa & Yoshida, 2007). Finally, ethnicity and race are only one aspect of an overall identity and self-concept, and there is very little guidance on how to support ERI as just one aspect of a multitude of social identities (e.g., gender, age, religious). Recently, intersectionality has been receiving increased attention as an important perspective for understanding how young people juggle multiple, intersecting identities (Settles & Buchanan, 2014); yet, research on this topic, and among AANHPI youth in particular, remains limited.

One of the key reasons foundational questions still remain in our understanding of ERI among AANHPI youth is that ERI development is bound by and situated within the current context. In our section on ERS, we cover various sources of how young people learn about their ERI. Each of these socialization agents operate within a cultural and historical context. Perhaps one of the most salient illustrations of how context shapes ERI development is the COVID-19 pandemic (Cheah et al., 2021; Yip et al., 2024). During this time, AANHPI youth were making sense of their self-concept against a backdrop of unprecedented levels of anti-Asian hate including highly visible physical attacks and politicized rhetoric (Huynh et al., 2022; Nhan et al., 2024). As a result, that particular period in history marks a time where there were few Asians globally, for whom, ERI was not salient (Monte & Shin, 2022; Yang et al., 2022).

Summary and Recommendations

ERI is multifaceted and complex, and its development spans childhood through adulthood. In some ways, it reflects how young people see themselves as members of ethnic and racial groups. Yet in other ways, it also reflects how they think others see them as members of their ethnic and racial groups (i.e., looking glass self (Cooley, 1902)). As a form of self-concept, ERI provides young people with a sense of belonging within a larger social milieu. These feelings of belonging and rootedness seem to confer positive associations for young people when they have a clear sense of their ERI, particularly in the face of discrimination. Given the challenges of growing up with racism and discrimination, and the observed benefits of ERI, how can we as a community support the healthy ERI development of AANHPI young people? Table 1.1 provides a summary of key concepts and recommendations.

Table 1.1 Summary of key concepts and recommendations.

Concept	Definition & importance	Examples	Recommendations
Ethnic-racial identity (ERI)	Multidimensional way in which one forms a social identity around ethnicity and or race. • Exploration (i.e., searching for the meaning of one's ethnicity and race; Phinney, 1992). • Commitment (i.e., a clear understanding of the role of ethnicity and race in one's life and identity; Phinney 1992). • Centrality (i.e., the relative importance of ethnicity and race in one's overall self-concept). • Private regard (i.e., how positively one feels about their ethnic and racial group membership). • Public regard (i.e., how positively one thinks that others view their ethnic and racial group; Sellers et al., 1997).	Asian American Chinese American Taiwanese American Japanese American Filipino/a American Indian American Korean American Pacific Islander	• Peer affinity and cultural groups in schools • Teachers who can create safe spaces and foster discussions • Community members who share aspects of one's ethnic-racial identity • Clinicians who can guide parents in ERI and ERS
Ethnic-racial socialization (ERS)	How parents, peers and broader society (e.g., media) convey messages about what it means to be Asian in the United States (Hughes et al., 2006). • Preparation for discrimination includes warnings about racism and discrimination. • Promotion of mistrust, warnings about potential negative interracial interactions, aimed to protecting from negative interactions with outgroup members. • Cultural socialization involves teaching about ethnic traditions, heritage and cultural behaviors	• Watching ethnic or Asian American movies • Traveling to Asia • Attending native language programs • Learning cultural dances or holiday traditions • Warnings about possible discrimination • Saying that you will need to work twice as hard to get half as far	• Incorporating Asian American history into school curricula, in addition to during AANHPI history month • Attending community cultural events • Seeking out Asian American media (e.g., books, movies, theater) • Traveling to historic Asian American places or other places of significance

(*Continued*)

Table 1.1 (Continued)

Concept	Definition & importance	Examples	Recommendations
Model minority myth (MMM)	Labels Asian Americans as successful, especially in comparison to other racial minorities, and ascribes academic success to superior cultural values and work ethic. The MMM in Asian Americans can increase stress to succeed academically, decrease help-seeking behaviors, and worsen mental health.	Beliefs that: • All Asians are hardworking and naturally good at math • Asians are not good at sports • Asians do not struggle with mental health challenges • Seeking mental health care is not accepted among Asian Americans	• School personnel made aware of the MMM and actively resist its impact on Asian students • School personnel trained to intervene when they witness students or other personnel invoke the MMM • School personnel name the MMM and dismantle it by seeing Asian students as unique individuals • Parental support and assisting in mental health-seeking behaviors • Parents modeling their own mental health care • Parents having open discussion about the impact of the MMM
Collectivism and filial piety	• Collectivism is putting the collective good above one's own individual needs. • Filial piety describes the Confucian-influenced value of respecting elders and a sense of duty toward one's family. ▪ The Dual Filial Piety Model defines the two factors of filial piety as reciprocal and authoritarian (Yeh & Bedford, 2003). Whereas authoritarian filial piety (AFP) describes obedience to hierarchy, reciprocal filial piety (RFP) describes gratitude and care to one's elders, especially parents.	• Deferring to family elders (e.g., letting them eat first) • Prioritizing collective needs over individual desires	• School personnel recognizing the unique roles that family and elders play in Asian cultures • Parents having conversations about how collectivist and filial duties conflict with American individualism

Concept	Definition & importance	Examples	Recommendations
Racism, discrimination, and microaggressions	Unfair or differential treatment due to one's racial or ethnic group membership. Microaggressions are everyday racial slights that demean, tease, or invalidate the victim and are often unintentional or unconsciously driven.	• Having one's race or ethnicity confused (i.e., Koreans mistaken as Japanese) • Being assumed to no bet American (e.g., "you speak English so well") • Target of racial jokes	• School personnel trained to intervene when they witness any form of racial or ethnic discrimination or microaggression • Peers encouraged to intervene at school and outside of school • Parents having open conversations about racism and discrimination (see ERS preparation for discrimination) and how to respond when it happens

One way in which communities can support ERI development is to support its healthy exploration and facilitate the development of ERI commitment. That is, communities can scaffold the exploration period as a normative component of ERI development, but also ensure that young people do not linger in a prolonged period of exploration. Research on socialization tells us that parents are the key socializing agents, especially for preadolescent young people. However, just 53% of AANHPI youth report feeling comfortable talking to their parents when going through emotional or mental distress (this number falls to a third for LGBTQ+ youth) (TAAF, 2024); therefore, AANHPI youth may not share discrimination experiences with parents, highlighting the importance of peers in ERI development. During adolescence, peers assume the role of key socializers, at a time where society and the media are also notable influences. Educational contexts also play an important role. Teachers with higher esteem in their ability to teach with culturally diverse students can also act as role models for students, connecting with students from different cultures to increase positive intercultural connections (Ulbricht et al., 2022). Similarly, a group-based workshop that emphasizes the value of diversity and respecting differences significantly improved ethnocultural empathy in healthcare students (Fleming et al., 2015). Similar workshops should be employed in schools to increase ethnocultural empathy for all students, potentially decreasing peer racial discrimination. To fight the effects of the stereotypes and discrimination, teachers, counselors, and other staff need to actively recognize and address areas that, like all students, Asian American students may struggle with.

Importantly, AANHPI youth do not experience stigma or stereotypes in isolation; mental health professionals, teachers, family members, and other figures together shape youth identity and mental health. Young AANHPIs tend to rely on alternative support networks such as friends rather than professional help, demonstrating the need for building culturally accessible mental health programming and culturally competent mental health professionals (Lee et al., 2009; TAAF, 2024).

Although ERI is just one aspect of a social identity that includes many facets (e.g., sex, gender, age, immigration status, language abilities, family roles, religion), it remains a highly salient aspect of life and health in the United States.

References

Academy of Motion Picture Arts and Sciences. (2023). Inside 'everything everywhere all at once's epic Oscars night. *Academy Newsletter*. https://newsletter.oscars.org/news/post/inside-everything-everywhere-all-at-onces-epic-oscars-night

Ahmed, S. M., & Lemkau, J. P. (2000). Cultural issues in the primary care of South Asians. *Journal of Immigrant Health*, *2*(2), 89–96. https://doi.org/10.1023/A:1009585918590

Ai, A. L., Nicdao, E. G., Appel, H. B., & Lee, D. H. (2015). Ethnic identity and major depression in Asian American subgroups nationwide: differential findings in relation to subcultural contexts. *Journal of Clinical Psychology*, *71*(12), 1225–1244. https://doi.org/10.1002/jclp.22214

Atkin, A. L., & Yoo, H. C. (2021). Patterns of racial-ethnic socialization in Asian American families: associations with racial-ethnic identity and social connectedness. *Journal of Counseling Psychology*, *68*(1), 17–26. https://doi.org/10.1037/cou0000435

Azhar, S., Alvarez, A. R. G., Farina, A. S. J., & Klumpner, S. (2021). "You're so exotic looking": an intersectional analysis of Asian American and Pacific Islander stereotypes. *Affilia*, *36*(3), 282–301. https://doi.org/10.1177/08861099211001460

Benet-Martínez, V., & Haritatos, J. (2005). Bicultural identity integration (BII): components and psychosocial antecedents. *Journal of Personality*, *73*(4), 1015–1049. https://doi.org/10.1111/j.1467-6494.2005.00337.x

Benner, A. D., Wang, Y., Shen, Y., Boyle, A. E., Polk, R., & Cheng, Y. P. (2018). Racial/ethnic discrimination and well-being during adolescence: a meta-analytic review. *American Psychologist*, *73*(7), 855–883. https://doi.org/10.1037/amp0000204

Branscombe, N., Schmitt, M., & Harvey, R. (1999). Perceiving pervasive discrimination among African Americans: implications for group identification and well-being. *Journal of Personality and Social Psychology*, *77*, 135–149. https://doi.org/10.1037/0022-3514.77.1.135

Bronfenbrenner, U. (1979). *The Ecology of Human Development: Experiments by Nature and Design*. Harvard University Press.

Brown, B. B., Bakken, J. P., Ameringer, S. W., & Mahon, S. D. (2008). A comprehensive conceptualization of the peer influence process in adolescence. In M. J. Prinstein, & K. A. Dodge (Eds.), *Understanding Peer Influence in Children and Adolescents* (pp. 17–44). The Guilford Press.

Budiman, A., & Ruiz, N. G. (2021). Key facts about Asian Americans, a diverse and growing population. Pew Research Center. https://www.pewresearch.org/short-reads/2021/04/29/key-facts-about-asian-americans/

Center, P. R. (2013). Chapter 2: Demographic portrait of adult children of immigrants. *Second-Generation Americans*. https://www.pewresearch.org/social-trends/2013/02/07/chapter-2-demographic-portrait-of-adult-children-of-immigrants/#:~:text=Among%20adult%20Asian%20Americans%2C%2019,23%25%20of%20Asian%20Americans%20overall

Charmaraman, L., & Grossman, J. M. (2010). Importance of race and ethnicity: an exploration of Asian, Black, Latino, and multiracial adolescent identity. *Cultural Diversity & Ethnic Minority Psychology*, *16*(2), 144–151. https://doi.org/10.1037/a0018668

Cheah, C. S. L., Wang, C., Ren, H., Zong, X., Cho, H. S., & Xue, X. (2020). COVID-19 racism and mental health in Chinese American families. *Pediatrics*, *146*(5). https://doi.org/10.1542/peds.2020-021816

Cheah, C. S. L., Zong, X., Cho, H. S., Ren, H., Wang, S., Xue, X., & Wang, C. (2021). Chinese American adolescents' experiences of COVID-19 racial discrimination: risk and protective factors for internalizing difficulties. *Cultural Diversity & Ethnic Minority Psychology*, *27*(4), 559–568. https://doi.org/10.1037/cdp0000498

Chen, J. M., Kteily, N. S., & Ho, A. K. (2019). Whose side are you on? Asian Americans' mistrust of Asian-White biracials predicts more exclusion from the ingroup. *Personality and Social Psychology Bulletin*, *45*(6), 827–841. https://doi.org/10.1177/0146167218798032

Chen, M., & Wu, X. (2021). Attributing academic success to giftedness and its impact on academic achievement: the mediating role of self-regulated learning and negative learning emotions. *School Psychology International*, *42*(2), 170–186. https://doi.org/10.1177/0143034320985889

Cheryan, S., & Monin, B. (2005). "Where are you really from?": Asian Americans and identity denial. *Journal of Personality and Social Psychology*, *89*(5), 717–730. https://doi.org/10.1037/0022-3514.89.5.717

Choi, S., Lewis, J. A., Harwood, S., Mendenhall, R., & Huntt, M. B. (2017). Is ethnic identity a buffer? Exploring the relations between racial microaggressions and depressive symptoms among Asian-American individuals. *Journal of Ethnic & Cultural Diversity in Social Work*, *26*(1–2), 18–29. https://doi.org/10.1080/15313204.2016.1263815

Chong, V., & Kuo, B. (2015). Racial identity profiles of Asian-White biracial young adults: testing a theoretical model with cultural and psychological correlates. *Asian American Journal of Psychology*, *6*. https://doi.org/10.1037/aap0000022

Chou, R. S., & Feagin, J. R. (2015). *Myth of the Model Minority: Asian Americans Facing Racism*. Rouledge. https://doi.org/10.4324/9781315636313

Chung, R. H. (2001). Gender, ethnicity, and acculturation in intergenerational conflict of Asian American college students. *Cultural Diversity & Ethnic Minority Psychology*, *7*(4), 376–386. https://doi.org/10.1037/1099-9809.7.4.376

Cooley, C. H. (1902). The looking-glass self. *The Production of Reality: Essays and Readings on Social Interaction* (Vol. 6) (pp. 126–128). mediastudies.press.

Cox, M. J., & Paley, B. (2003). Understanding families as systems. *Current Directions in Psychological Science*, *12*(5), 193–196. https://doi.org/10.1111/1467-8721.01259

Crocetti, E. (2017). Identity formation in adolescence: the dynamic of forming and consolidating identity commitments. *Child Development Perspectives*, *11*(2), 145–150. https://doi.org/10.1111/cdep.12226

de Waal, M. F., & Born, M. P. (2021). Where I'm from? Third culture kids about their cultural identity shifts and belonging. *International Journal of Intercultural Relations*, *83*, 67–83. https://doi.org/10.1016/j.ijintrel.2021.04.004

Deo, M. E., Lee, J. J., Chin, C. B., Milman, N., & Yuen, N. W. (2008). Missing in action: "framing" race on prime-time television. *Social Justice*, *35*(2 (112)), 145–162.

Desmarais, A., Christophe, N. K., & Robins, R. W. (2024). Mexican-origin children's trajectories of ethnic-racial pride from childhood through emerging adulthood: associations with mothers and fathers' trajectories. *Journal of Youth and Adolescence*, *53*(3), 685–700. https://doi.org/10.1007/s10964-023-01902-7

DuCros, F. M., Chin, C. B., Lee, J. J.-H., Yuen, N. W., Deo, M. E., & Milman, N. (2018). Asian Americans and Pacific Islanders on TV. *Contexts*, *17*(4), 12–17. https://doi.org/10.1177/1536504218812863

Erikson, E. H. (1968). *Identity Youth and Crisis (No. 7).* WW Norton & Company.
Fleming, B. D., Thomas, S. E., Burnham, W. S., Charles, L. T., & Shaw, D. (2015). Improving ethnocultural empathy in healthcare students through a targeted intervention. *Journal of Culture Diversity*, *22*(2), 59–63.
García Coll, C., Lamberty, G., Jenkins, R., McAdoo, H. P., Crnic, K., Wasik, B. H., & Vázquez García, H. (1996). An integrative model for the study of developmental competencies in minority children. *Child Development*, *67*(5), 1891–1914.
Gerard, J. M., & Booth, M. Z. (2015). Family and school influences on adolescents' adjustment: the moderating role of youth hopefulness and aspirations for the future. *Journal of Adolescence*, *44*, 1–16. https://doi.org/10.1016/j.adolescence.2015.06.003
Gonzales-Backen, M. A. (2013). An application of ecological theory to ethnic identity formation among biethnic adolescents. *Family Relations: An Interdisciplinary Journal of Applied Family Studies*, *62*(1), 92–108. https://doi.org/10.1111/j.1741-3729.2012.00749.x
Gonzales-Backen, M. A., Meca, A., Lorenzo-Blanco, E. I., Des Rosiers, S. E., Córdova, D., Soto, D. W., ... Unger, J. B. (2018). Examining the temporal order of ethnic identity and perceived discrimination among Hispanic immigrant adolescents. *Development Psychology*, *54*(5), 929–937. https://doi.org/10.1037/dev0000465
Graham, S., & Echols, L. (2018). Race and ethnicity in peer relations research. In W. M. Bukowski, B. Laursen, & K. H. Rubin (Eds.), *Handbook of Peer Interactions, Relationships, and Groups* (Second Edition) (pp. 590–614). The Guilford Press.
Greene, M. L., Way, N., & Pahl, K. (2006). Trajectories of perceived adult and peer discrimination among Black, Latino, and Asian American adolescents: patterns and psychological correlates. *Developmental Psychology*, *42*(2), 218–236. https://doi.org/10.1037/0012-1649.42.2.218
Gupta, A., Szymanski, D., & Leong, F. (2011). The "model minority myth": internalized racialism of positive stereotypes as correlates of psychological distress, and attitudes toward help-seeking. *Asian American Journal of Psychology*, *2*, 101–114. https://doi.org/10.1037/a0024183
Helms, J. E. (1995). An update of Helm's White and people of color racial identity models. In J. G. Ponterotto, J. M. Casas, L. A. Suzuki, & C. M. Alexander (Eds.), *Handbook of Multicultural Counseling* (pp. 181–198). Sage Publications, Inc.
Herman, M. (2004). Forced to choose: some determinants of racial identification in multiracial adolescents. *Child Development*, *75*(3), 730–748. https://doi.org/10.1111/j.1467-8624.2004.00703.x
Higuera, K. (2024). The immigrant linguistic maturation of Asian American and Latinx language brokers. *Sociology Compass*, *18*(7), e13221. https://doi.org/10.1111/soc4.13221
Hughes, D. L., Del Toro, J., & Way, N. (2017). Interrelations among dimensions of ethnic-racial identity during adolescence. *Development Psychology*, *53*(11), 2139–2153. https://doi.org/10.1037/dev0000401
Hughes, D., Rodriguez, J., Smith, E. P., Johnson, D. J., Stevenson, H. C., & Spicer, P. (2006). Parents' ethnic-racial socialization practices: a review of research and directions for future study. *Development Psychology*, *42*(5), 747–770. https://doi.org/10.1037/0012-1649.42.5.747
Huynh, V. W., Raval, V. V., & Freeman, M. (2022). Ethnic-racial discrimination towards Asian Americans amidst COVID-19, the so-called "China" virus and associations with mental health. *Asian American Journal of Psychology*, *13*(3), 259–269. https://doi.org/10.1037/aap0000264
Ibrahim, F., Ohnishi, H., & Sandhu, D. S. (1997). Asian American identity development: a culture specific model for South Asian Americans. *Journal of Multicultural Counseling and Development*, *25*(1), 34–50. https://doi.org/10.1002/j.2161-1912.1997.tb00314.x

Jorgensen, N. A., Lindquist, K. A., Prinstein, M. J., & Telzer, E. H. (2025). Early adolescents' ethnic-racial identity in relation to longitudinal growth in perspective taking. *Development Psychology*, *61*(1), 105–112. https://doi.org/10.1037/dev0001861

Juang, L. P., Shen, Y., Kim, S. Y., & Wang, Y. (2016). Development of an Asian American parental racial-ethnic socialization scale. *Cultural Diversity Ethnic Minority Psychology*, *22*(3), 417–431. https://doi.org/10.1037/cdp0000083

Juang, L., Yoo, H., & Atkin, A. (2017). A critical race perspective on an empirical review of Asian American parental racial-ethnic socialization. In Y. Choi, & H. Hahm (Eds.), *Asian American Parenting*. Springer. https://doi.org/10.1007/978-3-319-63136-3_2

Kelly, D. J., Quinn, P. C., Slater, A. M., Lee, K., Gibson, A., Smith, M., ... Pascalis, O. (2005). Three-month-olds, but not newborns, prefer own-race faces. *Development Science*, *8*(6), F31–F36. https://doi.org/10.1111/j.1467-7687.2005.0434a.x

Kiang, P. (2006). Issues of curriculum and community for first-generation Asian Americans in college. *New Directions for Community Colleges*, *1992*, 97–112. https://doi.org/10.1002/cc.36819928012

Kim, B. S., Brenner, B. R., Liang, C. T., & Asay, P. A. (2003). A qualitative study of adaptation experiences of 1.5-generation Asian Americans. *Cultural Diversity Ethnic Minority Psychology*, *9*(2), 156–170. https://doi.org/10.1037/1099-9809.9.2.156

Kim, S. E., Zhao, Z., Wong, S. H. M., & Toomey, R. B. (2023). Racial-ethnic socialization, racial discrimination, and internalization of the model minority myth in East Asian families. *Journal of Research on Adolescence*, *33*(2), 458–468. https://doi.org/10.1111/jora.12817

Knight, G. P., Bernal, M. E., Garza, C. A., Cota, M. K., & Ocampo, K. A. (1993). Family socialization and the ethnic identity of Mexican-American children. *Journal of Cross-Cultural Psychology*, *24*(1), 99–114. https://doi.org/10.1177/0022022193241007

Lee, J., & Zhou, M. (2014). The success frame and achievement paradox: the costs and consequences for Asian Americans. *Race and Social Problems*, *6*(1), 38–55. https://doi.org/10.1007/s12552-014-9112-7

Lee, J., Cheon, Y. M., Wei, X., & Chung, G. H. (2018). The role of ethnic socialization, ethnic identity and self-esteem: implications for bi-ethnic adolescents' school adjustment. *Journal of Child and Family Studies*, *27*(12), 3831–3841. https://doi.org/10.1007/s10826-018-1235-9

Lee, R. M., Grotevant, H. D., Hellerstedt, W. L., & Gunnar, M. R. (2006). Cultural socialization in families with internationally adopted children. *Journal of Family Psychology*, *20*(4), 571–580. https://doi.org/10.1037/0893-3200.20.4.571

Lee, S., Juon, H.-S., Martinez, G., Hsu, C. E., Robinson, E. S., Bawa, J., & Ma, G. X. (2009). Model minority at risk: expressed needs of mental health by Asian American young adults. *Journal of Community Health*, *34*(2), 144–152. https://doi.org/10.1007/s10900-008-9137-1

Li, G. (2005). Other people's success: impact of the "model minority" myth on underachieving Asian students in North America. In G. Li, & L. Wang (Eds.), *Model Minority Myth Revisited: An Interdisciplinary Approach to Demystifying Asian American Educational Experiences* (pp. 213–231). Emerald Publishing Limited.

Lim, A. J., Lau, C. Y. H., & Cheng, C. Y. (2021). Applying the dual filial piety model in the United States: a comparison of filial piety between Asian Americans and Caucasian Americans. *Frontiers in Psychology*, *12*, 786609. https://doi.org/10.3389/fpsyg.2021.786609

Lopez, L. K. (2021). Excessively Asian: crying, crazy rich Asians, and the construction of Asian American audiences. *Critical Studies in Media Communication*, *38*(2), 141–154. https://doi.org/10.1080/15295036.2021.1883193

Lou, E., Lalonde, R. N., & Wilson, C. (2011). Examining a multidimensional framework of racial identity across different biracial groups. *Asian American Journal of Psychology*, *2*(2), 79–90. https://doi.org/10.1037/a0023658

Marcia, J. E. (1980). Identity in adolescence. In J. Adelson (Ed.), *Handbook of Adolescent Psychology* (Vol. 9) (pp. 109–137). Wiley.

Miller-Cotto, D., & Byrnes, J. P. (2016). Ethnic/racial identity and academic achievement: a meta-analytic review. *Developmental Review*, *41*, 51–70. https://doi.org/10.1016/j.dr.2016.06.003

Monte, L. M., & Shin, H. B. (2022). 20.6 million people in the U.S. identify as Asian, Native Hawaiian or Pacific Islander. Census.gov. https://www.census.gov/library/stories/2022/05/aanhpi-population-diverse-geographically-dispersed.html#:~:text=The%202020%20Census%20shows%3A,in%20combination%20with%20another%20race

Nelson, S. C., Syed, M., Tran, A., Hu, A. W., & Lee, R. M. (2018). Pathways to ethnic-racial identity development and psychological adjustment: the differential associations of cultural socialization by parents and peers. *Developmental Psychology*, *54*(11), 2166–2180. https://doi.org/10.1037/dev0000597

Nhan, E. R., Williamson-Raun, A. R., Chan, R., & Yang, J. P. (2024). Ethnic identity protects and internalized racism harms health and coping in Asian Americans following COVID-19 discrimination: a mixed-methods study. *Journal of Racial and Ethnic Health Disparities*. https://doi.org/10.1007/s40615-024-02000-5

Oikawa, S., & Yoshida, T. (2007). An identity based on being different: a focus on biethnic individuals in Japan. *International Journal of Intercultural Relations*, *31*(6), 633–653. https://doi.org/10.1016/j.ijintrel.2007.05.001

Oyserman, D., & Sakamoto, I. (1997). Being Asian American: identity, cultural constructs, and stereotype perception. *The Journal of Applied Behavioral Science*, *33*(4), 435–453. https://doi.org/10.1177/0021886397334002

Park, K. (1999). "I really do feel I'm 1.5!": The construction of self and community by young Korean Americans. *Amerasia Journal*, *25*(1), 139–163.

Patel, P., Martin Romero, M. Y., Stein, G. L., & Raval, V. (2023). Promoting pride but missing the need for preparation for bias: racial-ethnic socialization among Indian American families living in the southeast U.S. *Asian American Journal of Psychology*, *14*(3), 250–261. https://doi.org/10.1037/aap0000296

Phinney, J. S. (1990). Ethnic identity in adolescents and adults: review of research. *Psychological Bulletin*, *108*(3), 499–514. https://doi.org/10.1037/0033-2909.108.3.499

Phinney, J. S. (1992). The multigroup ethnic identity measure: a new scale for use with diverse groups. *Journal of Adolescent Research*, *7*(2), 156–176.

Phinney, J. S., Romero, I., Nava, M., & Huang, D. (2001). The role of language, parents, and peers in ethnic identity among adolescents in immigrant families. *Journal of Youth and Adolescence*, *30*(2), 135–153. https://doi.org/10.1023/A:1010389607319

Piaget, J. (1971). The theory of stages in cognitive development. In D. R. Green, M. P. Ford, & G. B. Flamer (Eds.), *Measurement and Piaget* (pp. ix, 283). McGraw-Hill.

Priest, N., Doery, K., Truong, M., Guo, S., Perry, R., Trenerry, B., ... Paradies, Y. (2021). Updated systematic review and meta-analysis of studies examining the relationship between reported racism and health and well-being for children and youth: a protocol. *BMJ Open*, *11*(6), e043722. https://doi.org/10.1136/bmjopen-2020-043722

Quinn, P. C., Uttley, L., Lee, K., Gibson, A., Smith, M., Slater, A. M., & Pascalis, O. (2008). Infant preference for female faces occurs for same- but not other-race faces. *Journal of Neuropsychology*, *2*(1), 15–26. https://doi.org/10.1348/174866407x231029

Rajagopal, S. K., & Durkee, M. I. (2024). Internalizing the model minority myth: dangers for Asian American mental health and attitudes towards other minorities. *Social and Personality Psychology Compass*, *18*(5), e12959. https://doi.org/10.1111/spc3.12959

Rivas-Drake, D., Syed, M., Umaña-Taylor, A., Markstrom, C., French, S., Schwartz, S. J., ... Ethnic and Racial Identity in the 21st Century Study Group. (2014). Feeling good, happy, and proud: a meta-analysis of positive ethnic–racial affect and adjustment. *Child Development*, *85*(1), 77–102. https://doi.org/10.1111/cdev.12175

Rogers, L. O., Kiang, L., White, L., Calzada, E. J., Umaña-Taylor, A. J., Byrd, C., ... Whitesell, N. (2020). Persistent concerns: questions for research on ethnic-racial identity development. *Research in Human Development*, *17*(2–3), 130–153. https://doi.org/10.1080/15427609.2020.1831881

Root, M. P. P. (1997). Multiracial Asians: models of ethnic identity. *Amerasia Journal*, *23*(1), 29–42. https://doi.org/10.17953/amer.23.1.27475111p281288m

Rumbaut, R. G. (1994). The crucible within: ethnic identity, self-esteem, and segmented assimilation among children of immigrants. *International Migration Review*, *28*(4), 748–794. https://doi.org/10.1177/019791839402800407

Rumbaut, R. G., & Ima, K. (1988). The adaptation of Southeast Asian refugee youth: a comparative study. Final Report to the U.S. Office of Refugee Resettlement. San Diego State University.

Sangrigoli, S., & De Schonen, S. (2004). Recognition of own-race and other-race faces by three-month-old infants. *Journal of Child Psychology and Psychiatry*, *45*(7), 1219–1227. https://doi.org/10.1111/j.1469-7610.2004.00319.x

Schild, L., Ling, C., Blackburn, J., Stringhini, G., Zhang, Y., & Zannettou, S. (2020). "Go eat a bat, Chang!": an early look on the emergence of Sinophobic behavior on web communities in the face of COVID-19. *ArXiv:2004.04046*.

Sellers, R. M., Rowley, S. A. J., Chavous, T. M., Shelton, J. N., & Smith, M. A. (1997). Multidimensional inventory of black identity: a preliminary investigation of reliability and construct validity. *Journal of Personality and Social Psychology*, *73*(4), 805–815.

Settles, I. H., & Buchanan, N. T. (2014). Multiple groups, multiple identities, and intersectionality. In V. Benet-Martínez (Ed.), *The Oxford Handbook of Multicultural Identity* (pp. 160–180). Oxford University Press. https://doi.org/10.1093/oxfordhb/9780199796694.001.0001

Sladek, M. R., Umaña-Taylor, A. J., Hardesty, J. L., Aguilar, G., Bates, D., Bayless, S. D., ... Vázquez, M. A. (2022). "So, like, it's all a mix of one": intersecting contexts of adolescents' ethnic-racial socialization. *Child Development*, *93*(5), 1284–1303. https://doi.org/10.1111/cdev.13756

Smith, T. B., & Silva, L. (2011). Ethnic identity and personal well-being of people of color: a meta-analysis. *Journal of Counseling Psychology*, *58*(1), 42–60. https://doi.org/10.1037/a0021528

Spielman, B. (2012). Elderly, social attitudes toward. In R. Chadwick (Ed.), *Encyclopedia of Applied Ethics* (Second Edition) (pp. 56–62). Academic Press. https://doi.org/10.1016/B978-0-12-373932-2.00304-5

Sue, D. W., Capodilupo, C. M., Torino, G. C., Bucceri, J. M., Holder, A. M. B., Nadal, K. L., & Esquilin, M. (2007). Racial microaggressions in everyday life: implications for clinical practice. *American Psychologist*, *62*(4), 271–286. https://doi.org/10.1037/0003-066X.62.4.271

Suzuki-Crumly, J., & Hyers, L. L. (2004). The relationship among ethnic identity, psychological well-being, and intergroup competence: an investigation of two biracial groups. *Cultural Diversity & Ethnic Minority Psychology*, *10*(2), 137–150. https://doi.org/10.1037/1099-9809.10.2.137

Syed, M., & Juan, M. J. (2012). Birds of an ethnic feather? Ethnic identity homophily among college-age friends. *Journal of Adolescence*, *35*(6), 1505–1514. https://doi.org/10.1016/j.adolescence.2011.10.012

TAAF. (2024). *Beyond the Surface: Youth Mental Health Study 2024*. https://www.taaf.org/youthmentalhealth

Tan, J. B., & Yates, S. (2011). Academic expectations as sources of stress in Asian students. *Social Psychology of Education*, *14*(3), 389–407. https://doi.org/10.1007/s11218-010-9146-7

Thompson, G., McBride, R. B., Hosford, C. C., & Halaas, G. (2016). Resilience among medical students: the role of coping style and social support. *Teaching and Learning in Medicine*, *28*(2), 174–182. https://doi.org/10.1080/10401334.2016.1146611

Ting, J. Y., & Hwang, W.-C. (2009). Cultural influences on help-seeking attitudes in Asian American students. *American Journal of Orthopsychiatry*, *79*(1), 125–132. https://doi.org/10.1037/a0015394

Ting-Toomey, S., Yee-Jung, K. K., Shapiro, R. B., Garcia, W., Wright, T. J., & Oetzel, J. G. (2000). Ethnic/cultural identity salience and conflict styles in four US ethnic groups. *International Journal of Intercultural Relations*, *24*(1), 47–81. https://doi.org/10.1016/S0147-1767(99)00023-1

Torres, L., & Ong, A. D. (2010). A daily diary investigation of Latino ethnic identity, discrimination, and depression. *Cultural Diversity Ethnic Minority Psychology*, *16*(4), 561–568. https://doi.org/10.1037/a0020652

Tran, A. G. T. T., & Lee, R. M. (2010). Perceived ethnic–racial socialization, ethnic identity, and social competence among Asian American late adolescents. *Cultural Diversity & Ethnic Minority Psychology*, *16*(2), 169–178. https://doi.org/10.1037/a0016400

Ulbricht, J., Schachner, M. K., Civitillo, S., & Noack, P. (2022). Teachers' acculturation in culturally diverse schools - how is the perceived diversity climate linked to intercultural self-efficacy? *Frontiers in Psychology*, *13*, 953068. https://doi.org/10.3389/fpsyg.2022.953068

Umaña-Taylor, A. J., Yazedjian, A., & Bámaca-Gómez, M. (2004). Developing the ethnic identity scale using Eriksonian and social identity perspectives. *Identity*, *4*(1), 9–38. https://doi.org/10.1207/S1532706XID0401_2

Useem, J., Useem, R., & Donoghue, J. (1963). Men in the middle of the third culture: the roles of American and Non-Western people in cross-cultural administration. *Human Organization*, *22*(3), 169–179. https://doi.org/10.17730/humo.22.3.5470n44338kk6733

Vaghela, P., & Ueno, K. (2017). Racial-ethnic identity pairings and mental health of second-generation Asian adolescents. *Sociological Perspectives*, *60*(4), 834–852.

VandenBos, G. R. (Ed.). (2007). *APA Dictionary of Psychology*. American Psychological Association.

Wang, Y. (2021). Daily ethnic/racial context in peer groups: frequency, structure, and implications for adolescent outcomes. *Child Development*, *92*(2), 650–661. https://doi.org/10.1111/cdev.13509

Wang, Y., Zhang, Y., & Wadsworth, H. (2023). Family and peer ethnic-racial socialization in adolescents' everyday life: a daily transactional model with ethnic-racial identity and discrimination. *Child Development*, *94*(6), 1566–1580. https://doi.org/10.1111/cdev.13937

Wheeler, A., Anzures, G., Quinn, P. C., Pascalis, O., Omrin, D. S., & Lee, K. (2011). Caucasian infants scan own- and other-race faces differently. *PLoS One*, *6*(4), e18621. https://doi.org/10.1371/journal.pone.0018621

Williams, C. D., Byrd, C. M., Quintana, S. M., Anicama, C., Kiang, L., Umaña-Taylor, A. J., ... Whitesell, N. (2020). A lifespan model of ethnic-racial identity. *Research in Human Development*, *17*(2–3), 99–129. https://doi.org/10.1080/15427609.2020.1831882

Wing, J. Y. (2007). Beyond black and white: the model minority myth and the invisibility of Asian American students. *The Urban Review*, *39*(4), 455–487. https://doi.org/10.1007/s11256-007-0058-6

Wong, F., & Halgin, R. (2006). The "model minority": bane or blessing for Asian Americans? *Journal of Multicultural Counseling and Development*, *34*(1), 38–49. https://doi.org/10.1002/j.2161-1912.2006.tb00025.x

Wong-Padoongpatt, G., Zane, N., Okazaki, S., & Saw, A. (2020). Individual variations in stress response to racial microaggressions among Asian Americans. *Asian American Journal of Psychology*, *11*(3), 126–137. https://doi.org/10.1037/aap0000182

Woo, B., Maglalang, D. D., Ko, S., Park, M., Choi, Y., & Takeuchi, D. T. (2020). Racial discrimination, ethnic-racial socialization, and cultural identities among Asian American youths. *Cultural Diversity and Ethnic Minority Psychology*, *26*(4), 447–459. https://doi.org/10.1037/cdp0000327

Xie, M., Yip, T., Cham, H., & El-Sheikh, M. (2021). The impact of daily discrimination on sleep/wake problem trajectories among diverse adolescents. *Child Development*, *92*(5), e1061–e1074. https://doi.org/10.1111/cdev.13605

Yang, Y., Emmen, R. A. G., van Veen, D., & Mesman, J. (2022). Perceived discrimination, ethnic identity, and ethnic-racial socialization in Chinese immigrant families before and after the COVID-19 outbreak: an exploratory natural experiment. *International Journal of Intercultural Relations*, *91*, 27–37. https://doi.org/10.1016/j.ijintrel.2022.09.001

Yeh, K.-H., & Bedford, O. (2003). A test of the Dual Filial Piety model. *Asian Journal of Social Psychology*, *6*, 215–228. https://doi.org/10.1046/j.1467-839X.2003.00122.x

Yip, T. (2018). Ethnic/racial identity—a double-edged sword? Associations with discrimination and psychological outcomes. *Current Directions in Psychological Science*, *27*(3), 170–175. https://doi.org/10.1177/0963721417739348

Yip, T., & Fuligni, A. J. (2002). Daily variation in ethnic identity, ethnic behaviors, and psychological well-being among American adolescents of Chinese descent. *Child Development*, *73*(5), 1557–1572.

Yip, T., Chung, K., & Chae, D. H. (2024). Vicarious racism, ethnic/racial identity, and sleep among Asian Americans. *Cultural Diversity & Ethnic Minority Psychology*, *30*(2), 319–329. https://doi.org/10.1037/cdp0000534

Yip, T., Gee, C. G., & Takeuchi, T. D. (2008). Racial discrimination and psychological distress: the impact of ethnic identity and age among immigrant and United States-born Asian adults. *Developmental Psychology*, *44*(3), 787–800. https://doi.org/10.1037/0012-1649.44.3.787

Yip, T., Wang, Y., Mootoo, C., & Mirpuri, S. (2019). Moderating the association between discrimination and adjustment: a meta-analysis of ethnic/racial identity. *Developmental Psychology*, *55*(6), 1274–1298. https://doi.org/10.1037/dev0000708

Yoo, H. C., & Lee, R. M. (2005). Ethnic identity and approach-type coping as moderators of the racial discrimination/well-being relation in Asian Americans. *Journal of Counseling Psychology*, *52*(4), 497–506. https://doi.org/10.1037/0022-0167.52.4.497

Yoo, H. C., Miller, M. J., & Yip, P. (2015). Validation of the internalization of the Model Minority Myth Measure (IM-4) and its link to academic performance and psychological adjustment among Asian American adolescents. *Cultural Diversity & Ethnic Minority Psychology*, *21*(2), 237–246. https://doi.org/10.1037/a0037648

Zhang, J. (2024). The influence of cultural identity on language acquisition in "Third Culture Kids (TCKs)" in America with East Asian backgrounds. *Communications in Humanities Research, 45*, 45–50. https://doi.org/10.54254/2753-7064/45/20240078

2

Bridging Cultural Gaps in Parenting and Parent–Child Relationships in Asian American Families to Improve Child and Adolescent Mental Health

Aya Inamori Williams[1], Sara Chung[2], and Qing Zhou[3]

[1]*Santa Clara University, Santa Clara, CA, USA*
[2]*University of California, San Francisco, CA, USA*
[3]*University of California, Berkeley, CA, USA*

Asian American communities have persistently faced disparities in mental health service use and research (Cook et al., 2017; Đoàn et al., 2019). A recent national, large-scale study has found that compared to White children and youth, Black children were 17% less likely, Latine children 23% less likely, and Asian children 52% less likely to receive a diagnosis for a mental health condition before age 12. This gap widens into adolescence and young adulthood (Adams et al., 2024). Interestingly, these disparities in diagnosis and treatment are not as pronounced for those residing in Asia (see China, Taiwan, Thailand, Malaysia, Afghanistan, Sri Lanka; Chen et al., 2019; Feng et al., 2024; Liu et al., 2018; Ranjan et al., 2024), thus highlighting the importance of focusing on Asian immigrant communities. Meta-analyses have shown that when interventions are culturally adapted, parenting behaviors and child outcomes improve (Van Mourik et al., 2017), and for psychosocial treatment outcomes, the average effect size of cultural adaptations for Asian was more than twice those for Black and Latine samples (Smith et al., 2011). Thus, cultural fit of treatment may be especially critical for Asian American families and communities.

Parent–Child Relationships, Parenting Practices, and Emotional Communication in Asian American Families

A unique developmental experience for children in immigrant families is their exposure to multiple languages and multiple sets of cultural values and belief systems across their social milieu (family, school, peers, neighborhood, and community). Such multilingual and multicultural experiences are associated with opportunities (e.g., cognitive benefits; greater employment opportunities and earning potential; creativity; global awareness) and challenges (e.g., experience of racial discrimination, xenophobia, systematic racism, intergenerational acculturation gap, and acculturative stress). Thus, when working with Asian American youth, clinicians need to conduct a thorough assessment of youths and caregivers' cultural orientations and acculturation-related stressors to better understand the roles of cultural context, norms, and practices in symptoms, etiology, help-seeking, and treatment engagement processes.

For Asian American youth and parents/caregivers, cultural orientation is a bidirectional process consisting of acculturation or host cultural orientation (i.e., one's adaptation of, engagement in, or identification of the language, behaviors, and beliefs and values of the host culture) and enculturation or heritage cultural orientation (i.e., one's maintenance, acquisition, or adaptation of the language, behaviors, and beliefs/values of the heritage culture) (Tsai & Chentsova-Dutton, 2002). Due to generational, age, and contextual differences in acculturation process, Asian American children and their caregivers often acculturate (i.e., process of adapting to the host culture) and enculturate (i.e., process of maintaining the heritage culture) at different paces, resulting in intergenerational dissonance in cultural orientations (Lui, 2019). These intergenerational gaps can escalate parent–child conflict, obstruct parent–child open communication, and undermine the quality of parent–child relationships, all of which are risk factors for youth mental health adjustment (Chung et al., 2021; Lui, 2019).

To illustrate the complex and multiple roles of parent–child cultural orientations in shaping parenting, parent–child relationships and psychological adjustment in Asian American families, we have developed a heuristic model (see Figure 2.1). According to this model, parents' and children's cultural orientations and parent–child cultural fit can jointly shape parenting practices and parent–child relationships, which in turn shape parents' and children's psychological well-being. Furthermore, cultural orientations are dynamic processes such that children's and parents' psychological well-being can have reciprocal influences on their cultural orientations and parent–child cultural dissonance.

Empirical support for this model has been found in our longitudinal study of over 250 first-generation (foreign-born) and second-generation (US-born with at least one foreign-born parent) children (initially 6–9 years of age, 52% boys, 48% girls) in Chinese American immigrant families (Chen et al., 2014, 2015). For example, parents' Chinese proficiency and children's American proficiency were both associated with higher authoritative parenting. Moreover, a higher parent–child

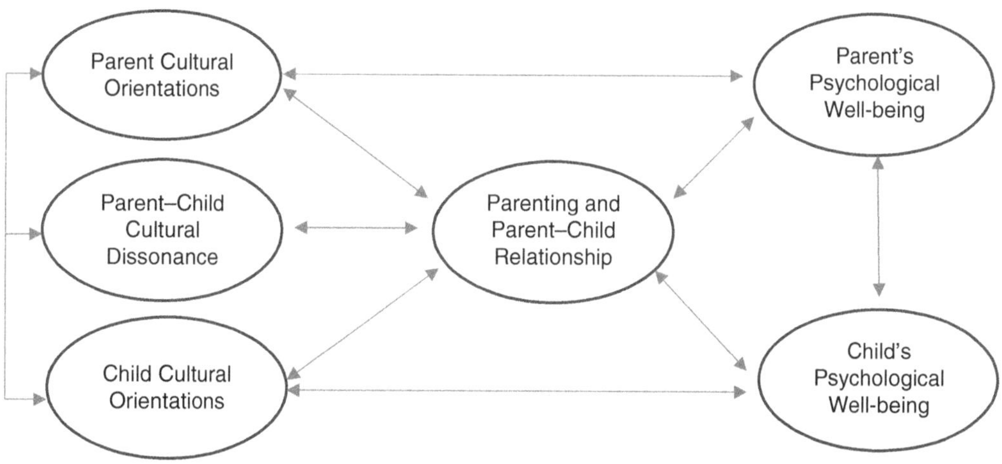

Figure 2.1 Heuristic model on associations between cultural orientations, parenting and parent–child relationships, and parent's and child's psychological well-being in immigrant families.

gap in Chinese proficiency was associated with parents' reduced use of authoritative parenting, which in turn predicted children's poorer psychological adjustment (Chen et al., 2014). Both parents' American and Chinese orientations were associated with higher self-reported emotional expressivity in the family (Chen et al., 2015). Furthermore, the relation between parents' Chinese orientation and their emotional expressivity varied by children's Chinese orientation, such that a higher parent–child gap in Chinese orientation was associated with reduced expressions of positive emotions (Chen et al., 2015). We also found that parents, children, and independent observers had low agreement in their perceptions of intrusive parenting: children perceived lower intrusive parenting in families with more acculturated parents and less enculturated children; parents displayed more intrusive parenting when interacting with children who were more acculturated (Kho et al., 2019).

Cultural Values and Practices Related to Family Relationship, Parenting, and Emotion

Cross-cultural research in developmental, social, and clinical psychology has identified a variety of differences and similarities in cultural values and practices related to parenting, parent–child relationships, and communication of emotion between White American, Asian, and Asian American groups (see Table 2.1). These cultural values and practices have important implications for clinical work with Asian American youth and families.

In Asian communities, individuals are often intricately connected with and embedded in groups, including family (Triandis, 2018; Chentsova-Dutton & Ryder, 2020). The cultural value of *familism* emphasizes family unity and loyalty, and individuals are expected to prioritize family needs and goals, make commitment to, and receive support from the family (Choi et al., 2021). This contrasts individualistic values of (1) autonomy (a person's capacity for independent thinking, judgment, and survival); (2) mutual self-responsibility (a person accepts responsibility for self and for their actions, and has confidence in one's abilities); and (3) uniqueness (a person sees oneself as being different from the others; Realo, 2002). Research conducted with Filipino American and Korean American adolescents (Choi et al., 2021) has identified six subdomains of Asian familism values: (1) traditional manners and etiquette (e.g., uses proper addressing terms); (2) respect for adults; (3) caring for aging parents (filial piety); (4) centrality of the family; (5) harmony and sacrifice; and (6) parental expectation of family obligation.

For immigrant children and youth, endorsement of heritage cultural values can serve as both protective and risk factors. Interestingly, none of the familism subdomains was significantly associated with Asian immigrant youths' acculturation levels, suggesting that immigrant youth's acculturation to the mainstream culture and engagement in the heritage culture (i.e., enculturation) are independent processes (Choi et al., 2021). Furthermore, different familism values showed divergent relations to youths' adjustment: while higher endorsement of respect for adults, caring for aging parents, harmony and sacrifice were associated with lower depressive symptoms and antisocial behaviors in Filipino American youth, perceived parental expectation of family obligation was associated with higher depressive symptoms in both Korean American and Filipino American youths (Choi et al., 2021).

Table 2.1 Comparison of Eastern and Western cultural values and practices on parenting, family relationships, emotion, and academic achievement.

	Asian American cultures	European American culture	Clinical considerations
Individualism vs. collectivism/ familism	*Familism*: emphasizes family unity and loyalty; individuals are expected to prioritize family needs/goals over individual needs/goals, make commitment to, and receive support from the family. *Familism values:* • Traditional manners and etiquette • Respect for adults • Caring for aging parents (filial piety) • Centrality of the family • Harmony and sacrifice • Parental expectation of family obligation	*Individualism*: individuals are independent from their groups and are primarily motivated by their own preferences, needs, and rights. *Individualism values:* • Autonomy • Mutual self-responsibility • Uniqueness	• Family migration and immigration history • Acculturation and language proficiencies and exposure • Family cultural values • Racial-ethnic identity *Clinical tools:* • Cultural Formulation Interview • Cultural Genogram • Family Ecomap • Social Identity Wheel
Family relationship	*Parent–child relationship*: family relationship is hierarchical; children are expected to show respect for, listen to, and obey parents/elders (even when they disagree). Parent–child communication is unidirectional, with parents giving instructions and commands while children listen, obey, and follow. *Sibling relationship*: older siblings are expected to care for, serve as role model, and guide younger siblings; young siblings are expected to show respect for and learn from older siblings; the oldest sibling (first son or first daughter) is expected to take on more family responsibilities than younger siblings.	*Parent–child relationship:* family relationship is egalitarian—both parents and children are expected to treat each other with respect. Parent–child communication is reciprocal and bidirectional. When disagreement occurs, family members (including parents and children) are expected to work collaboratively to resolve conflict through negotiation and compromise. *Sibling relationship*: siblings (regardless of age, birth order, and gender) are regarded as equal members of the family and treated fairly and equitably in terms of family obligations, benefits, and responsibilities.	• Family structure and household composition • Parent–child relationships and parent–child interactions • Sibling relationship • Interparental relationship • Relationships with extended family (e.g., grandparents) • Family conflict and family cohesiveness *Clinical tools:* • Attachment and Culture/Race-Related Interview • Adult Attachment Interview • Family Assessment Device • EFFT Cycle

(*Continued*)

Table 2.1 (Continued)

	Asian American cultures	European American culture	Clinical considerations
Parenting	*Training/Guan/ga-jung-kyo-yuk:* parents have the obligation to teach, train, and guide children in socially appropriate behaviors. *Care-oriented power-assertive parenting:* parental display of power-assertive behaviors (e.g., strict discipline, criticism, and demanding compliance) that are motivated by and reflect parental concern and care for the child. *Psychological control*: intrusive and manipulative parenting behaviors aimed at controlling children's decisions, thoughts, and feelings, reflects the opposite end of autonomy support (e.g., love withdrawal, guilt induction, shaming, invalidating, and intruding into children's personal domain). Asian parents displayed higher psychological control than White parents.	*Authoritative parenting*: the parenting style that balances warmth and control. Parents are expected to show love and affection, be sensitive to children's needs and emotions, and have an intimate relationship with their children. Discipline is best practiced by setting clear expectations, reasoning and induction (providing rationales and explaining consequences), and consistent behavioral consequences (e.g., verbal praises, rewards, and loss of privileges) *Autonomy support*: parents support children's development of independence and allow and encourage them to express themselves and make choices for themselves. White American parents endorsed higher autonomy support than Asian parents.	• Parenting styles • Coparenting (mother, father, grandparents, other caregivers) • Differential parenting across siblings *Clinical tools:* • Observation of caregiver–child free play • Eyberg Child Behavior Inventory • Parenting Styles and Dimensions Questionnaire—Short Form • Parenting Stress Inventory—Short Form • Grandparental Involvement Inventory • Parenting Sense of Competence Scale
Emotion	*Emotion expression:* Asian and Asian American contexts value suppression of emotions in some situations. *Ideal affect*: Asian and Asian American individuals prefer low-intensity positive affect more than high-intensity positive affect. *Emotion talk*: Chinese parents tended to use a "behavioral style" by emphasizing the consequences of children's behaviors.	*Emotion expression:* White American contexts value open expression of emotions. *Ideal affect*: White American individuals prefer high-intensity positive affect more than low-intensity positive affect. *Emotion talk*: White American parents tended to use a "cognitive style" by providing more elaborative explanations of emotions.	• Emotion expressiveness • Emotion values (e.g., ideal affect, values regarding emotion control) • Emotion communications within the family *Clinical tools:* • Affect Valuation Index • EFFT Cycle

Family Relationship: Egalitarianism and Hierarchy

These broad cultural values can shape family dynamics and parent–child relationships. In traditional Asian families, family relationships are hierarchical, ordered by generational status and birth order. Children are expected to show respect for, listen, and obey parents and elders (e.g., 尊老爱幼, respect the elderly and love the young). Parent–child communication tends to be unidirectional, with parents providing directions and children following and complying. Children's open expression of disagreement is often viewed as "impolite" to a slight degree or an act of questioning or intrusion on parental authority more seriously. Similarly, sibling relationship is hierarchical, often ordered by birth order and gender status. Older siblings are expected to care for and look after younger siblings, and younger siblings are expected to follow and obey older siblings (e.g., 長兄如父, 長嫂如母 the eldest brother is like a father, the eldest sister-in-law is like a mother). By contrast, White American families endorse relatively egalitarian values, whereby parent–child communication is reciprocal and bidirectional, and democratic participation is valued (e.g., children are encouraged to voice their opinions and desires, especially on matters related to personal domain; Wang & Fivush, 2005). These contrasting values are associated with different parental expectations for children's behaviors.

Parenting: Authoritative Style, Guan, and Autonomy Support

Cultural values regarding a person's relationship with their family can further shape parenting goals and practices, as a key goal of socialization is to bring children into conforming and contributing members of the society. Seen as "universally beneficial," authoritative parenting has been associated with favorable mental health and behavioral outcomes in Asian children from preschool-age to adolescents (Ng & Wang, 2019; Shen et al., 2018). Authoritative parenting is characterized by high parental warmth (i.e., high amounts of affection, acceptance of their child, and sensitivity to their needs and feelings), and high parental control (i.e., exertion of age-appropriate control of children's behaviors via setting clear expectations and (Baumrind, 1996). The balance between the two dimensions promotes children's emotional security and self-regulation (Lansford, 2017; Zhou et al., 2008). It is important to note that authoritative parenting has been consistently observed and endorsed by Asian parents of different ethnic, socioeconomic, political, and geographical backgrounds (see Ng & Wang, 2019, for a review).

However, there are many nuanced aspects of Asian parenting that are not captured by authoritative parenting. Most notably, the Asian parenting ideology of *guan* 管 (to govern) or *jiao xun* 教訓 (training) rooted in Confucianism entails that parents have the obligation to govern and train children out of love and care so that children can become thriving members of the society (Chao, 1994). In Korean culture, a similar parenting ideology to training is *ga-jung-kyo-yuk* (i.e., family socialization, Choi et al., 2013). Training can be reflected in parenting beliefs (e.g., 養不教, 父之過, raising a child without teaching them right from wrong is the father's fault) and parenting practices (e.g., maintain high control to make the child learn and thrive, criticize the child to push them to work harder). Asian parents' practice of training might sometimes resemble the form of strict, coercive, and punitive control characteristic of authoritarian parenting, although they are motivated by parents' love and care for children (Chen et al., 2019). Not surprisingly, Asian parents displayed higher levels of authoritarian parenting compared to White American parents in cross-national studies (Deater-Deckard et al., 2011). Chen (2025) characterized the combination of care and power in Chinese parenting as "care-based power-assertive parenting": the use of authority (e.g., strict discipline, criticism, and demanding compliance) motivated by parents' love and care for the child (Chen, 2025).

In Asian American families, children's developing autonomy and independence can clash with the collective values of interdependence, familism, and parenting etiologies such as *guan* and training. Thus, the socialization impact of parental autonomy support (practices that support development of independence and encourage children to express and make decisions themselves) and psychological control are more heterogeneous compared to White American samples. On the one hand, autonomy support predicted favorable outcomes among East Asian children and adolescents, whereas the opposite relations were found with psychological control (Pomerantz & Wang, 2009). On the other hand, the strength of relations between autonomy support or psychological control and children's emotional well-being and academic learning was found to be weaker in Asian American family contexts than in White American family contexts (Ng et al., 2019; Pomerantz & Wang, 2009). This is consistent with the perspective that cultural values and norms can moderate the psychological consequences of parenting practices, but cultural values cannot revert the harmful consequences of parenting practices that are inherently inconsistent with basic psychological needs of human nature (e.g., physical abuse, emotional abuse).

Emotion: Expressivity, Ideal Affect, and Emotion Talk

Extensive research has demonstrated that emotion plays an indispensable role in shaping parenting, parent–child and family relationships, as well as child well-being. In Asian communities, open expression of emotions can be viewed as disruptive to interpersonal harmony and undermine the individual's connectedness with the group. Asian cultural practices therefore encourage moderation and suppression of emotions (Matsumoto, 1990; Mauss & Butler, 2010) in contrast to individualistic contexts that support open expression of emotions (especially self-oriented emotions such as happiness, pride, and anger) that enable the individual to assert the self and be apart from the group (Markus & Kitayama, 1991; Rychlowska et al., 2005). The cultural "fit" of these practices matters in predicting mental health consequences. Individuals in Asian cultures suppressed emotions more than those of White American cultures, yet the associations between emotion suppression and adverse mental health outcomes were found to be weaker in Asian compared to White American samples (Tsai & Lu, 2018).

Culture and context shape psychological health by transmitting beliefs about which emotional states are valued (e.g., ideal affect, Tsai et al., 2006; Tsai, 2007, see Chapter 3). For example, those who endorse collective values prefer to experience low-arousal positive affect (e.g., calm, peaceful, and relaxed) more than high-arousal positive affect (e.g., excited, enthusiastic, and elated), likely because adjusting to others (emphasized in Asian cultures) often involves suspending actions and decreasing physiological arousal (Tsai, 2007). In contrast, those who endorse individualistic values prefer to experience high-arousal positive affect more than low-arousal positive affect, likely because influencing others (emphasized in White American cultures) usually involves actions and requires increased physiological arousal (Tsai, 2007). Individual differences in ideal affect have implications for mental health, as researchers have found that college students who valued high arousal positive affect were less likely to have depressive symptoms, but more likely to have anxiety and alcohol abuse symptoms (Swerdlow et al., 2019).

Emotion talk, or verbal communications addressing feeling states, emotion-related sensations, and physiological states, has been found to vary across cultural contexts. For example, when talking about past emotion-related experiences with children, Chinese mothers used a more "behavioral approach" by emphasizing the negative consequences of children's behaviors (Wang & Fivush, 2005), which is consistent with *guan* and training, where White American mothers used a "cognitive approach" by providing more elaborative explanations about the causes of emotions (Wang & Fivush, 2005). Cultural differences in emotion talk might be attributed to cultural differences in values toward emotion expression or regulation, or language differences in emotion words (e.g., there are more than 2,000 estimated emotion words in English and only about 953 estimated emotion words in Mandarin Chinese, Wallace & Carson, 1973; Ng et al., 2019). Because emotion talk is one pathway in which caregivers socialize children's emotion understanding and regulation, it is considered a key mechanism through which cultural values about emotion are transmitted across generations.

Below, we describe how these concepts may be implemented in clinical settings through a case illustration of attention deficit/hyperactivity disorder (ADHD), a condition that impacts approximately 10% of children and youth living in the United States. Importantly, we show how shifting treatment targets to parenting and parent–child relationships through the Asian American family and cultural lens led to improvements in the symptoms of ADHD.

Clinical Case Study: "Math Is Boring and I Am Just a Little Lazy"

Attention deficit/hyperactivity disorder (ADHD) is diagnosed in approximately 1 in 11 US children (Bitsko et al., 2024). Current estimates indicate underdiagnosis of ADHD in Asian youth, despite similar prevalence rates across North America and Asia (Polanczyk et al., 2014). Recent analyses of the 2018 National Survey of Children's Health found that Asian youth were 73% less likely than White youth to receive an ADHD diagnosis, followed by Latine (32%) and Black youth (22%; Zhao et al., 2023). Asian children with ADHD were 46% less likely than their White peers to have received treatment for ADHD (Shi et al., 2021). Importantly, Asian communities have historically been underrepresented in ADHD treatment studies for children and youth, represented by only 1.43% of 10,604 participants (see Merrill et al., 2024, for a review). There is a need to build on this limited research (Payakachat et al., 2019; Chung et al., 2019; Chung et al., 2024), particularly in the areas of mental health stigma and related help-seeking (Chung et al., 2025). Even within a single healthcare system—in which groups have relatively equal access to ADHD care, Asian had lower rates of treatment utilization than White, Black, and Latine youth (Chung et al., 2019). ADHD-related impairments may be especially detrimental to Asian youth, who are already at heightened risk for parent–child conflict, low self-esteem, suicidal ideation, and academically related anxiety (Shen et al., 2021).

Eleven-year-old Allie lived with her family in a first- and second-generation Chinese American household in greater Los Angeles area. Her mother was born in rural China and was raised by a single mother (i.e., first generation). Her father was born in the United States (i.e., second generation) and grew up a large immigrant family residing in a predominantly Chinese ethnic enclave. Allie was raised with a 7-year old younger brother Andy who did not participate in treatment. Her parents met one another in law school and became successful lawyers, achieving the "American Dream." After multiple attempts at IVF treatment, the family had their first daughter Allie. Once Allie was born, po po (maternal grandma) joined their home from China. Allie was raised in a multigenerational and bilingual (Mandarin and English) family in a high-income neighborhood.

Following Allie's diagnosis of ADHD, predominantly inattentive type (ADHD-I), her family was referred to a hospital specialty clinic. Her mother was relieved to have a medical label for a constellation of behaviors that led her to suspect for a long time that "something was wrong with Allie." Her father who "[saw] many parts of [him]self in Allie" understood his daughter's daily forgetting and time warps. Both parents were motivated to begin treatment and hoped that this specialty care would improve Allie's behaviors at home and school. Yet, both parents also agreed that ADHD was not to be discussed with po po or the rest of the family. In her first session, Allie described that she runs late, forgets and loses many things (e.g., backpack), and that her parents were "mad at me all the time." Having internalized the stigma, Allie described these ADHD-I symptoms as "Math is boring and I am just a little lazy."

Case Conceptualization: Parent Management Training (PMT)-as-Usual for ADHD

From a neurocognitive perspective, Allie has difficulty with executive functions—or the ability to regulate top-down cognitive resources to achieve goal-directed behaviors (Nigg, 2017). The condition is highly heritable with Allie's father endorsing similar symptoms. These challenges manifested in the home setting for Allie as daydreaming in the bathroom, running late to school, and multiple reminders from parents that resulted in daily conflicts. In school, teachers described Allie as "smart, but doesn't try very hard;" despite her math grades declining, no notable concerns were expressed. The teachers' muted concerns about Allie, in part illustrates the model minority myth, an externally imposed perception of Asian American communities as independently high achieving and free of psychological distress (Kim et al., 2023), often contributing to stigma and underdiagnosis of mental health conditions in this community. Allie's ADHD symptoms contributed to her anxiety, low self-esteem, and suicidal ideation (Hinshaw et al., 2022; Chung et al., 2024).

Parent management training (PMT), a first-line evidence-based intervention for ADHD-I in school-age children was selected for treatment. Notably, parenting interventions are created to support parents in implementing "authoritative" practices. Positive parental cognitions about treatment suggested benefits from this behavioral intervention (Chung et al., 2024). Allie's PMT treatment included components of building positive parent–child relationships, positive and negative consequences for child behaviors, and parental self-regulation. Allie's target behaviors were specified and antecedents (home routines, effective instructions) and consequences (praise, rewards, planned ignoring) were adjusted to increase appropriate and reduce problematic behaviors (Pfiffner et al., 2016). For Allie, like many school-aged children, target behaviors included morning and evening routines as well as completing and submitting homework.

Cultural Barriers to Treatment: "The Carrot and the Stick"

Child behaviors do not exist in a sociocultural vacuum. Focusing on Allie's behaviors highlighted differences in cultural norms and expectations for Allie across family members, resulting in explosive conflict, and difficulty implementing routines. In a context where *familism* and hierarchy are prioritized, Allie's mother and father set high expectations for Allie. Her mother would tell Allie, "You need discipline. Life is not just about play, play, play. You're not three; you are twelve. Your work is school and academics." Allie's target behaviors on the "home challenge" centered on successful academic work and extracurricular activities (e.g., check school assignment, start homework, complete one short writing assignment independently). Values of high parental expectations and respect for adults were repeated in sessions (e.g., "[She] need[s] to watch her attitude and how she speaks to us.")

Importantly, acculturation gaps within and across family members led to inconsistent expectations for Allie. For instance, from her first-generation mother's perspective, Allie's target behavior of "arrive to school by 8:05 am" seemed like a fundamental expectation that a 12-year old can independently meet. In China, her mother was expected to get ready and walk herself to school while *po po* worked morning shifts in the factory. It seemed appropriate that if Allie could not be on time, she would walk herself to school. From her second-generation father's perspective, this seemed "strict" and raised safety concerns. His immigrant parents had tried hard to assimilate and this behavior of walking in a neighborhood where most parents drove luxury cars seemed counter to the unspoken rules he was raised with. For 2.5-generation Allie, walking to school as a punishment made no logical sense ("I am already late, I would be even later!"), humiliating in the eyes of her rich White American friends, and overwhelming. Child behaviors do not exist in a vacuum, and cultural variations in norms and expectations for Allie created friction within the family unit and made implementation of routines difficult.

In implementing behavioral consequences, multiple sessions were dedicated to the discussion of positive consequences. Allie's father described the provision of rewards as "bribery," "excessive," "I am spoiling my child," and "I am raising her to be weak." The apparent anxiety and frustration of increasing positive consequences was often described by Allie's mother as "the carrot and the stick."

> "Just having a carrot is not fully sufficient for [Allie]. She has to have that stick before she's fully motivated... Don't think that I celebrate when I get to take one of [her] things. I don't enjoy it; it's not fun."

The parents' strategy appeared to be rooted in parental ideologies of *guan* and *jiao xun* to care for Allie through behavioral control and academic training (Chao, 1994). Teaching children appropriate behaviors are parental duty and responsibility. Further, Allie's parents may be endorsing dialectical values, whereby expression of positive must be balanced with the expression of negative (Peng & Nisbett, 1999). In traditional Chinese parenting, for example, parents have been found to evoke shame—a painful negative emotion accompanying failure and shortcoming—in children as a parenting strategy, while at the same time expressing love and care (e.g., "playful shaming," Fung, 1999).

However, for Allie, such implementations of behavioral strategies were inconsistent and ineffective. When asked about the home challenge, Allie would describe the negative consequences, tune out, and exhibit increased signs of inattention ("I don't remember, I don't remember, I don't remember... [Parents] yelled at me a lot and then they took away TV.") She described her parents as "strict" and "overloading" compared to her friends' parents. Over time, such parent–child cultural gaps in emotional communication impacted Allie's view of self: "I am a mistake" and "Daddy doesn't love me." It was as if parental motivations to love and care for Allie were lost-in-translation within this family. Without integrating the parent–child relationship, the parenting interventions were only reinforcing parents' attempts at behavioral control and resulting helplessness.

Shifting from Individual to System Perspective to Bridge Family Cultural Gap

While Allie had been presented as the identified patient (IP) and behavioral tools included high parental involvement, the increasing levels of family conflict required a shift to family therapy. While Allie's parents showed some hesitance, the salient value of familism appeared to match the focus on family relationships and communication. Emotion-focused family therapy (EFFT) is an integrative, process-focused approach to restoring attachment bonds in parent–child relationship through increasing felt security in the family system (Johnson, 2019; Furrow & Palmer, 2019). The approach places centrality and importance on family as a system, as well as the focus on attachment and emotion as catalysts for change (Furrow & Palmer, 2019). Below, we describe how for Allie's family, (1) the shift to EFFT provided space to translate training (e.g., *guan*) into emotional expressions of love and care, (2) provided language for intergenerational trauma and stigma, and (3) restored connection between Allie's mother and father, which re-established their authority as parents. These key ingredients in treatments contributed to greater cohesion and connectedness in Allie's family, which in turn, contributed to improvements in Allie's ADHD symptoms.

One inherent value of family therapy is that it simply provides opportunities to talk about what the family does not talk about, even though they share daily experiences together (Bowlby, 1979). Initial sessions shifted into family conversations about how Allie's father, mother, and Allie experienced the day-to-day struggles with morning and evening routines with a focus on attachment relationships. Familial terms (daughter, daddy, mommy, *po po*, 12-year old, older sister, the family) that focused on role relationships instead of individual identities were used in session, placing the values of familism central to the treatment. This also highlighted parent–child hierarchy, restoring authoritative roles for parents. As family interactional patterns were tracked and mapped using the Family Cycle (Figure 2.2), Allie's father, mother, and Allie began to put words to internal emotional experiences that accompany the behavioral implementation of daily routines, including cultural differences in parenting (e.g., *guan*) and expressions of love and care.

To secure parental investment and shift the view from Allie's problematic ADHD to improving parent–child relationships, reflections and validations were provided through caregiving lens and family roles (e.g., "Raising your daughter is your most important work." "You were so angry

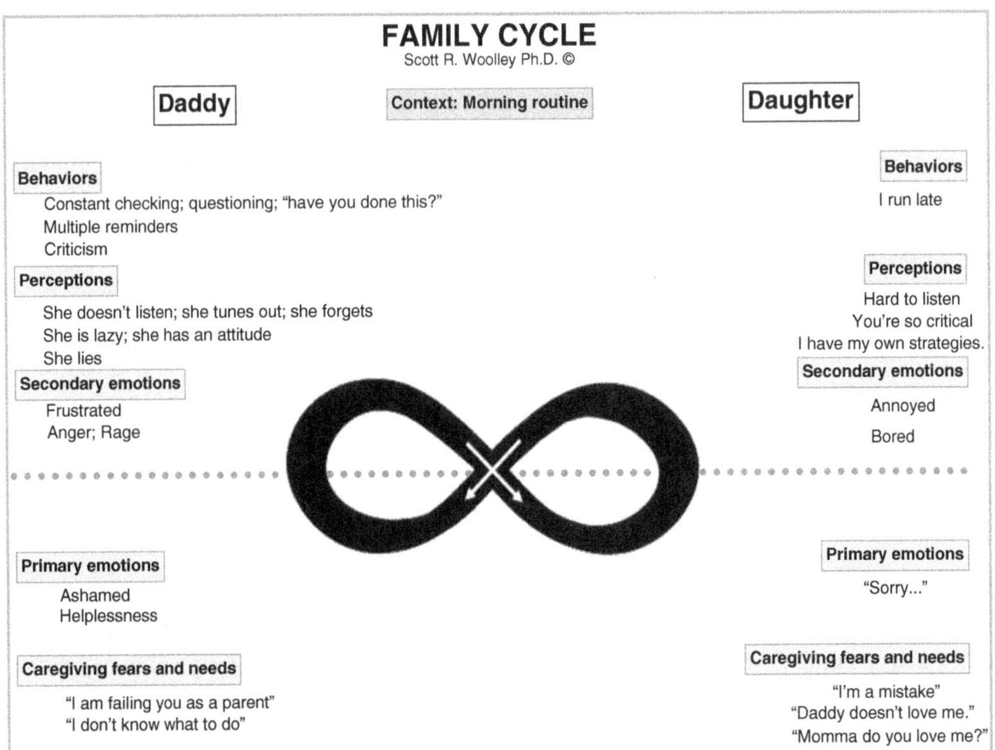

Figure 2.2 Family cycle illustrating interactional patterns between Allie and her father.

because you care so much." "Your daughter is so important to you. You get scared of hurting her in these moments of frustration. All you want to do is to protect her."). As safety for parents and Allie was gradually established, parents began to translate the behavioral training behaviors (*guan*) on the outside to emotional expressions of love and care on the inside.

> "You know that Mommy and Daddy love you. We love you. We put in the energy...all because we love you. We want to make life better for you. If we didn't care, it wouldn't matter if you were success, sick, or healthy. It's because all of those things matter."

Correspondingly, Allie began to send clearer emotional signals, in addition to behavioral signals, to her parents when she felt vulnerable ("This part is hard for me." "Mommy, do you love me?") and when she felt brave ("I have my own strategies [for ADHD-related symptoms].")

The relationship-focused intervention also created space for Allie's parents to explore and speak about their own intergenerational gaps, histories and trauma. Allie's mother was raised in a single-parent household, where academic expectations were remarkably high. Psychological control was used to instill these academic values. A less than perfect mark on an exam was met with punishment of sitting in the dark room alone for hours. Ironically, at the end of explosive fights with Allie, yelling, and taking away privileges, Allie's mother often felt like she wanted to "stumble through the hallway into my room entering a dark cave." For Allie's father, struggling with ADHD in silence as a child in a first-generation immigrant family was like a painful double-edged sword. On the one hand, he deeply understood Allie and was very involved in his daughter's day-to-day activities. On the other hand, he upheld high expectations because of the difficulties he faced and strategies he's had to build to survive on his own. Each step of engaging in Allie's ADHD treatment—assessment, weekly therapy visits, and taking medication—felt like a "secret" from *po po* and mark of "failure." In addition to breaking the silence of intergenerational experiences of mental illness, these family conversations shifted the narrative from fighting one another to fighting the challenges associated with ADHD together.

In one of the final treatment sessions, when asked about improvements, Allie's mother and father commented, "We've never been this good together." While the parents had never articulated their marital discord, their cultural gaps in expectations and parental goals and frustrations at one another often showed up in inconsistent parenting behaviors. Allie once described her father (the eldest male with most power in a traditional Asian family structure) as an "underwater surfboard" that she could ride and control. In spite of their harsh tone and controlling or punitive behaviors, Allie's parents often described their parenting experiences as "helpless." Permission to narrate their vulnerable feelings as parents bridged the couples' relationship, which in turn restored parental authority and hierarchy that enabled the provision of care-based power assertive parenting for Allie. The improved parent–child relationship, and consistent parenting behaviors, reduced Allie's ADHD symptoms.

Despite clear evidence for cultural adaptations in assessment and intervention for Asian American children and youth, clinicians are often faced with the question of *how*? How do practitioners apply research findings on culturally-varied and heterogeneous Asian American groups and apply it to the specific, individual child and family in real-world mental health settings? The present chapter offers one approach that honor multiple cultural and historical contexts, especially acculturation, family relationships that acknowledge traditional structures, and communication that enables translation and code-switching between heritage and present family values, expectations, and practices. Most importantly, this chapter raises the possibility that bridging the cultural dissonance in parenting and parent–child relationships may indeed be a treatment target, which in turn improves mental health in Asian American children and youth.

References

Abdoo, P. M. (2020). Social Identity Wheel [Worksheet]. University of Michigan, LSA Inclusive Teaching Initiative. https://sites.lsa.umich.edu/equitable-teaching/social-identity-wheel/

Adams, S. M., Riley, T., Quinn, P. D., Meraz, R., Karna, V., Rickert, M., & D'Onofrio, B. M. (2024). Racial-ethnic differences in ADHD diagnosis and treatment during adolescence and early adulthood. *Psychiatric Services*, *75*(6), 521–527.

Baumrind, D. (1996). The discipline controversy revisited. *Family Relations*, *45*(4), 405–414.

Bitsko, R. H., Holbrook, J. R., O'Masta, B., Maher, B., Cerles, A., Saadeh, K., ... Kaminski, J. W. (2024). A systematic review and meta-analysis of prenatal, birth, and postnatal factors associated with attention-deficit/hyperactivity disorder in children. *Prevention Science*, *25*(Suppl 2), 203–224.

Bowlby, J. (1979). *The Making and Breaking of Affectional Bonds*. London: Tavistock Publications.

Chao, R. K. (1994). Beyond parental control and authoritarian parenting style: understanding Chinese parenting through the cultural notion of training. *Child Development*, *65*(4), 1111–1119.

Chen, S. H., Hua, M., Zhou, Q., Tao, A., Lee, E. H., Ly, J., & Main, A. (2014). Parent–child cultural orientations and child adjustment in Chinese American immigrant families. *Developmental Psychology*, *50*(1), 189.

Chen, S. H., Zhou, Q., Main, A., & Lee, E. H. (2015). Chinese American immigrant parents' emotional expression in the family: relations with parents' cultural orientations and children's emotion-related regulation. *Cultural Diversity & Ethnic Minority Psychology*, *21*(4), 619.

Chen, V. C. H., Chan, H. L., Wu, S. I., Lee, M., Lu, M. L., Liang, H. Y., ... Lee, C. T. C. (2019). Attention-deficit/hyperactivity disorder and mortality risk in Taiwan. *JAMA Network Open*, *2*(8), e198714.

Chen, X., Zhou, J., Li, D., Li, Y., Wu, M., & Wang, J. (2025). Care-based power assertive parenting in changing Asian societies. In X. Chen (Ed.), *Asian Parenting: Meanings, Characteristics, and Implications* (pp. 1–19). Routledge.

Chentsova-Dutton, Y. E., & Ryder, A. G. (2020). Cultural models of normalcy and deviancy. *Asian Journal of Social Psychology*, *23*(2), 187–204.

Choi, Y., Kim, T. Y., Lee, J. P., Tan, K. P. H., Noh, S., & Takeuchi, D. (2021). Upholding familism among Asian American youth: measures of familism among Filipino and Korean American youth. *Adolescent Research Review*, *6*(4), 437–455.

Choi, Y., Kim, Y. S., Kim, S. Y., & Park, I. J. (2013). Is Asian American parenting controlling and harsh? Empirical testing of relationships between Korean American and Western parenting measures. *Asian American Journal of Psychology*, *4*(1), 19.

Chung, S., Goh, P., & Mikami, A. (2025). ADHD stigma and model minority myth beliefs among Asian Americans/Canadians and Native Hawaiian Pacific Islanders [Presentation]. *International Society for Research on Child and Adolescent Psychopathology 2025 Biennial Meeting*, Vancouver, Canada.

Chung, S., Williams, A., Owens, E., McBurnett, K., Hinshaw, S. P., & Pfiffner, L. J. (2024). Parental cognitions, treatment engagement, and child outcomes of ADHD behavioral treatment among Asian American families. *Research on Child and Adolescent Psychopathology*, *52*(3), 325–337.

Chung, S., Zhou, Q., Kho, C., & Main, A. (2021). Parent–child conflict profiles in Chinese American immigrant families: links to sociocultural factors and school-age children's psychological adjustment. *Family Process*, *60*(1), 169–185.

Chung, W., Jiang, S. F., Paksarian, D., Nikolaidis, A., Castellanos, F. X., Merikangas, K. R., & Milham, M. P. (2019). Trends in the prevalence and incidence of attention-deficit/hyperactivity disorder among adults and children of different racial and ethnic groups. *JAMA Network Open*, *2*(11), e1914344.

Cook, B. L., Trinh, N.-H., Li, Z., Hou, S. S., & Progovac, A. M. (2017). Trends in racial/ethnic disparities in access to mental health care, 2004–2012. *Psychiatric Services*, *68*(1), 9–16.

Deater-Deckard, K., Lansford, J. E., Malone, P. S., Alampay, L. P., Sorbring, E., Bacchini, D., ... Al-Hassan, S. M. (2011). The association between parental warmth and control in thirteen cultural groups. *Journal of Family Psychology*, *25*(5), 790.

Đoàn, L. N., Takata, Y., Sakuma, K. L. K., & Irvin, V. L. (2019). Trends in clinical research including Asian American, Native Hawaiian, and Pacific Islander participants funded by the US National Institutes of Health, 1992 to 2018. *JAMA Network Open*, *2*(7), e197432.

Feng, A., O'Neill, S., & Rostain, A. L. (2024). Contributors to underdiagnosis of ADHD among Asian Americans: a narrative review. *Journal of Attention Disorders*, *28*(12), 1499–1519.

Fung, H. (1999). Becoming a moral child: the socialization of shame among young Chinese children. *Ethos*, *27*(2), 180–209.

Furrow, J. L., Palmer, G., Johnson, S. M., Faller, G., & Palmer-Olsen, L. (2019). *Emotionally Focused Family Therapy: Restoring Connection and Promoting Resilience* (First Edition). Routledge. https://doi.org/10.4324/9781315669649

Hinshaw, S. P., Nguyen, P. T., O'Grady, S. M., & Rosenthal, E. A. (2022). Annual research review: attention-deficit/hyperactivity disorder in girls and women: underrepresentation, longitudinal processes, and key directions. *Journal of Child Psychology and Psychiatry*, *63*(4), 484–496.

Johnson, S. M. (2019). *Attachment Theory in Practice: Emotionally Focused Therapy (EFT) with Individuals, Couples, and Families*. Guilford Publications.

Kho, C., Main, A., Chung, S., & Zhou, Q. (2019). Intrusive parenting in Chinese American immigrant families: relations with cultural orientations and children's adjustment. *Asian American Journal of Psychology*, *10*(4), 341.

Kim, S. E., Zhao, Z., Wong, S. H., & Toomey, R. B. (2023). Racial-ethnic socialization, racial discrimination, and internalization of the model minority myth in East Asian families. *Journal of Research on Adolescence*, *33*(2), 458–468.

Lansford, J. E. (2017). An international perspective on parenting and children's adjustment. In N. J. Cabrera, & B. Leyendecker (Eds.), *Handbook on Positive Development of Minority Children and Youth* (pp. 107–122). Springer Science + Business Media.

Liu, A., Xu, Y., Yan, Q., & Tong, L. (2018). The prevalence of attention deficit/hyperactivity disorder among Chinese children and adolescents. *Scientific Reports*, *8*(1), 11169.

Lui, P. P. (2019). Rethinking the acculturation gap-distress theory among Asian Americans: testing bidirectional indirect relations. *American Journal of Orthopsychiatry*, *89*(6), 627.

Markus, H. R., & Kitayama, S. (1991). Cultural variation in the self-concept. In J. Strauss, & G. R. Goethals (Eds.), *The Self: Interdisciplinary Approaches* (pp. 18–48). New York, NY: Springer New York.

Matsumoto, D. (1990). Cultural similarities and differences in display rules. *Motivation and Emotion*, *14*(3), 195–214.

Mauss, I. B., & Butler, E. A. (2010). Cultural context moderates the relationship between emotion control values and cardiovascular challenge versus threat responses. *Biological Psychology*, *84*(3), 521–530.

Merrill, B. M., Hare, M. M., Piscitello, J., Schatz, N. K., Fabiano, G. A., Wells, E. L., ... Jones, H. A. (2024). Diversity and representation in ADHD psychosocial treatment research: a comprehensive synthesis with data from over 10,000 participants. *Clinical Psychology Review*, *112*, 102461.

Ng, B. C., Cui, C., & Cavallaro, F. (2019). The annotated lexicon of Chinese emotion words. *Word*, *65*(2), 73–92.

Ng, F. F. Y., & Wang, Q. (2019). Asian and Asian American parenting. In M. H. Bornstein (Ed.), *Handbook of Parenting* (pp. 108–169). Routledge.

Nigg, J. T. (2017). Annual research review: on the relations among self-regulation, self-control, executive functioning, effortful control, cognitive control, impulsivity, risk-taking, and inhibition for developmental psychopathology. *Journal of Child Psychology and Psychiatry*, *58*(4), 361–383.

Payakachat, N., Long, C. R., McElfish, P. A., Narcisse, M. R., Felix, H. C., Bursac, Z., & Hudson, T. J. (2019). Prevalence, health and resource utilization, and unmet healthcare needs of native Hawaiian and Pacific Islander children with developmental disabilities. *American Journal on Intellectual and Developmental Disabilities*, *124*(3), 234–247.

Peng, K., & Nisbett, R. E. (1999). Culture, dialectics, and reasoning about contradiction. *American Psychologist*, *54*(9), 741.

Pfiffner, L. J., Rooney, M., Haack, L., Villodas, M., Delucchi, K., & McBurnett, K. (2016). A randomized controlled trial of a school-implemented school–home intervention for attention-deficit/hyperactivity disorder symptoms and impairment. *Journal of the American Academy of Child & Adolescent Psychiatry*, *55*(9), 762–770.

Polanczyk, G. V., Willcutt, E. G., Salum, G. A., Kieling, C., & Rohde, L. A. (2014). ADHD prevalence estimates across three decades: an updated systematic review and meta-regression analysis. *International Journal of Epidemiology*, *43*(2), 434–442.

Pomerantz, E. M., & Wang, Q. (2009). The role of parental control in children's development in Western and East Asian countries. *Current Directions in Psychological Science*, *18*(5), 285–289.

Ranjan, J. K., Kumari, R., & Choudhary, A. (2024). Prevalence of attention deficit and hyperactive disorders in South Asian countries: a systematic review and meta-analysis of cross-sectional surveys from 1980 to 2023. *Asian Journal of Psychiatry*, *94*, 103970.

Realo, A., Koido, K., Ceulemans, E., & Allik, J. (2002). Three components of individualism. *European Journal of Personality*, *16*(3), 163–184.

Rychlowska, M., Miyamoto, Y., Matsumoto, D., Hess, U., Gilboa-Schechtman, E., Kamble, S., ... Niedenthal, P. M. (2015). Heterogeneity of long-history migration explains cultural differences in reports of emotional expressivity and the functions of smiles. *Proceedings of the National Academy of Sciences*, *112*(19), E2429–E2436.

Shen, J. J., Cheah, C. S., & Yu, J. (2018). Asian American and European American emerging adults' perceived parenting styles and self-regulation ability. *Asian American Journal of Psychology*, *9*(2), 140.

Shen, Y., Chan, B. S. M., Huang, C., Cui, X., Liu, J., Lu, J., ... Zhang, X. Y. (2021). Suicidal behaviors and attention deficit hyperactivity disorder (ADHD): a cross-sectional study among Chinese medical college students. *BMC Psychiatry*, *21*(1), 258.

Shi, Y., Guevara, L. R. H., Dykhoff, H. J., Sangaralingham, L. R., Phelan, S., Zaccariello, M. J., & Warner, D. O. (2021). Racial disparities in diagnosis of attention-deficit/hyperactivity disorder in a US national birth cohort. *JAMA Network Open*, *4*(3), e210321.

Smith, T. B., Domenech Rodríguez, M., & Bernal, G. (2011). Culture. *Journal of Clinical Psychology*, *67*, 166–175.

Swerdlow, B. A., Pearlstein, J. G., & Johnson, S. L. (2019). Multivariate associations of ideal affect with clinical symptoms. *Emotion*, *19*(4), 617.

Triandis, H. C. (2018). *Individualism and Collectivism*. Routledge.

Tsai, J. L. (2007). Ideal affect: cultural causes and behavioral consequences. *Perspectives on Psychological Science*, *2*(3), 242–259.

Tsai, J. L., & Chentsova-Dutton, Y. (2002). Models of cultural orientation: differences between American-born and overseas-born Asians. In K. S. Kurasaki, S. Okazaki, & S. Sue (Eds.), *Asian American Mental Health: Assessment Theories and Methods* (pp. 95–106). Boston, MA: Springer US.

Tsai, J. L., Knutson, B., & Fung, H. H. (2006). Cultural variation in affect valuation. *Journal of Personality and Social Psychology*, *90*(2), 288.

Tsai, W., & Lu, Q. (2018). Culture, emotion suppression and disclosure, and health. *Social and Personality Psychology Compass*, *12*(3), e12373. https://doi.org/10.1111/spc3.12373

Van Mourik, K., Crone, M. R., De Wolff, M. S., & Reis, R. (2017). Parent training programs for ethnic minorities: a meta-analysis of adaptations and effect. *Prevention Science*, *18*, 95–105.

Wallace, A. F., & Carson, M. T. (1973). Sharing and diversity in emotion terminology. *Ethos*, *1*, 1–29.

Wang, Q., & Fivush, R. (2005). Mother–child conversations of emotionally salient events: exploring the functions of emotional reminiscing in European-American and Chinese families. *Social Development*, *14*(3), 473–495.

Zhao, X., Hayes, T., Timmons, A. C., Wu, W., & Frazier, S. L. (2023). Unpacking inequities in ADHD diagnosis: examining individual-level race/ethnicity and state-level online information-seeking patterns. *Administration and Policy in Mental Health and Mental Health Services Research*, *50*(4), 576–590.

Zhou, Q., Wang, Y., Deng, X., Eisenberg, N., Wolchik, S. A., & Tein, J. Y. (2008). Relations of parenting and temperament to Chinese children's experience of negative life events, coping efficacy, and externalizing problems. *Child Development*, *79*(3), 493–513.

3

What Cultural Differences in Ideal Affect Can Teach Us About East Asian American Youth

Christy Wang[1], Angela M. Yang[2], and Jeanne L. Tsai[3]

[1]*Department of Psychological & Brain Sciences, Washington University in St. Louis, St. Louis, MO, USA*
[2]*Lynch School of Education and Human Development, Boston College, Chestnut Hill, MA, USA*
[3]*Department of Psychology, Stanford University, Stanford, CA, USA*

How do cultural differences in emotion—in particular the emotions that people value and ideally want to feel (their "ideal affect")—play a role in the life experiences of East Asian American youth? In this chapter, we attempt to answer this question. This chapter is divided into three parts. In the first part, we review decades of empirical research revealing US-East Asian differences in ideal affect, some of which include East Asian American samples. In the second part, we discuss the implications of these cultural differences in ideal affect for East Asian American youth. In the third part, we provide a list of recommendations for how teachers and clinicians might consider cultural differences in ideal affect when working with East Asian American youth and apply them to a case study.

Like many ethnic minority groups in the United States, East Asian Americans have historically been stereotyped every which way, ranging from passive, docile, and blindly obedient to predatory, conniving, and threatening. Current prevailing stereotypes depict East Asian Americans as the "model minority" but at the same time as "robotic," "cold," and "inscrutable." As political and economic tensions between the United States and China steadily increase, familiar stereotypes of East Asian Americans—such as the "Tiger Mom"—resurface, portraying mothers as ultra-competitive and achievement-obsessed, even at the expense of their children's emotional well-being. Where do these stereotypes come from?

In this chapter, we argue that cultural differences in emotion—in particular the emotions that people value and ideally want to feel (their "ideal affect")—play an important role in the life experiences of East Asian American youth and may be one source of prevailing stereotypes of East Asian Americans by mainstream American culture. By "culture," we refer to the socially shared and historically transmitted foundational ideas that are reflected in and reinforced by practices, institutions, and artifacts (Adams & Markus, 2004). Our cultures teach us what is good, moral, and virtuous, as well as what is bad, immoral, and sinful, and therefore, they guide much of our behavior, whether we are aware of it or not (Shweder, 2003).

Cultural Shaping of Emotion: US-East Asian Differences

Decades of research have demonstrated robust cultural differences in emotion between US and East Asian cultural contexts (see Tsai & Clobert, 2019, for review). One of the reasons so much attention has been paid to US and East Asian contexts is because they promote different models of self, which have important implications for emotion, cognition, and motivation (Markus & Kitayama, 1991, 2010). Specifically, US contexts tend to promote more *independent* models of the self, in which people are defined in terms of their internal traits and beliefs and are encouraged to differentiate themselves from others (Markus & Kitayama, 2010). As a result, emotions in US contexts tend to be more focused on individual aspects of the self (Chentsova-Dutton & Tsai, 2010; Kitayama et al., 2006; Mesquita, 2022); people in US contexts are encouraged to express their emotions (e.g., Matsumoto, 1990); and people in US contexts want to feel more positivity—especially excitement, enthusiasm, and other "high-arousal positive states"—compared to people in many East Asian contexts (Tsai et al., 2006).

In contrast, many East Asian contexts tend to promote more *interdependent* models of self, in which people are defined in terms of their roles and relationships with others and are encouraged to fulfill their duties and responsibilities (Markus & Kitayama, 2010). As a result, emotions are more focused on relational aspects of the self (e.g., Chentsova-Dutton & Tsai, 2010; Kitayama et al., 2006; Mesquita, 2022); people in East Asian contexts are encouraged to moderate and control their emotions (Matsumoto, 1990); and people in East Asian contexts want to feel more of a balance between positive and negative states, as well as calm, peacefulness, and other "low-arousal positive states" more than people in US contexts (Sims et al., 2015; Tsai et al., 2006). To the degree that East Asian Americans are exposed to and influenced by US and East Asian contexts, these differences in emotion are likely to influence them.

Affect Valuation Theory

In affect valuation theory (AVT) (Tsai et al., 2006; Tsai, 2007, 2017, 2024), we proposed that: (1) how people ideally want to feel (their "ideal affect") differs from how they actually feel (their "actual affect"), (2) cultural factors shape people's ideal affect more than their actual affect, whereas temperamental factors shape people's actual affect more than their ideal affect, and (3) people's ideal affect has important implications for what they do to feel good and how they engage with other people. Since we first proposed AVT, our research team and others have amassed a significant body of empirical research supporting each of these claims (see Tsai, 2024 for review; Tsai et al., 2025). Much of this work has compared European American, East Asian American, and East Asian groups because of our predictions that people's ideal affect would reflect their different models of self. *European Americans* refer to people who identify as Anglo, White, Caucasian, or European American; were born and raised in the United States; whose parents and grandparents were born in the United States or a Western European country; whose ancestors were from parts of Western Europe; and who represent mainstream American culture. *East Asians* refer to people who were born and raised in China, Japan, South Korea, or Taiwan; and whose parents and ancestors were born and raised in these countries; and *East Asian Americans* are people who live in the United States; were born in the United States or in an East Asian country; and whose parents were born and raised in an East Asian country (e.g., Japan, South Korea, China, Taiwan).

In our studies, participants complete the Affect Valuation Index (AVI), which asks them to use a 5-point rating scale to indicate how much they actually feel a number of states on average and how much they ideally would like to feel those same states on average (Tsai et al., 2006; Tsai et al., 2025). These states differ in terms of arousal (from low to high) and valence (from negative to positive) and sample each octant of the affective circumplex (see Figure 3.1). We average across the items in each octant to sample *high-arousal positive* states (HAP; e.g., excitement, enthusiasm), *positive* states (P; happiness, contentment), *low-arousal positive* states (LAP; calm, peacefulness), *low-arousal* states (LA; quiet, stillness), *low-arousal negative* states (LAN; dull, sluggish); *negative* states (N: sad, unhappy); *high-arousal negative* states (HAN; nervous, hostile); and *high-arousal* states (HA: aroused, surprised). The AVI can be downloaded from the Stanford Culture and Emotion Lab website (https://culture-emotion-lab.stanford.edu/).

Across cultural groups, people want to feel more positive than negative, and they want to feel more positive and less negative than they actually feel. These findings (along with results from other statistical analyses) suggest that how people want to feel differs from how they actually feel (Tsai et al., 2006; Tsai et al., 2025), the first premise of AVT.

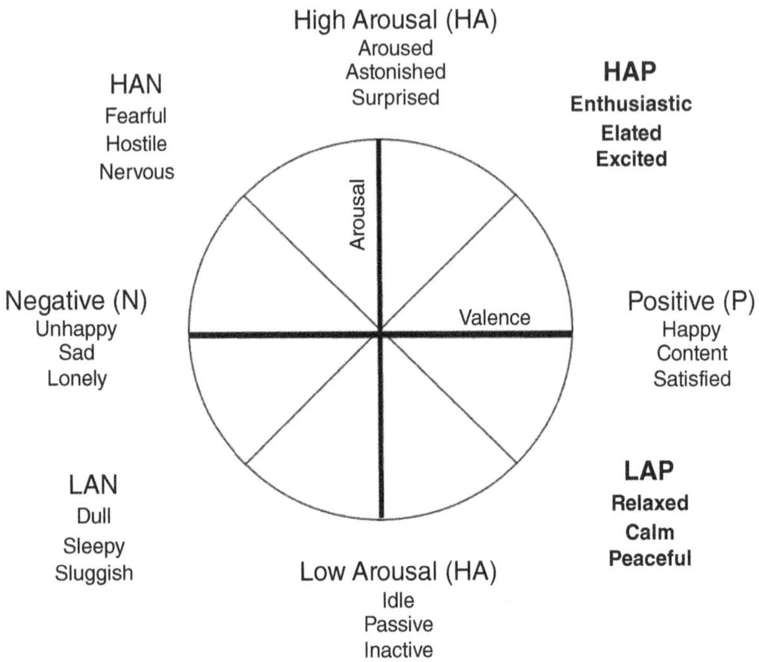

Figure 3.1 Affective circumplex. *Source:* Reproduced from Tsai et al. (2025)/with permission of the American Psychological Association.

Cultural Differences in Ideal Affect: European American vs. East Asian Contexts

We distinguished between people's ideal and actual affect because we predicted that while cultural factors shape both actual and ideal affect, they might shape people's ideal affect even more than their actual affect, in part because people's actual affect might be influenced by a host of other factors (e.g., temperament, ability to regulate emotions). More specifically, we predicted that because European Americans tend to have independent models of self in which they are encouraged to influence others (i.e., change their surroundings to be consistent with their internal beliefs and desires, such as trying to get people to do what they want), they would like to feel HAP more because influencing others requires action, and action involves increases in arousal (Cachia & Tsai, 2026; Tsai et al., 2006, 2007). In contrast, because East Asians tend to have more interdependent models of self in which they are encouraged to adjust to others (i.e., change their internal beliefs and desires to be consistent with those in their social groups, such as going along with what another person wants), we predicted that they would want to feel LAP more because adjustment requires suspending action in order to attend to one's environment, and suspended action is associated with decreases in arousal (Tsai et al., 2007). We found consistent correlational and experimental evidence in support of these predictions: European Americans wanted to feel HAP more and LAP less than East Asians, and these cultural differences in ideal HAP and ideal LAP were linked to broader cultural differences in influence and adjustment goals, respectively. In a recent meta-analysis examining ideal affect data including over 31K participants over the course of the last two decades, we observed that the cultural differences in ideal HAP have endured over time, whereas the cultural differences in ideal LAP have changed, driven by increases in the valuation of LAP among European Americans (Tsai et al., 2025). Furthermore, the cultural differences in ideal affect were greater in magnitude than the cultural differences in actual affect, consistent with the second premise of AVT.

Cultural differences in ideal affect are reflected in the dominant media in the United States and many East Asian countries. For instance, best-selling children's storybooks in the United States contain characters with more excited expressions and engaged in higher arousal activities compared to those in Taiwan (Tsai et al., 2007). Official website photos of government, industry, and university leaders in the United States are 6.25 times more likely to contain open toothy excited smiles than those in China (Tsai et al., 2016). Even the Twitter/X posts and Facebook profiles of US users contain more high-arousal positive content than that of East Asian users in Japan, China, and Taiwan (Blevins et al., 2023; Hsu et al., 2021; Huang & Park, 2013). In other words, these cultural differences in ideal affect are reflected in and reinforced by the media in people's environments, and to the degree that people are exposed to these media, they learn to want to feel the emotions reflected in them.

Implications for Daily Life

Why are these differences in ideal affect important? In a series of studies, we have shown that how people want to feel predicts various aspects of their daily lives, including their consumer and leisure preferences; how they view happiness, love, and aging; and even how they judge and treat other people. For example, European Americans are more likely to prefer stimulating (vs. soothing) products, physically rigorous vs. calming activities, and more adventurous leisure activities compared to East Asian Americans (Tsai et al., 2015; Tsai, 2007). They are also more likely to view happiness in terms of excitement (Tsai, 2024), to desire passion in their relationships (Cachia et al., 2026, under review), and to dread old age compared to East Asians (Tsai et al., 2018). Finally, when presented with excited and calm targets, European Americans are more likely to perceive the excited targets as warm and friendly compared to East Asians, regardless of the targets' sex or race (Blevins & Tsai, 2025; Tsai et al., 2019). These perceptions have important consequences: European Americans are more likely to share resources with excited (vs. calm and neutral) targets (Cachia et al., 2024; Park et al., 2017), hire them for hypothetical internships (Bencharit et al., 2019), and even choose them as leaders (Bencharit et al., 2026) compared to East Asians. In other words, cultural differences in ideal affect have important implications for how people behave and interact with others in their daily lives.

Ideal Affect Among East Asian Americans

What about East Asian Americans? As mentioned above, we have included East Asian American samples in many of our studies, predicting that East Asian Americans' ideal affect should reflect their orientation to US and East Asian cultural contexts. In Tsai et al. (2006), East Asian Americans resembled their European American peers in wanting to feel HAP more than East Asians, but they also resembled their East Asian peers in wanting to feel LAP more than European Americans (see Figure 3.2, right). Both findings were replicated in our meta-analytic review of cultural differences in ideal affect (Tsai et al., 2025).

East Asian American ideal affect also differs from European Americans and East Asians in several ways. First, while in some studies they valued HAP as much as their European American peers, in others, they valued HAP *less* than European Americans, but still more than East Asians (see Figure 3.2 left; Tsai et al., 2025). Second, in the early work, not only did East Asian Americans value LAP more than European Americans, but contrary to our prediction, they also wanted to feel LAP even *more* than East Asians. Indeed, these differences have persisted across

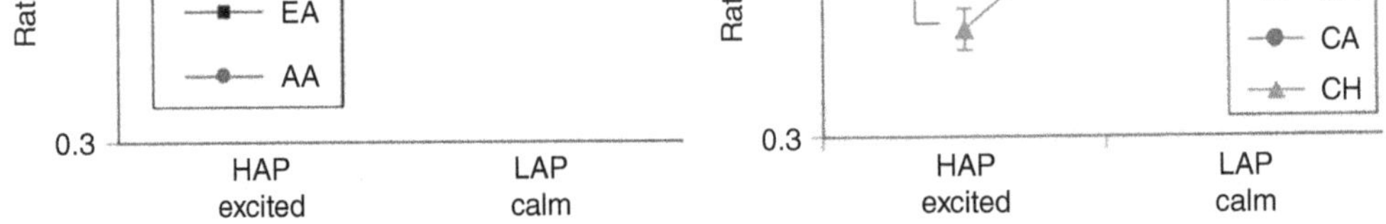

Figure 3.2 Cultural differences in ideal affect as reported in Tsai et al. (2006) for Study 1 (left) and Study 2 (right). EA = European Americans, AA = East Asian Americans, CA = Chinese Americans, CH = Hong Kong Chinese. *Source:* Reproduced from Tsai et al. (2006)/with permission of American Psychological Association.

two decades of research (Tsai et al., 2025). This might be because in our studies, East Asian Americans were primarily first- or second generation, raised by parents who had immigrated to the United States many years ago. Thus, the East Asian cultural ideas and practices that they were exposed to, if primarily through their parents, might have been even more traditional than those that exist in contemporary East Asia. It is also possible that as minorities in the United States, East Asian Americans experience greater discomfort, stress, or other high-arousal negative emotions, increasing their desire for calm and other LAP states even more.

The consequences of ideal affect also seem to reflect the multiple cultures that East Asian Americans are exposed to. For instance, in Tsai et al. (2006), we observed that across cultural groups, the greater the discrepancy between how people wanted to feel and how they actually felt, the more depressed they were. However, for European Americans, it was the discrepancy between ideal and actual HAP that predicted depression the most, whereas for East Asians (Hong Kong Chinese), it was the discrepancy between ideal and actual LAP that predicted depression the most. For East Asian Americans, discrepancies between ideal and actual HAP and between ideal and actual LAP predicted depression. These findings suggest that because of their exposure to multiple cultures, East Asian Americans may have duals paths to both happiness and depression.

When examining the behavioral consequences of ideal affect, however, East Asian Americans sometimes resemble European Americans, sometimes resemble East Asians, and sometimes fall in between the two cultural groups. For instance, when choosing an intern to hire or a candidate to lead, East Asian Americans were as likely to choose excited candidates as their European American peers and more likely to do so than Hong Kong Chinese (Bencharit et al., 2019; Bencharit et al., 2026). When choosing a physician, however, Chinese Americans were less likely than their European American counterparts (and as likely as their Hong Kong Chinese counterparts) to choose an excitement-focused physician (Sims et al., 2018).

There are multiple reasons why these different patterns might emerge, which speak to some of the challenges of studying East Asian Americans. First, these different patterns might reflect variability in cultural orientation among East Asian Americans. In the intern and leader choice studies, for instance, East Asian Americans were primarily second-generation college students, and therefore, it is likely that most had been primarily exposed to US norms regarding ideal job candidates and leaders. In the physician preference studies, however, Chinese Americans were primarily first-generation and in their mid-40s, and therefore, their physician choices might have been influenced by their greater exposure to Chinese culture.

In the meta-analysis described above, East Asian Americans showed the greatest variability in their ideal affect depending on different characteristics of the studies (e.g., whether the study was conducted by our team vs. another research team), very likely because different research teams recruited different subgroups of East Asian Americans (Tsai et al., 2025). For instance, because the Asian American population in the United States varies so widely—ranging from well over 30% of the population in San Francisco (Association of Bay Area Governments and Metropolitan Transportation Commission, 2020) and 40% in Honolulu (State of Hawai'i Department of Business, Economic Development, and Tourism, 2025) to less than 2% in parts of the South (United States Census Bureau, 2021)—the degree to which East Asian Americans are actually exposed to East Asian culture outside the home may vary considerably. Therefore, how East Asian Americans, European Americans, or East Asians compare may depend on where those samples live in the U.S.

These different patterns might also be due to the different outcomes studied. East Asian Americans might have greater exposure to US American ideals in the workforce, and therefore, may base their hiring decisions on European American ideals. In contrast, they may have greater exposure to East Asian ideals in the context of family and caregiving, making them more likely to choose physicians based on these East Asian ideals.

Implications for Understanding East Asian American Youth

In this section, we examine how cultural differences in ideal affect may shape East Asian American youth, including their communication with parents, their connections at school, and their behaviors in the clinic. In Table 3.1, we review the empirical findings discussed above and their implications for understanding East Asian American experiences.

Table 3.1 Summary of empirical findings and their potential implications for East Asian Americans.

Outcome	Findings for European Americans	Findings for East Asians	Findings/Implications for East Asian Americans
Self-reported ideal affect	Value HAP (i.e., excited) more than East Asians	Value HAP (i.e., excited) less than European Americans	Finding: East Asian Americans value HAP and LAP (i.e., calm) more than East Asians and value HAP less and LAP more than European Americans
Individual preferences	Prefer more stimulating products, physically rigorous activities, and passion in relationships	Prefer more soothing products, calming activities, and steady relationships	Finding: East Asian Americans resemble European Americans more for some preferences, East Asians more for others, and a combination for yet others
Social judgments	Judge targets with big, toothy "excited" smiles as more friendly, warm, and trustworthy than targets with small, closed "calm" smiles and targets with no expression (neutral)	Judge targets with excited smiles as less friendly, warm, and trustworthy than European Americans do	Implication: East Asian Americans who value and show less HAP may be mistakenly judged as less friendly, warm, and trustworthy by European American judges
Resource sharing and career opportunities	More likely to share resources and hire excited candidates (compared to calm and neutral ones)	More likely to share resources and hire calm candidates (compared to excited and neutral ones)	Implication: East Asian Americans who value and show less HAP may receive fewer resources from and be hired less by European American employers
Depression and well-being	Depression linked most to not feeling enough HAP (i.e., excitement); depressed individuals show flattened emotions that oppose cultural ideal of HAP	Depression linked most to not feeling enough LAP (i.e., calm); depressed individuals show stronger emotions that oppose cultural ideal of LAP	Implication: East Asian Americans who value and show less HAP may be viewed as more depressed than they actually are, and their actual depressive symptoms may be overlooked by European American clinicians

Communication with Parents

Family relationships are crucial to the well-being of youth. Positive parent–child relationships, parental involvement, and family cohesion serve as protective factors against depression and suicidal ideation in Asian American youth (Wyatt et al., 2015; Zou et al., 2021). Yet intergenerational cultural conflict has consistently been identified as a risk factor for mental health challenges (Lui, 2015; Wyatt et al., 2015; Zou et al., 2021). Such culture clashes may be particularly common in immigrant families, where intergenerational differences in levels and rates of acculturation are most pronounced (Cheung et al., 2011, Titzmann & Lee, 2018; Ying & Han, 2007).

Ideal affect may be an important area in which immigrant parents and their children acculturate differently, leading to different communication styles between the two generations that ultimately impact children's mental health. The expression of warmth within families is one example. Although Chinese American parents place as much value on expressing warmth to their children as European American parents do (Cheah et al., 2015), Wu & Chao (2005) found that Chinese American adolescents ideally wanted to receive more warmth from their parents. This discrepancy between desired and perceived warmth was larger, and predicted greater adjustment difficulties, for Chinese Americans compared to their European American peers (Wu & Chao, 2005). Although not studied directly, it is possible that East Asian American youth are yearning for more HAP expressions of warmth commonly seen in mainstream American media, including open declarations of love (e.g., "I love you!"; "You are so precious to me!"), enthusiastic affirmations (e.g., "Amazing job!" "I am so proud of you!"), and physical affection (e.g., hugs, high-fives). These expressions of warmth are open, uninhibited, and physically active. However, parents who are more deeply rooted in their East Asian cultures may express warmth in more subtle and quiet ways that support the child's well-being (e.g., cooking the child's favorite dish, reminding the child to dress warmly), offering realistic affirmations or constructive criticism (e.g., "You did okay this time."; "Next time, do this..."), and pushing their children when necessary (e.g., "You can do better"). These expressions of warmth focus on nurturance and instrumental support (Cheah et al., 2015) and aim to promote peace and stability within their children's lives but may be misunderstood as cold and critical when viewed through a cultural lens of ideal HAP, fueling stereotypes of "Tiger mothers."

Connections at School

Beyond their relationships at home, children's relationships with teachers and peers at school are as important and may also be shaped by differences in ideal affect.

Youth and their teachers. Strong child–teacher relationships are consistently linked to higher academic achievement, greater engagement, and stronger social adjustment (Cherng, 2017), and yet national data show that compared to other ethnic groups, East Asian American students are often rated as the least close to their teachers (Yiu, 2013). Cultural differences in ideal affect between teachers and East Asian American students may be one key barrier to building strong child–teacher relationships. In classroom settings where students are expected to express engagement and motivation through their enthusiasm and passion (HAP), fewer expressions of HAP and more expressions of LAP may be misread as disinterest or disengagement (Kim & Yeh, 2002; Liu, 2002; Okura, 2022; Yamamoto & Li, 2012). In some situations, as illustrated in the case study below, the presentation of LAP states (or the absence of HAP states) may even be misinterpreted as signs that a student is depressed or otherwise unwell. Conversely, expressions of LAP may also contribute to teachers' perceptions that East Asian American students are motivated only by academic pursuits and that they require less attention or support (Kao, 1995; Tuan, 1998; Chang & Demyan, 2007; Tenenbaum & Ruck, 2007). This leads to the risk that, when East Asian American students do experience social, emotional, and academic challenges in school, their struggles may be overlooked and go unaddressed.

Youth and their peers. Peer relationships also play a critical role in shaping the mental health of youth, and East Asian Americans are no exception (Benner & Kim, 2009; Greene et al., 2006). Cross-ethnic friendships promote well-being and can buffer the effects of discrimination on students' feelings of belonging at school (Bagci et al., 2014; Park & Killen, 2010). In US cultural contexts where the broad toothy smile is the signal of friendliness, East Asian American expressions of LAP may be misread as "unfriendly" and unapproachable by some cross-ethnic peers (Tsai et al., 2019). These cultural mismatches in ideal affect may reduce well-being and increase depressive symptoms, particularly if East Asian Americans feel pressure to express emotions that conflict with their cultural ideals (Butler et al., 2007; Chentsova-Dutton et al., 2014). Coupled with the "model minority" stereotype, expressions of LAP can make East Asian Americans appear academically competent but socially distant, "cold," and "robotic," potentially eliciting resentment or exclusion from cross-ethnic peers (Kiang et al., 2016; Thompson et al., 2020; Huang & Vidourek, 2019; Cooc & Gee, 2014). This may be particularly true in regions of the United States with fewer Asian Americans where affective mismatches could increase their vulnerability to being dehumanized, discriminated against, and bullied. For instance, in the northeastern United States, bullying victimization rates among Asian students were high and comparable to those of other racial groups (66–75%; Connell et al., 2015); in contrast, in California, Asian American youth reported the lowest prevalence (6.5%) of being bullied compared to African American (24%), White (17.5%), and Latino (15.2%) youth (Rhee et al., 2017). In regions of the United States with larger East Asian American populations, East Asian cultural ideals may be more intertwined with the regional culture, and East Asian American youth may experience greater ideal affect alignment with both same-ethnic and cross-ethnic peers, which may reduce their vulnerability to dehumanization, discrimination, and bullying.

Parents and teachers. These cultural mismatches may also result in misunderstandings between parents and teachers, impacting their ability to effectively communicate about and address concerns regarding East Asian American students' well-being and performance. Many East Asian parents, shaped by Confucian values that emphasize hierarchy and respect for authority, tend to defer to teachers and adopt a role of respectful compliance (Yang & McMullen, 2003; Yamamoto et al., 2022). They often prioritize academic support at home over visible school-based involvement (Kim et al., 2018; Uy, 2015). In contrast, White American teachers often expect direct communication and active parental engagement at school (Antony-Newman, 2018; Lin & Yang, 2024). As a result, East Asian American parents' quiet, emotionally restrained communication may be perceived as disengagement by teachers who expect more overt expressions of interest. This misalignment in both behavior and emotional style can lead to missed opportunities for collaboration, as reflected in studies showing that immigrant Asian parents are contacted less frequently by teachers than third-generation White parents (Cherng, 2016).

Behavior in Clinical Settings

Cultural differences in ideal affect can also influence expressions of emotional distress. The "cultural norm hypothesis" provides a useful framework, suggesting that depression "reduces individuals' abilities to react in culturally normative or ideal ways" (Chentsova-Dutton et al., 2010). For example, while watching a sad or amusing film clip, depressed European Americans tended to have *less intense* negative or positive reactions, respectively, compared to nondepressed European Americans (Chentsova-Dutton et al., 2007, 2010). These less intense emotional responses are the opposite of the high-arousal states that are valued in European American cultural contexts, signaling an inability to comply with norms and ideals to openly express emotions. This pattern aligns with dominant measures and assessments of depression in Western cultures, which often characterize depression in terms of flattened affect and diminished interest (Beck et al., 1996; Clark & Watson, 1991; Hamilton, 1960; Ryder et al., 2008). On the other hand, depressed East Asian Americans actually showed *more intense* negative and positive reactions while watching sad and amusing films, respectively, compared to nondepressed East Asian Americans (Chentsova-Dutton et al., 2007, 2010). These stronger emotional reactions are the opposite of the low-arousal states that are valued in many East Asian contexts, signaling an inability to comply with norms and ideals to control or moderate strong emotions.

Interestingly, when asked to choose the emotions they most associated with feeling depressed, East Asian Americans resembled their European American peers and chose more low-arousal negative states (dull, sleepy, sluggish—the opposite of high-arousal positive states) and fewer high-arousal negative states (nervous, hostile, fearful—the opposite of low-arousal positive states) than did Hong Kong Chinese. Similarly, when they were asked to choose emotions that they most associated with feeling happiness and well-being, East Asian Americans again resembled their European American peers and chose more HAP and fewer LAP states than Hong Kong Chinese (see Tsai, 2024). This is particularly important when considering the findings discussed above that for East Asian Americans, discrepancies in both ideal and actual HAP and LAP are associated with greater depressive symptoms (Tsai et al., 2006). These findings suggest that while East Asian Americans may have conceptions of depression and well-being that reflect US ideals, their own expressions of emotional distress may reflect a mixture of US and East Asian ideals.

Youth and clinicians. As mentioned above, East Asian American youth are less likely to engage with professional mental health services (Li & Seidman, 2010; Arora & Khoo, 2020; Ngo-Metzger et al., 2004). While youth who receive care in culturally matched clinics are more likely to return for follow-up sessions (Yeh et al., 1994), many still report feeling unsure whether clinicians truly understand their cultural background or emotional needs (Arora & Algios, 2019; George et al., 2025). These concerns may stem from mismatched emotional expectations between youth and clinicians (Tsai et al., 2007). As with teachers, Western clinicians often use high-arousal emotional expressions as signs of health and therefore are concerned when their East Asian American clients show low-arousal emotions and are more restrained in emotional expression, even though some research shows that not all emotion restraint is harmful, even in the United States (Bonanno & Burton, 2013; Butler et al., 2007; Ford & Mauss, 2015). Such misalignment can affect healthcare decision-making and satisfaction. For example, patients are more likely to prefer and trust physicians whose emotional styles match their own ideal affect (Sims et al., 2014; Sims & Tsai, 2015).

Parents and clinicians. These communication and cultural gaps extend to parent–clinician interactions as well. Parents of East Asian American youth often face health literacy challenges, including navigating the US healthcare system, understanding medical terminology, and accessing culturally appropriate services (Na et al., 2016; Kim & Lee, 2022), making them feel unequipped to advocate for their children (Liu et al., 2020). When clinicians project high-arousal styles not aligned with East Asian American parents' cultural preferences, this can lead to feelings of discomfort, mistrust, or disengagement from care. Therefore, understanding cultural variation in ideal affect and integrating this variation into clinical practice may be key to improving communication and trust in parent–clinician relationships, ultimately strengthening and extending East Asian American youth's mental health support network.

How can we leverage our understanding of cultural differences in ideal affect to help teachers, clinicians, and parents of East Asian American youth? In Table 3.2, we provide a list of recommendations. To make these recommendations more concrete, we also present a case study and then apply the recommendations to the case study.

Table 3.2 Recommendations for teachers and clinicians.

Recommendations	Rationale	Sample guiding questions
1. Consider the possibility that presentation reflects cultural differences in ideal affect.	Prevents misinterpretation/misdiagnosis of culturally normative affective styles (e.g., lack of excitement) as disengagement, disinterest, or psychopathology (e.g., depression).	*Does calm expression or lack of excitement reflect ideal affect, rather than disengagement or depression?*
2. Consider ideal affect mismatches as potential contributors to interpersonal stress or exclusion at home or at school.	Misalignment in ideal affect (e.g., calm vs. excitement) can create social distance and misunderstanding; awareness of cultural differences in ideal affect can improve inclusion and trust.	*What ideal affect am I encouraging in the classroom or clinic? Is this consistent with what my students or clients value? If not, could this be a source of stress for them?*
3. Assess ideal affect to understand preferred emotional states.	To clarify when differences in energy level or expressiveness reflect cultural norms rather than disengagement or negativity, improving understanding and reducing bias.	*What do the students' or patients' responses to the AVI reveal about their ideal affect?*
4. Provide multiple ways in which youth can participate and show engagement and interest.	Accommodates diverse communication styles, reducing cultural bias in academic, clinical, or social evaluations.	*Might the student/patient respond better to providing written responses or meeting during office hours?*
5. Educate youth, parents, teachers, and clinicians about cultural variation in ideal affect.	Promotes empathy, reduces misinterpretation, and supports culturally responsive parenting, teaching, and care.	*Are all parties involved aware of cultural differences in ideal affect?*
6. Recognize different emotion expression and regulation strategies to be culturally sensitive.	Helps youth navigate settings with differing emotional norms, promoting smoother interactions and resilience.	*Might the student/patient be expressing and regulating emotion in different ways that are appropriate to their cultures?*
7. Consider cultural fit in prevention and intervention planning.	Incorporating ideal affect alignment into program design can improve engagement, mental health outcomes, and peer relations.	*When creating school-wide engagement programs, are we including different activities that promote various ideal affects (e.g., calming and exciting activities)?*

Clinical Case Study

East Asian American Ideal Affect in the Classroom and at Home

Mr. Z prides himself on being able to spark enthusiasm in his seventh grade social studies class through historical reenactments and lively debates. However, despite his best efforts this year, Mr. Z finds himself unable to bring Klara, a Chinese American student, "out of her shell." During reenactments, for example, Klara reads her script quietly and without much inflection, even when the role calls for strong emotions. She also tends not to speak during debates and doesn't cheer along with her classmates when her team wins. Sometimes, she puts her head down when he cold-calls on students to participate. Although her written homework is typically completed well, her grades in the class have been negatively impacted by her lack of participation during class discussion, which her mother asks about during a parent–teacher conference. Mr. Z responds that, more so than Klara's grades, he is concerned about her mental health. She seems tired in class, displaying flat affect and lacking interest in activities that energize other students—behaviors which he learned in his training program align with the warning signs for depression. He offers to connect her with the school's counselor. Upon hearing his concerns, Klara's mother notes, "She seems to be acting like her usual self at home, but I'll tell her to participate more to boost her grades." Mr. Z leaves the meeting feeling frustrated at what he believes to be Klara's mother's disinterest in her mental health.

At dinner that evening, as Klara's mother spoons vegetables into Klara's bowl, she says, "Mr. Z says you're too quiet in class. You need to speak up more."

"But I've been doing my homework and getting good grades in the other subjects," Klara says. She has worked particularly hard this semester, looking forward to the positive things her mother would report from the parent–teacher conference. But this is always how it went: her mother would focus on what she should do better instead of what she was already doing well. In contrast, when her classmates' parents dropped them off at school or picked them up from sports practice, she would often hear them saying things like Love you! or Great job! "Did Mr. Z say anything else?" she asks.

"He thinks you're unhappy and even asked if you need to see a counselor," her mother replies, worried at the tears forming in Klara's eyes. "Are you actually unhappy?"

Recommendations

What can Mr. Z, the school counselor, and Klara's mother do to support her? To answer this question, we apply the recommendations outlined in Table 3.2 to Klara and Mr. Z:

- Consider the possibility that behavior reflects cultural differences in ideal affect. Mr. Z might first consider the possibility that Klara's "quiet" demeanor, "flat affect," and "lack of interest" may reflect her greater valuation of calm and other low-arousal positive states.
- Consider affective mismatches as potential contributors to interpersonal stress or exclusion. In a cultural context that often equates high-arousal positive (HAP) emotions with well-being, it seems apparent to Mr. Z that Klara—who doesn't present the same level of excitement and enthusiasm as other students—is not well. Furthermore, when Klara's mother does not share his concern about Klara's affect, he assumes it is because she is not attuned to her daughter's mental health rather than that she might share the same ideal affect as her daughter. In reality, however, the HAP states that he encourages in his classroom may not align with the low-arousal positive (LAP) emotions that are valued by Klara and her family. Her lower-arousal demeanor and her discomfort with embodying the HAP norms of the classroom may be misconstrued as signs of depression.

(Continued)

Clinical Case Study (Continued)

Additionally, when a school counselor evaluates Klara's challenges with both fitting into Mr. Z's classroom and communicating with her mother at home, it is important to consider that she has grown up with both East Asian and European American cultural influences, which may show up differently in various situations. For example, while she shares some of her mother's preference for LAP states, she may have internalized certain HAP norms for expressing affection from exposure to American media and her European American peers' families, resulting in her disappointment when her mother does not do the same.

- Assess ideal affect to understand individuals' preferred emotional states. Notably, however, the opposite may happen as well. Some teachers may stereotype students like Klara as quiet and disinterested, overlooking what are, in fact, signs of mental health struggles. Therefore, it is important for Mr. Z and/or the school counselor to assess Klara's ideal affect when assessing her mental health.
- Provide multiple ways in which youth can participate and show engagement and interest. Given that there are both cultural and individual differences in ideal affect, it would be important for Mr. Z to provide different ways in which Klara and others can show interest and engagement. While some students may feel more comfortable raising their hands and asking questions in class, or expressing their enthusiasm in front of their classmates, others may feel more comfortable expressing this in writing or one-on-one during office hours. Mr. Z might consider small group discussions where students share elements of their written responses with one another. Mr. Z might also occasionally reward and reinforce those who are calm and attentive in class, saying that he appreciates when students are quietly and thoughtfully engaged.
- Educate youth, parents, teachers, and clinicians about cultural variation in ideal affect. Given the potential for misunderstanding among youth and their support systems, it would be important to recognize that cultural differences in ideal affect exist, and that they could result in misunderstandings. For example, one prominent early intervention was Strengthening of Intergenerational/Intercultural Ties in Immigrant Chinese American Families (SITICAF) intervention (Ying, 1999, 2009), aimed at helping Chinese immigrant parents understand cultural differences between themselves and their children, and develop cross-cultural parenting, communication, and coping skills. This intervention improved the quality of the intergenerational relationship and increased children's esteem (Ying, 1999, 2009). Several other Asian American parent–child interventions have also been proposed (e.g., Lau et al., 2010, 2011; Wong et al., 2011; Wang et al., 2024). Albeit to varying degrees, all of them address cultural differences in emotion between immigrant parents and their children, focusing on helping parents learn to express emotions in ways that their more US-acculturated children might perceive as supportive.
- Recognize different emotion expression and regulation strategies. Ultimately, in multicultural societies, it would benefit youth, teachers, and parents to understand cultural differences in how people regulate their emotions. Klara's mother may be able to improve her communication with Klara by learning and adapting to the more explicit ways of expressing warmth and care that Klara yearns to receive. Similarly, Klara may also benefit from understanding and recognizing the ways in which her mother already expresses these things by offering her food and advice. Mr. Z might be able to improve his communication

with Klara's mother by recognizing her more subtle ways of supporting Klara. A school counselor who is well-versed in these cultural differences and interventions may be able to support students, parents, and teachers in recognizing each other's expectations and preferred ways of expressing emotion.

- Consider cultural fit in prevention and intervention planning. One way of doing this would be to incorporate cultural differences in emotion in school-wide socioemotional curricula. Ultimately, if Mr. Z and other teachers were interested in launching a school-wide program to increase student involvement, it would be important for them to incorporate an understanding of cultural differences in ideal affect in this programming to maximize its effectiveness with East Asian American youth and other ethnic groups that might be influenced by different cultural ideals.

Conclusions

To better understand East Asian American youth, we must recognize the cultural factors that shape their lives. In this chapter, we have focused on US-East Asian cultural differences in ideal affect and described the role they may play for East Asian American youth. Indeed, many of the stereotypes of East Asian Americans that prevail in the United States may be due to mismatches between European American and East Asian ideals. In Table 3.2, we describe seven ways in which teachers, clinicians, and other practitioners might take cultural differences in ideal affect into account when working with their students and clients. Ultimately, we hope that these recommendations will help promote greater understanding of the needs and strengths of East Asian American youth, many of which are related to how their cultures view emotion.

Authors' Note

The first two authors share equal authorship, and their names are listed alphabetically. The authors would like to thank Nancy Liu for her helpful comments and suggestions on this chapter, as well as the members of the Stanford Culture and Emotion Lab for their feedback, including M. Park, E. Blevins, R. Uricher, V. Lua, E. Leppert, A. Devgan, J. Xu, and J. Schoene.

References

Adams, G., & Markus, H. R. (2004). Toward a conception of culture suitable for a social psychology of culture. In M. Schaller, & C. S. Crandall (Eds.), *The Psychological Foundations of Culture* (pp. 335–360). Lawrence Erlbaum Associates Publishers.

Antony-Newman, M. (2018). Parental involvement of immigrant parents: a meta-synthesis. *Educational Review*, *71*, 362–381. https://doi.org/10.1080/00131911.2017.1423278

Arora, P. G., & Algios, A. (2019). School-based mental health for Asian American immigrant youth: perceptions and recommendations. *Asian American Journal of Psychology*, *10*(2), 166.

Arora, P. G., & Khoo, O. (2020). Sources of stress and barriers to mental health service use among Asian immigrant-origin youth: a qualitative exploration. *Journal of Child and Family Studies*, *29*(9), 2590–2601.

Association of Bay Area Governments and Metropolitan Transportation Commission. (2020). Bay Area Census. https://census.bayareametro.gov/population?location=san_francisco

Bagci, S. C., Rutland, A., Kumashiro, M., Smith, P. K., & Blumberg, H. (2014). Are minority status children's cross-ethnic friendships beneficial in a multiethnic context? *The British Journal of Developmental Psychology*, *32*(1), 107–115. https://doi.org/10.1111/bjdp.12028

Beck, A. T., Steer, R. A., & Brown, G. (1996). *Beck Depression Inventory–II (BDI-II)* [Database record]. APA PsycTests. https://doi.org/10.1037/t00742-000

Bencharit, L. Z., Blevins, E., Ko, M., Qu, Y., Tse, D., Fung, H. H., & Tsai, J. L. (2026). Leader choices reflect cultural differences in ideal affect more during organizational growth than decline. *Emotion* (Washington, D.C.). Advance online publication. https://doi.org/10.1037/emo0001634

Bencharit, L. Z., Ho, Y. W., Fung, H. H., Yeung, D. Y., Stephens, N. M., Romero-Canyas, R., & Tsai, J. L. (2019). Should job applicants be excited or calm? The role of culture and ideal affect in employment settings. *Emotion*, *19*(3), 377–401. http://dx.doi.org/10.1037/emo0000444

Benner, A. D., & Kim, S. Y. (2009). Experiences of discrimination among Chinese American adolescents and the consequences for socioemotional and academic development. *Developmental Psychology*, *45*(6), 1682–1694. https://doi.org/10.1037/a0016119

Blevins, E., Ko, M., Park, B. K., Qu, Y., Knutson, B., & Tsai, J. L. (2023). Cultural variation in neural responses to social but not monetary reward outcomes. *Social Cognitive and Affective Neuroscience*, *18*, 1–10. https://doi.org/10.1093/scan/nsad068

Blevins, E., & Tsai, J. L. (2025). The smiles we trust: interpersonal implications of cultural differences in ideal affect. In U. Hess, S. Hareli, & K. Kafetsios (Eds.), *Research Handbook on Culture and Emotion*. Edward Elgar Press.

Bonanno, G. A., & Burton, C. L. (2013). Regulatory flexibility: an individual differences perspective on coping and emotion regulation. *Perspectives on Psychological Science: A Journal of the Association for Psychological Science*, *8*(6), 591–612. https://doi.org/10.1177/1745691613504116

Butler, E. A., Lee, T. L., & Gross, J. J. (2007). Emotion regulation and culture: are the social consequences of emotion suppression culture-specific? *Emotion*, *7*(1), 30–48. https://doi.org/10.1037/1528-3542.7.1.30

Cachia, J., & Tsai, J. L. (2026). The cultural logic of models of self and emotion. In J. DeLeersnyder (Ed.), *The Cultural Shaping of Emotion* (pp. 56–84). Cambridge University Press.

Cachia, J. Y. A., Blevins, E., Chen, Y. C., Ko, M., Yen, N. S., Knutson, B., & Tsai, J. L. (2024). Cultural variation in the smiles we trust: the effects of reputation and ideal affect on resource sharing. *Emotion*. https://dx.doi.org/10.1037/emo0001450

Cachia, J. Y. A., Chen, D., Tanaka, M., Collardin, L., Uchida, Y., & Tsai, J. L. (2026). Ideal romantic love in the U.S. and Japan: cultural differences in the importance of passion, closeness, and appropriate distance. *Manuscript under review*.

Chang, D. F., & Demyan, A. L. (2007). Teachers' stereotypes of Asian, Black, and White students. *School Psychology Quarterly*, *22*(2), 91–114. https://doi.org/10.1037/1045-3830.22.2.91

Cheah, C. S. L., Li, J., Zhou, N., Yamamoto, Y., & Leung, C. Y. Y. (2015). Understanding Chinese immigrant and European American mothers' expressions of warmth. *Developmental Psychology*, *51*(12), 1802–1811. https://doi.org/10.1037/a0039855

Chentsova-Dutton, Y. E., Chu, J. P., Tsai, J. L., Rottenberg, J., Gross, J. J., & Gotlib, I. H. (2007). Depression and emotional reactivity: variation among Asian Americans of East Asian descent and European Americans. *Journal of Abnormal Psychology*, *116*(4), 776.

Chentsova-Dutton, Y. E., Senft, N., & Ryder, A. G. (2014). Listening to negative emotions: how culture constrains what we hear. In W. G. Parrott (Ed.), *The Positive Side of Negative Emotions* (pp. 146–178). The Guilford Press.

Chentsova-Dutton, Y. E., & Tsai, J. L. (2010). Self-focused attention and emotional reactivity: the role of culture. *Journal of Personality and Social Psychology, 98*(3), 507–519. https://doi.org/10.1037/a0018534

Chentsova-Dutton, Y. E., Tsai, J. L., & Gotlib, I. H. (2010). Further evidence for the cultural norm hypothesis: positive emotion in depressed and control European American and Asian American women. *Cultural Diversity and Ethnic Minority Psychology, 16*(2), 284.

Cherng, H.-Y. S. (2016). Is all classroom conduct equal?: teacher contact with parents of racial/ethnic minority and immigrant adolescents. *Teachers College Record, 118*(11). https://eric.ed.gov/?id=EJ1114995

Cherng, H.-Y. S. (2017). The ties that bind: teacher relationships, academic expectations, and racial/ethnic and generational inequality. *American Journal of Education, 124*(1), 67–100. https://doi.org/10.1086/693955

Cheung, B. Y., Chudek, M., & Heine, S. J. (2011). Evidence for a sensitive period for acculturation: younger immigrants report acculturating at a faster rate. *Psychological Science, 22*, 147–152. https://doi.org/10.1177/0956797610394661

Clark, L. A., & Watson, D. (1991). Tripartite model of anxiety and depression: psychometric evidence and taxonomic implications. *Journal of Abnormal Psychology, 100*(3), 316–336. https://doi.org/10.1037//0021-843x.100.3.316

Connell, N. M., El Sayed, S., Reingle Gonzalez, J. M., & Schell-Busey, N. M. (2015). The intersection of perceptions and experiences of bullying by race and ethnicity among middle school students in the United States. *Deviant Behavior, 36*(10), 807–822. https://doi.org/10.1080/01639625.2014.977159

Cooc, N., & Gee, K. A. (2014). National trends in school victimization among Asian American adolescents. *Journal of Adolescence, 37*(6), 839–849. https://doi.org/10.1016/j.adolescence.2014.05.002

Ford, B. Q., & Mauss, I. B. (2015). Culture and emotion regulation. *Current Opinion in Psychology, 3*, 1–5. https://doi.org/10.1016/j.copsyc.2014.12.004

George, N., Lee, A. H., Gonzalez-Gaspar, J., & Kwan, M. Y. (2025). A systematic review of barriers and facilitators impacting the utilization of mental health services among Asian American youth. *Evidence-Based Practice in Child and Adolescent Mental Health, 10*, 1–15.

Greene, M. L., Way, N., & Pahl, K. (2006). Trajectories of perceived adult and peer discrimination among Black, Latino, and Asian American adolescents: patterns and psychological correlates. *Developmental Psychology, 42*(2), 218–236. https://doi.org/10.1037/0012-1649.42.2.218

Hamilton, M. (1960). A rating scale for depression. *Journal of Neurology, Neurosurgery, and Psychiatry, 23*(1), 56–62. https://doi.org/10.1136/jnnp.23.1.56

Hsu, T. W., Niiya, Y., Thelwall, M., Ko, M., Knutson, B., & Tsai, J. L. (2021). Social media users produce more affect that supports cultural values, but are more influenced by affect that violates cultural values. *Journal of Personality and Social Psychology, 121*(5), 969–983. https://doi.org/10.1037/pspa0000282

Huang, C. M., & Park, D. (2013). Cultural influences on Facebook photographs. *International Journal of Psychology, 48*(3), 334–343.

Huang, S. T., & Vidourek, R. A. (2019). Bullying victimization among Asian-American youth: a review of the literature. *International Journal of Bullying Prevention, 1*(3), 187–204. https://doi.org/10.1007/s42380-019-00029-3

Kao, G. (1995). Asian Americans as model minorities? A look at their academic performance. *American Journal of Education, 103*(2), 121–159. https://doi.org/10.1086/444094

Kiang, L., Witkow, M. R., & Thompson, T. L. (2016). Model minority stereotyping, perceived discrimination, and adjustment among adolescents from Asian American backgrounds. *Journal of Youth and Adolescence, 45*(7), 1366–1379. https://doi.org/10.1007/s10964-015-0336-7

Kim, A., & Yeh, C. J. (2002). Stereotypes of Asian American students (ERIC Digest No. ED462510). ERIC Clearinghouse on Urban Education. https://files.eric.ed.gov/fulltext/ED462510.pdf

Kim, S. B., & Lee, Y. J. (2022). Factors associated with mental health help-seeking among Asian Americans: a systematic review. *Journal of Racial and Ethnic Health Disparities*, *9*(4), 1276–1297. https://doi.org/10.1007/s40615-021-01068-7

Kim, Y. A., An, S., Kim, H. C. L., & Kim, J. (2018). Meaning of parental involvement among Korean immigrant parents: a mixed-methods approach. *The Journal of Educational Research*, *111*(2), 127–138. https://doi.org/10.1080/00220671.2016.1220355

Kitayama, S., Mesquita, B., & Karasawa, M. (2006). Cultural affordances and emotional experience: socially engaging and disengaging emotions in Japan and the United States. *Journal of Personality and Social Psychology*, *91*(5), 890–903. https://doi.org/10.1037/0022-3514.91.5.890

Lau, A. S., Fung, J. J., Ho, L. Y., Liu, L. L., & Gudiño, O. G. (2011). Parent training with high-risk immigrant Chinese families: a pilot group randomized trial yielding practice-based evidence. *Behavior Therapy*, *42*(3), 413–426.

Lau, A. S., Fung, J. J., & Yung, V. (2010). Group parent training with immigrant Chinese families: enhancing engagement and augmenting skills training. *Journal of Clinical Psychology*, *66*(8), 880–894.

Li, H., & Seidman, L. (2010). Engaging Asian American youth and their families in quality mental health services. *Asian Journal of Psychiatry*, *3*(4), 169–172. https://doi.org/10.1016/j.ajp.2010.08.008

Lin, X., & Yang, C. (2024). Parental involvement to promote the social-emotional well-being of Asian immigrant youth: a cultural mismatch of teachers' and parents' perspectives. *School Psychology Review*, 1–23. https://doi.org/10.1080/2372966X.2024.2387529

Liu, J. (2002). Negotiating silence in American classrooms: three Chinese cases. *Language and Intercultural Communication*, *2*(1), 37–54. https://doi.org/10.1080/14708470208668074

Liu, C. H., Li, H., Wu, E., Tung, E. S., & Hahm, H. C. (2020). Parent perceptions of mental illness in Chinese American youth. *Asian Journal of Psychiatry*, *47*, 101857. https://doi.org/10.1016/j.ajp.2019.101857

Lui, P. P. (2015). Intergenerational cultural conflict, mental health, and educational outcomes among Asian and Latino/a Americans: qualitative and meta-analytic review. *Psychological Bulletin*, *141*(2), 404.

Markus, H. R., & Kitayama, S. (1991). Cultural variation in the self-concept. In J. Strauss, & G. R. Goethals (Eds.), *The Self: Interdisciplinary Approaches* (pp. 18–48). New York, NY: Springer New York.

Markus, H. R., & Kitayama, S. (2010). Cultures and selves: a cycle of mutual constitution. *Perspectives on Psychological Science*, *5*(4), 420–430.

Matsumoto, D. (1990). Cultural similarities and differences in display rules. *Motivation and Emotion*, *14*, 195–214. https://doi.org/10.1007/BF00995569

Mesquita, B. (2022). *Emotions Between Us: How Culture Creates Emotions*. Norton & Company.

Na, S., Ryder, A. G., & Kirmayer, L. J. (2016). Toward a culturally responsive model of mental health literacy: facilitating help-seeking among East Asian immigrants to North America. *American Journal of Community Psychology*, *58*(1–2), 211–225. https://doi.org/10.1002/ajcp.12085

Ngo-Metzger, Q., Legedza, A. T., & Phillips, R. S. (2004). Asian Americans' reports of their health care experiences: results of a national survey. *Journal of General Internal Medicine*, *19*(2), 111–119. https://doi.org/10.1111/j.1525-1497.2004.30143.x

Okura, K. (2022). Stereotype promise: racialized teacher appraisals of Asian American academic achievement. *Sociology of Education*, *95*(4), 302–319. https://doi.org/10.1177/00380407221119746

Park, B., Blevins, E., Knutson, B., & Tsai, J. L. (2017). Neurocultural evidence that ideal affect match promotes giving. *Social Cognitive and Affective Neuroscience*, *12*(7), 1083–1096.

Park, Y., & Killen, M. (2010). When is peer rejection justifiable? Children's understanding across two cultures. *Cognitive Development*, *25*(3), 290–301. https://doi.org/10.1016/j.cogdev.2009.10.004

Rhee, S., Lee, P. A., & Jung, S. Y. (2017). Racial and ethnic differences in bullying victimization among adolescents in California. *The Journal of School Health*, *87*(5), 347–355. https://doi.org/10.1111/josh.12499

Ryder, A. G., Yang, J., Zhu, X., Yao, S., Yi, J., Heine, S. J., & Bagby, R. M. (2008). The cultural shaping of depression: somatic symptoms in China, psychological symptoms in North America?. *Journal of Abnormal Psychology*, *117*(2), 300.

Shweder, R. (2003). *Why Do Men Barbeque?: Recipes for Cultural Psychology*. Cambridge: Harvard University Press.

Sims, T., Koopmann-Holm, B., Young, H. R., Jiang, D., Fung, H., & Tsai, J. L. (2018). Asian Americans respond less favorably to excitement (vs. calm)-focused physicians compared to European Americans. *Cultural Diversity and Ethnic Minority Psychology*, *24*(1), 1–14. https://doi.org/10.1037/cdp0000171

Sims, T., & Tsai, J. L (2015). Patients respond more positively to physicians who focus on their ideal affect. *Emotion*, *15*, 303–318.

Sims, T., Tsai, J. L., Koopmann-Holm, B., Thomas, E., & Goldstein, M. (2014). Choosing a physician depends on how you want to feel: the role of ideal affect in health-related decision-making. *Emotion*, *14*, 187–192.

Sims, T., Tsai, J. L., Jiang, D., Wang, Y., Fung, H. H., & Zhang, X. (2015). Wanting to maximize the positive and minimize the negative: Implications for mixed affective experience in American and Chinese contexts. *Journal of Personality and Social Psychology*, *109*, 292–315.

State of Hawai'i Department of Business, Economic Development, and Tourism. (2025). Hawaii Population Characteristics 2024. Retrieved October 22, 2025. https://files.hawaii.gov/dbedt/census/popestimate/2024/state-county-char/Highlights_Hawaii-Population-Characteristics-2024.pdf

Tenenbaum, H. R., & Ruck, M. D. (2007). Are teachers' expectations different for racial minority than for European American students? A meta-analysis. *Journal of Educational Psychology*, *99*(2), 253–273. https://doi.org/10.1037/0022-0663.99.2.253

Thompson, T. L., Kiang, L., & Witkow, M. R. (2020). Discrimination, the model minority stereotype, and peer relationships across the high school years. *Journal of Youth and Adolescence*, *49*(9), 1884–1896. https://doi.org/10.1007/s10964-020-01268-0

Titzmann, P. F., & Lee, R. M. (2018). Adaptation of young immigrants: a developmental perspective on acculturation research. *European Psychologist*, *23*(1), 72–82. https://doi.org/10.1027/1016-9040/a000313

Tsai, J. L. (2007). Ideal affect: cultural causes and behavioral consequences. *Perspectives on Psychological Science*, *2*(3), 242–259.

Tsai, J. L. (2017). Ideal affect in daily life: implications for affective experience, health, and social behavior. *Current Opinion in Psychology*, *17*, 118–128.

Tsai, J. L. (2024). Investigating culture and emotion: from responses to ideals. In M. J. Gelfand, C.-Y. Chiu, & Y.-Y. Hong (Eds.), *Handbook of Advances in Culture and Psychology* (pp. 54–117). Oxford University Press.

Tsai, J. L., Ang, J., Blevins, E., Goernandt, J., Fung, H., Jiang, D., ... Haddouk, L. (2016). Leaders' smiles reflect cultural differences in ideal affect. *Emotion*, *16*, 183–195.

Tsai, J. L., Blevins, E., Bencharit, L. Z., Chim, L., Fung, H. H., & Yeung, D. Y. (2019). Cultural variation in social judgments of smiles: the role of ideal affect. *Journal of Personality and Social Psychology*, *116*(6), 966–988. http://dx.doi.org/10.1037/pspp0000192

Tsai, J. L., Chen, D., Yang, A., Cachia, J. Y. A., Blevins, E., Ko, M., Mathur, M., ... Zhou, X. (2025). A meta-analytic review of cultural variation in affect valuation. *Psychological Bulletin*, *151*(12), 1486–1524. https://doi.org/10.1037/bul0000499

Tsai, J. L., Chim, L., & Sims, T. (2015). Consumer behavior, culture, and emotion. In S. Ng, & A. Y. Lee (Eds.), *Handbook of Culture and Consumer Behavior* (pp. 68–98). Oxford University Press. https://doi.org/10.1093/acprof:oso/9780199388516.003.0004

Tsai, J. L., & Clobert, M. (2019). Cultural influences on emotion: established patterns and emerging trends. In D. Cohen, & S. Kitayama (Eds.), *Handbook of Cultural Psychology* (Second Edition) (pp. 292–318). The Guilford Press.

Tsai, J. L., Knutson, B., & Fung, H. H. (2006). Cultural variation in affect valuation. *Journal of Personality and Social Psychology*, *90*(2), 288–307. https://doi.org/10.1037/0022-3514.90.2.288

Tsai, J. L., Louie, J. Y., Chen, E. E., & Uchida, Y. (2007). Learning what feelings to desire: socialization of ideal affect through children's storybooks. *Personality and Social Psychology Bulletin*, *33*(1), 17–30. https://doi.org/10.1177/0146167206292749

Tsai, J. L., Sims, T., Qu, Y., Thomas, E., Jiang, D., & Fung, H. H. (2018). Valuing excitement makes people look forward to old age less and dread it more. *Psychology and Aging*, *33*, 975–992. http://dx.doi.org/10.1037/pag0000295

Tuan, M. (1998). *Forever Foreigners or Honorary Whites? The Asian Ethnic Experience Today*. Rutgers University Press.

United States Census Bureau. (2021). Racial and ethnic diversity in the United States: 2010 Census and 2020 Census. https://www.census.gov/library/visualizations/interactive/racial-and-ethnic-diversity-in-the-united-states-2010-and-2020-census.html

Uy, P. S. (2015). Supporting Southeast Asian American family and community engagement for educational success. *Journal of Southeast Asian American Education and Advancement*, *10*(2), 3. https://doi.org/10.7771/2153-8999.1131

Wang, C., Havewala, M., Bali, D., Hui, J., Stancofski, R. M., & Patel, A. (2024). Parent and youth interventions for Chinese American families to address COVID-19 related discrimination and promote youth mental health. *School Psychology Review*, *55*(2), 224–240. https://doi.org/10.1080/2372966X.2024.2441648

Wong, Y. J., Tran, K. K., Schwing, A. E., Cao, L. H., Ho, P. P. H., & Nguyen, Q. T. (2011). Vietnamese American immigrant parents: a pilot parenting intervention. *The Family Journal*, *19*(3), 314–321.

Wu, C., & Chao, R. K. (2005). Intergenerational cultural conflicts in norms of parental warmth among Chinese American immigrants. *International Journal of Behavioral Development*, *29*(6), 516–523.

Wyatt, L. C., Ung, T., Park, R., Kwon, S. C., & Trinh-Shevrin, C. (2015). Risk factors of suicide and depression among Asian American, Native Hawaiian, and Pacific Islander youth: a systematic literature review. *Journal of Health Care for the Poor and Underserved*, *26*(2), 191–237.

Yamamoto, Y., & Li, J. (2012). Quiet in the eye of the beholder: teacher perceptions of Asian immigrant children. In C. Garcia Coll (Ed.), *The Impact of Immigration on Children's Development* (Contributions to Human Development, Vol. 24) (pp. 1–17). Karger. https://doi.org/10.1159/000331030

Yamamoto, Y., Li, J., & Bempechat, J. (2022). Reconceptualizing parental involvement: a sociocultural model explaining Chinese immigrant parents' school-based and home-based involvement. *Educational Psychologist*, *57*(4), 267–280. https://doi.org/10.1080/00461520.2022.2094383

Yang, H., & McMullen, M. (2003). Understanding the relationships among American primary-grade teachers and Korean mothers: the role of communication and cultural sensitivity in the linguistically diverse classroom. *Early Childhood Research & Practice*, *5*(1). https://ecrp.illinois.edu/v5n1/yang.html#:~:text=Volume%205%20Number%201%20%C2%A9The%20Author(s)%20 2003.,and%20Korean%20Mothers:%20The%20Role%20of%20Communication

Yeh, M., Takeuchi, D. T., & Sue, S. (1994). Asian-American children treated in the mental health system: a comparison of parallel and mainstream outpatient service centers. *Journal of Clinical Child Psychology*, *23*(1), 5–12. https://doi.org/10.1207/s15374424jccp2301_2

Ying, Y. W. (1999). Strengthening intergenerational/intercultural ties in migrant families: a new intervention for parents. *Journal of Community Psychology*, *27*(1), 89–96.

Ying, Y. W. (2009). Strengthening Intergenerational/Intercultural Ties in Immigrant Families (SITIF): a parenting intervention to bridge the Chinese American intergenerational acculturation gap. In N.-H. Trinh, Y. C. Rho, F. G. Lu, & K. M. Sanders (Eds.), *Handbook of Mental Health and Acculturation in Asian American Families* (pp. 45–64). Humana Press/Springer Nature.

Ying, Y. W., & Han, M. (2007). The longitudinal effect of intergenerational gap in acculturation on conflict and mental health in Southeast Asian American adolescents. *American Journal of Orthopsychiatry*, *77*(1), 61–66.

Yiu, H. L. (2013). The influence of student–teacher racial match on student–teacher closeness: a focus on Asian and Asian American students. *Asian American Journal of Psychology*, *4*(2), 126–135. https://doi.org/10.1037/a0027785

Zou, P., Siu, A., Wang, X., Shao, J., Hallowell, S. G., Yang, L. L., & Zhang, H. (2021). Influencing factors of depression among adolescent Asians in North America: a systematic review. *Healthcare*, *9*(5), 537.

4

Asian American Religious Identities: Influences on Mental Health and Well-being from Childhood Through Emerging Adulthood

Stephen H. Chen

Department of Psychology, Wellesley College, Wellesley, MA, USA

Corresponding author: stephen.chen@wellesley.edu

The growth and diversity of the Asian American[1] population over the past three decades are mirrored in their religious identities. Asian American religious organizations are the largest and fastest-growing Asian American organizations in the United States (Wong, 2018). Two-thirds of AAs identify as Christian (34%) or religiously unaffiliated (32%), while the remaining third identify as Buddhist (11%), Hindu (11%), Muslim (6%), or with another faith tradition (4%) (Pew Research Center, 2023). The importance of religion to Asian Americans' everyday lives also varies both by religious affiliation and by ethnic group. Only 20% of Japanese Americans and 14% of Chinese Americans considered religion very important to their lives, compared to more than a third of Indian, Vietnamese, Korean, and Filipino Americans, and to 41% of US adults as a whole. At the same time, religion is more important to the everyday lives of Asian American Muslims (60%) and Asian American Christians (54%). Adding to this complexity, though close to a third of Asian Americans are religiously-unaffiliated, almost two-thirds of this group still report feeling close to the religious or philosophical traditions of their family or ancestral culture, such as Buddhism, Christianity, Confucianism, or Daoism.

Religious identities have been identified as effective targets for mental health interventions with other racial-ethnic minority youth, yet their role in Asian American mental health remains largely unexplored. For example, among Black and Latino/a adolescents and young adults, a sense of belonging to religious communities has been found to buffer negative effects of stressors such as ethnic-racial discrimination on multiple mental health outcomes, including depressive symptoms (Butler-Barnes et al., 2018; Ellison et al., 2017), diagnoses of psychiatric disorders (Hope et al., 2017), and dysregulated stress responses (Lee et al., 2021). Likewise, although a number of investigations have examined the effectiveness of faith-based interventions with racial-ethnic minorities (Hays & Aranda, 2016; Villatoro et al., 2016), similar efforts with Asian American religious communities are sparse by comparison. Thus, while a growing number of interventions and research have focused on Asian American racial-ethnic identities as targets for mental health and

1 In comparison to research with Asian Americans, there is relatively little work on Pacific Islanders' religious development. We use the term Asian American, rather than Asian American Pacific Islander, to reflect the focus of this chapter and stress the need for more research in this area.

well-being, we know little of how their experiences as racial-ethnic minorities interact with their religious identities, and how they jointly serve as risk, protective, or promotive factors in their mental health.

This chapter addresses this gap by synthesizing existing research on how Asian American racial-ethnic and religious identities jointly shape their mental health and well-being, from early childhood to emerging adulthood. Across these stages of development, the chapter considers how biological, psychological, and social processes interactively shape, and are shaped by Asian American religious and racial-ethnic identities and experiences.

Theoretical Framework: Bioecological Model of Development

Bronfenbrenner's bioecological model (Bronfenbrenner & Morris, 2006) proposes that human development is shaped by the dynamic and interactive relationships between *process*, *person*, *context*, and *time*. Process refers primarily to the interactions between an individual and those in their direct, or most proximal environment, such as their interactions with their parents and peers. These processes are themselves influenced by characteristics of the individual person; the broader, nested contexts in which these processes unfold; as well as the *time* period—both the socio-historical period and the individual's developmental stage—in which these processes took place. A clinician, teacher, or religious leader seeking to apply a bioecological framework to their work with Asian American clients or community members may ask how a person's (a) individual traits, beliefs, and values; (b) their family, community and broader cultural contexts; and (c) the current historical period and their current developmental age are interacting to shape their mental health and well-being.

In each of the following sections, this chapter applies this question to Asian American youth at four different stages of development—early childhood, middle childhood, adolescence, and emerging adulthood—and focuses on the interactions between religious and racial-ethnic identities in shaping mental health and well-being.

Early Childhood

Early childhood is generally conceptualized as the period from birth through age six, and during this stage, parents and other primary caregivers are the most proximal and salient influences on children's development and well-being. Their influences are manifested through direct processes, such as daily interactions with their children and more global parenting styles, as well as through more indirect processes, such as decisions regarding health care, education, and community. Understanding the factors influencing children's mental health and well-being in early childhood can therefore begin by looking at their parents and caregivers, and identifying the factors influencing both their day-to-day interactions with their children as well as their longer-term behaviors related to health and well-being. For example, parents' everyday interactions with their young children—when and how to discipline, how to express affection and care, or even what books to read at bedtime—can reflect the values, beliefs, and norms of their embedded cultural contexts, including their proximal and broader religious communities (Mahoney & Boyatzis, 2019).

Likewise, the stress of exosystem-level interactions that the caregiver encounters outside the home—e.g., a demanding workplace, encounters with racism, discrimination, or community violence—can "spillover" into the parents' interactions with their children inside the home, particularly if the family lacks resources to buffer the effects of these stressors.

These processes are particularly salient for immigrant parents across different racial-ethnic minority groups, and they also present a key entry point for religious influence. Religious communities often provide the first point of co-ethnic community contact for recent Asian American immigrants, whether or not they themselves are religiously- or spiritually-identified (Hirschman, 2004; Min, 1992). These communities also function as a primary source of social support for issues ranging from navigating workplace/legal issues, providing assistance with translation or transportation, and assisting with childcare (Bankston & Zhou, 2000 Derr et al., 2018; Zhou et al., 2002). Each of these forms of support can buffer stressors of immigration and acculturation and prevent these from spilling over into parent–child interactions.

Religion and Parenting in Early Childhood

At the broader, macrosystem level, religious/spiritual teachings provide parents with cultural scripts for caring for their young children (Bornstein, et al., 2022). Individual and cross-cultural variations in caregiving behaviors emerge beginning from infancy, and for members of religious communities, these behaviors can reflect the beliefs, norms, and values of those groups (Bornstein et al., 2022; Mahoney, 2010). For example, the theistic sanctification of parenting is the view of parenting as a manifestation of one's images, beliefs, or experiences of God (Mahoney et al., 2003). Parents' beliefs in the sanctification of parenting have been positively associated with aspects of young children's moral conscience (e.g., feeling bad about wrongdoing) as well as greater use of positive socialization practices (e.g., praise) (Volling et al., 2009). An interview (Lu, 2012) with a Chinese-American mother of a young infant illustrates this sanctified view of parenting:

> Maybe she doesn't understand, she babbles, but I pray with her during mealtime and like I said before, sometimes it is hard for me, having [her and trying] to pray or to read. These past few weeks, I've been, when she is playing, I hold her, and I pray. That's my prayer time. I just want her to see that [a true] Christian life is just not on Sundays. It is throughout the whole week. I think that will be a challenge... I think that is very important to them when they develop their own faith—to know it is not just about going to church on Sunday, and that is it. Throughout the week, it is part of our lives (Lu, 2012, p. 86).

Children's own religious beliefs, as well as their beliefs in divine or supernatural entities, also begin developing in early childhood. During this stage of development, these beliefs primarily reflect direct socialization practices of their parents and primary caregivers, rather than formal education (Gauvain & Perez, 2015; Saide & Richert, 2020). For example, children's beliefs in unobservable entities (McLoughlin et al., 2021a) and their attribution of human-like qualities to divine beings (Richert et al. 2016) have all been linked to ways in which their caregivers talk to them about religious beliefs and practices (McLoughlin et al., 2021a, 2021b; Richert & Corriveau, 2022; Richert et al., 2016). An interview with a Taiwanese-American mother, also from the Lu (2012) study, reflects both the sanctification of parenting as well as her efforts to pass on beliefs about God to her daughter:

> It's easy for children to believe in God if they grow up in Christian family. It's easy for them to be children of God. We should help our children to form a personality of deifying and loving God. We see the mystery and beauty of the creation of God through the children whom God gives us (Lu, 2012, p. 86).

Attachment

One of the most formative processes of early childhood is the establishment of the attachment relationship between the child and a primary caregiver (Ainsworth et al., 1978; Bowlby, 1969, 1973). In addition to setting the stage for socioemotional well-being in adolescence and beyond (Cassidy & Shaver, 1999), individuals' early attachment relationships have also been linked to their concepts of God and the Divine (De Roos et al., 2004; Kirkpatrick & Shaver, 1992). In support of this "correspondence hypothesis" (Kirkpatrick, 1999), securely attached young children and young children who perceive their parents positively view God with similarly positive qualities, such as being nurturing (Dickie et al., 1997) or being close in times of sickness (Granqvist et al., 2007). The correspondence hypothesis has also been supported beyond the parent–child relationship. In a study of preschoolers in the Netherlands, children with close and harmonious relationships with their teacher were more likely to have concepts of God as a loving and caring being, whereas children with negative relationships with parents and teachers were less likely to perceive God as close, warm, or personal (De Roos, 2006).

Though we are unaware of research specifically examining attachment and religion in young Asian American children, some studies have extended the attachment framework to the religious beliefs of older Asian American youth and young adults. Among Korean American adolescents, insecure parental attachments were associated with more negative strategies of religious coping, such as feeling punished for their lack of devotion, or questioning God's love for them (Roh, 2016). Another study found that Chinese American and Korean American college students with lower attachment security to their parents reported more instability and disappointment in their relationship with God (Shin, 2009). Insecure attachment to God among Chinese American Christian college students, in turn, has been associated with lower life satisfaction in response to stress (Wei et al., 2012).

While limited in number and in their focus on Asian American Christians, these studies provide some evidence that Asian Americans' religious beliefs may be shaped in part by their parental attachments, the patterns of which are established beginning in early childhood. Indeed, a much more established body of research has examined predictors of parental attachment in young Asian American children. In a study of a nationally representative sample of Asian American families, insecure attachment was more common in Asian American infants and toddlers whose mothers were foreign-born, compared to US born, and whose mothers were lower in sensitivity (Huang et al., 2012). Similarly, among 2–6-year-old children of South Asian immigrants in Canada, children whose mothers reported more depressive symptoms were rated as being less securely attached (Lecompte et al., 2018). Our own research with older (elementary-age) children suggests that within Asian American immigrant families in particular, attachment security may be influenced by differences between parents' and children's cultural orientations, such that culturally-specific expressions of parental love and care (e.g., criticism, providing food) may be "lost in translation" when communicated to more acculturated Asian American children (Williams et al., 2024).

Middle Childhood

Though often overlooked as the "forgotten years" in developmental research, middle childhood (ages 7–11) represents a period of pronounced social and cognitive development with particular relevance to the well-being of racial-ethnic minority youth. One of the hallmarks of middle childhood is an increase in autonomy and a corresponding decrease in direct parental supervision. This increased autonomy is accompanied by an increase in nonparental influences. In infancy and early childhood, the child's microsystem is comprised almost exclusively of their immediate family members and childcare providers. Peer contacts—other children in their childcare centers/preschools, children from their neighborhood or community—are largely curated and supervised by the adults in their microsystem. By middle childhood, the roster of agents in the child's microsystem has expanded to include teachers, coaches, and other adults; as well as peers who have been increasingly self- or reciprocally-selected by the children themselves, rather than by their parents.

For Asian American youth, particularly those from immigrant families, this expanded microsystem provides exposure to cultural scripts that may differ dramatically from those in their family context (Chen et al., 2014). For example, friends may provide different ways of interacting with their parents and operate under different sets of expectations for schoolwork and family responsibilities. These changes in microsystem composition dovetail with changes in capacities for social cognition. A hallmark of cognitive development in middle childhood is the capacity to consider multiple identities and group membership. For example, our previous research with elementary age Chinese American children demonstrates how they integrate socioeconomic status and racial-ethnic identity into their views of themselves and others (Chen et al., 2019; Wang et al., 2025), and are able to consider the relative importance of multiple identities (e.g., gender, ethnicity) in their sense of who they are (Wong et al., 2024). Critically, these aspects of identity are linked to their socioemotional development and well-being (Chen et al., 2019; Wong et al., 2024).

Given these changes in their children's social spheres, as well as their maturing considerations for group membership and identities, Asian American parents' efforts at religious socialization may draw from religious communities to construct their elementary age children's social networks (Windzio & Windgens, 2014). For Asian American immigrant parents, in particular, these religious communities are often comprised of co-ethnic peers, and as such, serve the dual function of socializing both religious and ethnic identities. Joshi's (2006) observation of a Hindu American community notes that members "either conflated Indian culture and Hinduism, saw Hinduism as an inseparable component of Indian culture, or intellectually understood the distinctions but nevertheless considered Hinduism and Indian culture to be irreducibly related" (p. 48). Likewise, Ganapathy-Coleman (2014) captures this dual function in interviews with Hindu American parents in Baltimore, when asking why they sent their children to Bal Vihar, religious classes held at a Hindu temple.

RAJ: Rahul is [going there] to learn Hindi and to know little bit of religion.
NEETA: And Indian culture.
NEETA: To him it means going and playing with his friends.
RAJ: But he knows why we take him.

NEETA: ...and the fun part for him is that he is getting to meet his friends. And you know what...this year he is enjoying it. He will tell me, oh, can you practice my Hindi letters...and he is also getting into the religion one also because it's the shlokas they are learning now, so he wants to learn some of these...It is not because I am telling him, he wants to do it now, wants to learn this, so before it was friends only, which is still there, but I think he is taking interest in other things that he is learning at the same time.

(Ganapathy-Coleman, 2014, p. 130)

Ganapathy-Coleman's interviewees note that these religion classes serve three socialization functions for their children: teaching about Indian culture, teaching about Hindu religious teachings, and also allowing him to socialize with co-ethnic peers. For Asian American youth, particularly those doubly-minoritized as ethnic and religious minorities, having peers who share both their religious and ethnic identities can buffer against both religious and racial-ethnic discrimination.

While these examples spotlight the function of community religious sites, an ethnographic study of Vietnamese American Buddhist families in Southern California provides a vivid picture of how religious socialization also occurs within the home, through the intentional placement and maintenance of altars and Buddhist artifacts, routines of family prayer, and recitation of sacred phrases (Mazumdar & Mazumdar, 2015). Critically, the performance of rituals is accompanied by explicit explanations of their meaning. In recalling one of these childhood rituals, one interviewee demonstrates how she has internalized its purpose:

> [It] is a phrase that pays respect to Buddha. You say it during prayer...My mom taught me to say it when I have trouble falling asleep. Saying it helps you concentrate your thoughts and drives out the bad ones, it keeps you at peace and helps you stay calm.
>
> *(Mazumdar & Mazumdar, 2015, p. 50).*

Questions for Parents of Preschool and Elementary-age Children

- *In what ways do you see your religious beliefs and values shaping your parenting?*
- *In what ways do your parenting practices differ from (a) other Asian Americans who do not share your religious beliefs, or (b) other parents who share your religious beliefs, but who are not Asian American?*

Adolescence

The marked biological, psychological, and social changes during adolescence lay the foundation for identity formation, one of the key tasks in this period of development. These developmental changes also allow for pronounced changes in religion and spirituality (Erikson, 1968). Adolescents' growing capacity for abstract thought, coupled with increased reward sensitivity, set the stage for emotionally-salient religious and spiritual experiences (DeHaan et al., 2011). These maturational capacities of adolescence also enable the pursuit of existential questions, such as a sense for a search for self and life purpose (King, 2008; Mariano, & Damon, 2008). The pursuit of these questions may be reflected in different trajectories of religious identity development: adolescents may maintain, reject, or even deepen their commitment to their family's religious traditions; they may convert to a new religious affiliation; or even cease to identify with any religious tradition (Ream & Savin-Williams, 2003).

For religiously-identified Asian American adolescents, or those who have been raised in religious households, this process of identity exploration occurs on both racial-ethnic and religious-spiritual fronts. In a longitudinal study of religious identity among ethnically diverse adolescents, Asian American adolescents reported higher levels of religious identity compared to their European American counterparts, suggesting that ethnic minority identity may contribute to religious identification (Lopez et al., 2011). In another study, Vietnamese American adolescents who participated in ethnic churches also demonstrated stronger ethnic identity (Bankston & Zhou, 1995). Through these co-occurring processes of identity exploration, Asian American adolescents may be weighing the importance of, and their feelings toward their Asian American identity, while simultaneously posing similar questions in regards to the religious-spiritual traditions in which they were raised. These identities also work together to shape mental health and well-being, with beneficial, as well as deleterious effects. In a study of Asian American adolescents from varying religious backgrounds, religious identity positively predicted adolescents' self-esteem, positive affect, and the presence of meaning in life over a four-year period (Davis & Kiang, 2016).

The transition from middle childhood to adolescence also sees a microsystem-level shift in religious influence, from parents to peers. While parents continue to serve as agents of religious socialization in adolescence, adolescents' religion and spirituality is also highly influenced by the beliefs and practices of their peers (Desmond et al., 2010; Schwartz, 2006; Smith & Denton, 2005). In this way, some Asian American parents may continue to emphasize their adolescents' participation in religious communities as a way of shaping their social circles. In a study of South Asian Muslim mothers in the United States, Ross-Sheriff and colleagues (2007) noted how parents of teenage daughters did so through joint participation in these activities. As described by one of their participants:

> "When I was growing up, I did not fast or go to mosque regularly. However, since my children were born, I have started fasting, going for Friday prayers, and getting involved in social and religious activities at the mosque, including teaching children's religion classes. My daughter looks forward to Fridays and all the programs we enjoy together. She even likes to go to Sunday school at the mosque. Not only has she learned about Islam, but she also has made friends and feels good. She has learned other Islamic values such as respect for the elders in the community, modesty, *adab* [translated in English, appropriate behaviors toward different groups of people]. We both enjoy going to programs organized at our mosque. All this without arguing with her!" (Ross-Sheriff et al., 2007, p. 203).

This example demonstrates one Asian American adolescent's acceptance of her family's religious traditions. For others, however, the increased exploration of issues around gender and sexuality during adolescence may also lead to conflicts with family members whose religious views hold proscriptions against certain sexual identities, gender identities, and which may endorse strict gender roles and expectations (Hardy & Taylor, 2024; Wolf & Platt, 2022). These conflicting views may lead some adolescents to de-identify with their previous religious affiliations altogether (Hardy & Taylor, 2024). For example, in in-depth interviews with second-generation Filipina American emerging adults (Hufana, 2021), interviewees noted the emergence of these intergenerational conflicts during adolescence and their impact on mental health. As described by one interviewee:

"For most of my middle school and high school I had pretty severe depression, which was a huge arguing point for my parents and I. They asked me why I was sad and I literally had no idea. Then the closeted stuff was another thing and it meant I was 'unholy'. I don't know, maybe it's because I grew up in this Catholic household" (Hufana, 2021, p. 63).

For Asian American adolescents in co-ethnic religious-spiritual communities, these conflicting views on gender and sexuality may lead them to be "doubly marginalized" and separated from both their racial-ethnic and religious-spiritual communities (Cheng, 2006; Pak, 2020).

Discrimination

Asian American identity development during adolescence is closely linked to their experiences with racism and discrimination. For example, in the process of exploring and becoming more committed to their ethnic-racial identities, Asian American adolescents may also be more aware of, and even exposed to, more discriminatory behaviors (Cheon & Yip, 2019). Critically, Asian Americans' experiences of discrimination in adolescence negatively impact multiple domains of well-being, including mental health, social relationships, and academic performance (Benner & Kim, 2009; Benner et al., 2018; Greene et al., 2006).

Asian Americans' experiences of racial discrimination have received increasing attention in research over the past decade, and they have been amplified in public discourse through movements such as Stop AAPI Hate. By comparison, Asian Americans' experiences of religious discrimination are still overlooked. For Asian American Sikhs, Muslims, and Hindus in particular, experiences of racial-ethnic discrimination are often inextricable from their religious-spiritual identities. At the same time, whereas overt acts of racial discrimination commonly target Asian American physical features (e.g., skin color) over which they have no voluntary control, religious discrimination frequently targets individuals' voluntary, religious practices (e.g., wearing a hijab, praying in public). For Asian American adolescents with stigmatized religious identities, the nature of these discriminatory encounters presents an additional challenge to their identity formation: namely, the social cost of identity commitment.

A study by Abo-Zena (2019) underscores how experiences of gender, race-ethnicity and religious identity intersect in the everyday lives of Muslim American adolescent girls. As noted by Abo-Zena (2019), for devoted Muslim females, puberty marks a transition to adult levels of religious accountability, which includes fasting during Ramadan, praying five times a day, and adhering to Islamic dress. In this way, "menarche is the biological vehicle that transports her into a social and cultural world with an adult level of religious accountability" (p. 310). Abo-Zena's interviews and focus groups with 26 Muslim American adolescent girls identified how religious identities functioned as both a risk and protective factor in their well-being. For some respondents, adherence to religious regulations for dress—namely, wearing *hijab*—elicited stares, insults, and other discriminatory behavior, often from strangers. At the same time, religious identity also served as a buffer against these stressors, through support from peers in their religious community, and most frequently, by reliance on Allah through prayers. Taken together, this study exemplifies how person-level psychobiological factors such as gender and biological changes interact, at a given time in history and development (adolescence) with microsystem-level encounters of discrimination that are nested within macrosystem-level religious teachings and broader attitudes of Islamophobia.

Indeed, for Asian American youth, co-ethnic religious communities can provide peers who not only share similar experiences of racial discrimination, but who can also help provide spiritual support. In a study of Chinese American Christians in Memphis, Tennessee, two interviewees recounted how church youth groups served this function during their adolescence:

> In the church youth group, the friends you grew up with are Christians, you can be open and vulnerable. We grew up together. We developed that bond and relationship where we feel safe. We see each other every Sunday, we do things together, and we trust each other.
>
> I am no longer being ashamed of my Asian appearance. I am proud. Even though I am American, speaking English, and going to American schools, [the fellow youth group members] were able to teach me to learn about my Chinese identity.
>
> *(Yu, 2018, p. 187)*

Questions for Adolescents

- *Think about the things you believe and do that are related to being Asian American, and the things you believe and do that are related to your religious identity. Are there ways that your religious and Asian American identities are in tension with one another? Are there ways in which they are complementary, or do you see them as being largely unrelated?*
- *Do you feel differently about your religious and Asian American identities? For example, do you see one as being more important than the other, or do you have more positive or negative feelings toward one identity?*

Emerging Adulthood

Emerging adulthood refers to the period of time between late adolescence and early adulthood and has been identified over the past two decades as a period of increased autonomy, exploration, and instability across multiple life domains (2004). Despite ongoing debates regarding emerging adulthood as a distinct stage of development (Arnett et al., 2011; Côté, 2014; Syed, 2015), its framework suggests that the ages of 18–29 represent one of the most unstable periods of the lifespan: it is a decade in which emerging adults explore and take on new roles, relationships, and responsibilities in both personal and professional domains; while also navigating numerous crossroads pivotal to their long-term professional and personal trajectories (Arnett et al., 2014).

This period of instability coincides with what Arnett (2000, 2004) and Erikson (1968) identify as a key developmental task of emerging adulthood: the exploration of, and the eventual commitment to, a unique set of values, beliefs, and worldviews. This process of exploration and commitment sets the stage for emerging adulthood as a dynamic period of religious-spiritual development, albeit one with varying endpoints. On the one hand, a robust body of research indicates a general decline in religious identity during emerging adulthood across multiple domains, including religious attendance, private religious practice, and salience of religious identity (Chan et al., 2015; Dyer et al., 2022; Hardy et al., 2019). At the same time, individuals who maintain or increase their religious involvement in the transition to young adulthood show better outcomes, including overall better psychological well-being (Davis & Kiang, 2016; Hwang et al., 2022), a higher sense of purpose (Pfund et al., 2022), and self-regulation (Hardy et al., 2019; Zong & Cheah, 2023).

The research on religious development among Asian American emerging adults reveals a rich tapestry of trajectories, with some deepening or renewing religious commitments from adolescence, others rejecting them in favor of new religious or spiritual identities, and still others who do all of the above. The following examples illustrate each of these trajectories.

First, for many Asian American college students, co-ethnic or pan-Asian American religious groups provide a salient opportunity for exploring the intersection of both their racial-ethnic and religious identities, and importantly, to do so with relative autonomy from their parents. Driven primarily by Christian-affiliated groups, Asian American religious organizations at colleges and universities have proliferated over the past decades; indeed, Asian American chapters often represent the largest or fastest-growing groups within broader campus religious organizations (Kim, 2006; Park et al., 2013). Occupying the intersection of racial-ethnic and religious identities allows for a unique approach to issues such as racial-ethnic discrimination. Hufana (2021) describes how a Filipina American student's Catholic campus ministry encouraged her to dress in traditional Filipino clothing for a special Mass. The resulting experience was dramatically different from the embarrassment she had felt in the past:

> "I was a part of the team that recruited people to dress up and I got to speak on this experience. It was a different experience of walking and having everyone look at me wearing a *barong*. People said you look so nice doing that. It felt crazy that I went from 'Oh no, everyone's looking at me' to 'Wow, everyone is looking at me!' kind of thing. It was different. I don't know, it was a definitely a whole shift" (Hufana, 2021, p. 61).

Asian American campus religious groups can also serve as a bridge for individuals who already hold positive views toward their ethnic identities, but who have no previous religious affiliations. These individuals may be initially drawn to co-ethnic religious groups out of what Hall (2006) describes as "ethnic seekership"—a desire to be with co-ethnic peers, and at the very least, an openness to the group's religious views. In his ethnographic study of Chinese Americans who converted to Christianity through a Chinese American campus ministry, Hall (2006) concludes that conversion among religious seekers is driven in large part by the strength and quality of the social bonds within these co-ethnic groups.

Hall's (2006) Asian American interviewees experienced these co-ethnic religious spaces as places of belonging that ultimately fostered their religious exploration and commitment. By contrast, for other Asian American emerging adults, the process of religious exploration—and eventual commitment—involves stepping into minoritized spaces. These experiences are exemplified in Han's (2017, 2019) interviews with young adult Asian American Buddhists who were not raised in Buddhist households. Han's interviewees articulate shared challenges of belonging: they struggle to fit in with either American Buddhist communities, which are dominated by white Americans, or with Buddhist temples, which primarily serve immigrant communities and thus present language barriers. In their process of religious exploration, "first generation Buddhists" also encounter tensions with friends and family members. As recounted by one interviewee, "[My family members] constantly tell me to convert and that I need to come back to Jesus... [t]he Korean Christians that I've met have not been understanding of my religion and they criticize my religion at every opportunity" (Han, 2019, p. 3). Han notes that some young adults resolve these tensions by re-envisioning Buddhism as part of their cultural heritage and finding areas of alignment with the beliefs and practices of their immediate family members. One Chinese American Buddhist who was raised in a Christian family described the process in this way:

> I see just how much my family (although they did not identify with it) practiced (when we could) Buddhism in many ways—such as respect for all life; minding our impact on others; having compassion for suffering and doing what we can to decrease it; generosity with friends, neighbors, and family; and trying to appreciate what we have (Han, 2019, p. 11).

Despite their differences, these examples both demonstrate that for Asian Americans, the increased autonomy and instability of emerging adulthood make it a rich period for exploring the intersections of racial-ethnic and religious identities. A final example illustrates how religious experiences during emerging adulthood can provide a framework for life beyond it. In our study of status and social mobility in Chinese American families, one parent recounted how her religious experiences from late adolescence through college shaped her long-term perspectives on what it means to be successful:

> "I just feel very fortunate that I [was] able to meet some Christians who really guided me through those difficult times and became really positive role models for me and... I was able to...go to college and just have [a] kind of focus...I wasn't really distracted by a lot of other things and did really well in college because of my involvement with the Christian group there. And then, and then ended up going to a Bible school training program for two years, which really just set the right direction in my life and then ended up going to law school after that.
>
> And just step by step, I think I was always very clear as to what my primary goal was in life, which was not status or money...you know, things that would satisfy me inwardly rather than these things externally. And I think in part that helped me succeed, you know just having that perspective. Nevertheless, you know there's a lot of hard work involved, but you know, it was helpful to have another Center rather than just me, myself, and I."

Clinical Case Study

Joanna is an Asian American woman struggling to adjust to her first year in college. She grew up in what she describes as a "very loving, very religious" family, and her closest friends throughout high school were others in their co-ethnic, religious community. Since coming to college, Joanna has struggled to establish a sense of community. There are organizations on campus for students who share her religious affiliation, which she has visited on occasion, but she felt out of place as one of the only non-White students there. On the other hand, Joanna has made a number of good Asian American friends, but none of them share her religious values or beliefs.

Joanna is also questioning whether the beliefs she was raised with are actually her own, or just those of her family and childhood friends. As a result, the ways she has always coped with stress, loneliness, and anxiety in the past—by praying and seeking support from others in her faith community—now feel inaccessible and inauthentic. She is hesitant to engage in therapy, as she had been taught that "secular" mental health treatments were often at odds with their religious beliefs.

1. *How would you address Joanna's struggle to find friendships with those who share both her religious-spiritual and racial-ethnic identity?*
2. *How might you approach her reservations toward "secular" therapy, while acknowledging both (a) the importance of her religious identity and (b) her current doubts about her religious beliefs?*

Conclusion

The wide array of experiences captured in this chapter challenges any broad conclusions regarding religion's effect on the mental health and well-being of Asian American youth. As illustrated in these sections, the religious identities of Asian American youth are not easily disentangled from their experiences as racial-ethnic minorities—indeed, in many cases, the contexts in which these identities are socialized are one and the same. Likewise, we cannot consider the effects of Asian American religious identities on mental health and well-being without considering characteristics of the individual person, such as their gender, sexual orientation, social status, and perhaps most critically, their stage of development. Together, they complicate the Confucian and Daoist concepts traditionally applied to frameworks of Asian American mental health, such as filial piety, harmony, and collectivism; and underscore the need for more dynamic and nuanced conceptualizations of cultural influence.

These complexities notwithstanding, two things are clear. First, there are pronounced gaps in the existing research. Relative to studies of Asian Americans' religious development in adolescence and emerging adulthood, we know little of how these processes play out in middle childhood, and even less in early childhood. Likewise, in its focus on Asian Americans' religious identities, this chapter has set aside investigations of Asian American spirituality—what Mahoney (2013) defines as "search for the sacred." Also omitted in this chapter is a substantial discussion of Asian American "religious nones": while nearly a third of Asian Americans may not identify with any formal religious group, they may nonetheless share traditions that function similarly to religion by providing meaning, ethics, identity, and a central narrative for their lives (Jeung et al., 2019).

These gaps point to the second and final conclusion of this chapter: while there is much we do not know about religion, mental health, and well-being in Asian American youth, there is no doubt that these are questions well-worth pursuing.

Author Note

We have no conflicts of interest to disclose.

Acknowledgments

I am grateful to Marie Kung, Samantha Khemlani, Sherry Sze, and Yixuan Zhang from the Wellesley Culture, Family & Development Lab for their assistance on this chapter.

References

Abo-Zena, M. M. (2019). Being young, Muslim, and female: youth perspectives on the intersection of religious and gender identities. *Journal of Research on Adolescence*, *29*(2), 308–320.

Ainsworth, M. D. S., Blehar, M. C., Waters, E., & Wall, S. (1978). *Patterns of Attachment: A Psychological Study of the Strange Situation*. Hillsdale, NJ: Lawrence Erlbaum. https://doi.org/10.4324/9780203758045

Arnett, J. J. (2000). Emerging adulthood: a theory of development from the late teens through the twenties. *American Psychologist*, *55*(5), 469.

Arnett, J. J. (2004). Emerging adulthood: the winding road from the late teens through the twenties. New York: Oxford University Press.

Arnett, J. J., Kloep, M., Hendry, L. B., & Tanner, J. L. (2011). *Debating Emerging Adulthood: Stage or Process*? Oxford, NY: Oxford University Press. https://doi.org/10.1093/acprof:oso/9780199757176.001.0001

Arnett, J. J., Žukauskienė, R., & Sugimura, K. (2014). The new life stage of emerging adulthood at ages 18–29 years: Implications for mental health. *The Lancet Psychiatry*, *1*(7), 569–576. https://doi.org/10.1016/S2215-0366(14)00080-7

Bankston III, C. L., & Zhou, M. (2000). De facto congregationalism and socioeconomic mobility in Laotian and Vietnamese immigrant communities: A study of religious institutions and economic change. *Review of religious research*, 453–470.

Bankston III, C. L., & Zhou, M. (1995). Religious participation, ethnic identification, and adaptation of Vietnamese adolescents in an immigrant community. *Sociological Quarterly*, *36*(3), 523–534. https://doi.org/10.1111/j.1533-8525.1995.tb00451.x

Benner, A. D., & Kim, S. Y. (2009). Experiences of discrimination among Chinese American adolescents and the consequences for socioemotional and academic development. *Developmental Psychology*, *45*(6), 1682. https://doi.org/10.1037/a0016119

Benner, A. D., Wang, Y., Shen, Y., Boyle, A. E., Polk, R., & Cheng, Y. P. (2018). Racial/ethnic discrimination and well-being during adolescence: a meta-analytic review. *American Psychologist*, *73*(7), 855. https://doi.org/10.1037/amp0000204

Bornstein, M. H., Putnick, D. L., Lansford, J. E., Al-Hassan, S. M., Bacchini, D., Bombi, A. S., ... & Alampay, L. P. (2017). 'Mixed blessings': parental religiousness, parenting, and child adjustment in global perspective. *Journal of child psychology and psychiatry, and allied disciplines*, *58*(8), 880–892. https://doi.org/10.1111/jcpp.12705

Bowlby, J. (1969). *Attachment and Loss: Vol. 1. Attachment*. New York: Basic Books.

Bowlby, J. (1973). *Separation Anxiety and Anges:* Vol. 2. *Attachment and Loss*. New York: Basic Books.

Bowlby, J. (1980). *Attachment and Loss: Vol. 3. Loss*. New York: Basic Books.

Bronfenbrenner, U., & Morris, P. A. (2006). The bioecological model of human development. In R. M. Lerner, & W. Damon (Eds.), *Handbook of Child Psychology: Theoretical Models of Human Development* (Sixth Edition) (pp. 793–828). John Wiley & Sons, Inc. https://doi.org/10.1002/9780470147658.chpsy0114

Butler-Barnes, S. T., Martin, P. P., Copeland-Linder, N., Seaton, E. K., Matusko, N., Caldwell, C. H., & Jackson, J. S. (2018). The protective role of religious involvement in African American and Caribbean Black adolescents' experiences of racial discrimination. *Youth & Society*, *50*(5), 659–687.

Cassidy, J., & Shaver, P. R. (Eds.). (1999). *Handbook of Attachment: Theory, Research, and Clinical Applications*. New York: Guilford. https://doi.org/10.1002/imhj.21730

Chan, M., Tsai, K. M., & Fuligni, A. J. (2015). Changes in religiosity across the transition to young adulthood. *Journal of Youth and Adolescence*, *44*(8), 1555–1566. https://doi.org/10.1007/s10964-014-0157-0

Chen, S. H., Gleason, T. R., Wang, M. M., Liu, C. H., & Wang, L. K. (2019). Perceptions of social status in Chinese American children: associations with social cognitions and socioemotional well-being. *Asian American Journal of Psychology*, *10*(4), 362.

Chen, S. H., Hua, M., Zhou, Q., Tao, A., Lee, E. H., Ly, J., & Main, A. (2014). Parent–child cultural orientations and child adjustment in Chinese American immigrant families. *Developmental Psychology*, *50*(1), 189.

Cheng, P. S. (2006). Reclaiming our traditions, rituals, and spaces: spirituality and the queer Asian Pacific American experience. *Spiritus: A Journal of Christian Spirituality*, *6*(2), 234–240. https://dx.doi.org/10.1353/scs.2006.0051

Cheon, Y. M., & Yip, T. (2019). Longitudinal associations between ethnic/racial identity and discrimination among Asian and Latinx adolescents. *Journal of Youth and Adolescence*, *48*, 1736–1753. https://doi.org/10.1007/s10964-019-01055-6

Côté, J. E. (2014). The dangerous myth of emerging adulthood: an evidence-based critique of a flawed developmental theory. *Applied Developmental Science*, *18*(4), 177–188.

Davis III, R. F., & Kiang, L. (2016). Religious identity, religious participation, and psychological well-being in Asian American adolescents. *Journal of Youth and Adolescence*, *45*(3), 532–546. https://doi.org/10.1007/s10964-015-0350-9

DeHaan, L. G., Yonker, J. E., & Affholter, C. (2011). More than enjoying the sunset: conceptualization and measurement of religiosity for adolescents and emerging adults and its implications for developmental inquiry. *Journal of Psychology and Christianity*, *30*, 184–195.

De Roos, S. A. (2006). Young children's God concepts: influences of attachment and religious socialization in a family and school context. *Religious Education*, *101*(1), 84–103.

De Roos, S. A., Iedema, J., & Miedema, S. (2004). Influence of maternal denomination, God concepts, and child-rearing practices on young children's God concepts. *Journal for the Scientific Study of Religion*, *43*(4), 519–535.

Derr, A., Lindhorst, T., & Oesterle, S. (2018). Examining heterogeneity of social support among Asian and Latino immigrants in the United States: a latent class analysis. *The International Journal of Health, Wellness and Society*, *8*(2), 17. https://doi.org/10.18848/2156-8960/CGP/v08i02/17-33

Desmond, S. A., Morgan, K. H., & Kikuchi, G. (2010). Religious development: how (and why) does religiosity change from adolescence to young adulthood? *Sociological Perspectives*, *53*(2), 247–270. https://doi.org/10.1525/sop.2010.53.2.247

Dickie, J. R., A. K. Eshleman, D. M. Merasco, A. Shepard, M. V. Wilt, & M. Johnson. (1997). "Parent-child Relationships and Children's Images of God." *Journal for the Scientific Study of Religion* *36*:25–43.

Dyer, W. J., Goodman, M. A., & Hardy, S. A. (2022). Adolescent suicide ideation in Utah: the role of religion and family. *Psychology of Religion and Spirituality*, *14*(1), 86–96. https://doi.org/10.1037/rel0000319

Ellison, C. G., DeAngelis, R. T., & Güven, M. (2017). Does religious involvement mitigate the effects of major discrimination on the mental health of African Americans? Findings from the Nashville Stress and Health Study. *Religions*, *8*(9), 195. https://doi.org/10.3390/rel8090195

Erikson, E. H. (1968). *Identity: Youth and Crisis*. New York, NY: Norton.

Ganapathy-Coleman, H. (2014). 'He thinks Krishna is his friend': domestic space and temple sociality in the socialisation beliefs of immigrant Indian Hindu parents. *Culture and Religion*, *15*(1), 118–146.

Gauvain, M., & Perez, S. M. (2015). The socialization of cognition. In J. E. Grusec, & P. D. Hastings (Eds.), *Handbook of Socialization: Theory and Research* (Second Edition) (pp. 566–589). The Guilford Press.

Granqvist, P., Ljungdahl, C., & Dickie, J. R. (2007). God is nowhere, God is now here: attachment activation, security of attachment, and God's perceived closeness among 5–7-year-old children from religious and non-religious homes. *Attachment & Human Development*, *9*(1), 55–71.

Greene, M. L., Way, N., & Pahl, K. (2006). Trajectories of perceived adult and peer discrimination among Black, Latino, and Asian American adolescents: patterns and psychological correlates. *Developmental Psychology*, *42*(2), 218. https://doi.org/10.1037/0012-1649.42.2.218

Hall, B. (2006). Social and cultural contexts in conversion to Christianity among Chinese American college students. *Sociology of Religion*, *67*(2), 131–147. https://doi.org/10.1093/socrel/67.2.131

Han, C. (2017). Diverse practices and flexible beliefs among young adult Asian American Buddhists. *Journal of Global Buddhism*, *18*, 1–24. https://doi.org/10.5281/zenodo.1247854

Han, C. (2019). Contesting "conversion" and "reversion" among young adult Asian American Buddhists. *Religions*, *10*(4), 261. https://doi.org/10.3390/rel10040261

Hardy, S. A., Dollahite, D. C., & Baldwin, C. R. (2019). Parenting, religion, and moral development. In D. J. Laible, G. Carlo, & L. M. Padilla-Walker (Eds.), *The Oxford Handbook of Parenting and Moral Development* (pp. 179–196). Oxford University Press.

Hardy, S. A., & Taylor, E. M. (2024). The past, present, and future of research on religious and spiritual development in adolescence, young adulthood, and beyond. *Archiv für Religionspsychologie / Archive for the Psychology of Religion*, *46*(2), 109–120. https://doi.org/10.1177/00846724241235172

Hays, K., & Aranda, M. P. (2016). Faith-based mental health interventions with African Americans: a review. *Research on Social Work Practice*, *26*(7), 777–789. https://doi.org/10.1177/1049731515569356

Hirschman, C. (2004). The role of religion in the origins and adaptation of immigrant groups in the United States. *International Migration Review*, *38*(3), 1206–1233. https://doi.org/10.1111/j.1747-7379.2004.tb00233.x

Hope, M. O., Assari, S., Cole-Lewis, Y. C., & Caldwell, C. H. (2017). Religious social support, discrimination, and psychiatric disorders among Black adolescents. *Race and Social Problems*, *9*, 102–114. https://doi.org/10.1007/s12552-016-9192-7

Huang, Z. J., Lewin, A., Mitchell, S. J., & Zhang, J. (2012). Variations in the relationship between maternal depression, maternal sensitivity, and child attachment by race/ethnicity and nativity: findings from a nationally representative cohort study. *Maternal and Child Health Journal*, *16*, 40–50. https://doi.org/10.1007/s10995-010-0716-2

Hufana, A. M. A. (2021). Exploring the lived experiences of second-generation Filipina American emerging adults: navigating challenges and meaning-making of intersecting identities and cultural values. University of California, Santa Barbara.

Hwang, W., Cheng, K. J., Brown, M. T., & Silverstein, M. (2022). Religiosity of baby-boomers in young adulthood: associations with psychological well-being over the life course. *Advances in Life Course Research*, *52*, 100477.

Jeung, R. M., Fong, S. S., & Kim, H. J. (2019). *Family Sacrifices: The Worldviews and Ethics of Chinese Americans*. Oxford University Press. https://doi.org/10.1093/oso/9780190875923.001.0001

Joshi, K. Y. (2006). *New Roots in America's Sacred Ground: Religion, Race, and Ethnicity in Indian America*. Rutgers University Press.

Kim, R. Y. (2006). *God's New Whiz Kids?: Korean American Evangelicals on Campus*. NYU Press.

King, P. E. (2008). Spirituality as fertile ground for positive youth development. In R. M. Lerner, R. Roeser, & E. Phelps (Eds.). *Positive Youth Development and Spirituality: From Theory to Research* (pp. 55–73). West Conshohocken, PA: Templeton Foundation Press.

Kirkpatrick, L. A. (1999). Attachment and religious representations and behavior. In *Handbook of Attachment: Theory, Research, and Clinical Applications* (pp. 803–822). New York: Guilford Press.

Kirkpatrick, L. A., & Shaver, P. R. (1992). An attachment-theoretical approach to romantic love and religious belief. *Personality and Social Psychology Bulletin*, *18*(3), 266–275.

Lecompte, V., Miconi, D., & Rousseau, C. (2018). Challenges related to migration and child attachment: a pilot study with South Asian immigrant mother–child dyads. *Attachment & Human Development*, *20*(2), 208–222. https://doi.org/10.1080/14616734.2017.1398765

Lee, D. B., Peckins, M. K., Miller, A. L., Hope, M. O., Neblett, E. W., Assari, S., ... Zimmerman, M. A. (2021). Pathways from racial discrimination to cortisol/DHEA imbalance: protective role of religious involvement. *Ethnicity & Health*, *26*(3), 413–430. https://doi.org/10.1080/13557858.2018.1520815

Lopez, A. B., Huynh, V. W., & Fuligni, A. J. (2011). A longitudinal study of religious identity and participation during adolescence. *Child Development*, *82*(4), 1297–1309. https://doi.org/10.1111/j.1467-8624.2011.01609.x

Lu, Y. (2012). "Faith is Life": a qualitative study of Christian faith and Chinese immigrant families. [Doctoral Dissertation, Louisiana State University and Agricultural & Mechanical College].

Mahoney, A. (2010). Religion in families 1999–2009: a relational spirituality framework. *Journal of Marriage and Family*, *72*, 805–827. https://doi.org/10.1111/j.1741-3737.2010.00732.x

Mahoney, A. (2013). The spirituality of us: relational spirituality in the context of family relationships. In K. I. Pargament, J. J. Exline, & J. W. Jones (Eds.), *APA Handbook of Psychology, Religion, and*

Spirituality (Vol 1): Context, Theory, and Research (pp. 365–389). Washington, DC: American Psychological Association. https://doi.org/10.1037/14045-020

Mahoney, A., & Boyatzis, C. J. (2019). Parenting, religion, and spirituality. In M. H. Bornstein (Ed.), *Handbook of Parenting: The Practice of Parenting* (3rd ed., pp. 515–552). Routledge/Taylor & Francis Group. https://doi.org/10.4324/9780429401695-18

Mahoney, A., Pargament, K. I., Murray-Swank, A., & Murray-Swank, N. (2003). Religion and the sanctification of family relationships. *Review of Religious Research*, *44*, 220–236. https://doi.org/10.2307/3512384

Mariano, J. M., & Damon, W. (2008). The role of spirituality and religious faith in supporting purpose in adolescence. In R. M. Lerner, R. W. Roeser, & E. Phelps (Eds.), *Positive Youth Development and Spirituality: From Theory to Research* (pp. 210–230). West Conshohocken, PA: Templeton Foundation Press.

Mazumdar, S., & Mazumdar, S. (2015). Religious ritual, place, and family: Vietnamese-American Buddhists in Southern California. *Journal of Ritual Studies*, 45–56. http://www.jstor.org/stable/44735501

McLoughlin, N., Davoodi, T., Cui, Y. K., Clegg, J., Harris, P. L., & Corriveau, K. H. (2021a). Parents' belief about their influence on children's scientific and religious view: perspectives from Iran, China and the United States. *Journal of Cognition and Culture*, *21*(1–2), 49–75. https://doi.org/10.1163/15685373-12340096

McLoughlin, N., Jacob, C., Samrow, P., & Corriveau, K. H. (2021b). Beliefs about unobservable scientific and religious entities are transmitted via subtle linguistic cues in parental testimony. *Journal of Cognition and Development*, *22*(3), 379–397. https://doi.org/10.1080/15248372.2020.1871351

Min, P. G. (1992). The structure and social functions of Korean immigrant churches in the United States. *International Migration Review*, *26*(4), 1370–1394. https://doi.org/10.1177/019791839202600413

Pak, J. (2020). Korean Americans, the protestant Christian church, and the future of Asian American LGBTQ rights. *Hastings Race and Poverty Law Journal*, *17*(2), 553–576.

Park, J. J., Lew, J. W., & Chiang, W. (2013). Asian American evangelical Christian students on campus. In S. D. Museus, D. C. Maramba, & R. T. Teranishi (Eds.), *The Misrepresented Minority: New Insights on Asian Americans and Pacific Islanders, and the Implications for Higher Education* (pp. 165–181). Sterling, VA: Stylus.

Pew Research Center. (2023). "Religion among Asian Americans: key findings from a Pew Research Center survey." United States of America. https://coilink.org/20.500.12592/5d1ckj

Pfund, G. N., Schultz, L. H., Andrews, J. A., & Hill, P. L. (2022). Individual-level trajectories of religiosity during adolescence and their implications for purpose. *Psychology of Religion and Spirituality*, *14*(3), 386–389. https://doi.org/10.1037/rel0000317

Ream, G. L., & Savin-Williams, R. C. (2003). Religious development in adolescence. In G. R. Adams & M. D. Berzonsky, *Blackwell Handbook of Adolescence*, 51–59.

Richert, R. A., & Corriveau, K. H. (2022). Development of religious cognition. *Annual Review of Developmental Psychology*, *4*(1), 185–206.

Richert, R. A., Shaman, N. J., Saide, A. R., & Lesage, K. A. (2016). Folding your hands helps god hear you: prayer and anthropomorphism in parents and children. *Research in the Social Scientific Study of Religion*, *27*, 140–157. https://doi.org/10.1163/9789004322035_010

Roh, P. (2016). *The Relationship Between Parental Attachment, Religious Coping, and Self-Esteem in Korean-American Adolescents*. Liberty University.

Ross-Sheriff, F., Tirmazi, M. T., & Walsh, T. R. (2007). Cultural and religious contexts of parenting by immigrant South Asian Muslim mothers. In J. E. Lansford, K. Deater-Deckard, & M. H. Bornstein (Eds.), *Immigrant Families in Contemporary Society* (pp. 194–211). New York, NY: Guilford Press.

Saide, A. R., & Richert, R. A. (2020). Socio-cognitive and cultural influences on children's concepts of God. *Journal of Cognition and Culture*, *20*(1–2), 22–40. https://doi.org/10.1163/15685373-12340072

Schwartz, K. D. (2006). Transformations in parent and friend faith support predicting adolescents' religious faith. *International Journal for the Psychology of Religion*, *16*(4), 311–326. https://doi.org/10.1207/s15327582ijpr1604_5

Shin, H. (2009). Asian American college students' parental attachment and their relationship with God. *Christian Education Journal*, *6*(2), 353–375. https://doi.org/10.1177/073989130900600212

Smith, C., & Denton, M. L. (2005). *Soul Searching: The Religious and Spiritual Lives of American Teenagers* (Online Edition). New York: Oxford Academic. https://doi.org/10.1093/0195180 95X.001.0001

Syed, M. (2015). Emerging adulthood: developmental stage, theory, or nonsense? In J. J. Arnett (Ed.), *Oxford Handbook of Emerging Adulthood* (pp. 11–25). London: Oxford University Press.

Villatoro, A. P., Dixon, E., & Mays, V. M. (2016). Faith-based organizations and the affordable care act: reducing Latino mental health care disparities. *Psychological Services*, *13*(1), 92. https://doi.org/10.1037/a0038515

Volling, B. L., Mahoney, A., & Rauer, A. J. (2009). Sanctification of parenting, moral socialization, and young children's conscience development. *Psychology of Religion and Spirituality*, *1*(1), 53. https://doi.org/10.1037/a0014958

Wang, M. M., Gleason, T. R., & Chen, S. H. (2025). Effortful control is associated with ethnic minority children's pro-wealth biases and explanations across social domains. *Developmental Psychology*, *61*(9), 1707–1720. https://doi.org/10.1037/dev0001853

Wei, M., Ku, T. Y., Chen, H. J., Wade, N., Liao, K. Y. H., & Guo, G. J. (2012). Chinese Christians in America: attachment to God, stress, and well-being. *Counseling and Values*, *57*(2), 162–180. https://doi.org/10.1002/2161007X-05702003

Williams, A. I., Liu, C., Zhou, Q., Wu, J., Meng, L., Deng, X. F., & Chen, S. H. (2024). Parental expressions of love in Chinese American immigrant families: implications for children's attachment security. *Developmental Science*, *27*(6), e13549. https://doi.org/10.1111/desc.13549

Windzio, M., & Wingens, M. (2014). Religion, friendship networks and home visits of immigrant and native children. *Acta Sociologica*, *57*(1), 59–75. https://doi.org/10.1177/0001699313481226

Wolf, J. K., & Platt, L. F. (2022). Religion and sexual identities. *Current Opinion in Psychology*, *48*, 101495. https://doi.org/10.1016/j.copsyc.2022.101495

Wong, J. S. (2018). *Immigrants, Evangelicals, and Politics in an Era of Demographic Change*. Russell Sage Foundation.

Wong, S. H., Zhang, E., Liu, C. H., & Chen, S. (2024). Ethnic-racial socialization in Chinese American immigrant families: associations with middle childhood ethnic identity. *Social Development*, *33*(4), 12746. https://doi.org/10.1111/sode.12746

Yu, S. (2018). "We are all children of God": the intersectionality of religion, race and ethnicity, and immigration in Chinese churches in Memphis, Tennessee. *Papers in Applied Geography*, *4*(3), 256–273. https://doi.org/10.1080/23754931.2017.1401955

Zhou, M., Bankston, C. L., & Kim, R. Y. (2002). Rebuilding spiritual lives in the new land: religious practices among Southeast Asian refugees in the United States. In *Religions in Asian America*, 37–70.

Zong, X., & Cheah, C. S. L. (2023). Multiple dimensions of religiosity, self-regulation, and psychological adjustment among emerging adults. *Current Psychology*, *42*, 4133–4142. https://doi.org/10.1007/s12144-021-01780-x

5

Adapting Mental Health Interventions for Asian American and Pacific Islander Youth

Stephanie H. Yu[1]*, Belinda C. Chen*[2]*, Summer Pascual*[2]*, and Anna S. Lau*[2]

[1]*Department of Psychiatry and Behavioral Sciences, University of California, San Francisco, CA, USA*
[2]*Department of Psychology, University of California, Los Angeles, CA, USA*

Adapting interventions involves making intentional changes to an intervention's design or delivery to better fit a specific population, setting, or context (Stirman et al., 2019). Cultural adaptations are those that make an intervention more resonant with a client's culture, language, and context (Bernal et al., 2009).

Asian Americans and Pacific Islanders (AAPIs) trace their roots to more than 30 countries—each with distinct histories, cultures, and languages. Evidence-based interventions (EBIs) for mental health are interventions shown in research studies to successfully treat a targeted mental health problem. However, EBIs for youth have been historically developed from Western, Eurocentric frameworks and tested among White and WEIRD (Western, educated, industrialized, rich, and democratic) populations (Henrich et al., 2010). Thus, they do not inherently attend to the unique experiences of AAPI youth and families.

The question of "to adapt or not to adapt" has been much debated (von Thiele Schwarz et al., 2019). On the one hand, adapting interventions may improve their effectiveness, acceptability, and client engagement through enhanced cultural relevance (Steinka-Fry et al., 2017; Rathod et al., 2018; Hall et al., 2016). On the other, AAPI communities can benefit from existing EBIs (Huey Jr. et al., 2018; Park et al., 2023; Xin et al., 2022), and adaptations may remove key aspects of the interventions that make them work (Castro et al., 2004; Pérez et al., 2016). Intentional adaptation offers a compromise between applying EBIs universally without alteration and developing a new intervention for every possible clinical presentation. In this chapter, we consider the why, when, and how of adapting mental health interventions for AAPI youth, ultimately with the goal of better serving the mental health needs of AAPI communities.

Why Adapt Mental Health Interventions for AAPI Youth?

Though the longstanding model minority myth[1] has led to the widespread misperception that AAPIs are an exemplar group with few mental and physical health problems, AAPI youth face significantly underserved yet high acuity mental health needs (George et al., 2024; Lui et al., 2024). Despite this high need, 92% of Asian American (AA) adolescents and 67% of Native Hawaiian and Pacific Islander (NHPI) adolescents do not receive mental health services (MHS; The Children's Partnership, 2023a; 2023b). Systematic underfunding of AAPI-focused health research and lack of disaggregated data focused on unique AAPI subgroups (e.g., South Asian and Pacific Islander youth) further obscures mental health disparities (Kim et al., 2021; Rastogi et al., 2025; Sharma et al., 2020; Morey et al., 2020). Thus, AAPI youth face a concerning mental healthcare gap. To better meet their needs, providers and advocates may adapt existing EBIs to meet group-specific stressors and leverage the rich cultural resources and knowledge embedded within the AAPI community.

When to Adapt and for What Purpose

The term "AAPI" invokes a widely heterogeneous group. Ethnic group membership encompasses many dimensions including cultural processes, values, and strengths that are dynamic and differ by lived experience across AAPI ethnic groups. These lived experiences are also contextualized within varied historical and present-day sociocultural contexts. Notably, AAPIs have experienced racial subjugation and oppression throughout US history ranging from the Chinese Exclusion Act of 1882, the incarceration of Japanese Americans during World War II, and the colonization of Hawai'i, the Philippines, and Pacific Islands (Millner et al., 2021). Their diverse experiences can produce different strengths and mental health risks that impact individuals' clinical presentations and how they respond to EBIs (Barrera Jr. & Castro, 2006; Lau, 2006). Therefore, adaptations should not be made based on stereotyped assumptions. While someone's racial/ethnic group provides meaningful information, relying on it as a sole proxy to understand AAPI experiences will result in interventions and adaptations falling short. Furthermore, AAPI youth may be multiracial/ethnic and hold multiple identities based on gender, sexuality, religion, socioeconomic status, and so on, all of which deserve attention and shape AAPI experience. Collectively, these cultural and contextual dynamics likely have more bearing on AAPI youth mental health and treatment response than racial or ethnic group membership alone.

A Selective and Directed Approach to Adaptation

Given this heterogeneity, those seeking to adapt interventions for AAPI youth should consider the purpose and target of their adaptations. One challenge to be mindful of is the balance between designing adaptations to address suboptimal fit and maintaining the therapeutic value of the original intervention. Lau (2006) provides a framework for a *selective* and *directed* approach to adaptation that involves using data to (1) *selectively* determine **when** a cultural adaptation may be needed based on a problem, and (2) *direct* the adaptation toward **an identified purpose**

1 The misperception that Asian Americans are an exemplary racial/ethnic minoritized group who face little to no barriers to academic and career success (Kiang et al., 2017).

or mechanism of change. "Data" in this chapter includes multiple ways of knowing—from the body of empirically-supported studies to lessons gleaned from AAPI lived experiences and perspectives. Adaptation may be warranted if data indicate the need to: (1) enhance engagement so AAPI youth can benefit from the EBI, (2) augment content for sociocultural contexts not considered by the EBI, (3) intensify learning for culturally unfamiliar skills, and (4) leverage unique cultural strengths.

To consider when interventions may need to be adapted, we touch briefly on examples of adaptation-relevant mental health risks, cultural values, and strengths *that are not universal across AAPI youth and families*. Though it is beyond the chapter's scope to characterize the range of AAPI experiences, attending to each unique experience during intervention is critical.

Adapting to Enhance Engagement

Engagement involves motivating individuals to seek, attend, participate, and stay in treatment. Given research that AAPI youth and families underutilize MHS, intervention adaptations may be directed toward enhancing engagement (Garrett et al., 2025; George et al., 2024).

Structural, Logistical, and Attitudinal Barriers. Structural racism and xenophobia targeting AAPIs have resulted in systemic barriers that deter AAPI communities from accessing care (Guan et al., 2024). Nearly half of AAs have experienced restricted access to MHS due to lack of multilingual providers in the psychology workforce (Augsberger et al., 2015). This is particularly concerning given that in California, the state with the largest population of AAPIs, 21% of AA and 13% of NHPI students are English Language Learners, and 86% of AA and 38% of NHPI children live in immigrant families with at least one parent born outside the United States (The Children's Partnership, 2023a; 2023b). Since caregivers must consent to MHS for their children and are often active participants in youth treatments, AAPI children bear the downstream consequences of marginalization as AAPI caregivers are also more likely to lack the time, finances, and insurance coverage for MHS (Gudiño et al., 2008; Kim & Lee, 2022). AAPI youth with immigrant or undocumented family members, or who are immigrants or undocumented themselves, may be further impacted by immigration-related fears (Wright et al., 2024). In California, 10% of AAs and 11% of NHPIs avoided accessing government-funded health benefits due to fears of disqualifying themselves or their family members from a green card/citizenship (The Children's Partnership, 2023a; 2023b). Stigma toward MHS is also amplified within this environment as AAPI caregivers may worry that others finding out about their child's mental health concerns will harm their life prospects (Wang et al., 2019). Anti-immigrant discourse and policies only worsen these issues (López-Hinojosa et al., 2024)—as youth internalize a hostile sociocultural context, it becomes increasingly difficult for them to seek help when in need (Arora & Khoo, 2020; Yu et al., 2025).

To address these wide-ranging barriers, adaptations to increase engagement include culturally-informed peer-led interventions (Hwang & Chan, 2019; Lin et al., 2018), digital interventions (Song et al., 2022; Sit et al., 2020; Wong et al., 2024), and school-based MHS that serve youth where they are (Bear et al., 2014). Mental health crises among AAPI youth are most often identified by school personnel, highlighting the importance of school-based MHS for these populations (Chen et al., 2022). Parent trainings and workshops (Wang et al., 2020; 2021; 2022), as well as education through informal networks (e.g., local ethnic radio stations, lay/community health workers), can expand health and mental health outreach to AA communities (Cheng et al., 2022; Han et al., 2015; Islam et al., 2015; Weng & Spaulding-Givens, 2016; Woo, 2012). For example, workshops highlighting

Table 5.1 Examples of alternative mental health terms.

Mental health terms	Alternative terms
Mental health	Mental balance; Being at peace/ease; Contentment
Mental health treatment	Emotional support or guidance; Problem-solving; Decreasing stress and overwhelm
Mental illness	Emotional/mental stress or imbalance; Overwhelm
Depression	Sadness; Heart pain; Heaviness; Mood
Anxiety	Nervousness; Fear; Stomach pain; Tension; Heart racing

Source: Stephanie H. Yu

scenes from Korean dramas to facilitate discussions on mental health-related topics like depression and help-seeking improved mental health knowledge, attitudes, and behaviors in diverse AAs (Ta Park et al., 2019; 2020; 2021). Finally, integrating complementary cultural and religious practices into treatment (e.g., holistic mind-body practices, traditional medicine), or using culturally-resonant terms, framing, and explanatory beliefs for mental health (e.g., as a social or medical problem) may also address cultural aspects of stigma in AAPI communities (see Table 5.1; Fancher et al., 2010; Misra et al., 2021; Sung et al., 2013).

Adapting to Augment Content for Distinct Sociocultural Contexts

Adaptations to augment content may be necessary when a clinical problem emerges within a distinct sociocultural context for a given community (Lau, 2006). Data may indicate this need if an EBI is not improving expected outcomes or AAPI youth exhibit symptoms that existing EBIs do not address. In these situations, a culturally-relevant theory may more precisely leverage strengths or target risk factors to achieve desired outcomes (Barrera Jr. & Castro, 2006).

Acculturative Stress. AAPI youth may disproportionately experience acculturative stress, or the stress from adapting to or integrating the characteristics of a new culture with those of one's heritage culture (Hwang & Ting, 2008; Tummala-Narra et al., 2016). Acculturative stress can vary by immigrant generation and the circumstances under which individuals or their families came to the United States, whether forcibly (e.g., as refugees) or by choice (d'Abreu et al., 2019; Sangalang et al., 2019; Singh et al., 2015). Relatedly, acculturation gaps, or differences in values and cultural identity between immigrant parents and their children, may be a source of stress, distance, or conflict in AAPI families, with mental health consequences for youth (Hwang, 2006; Nguyen et al., 2018; Telzer, 2011). See *Design-Time Adaptation Case Study* for one way this was addressed.

Racial Stress and Trauma. AAPI communities face a legacy of structural racism that shapes downstream experiences of discrimination, microaggressions, and race-related stress. Racial stress and trauma, characterized by symptoms like fear, anxiety, shame, anger, and hypervigilance (Carter, 2007), can arise among AAPI youth due to chronic exposure to racism (Hahm et al., 2021; Zhang et al., 2022). Interventions and frameworks for adapting therapy to address racial stress and trauma are listed in Table 5.2. For example, Williams and colleagues provide guidance on adapting cognitive-behavioral therapy (CBT), an EBI shown to be effective for a wide range of mental health problems (Huey Jr. et al., 2023; Xin et al., 2022). CBT is rooted in the principle that how individuals react to a situation is shaped more by their perception of it

Table 5.2 Interventions or frameworks for addressing racial stress and trauma.

Intervention or framework	Reference
Racial, Ethnic, and Cultural Healing (REACH)	DeLapp & Gallo (2022)
Trauma and Racism Addressed by Navigating Systemic Forms of Oppression using Resistance Methods (TRANSFORM)	Lau Johnson et al. (2024)
Antiracist Cognitive-Behavioral Therapy	Williams et al. (2023), Cénat et al. (2024)
Psychological Framework of Radical Healing	French et al. (2020), Adames et al. (2023)

Source: Stephanie H. Yu

than by the situation itself. CBT skills, such as cognitive restructuring, focus on identifying and changing unhelpful thinking patterns and behaviors. However, if not applied carefully, cognitive restructuring can invalidate youths' reactions to discrimination by "blaming" them on youths' perceptions rather than on the experience itself. Effectively adapting CBT to address racialized stress includes: validating the client while using CBT to process and make sense of racist experiences; contextualizing experiences within societal prejudice to reduce internalization of racism; practicing skills to confront racism and microaggressions; and using identify-affirming coping strategies (e.g., leaning into community and family; Williams et al., 2023).

Adapting to Intensify Learning

AAPI youth and families may need more time and support to fully benefit from evidence-based skills that are culturally unfamiliar or less initially acceptable.

Parenting Skills. Lau et al. (2010; 2011; 2012) conducted a series of studies examining the effectiveness of culturally-adapted parent behavioral training for Chinese immigrant families. Parent training teaches caregivers how to change child behaviors using positive reinforcement[2] skills (e.g., praise, rewards, selective attention) for desired behaviors, and limit-setting (e.g., removing attention by ignoring) for nondesired behaviors (Kazdin, 2005). Lau and colleagues recognized that positive reinforcement skills were often incongruent with parenting practices and child-rearing ideologies. This incongruence complicated engagement and required collaboration and motivational enhancement. Once parents were invested in making changes, the unfamiliarity of skills such as labeled praise also impacted learning. Adaptations to support learning likely involve increasing treatment dosage (e.g., spending more time on parents' concerns to tailor the teaching of positive reinforcement skills), while slowing down the treatment pace to provide more support for parents to learn through repeated rehearsal of unfamiliar skills.

Leveraging Unique Cultural Strengths

Providers should identify and build on the strengths, resources, and expertise of AAPI youth and their community supports. For example, AA young adults have expressed appreciation for their unique familial strengths, including parental provision of practical help, respect for their child's

2 Where presenting desirable behavior with a reward or positive stimulus increases the likelihood that it will be repeated.

autonomy, and sacrificial love (Wong et al., 2012). Furthermore, fostering cultural identity and establishing a sense of pride around family, community, and cultural heritage can be protective for AAPI youth mental health (Nieri et al., 2024; Park et al., 2021). As such, ethnic-racial socialization interventions and frameworks are being developed to assist AAPI and other racial/ethnic minoritized caregivers with how to have conversations about race and culture with their children (Bo et al., 2023; Stein et al., 2021; Tsong et al., 2022; Wang et al., 2024). This includes guiding youth to understand their and their family's experiences through a contextual lens of demands placed upon them by racism, discrimination, and acculturative stress in the United States (Doan et al., 2022).

How to Make Adaptations

Once data suggest a need to adapt, it is helpful to identify a framework to guide adaptions toward the identified purpose. Below, we name a few prominent frameworks that suit different purposes. Additional frameworks can be found at Domenech Rodríguez & Bernal (2012).

Conceptual Content Frameworks

Some frameworks provide the conceptual foundation for how to adapt. The Ecological Validity Framework (Bernal et al., 1995) outlines how to align an intervention along eight dimensions of cultural sensitivity: language, persons, metaphors, content, concepts, goals, methods, and context (see Table 5.3).

Table 5.3 Culturally sensitive elements drawn from Bernal et al. (1995)'s ecological validity framework.

Intervention	Culturally sensitive elements
1. Language	Culturally appropriate; culturally syntonic language
2. Persons	Role of ethnic/racial similarities and differences between client and therapist in shaping therapy relationship
3. Metaphors	Symbols and concepts shared with the population; sayings in treatment
4. Content	Cultural knowledge: values, costumes and traditions; uniqueness of groups (social, economic, historical, political)
5. Concepts	Treatment concepts consonant with culture and context; dependence vs. interdependence vs. independence; emic (within culture, particular) over etic (outside culture, universal)
6. Goals	Transmission of positive and adaptive cultural values; support adaptive values from the culture of origin
7. Methods	Development and/or cultural adaptation of treatment methods. Examples: "modeling" to include culturally consonant traditions (e.g., therapy based on folk tales); "cultural reframing" of intergenerational cultural conflicts; use of language (formal and informal); cultural hypothesis testing; use of genograms, "cultural migration dialogue"
8. Context	Consideration of changing contexts in assessment during treatment or intervention: acculturative stress, phase of migration; developmental stage; social supports and relationship to country of origin; economic and social context of intervention

Note: Definitions drawn directly from Table I on p. 74 of Bernal et al. (1995) and only slightly tailored.
Source: Bernal et al. (1995)/Springer Nature.

Resnicow et al. (2000) further distinguish *surface structure* and *deep structure* adaptations. Surface structure adaptations are made to the surface-level aspects of an intervention—adapting materials, activities, and examples to better align with observable characteristics of AAPI culture, such as foods, music, language, and traditions. For example, a collective rhythm activity was used to build community spirit in a multifamily group parenting intervention coadapted with Hmong elders (McDonald et al., 2012). Surface structure adaptations are recommended to enhance cultural resonance, comprehension, and motivation and are generally not thought to risk integrity to the intervention's theoretical principles (Castro et al., 2004; Chu & Leino, 2017).

Deep structure adaptations incorporate cultural ideas, belief systems, and values within the processes that directly impact mental health concerns of interest. For example, in a culturally-grounded health promotion program (Project Talanoa) for Pacific Islander youth, the curriculum centered cultural identity/pride and family ties along with adolescent health and peer relations (McGrath & Ka'ili, 2010). Deep structure adaptations may require more caution as they are more likely to alter theoretical principles of EBIs; however, they may have greater potential for improving outcomes for AAPIs (Hwang, 2016).

Process Frameworks

Process frameworks describe the steps to making adaptations. For example, the Heuristic Framework for the Cultural Adaptation of Interventions (Barrera Jr. & Castro, 2006) describes a four-phase sequence: (1) information gathering, (2) preliminary adaptation design, (3) preliminary adaptation tests, and (4) adaptation refinement. To apply these steps, it can help to name where you are in the intervention implementation process. "Design-time" adaptations are proactively planned before an intervention is implemented in a new setting (Alvidrez et al., 2019), while "run-time" adaptations are made reactively during real-time EBI delivery (Barrera Jr. et al., 2017; Chorpita & Daleiden, 2014).

Design-time Adaptation Case Study

Proactive design-time adaptation presents an opportunity to make intervention improvements guided by theory, empirical knowledge, and importantly, collaboration with the local AAPI community (Cahill & Dadvand, 2018; Collins et al., 2018; Rodriguez Espinosa & Verney, 2021). AAPI youth, caregivers, and communities can provide lived experience expertise to help adaptations address their targeted mechanisms. Community engagement can range from consultation (e.g., needs assessment interviews), to ongoing collaboration (e.g., peer-led youth programming), to cocreation (e.g., codesigning interventions/adaptations with AAPI communities). To determine the appropriate level of community partnership, consider how much decision-making, power, and ownership will be shared, what activities partners will lead or be involved in, and the available resources given that community members should be compensated for their contributions.

We share a case study of design-time adaptation through the SAFETY-A for Promoting Equity in Suicide Prevention Outcomes in Schools study (R34MH126670; PI: Dr. Anna Lau).

Clinical Case Study 1

Safe Alternatives for Teens and Youth-Acute (SAFETY-A)

SAFETY-A is a trauma-informed, strengths-based suicide prevention intervention. It improved linkage to follow-up mental healthcare among youth presenting with suicide risk in the emergency department, with the greatest benefit for racial/ethnic minoritized youth including AAs (Asarnow et al., 2011; Kodish et al., 2023). As a family-centered model, SAFETY-A involves an in-person crisis session with youth and caregiver(s), followed by caring contacts[3] to support follow-up care linkage. During the in-person crisis session, session components are delivered individually to the youth and caregiver, followed by the family together. All components start with identifying youth and family strengths to build hope. The youth session focuses on developing a safety plan informed by an emotional thermometer to identify situations and emotional reactions that increase risk of suicidal thoughts and behaviors. The caregiver session focuses on restricting youth access to lethal means and coaching caregivers on providing protective support and monitoring during times of distress. The family session then brings the youth and caregiver together to review, practice, and affirm commitment to the safety plan. SAFETY-A was identified as a promising EBI to improve school-based risk assessment procedures that were seeing lower rates of follow-up care linkage in racial/ethnic minoritized students identified with suicide risk (Kim et al., 2018; Kodish et al., 2020). SAFETY-A was implemented in four public school districts primarily serving racial/ethnic minoritized youth, the majority who are from AA and Latine immigrant families.

Selective and Directed Adaptation Through the Ecological Validity Framework

Prior to implementation, the research team conducted a process of selective and directed adaptation to enhance SAFETY-A's fit, shaped by the voices of the local school communities (Table 5.4) (Vargas et al., in press).

The research team conducted needs assessment interviews with students, caregivers, and school providers from the partnered school districts. After viewing video clips of SAFETY-A components, interviewees were asked about SAFETY-A's fit with the needs of their school communities, including families' cultural backgrounds and norms. The research team designed adaptations to target identified barriers of SAFETY-A implementation (Vargas et al., under review), and presented them in focus groups with school district leaders to elicit feedback and align them with school policies and infrastructures. Cultural adaptations were designed to address four concerns relevant to AA families.

1. **(L)earned Mistrust of Schools due to Historical Overinvolvement with Racial/Ethnic Minoritized Communities**. Interviews revealed a *history of school overinvolvement* with racial/ethnic minoritized communities, within a broader sociopolitical context of discriminatory treatment across healthcare, social service, law enforcement, and immigration systems. Families often experience school-based risk assessments and hospitalization as

3 Caring Contacts is a low-cost suicide prevention intervention consisting of brief messages sent to express care and support, such as by phone or text (Skopp et al., 2023). In SAFETY-A, they are further used to facilitate follow-up care linkage (Asarnow et al., 2020).

Table 5.4 Selective and directed adaptation approach through the ecological validity framework.

Selective (community-raised concerns)	Directed (ecological validity framework)	Directed adaptation strategy
(L)earned mistrust of schools by families	**Context:** Schools' historical over-involvement with racial/ethnic minoritized communities, within a broader sociopolitical context of discriminatory treatment across systems	Begin youth session by reassuring students they are not in trouble and that the meeting is motivated by care not discipline Begin caregiver session by reassuring caregivers that any discussion of student mental health concerns is confidential and never included in their child's academic record
SAFETY-A expectations of emotional and bidirectional communication in families	**Context:** Intergenerational acculturation gaps	Added a module on navigating intergenerational acculturation gaps for providers as "cultural brokers"
Caregiver mental health stigma	**Concepts:** Incongruence in belief systems about mental health	Reduced stigmatizing language in intervention materials and trainings
Linguistic barriers	**Language:** Linguistic differences between both providers-to-families and youth-to-caregivers	Encouraged schools to hire bilingual staff Provided translated SAFETY-A handouts and introductory training in SAFETY-A to staff who provide interpretation Built in comprehension checks to assess second-language, English-speaking caregivers' understanding

Source: Stephanie H. Yu

traumatic and coercive, which can be unintentionally perpetuated by school practices that exclude families from decision-making and erode trust (Kodish et al., 2020). Providers in low-resource school settings may lack adequate time, resources, and training to engage in the necessary relationship-building to earn families' trust. Thus, they fall back on coercive and retraumatizing practices. For instance, schools often rely on emergency services—including psychiatric mobile response teams, police, and school resource officers—to transport students to hospitals, often involuntarily, instead of providing on-site intervention (Kodish et al., 2020; Yu et al., 2023). Likewise, when caregivers are reluctant to accept MHS referrals, school personnel may involve child protective services. In this way, providers may be seen as extensions of coercive systems, rather than as supportive resources, contributing to *mistrust*.

Already, SAFETY-A was chosen for school-based implementation due to its family-centered, trauma-informed approach focused on strengths, which was hypothesized to foster trust, collaboration, and thus positive views of mental healthcare (O'Neill et al., 2021). From there, two adaptations were made to further position providers to promote collaboration and trust. In the manual, providers were instructed to (1) assure youth at the outset of the session that they are **not in trouble and that the meeting is motivated by care and not discipline**, and (2) reassure caregivers that any **discussion of student mental health concerns is confidential and never included in their child's academic record.**[4]

2. **SAFETY-A Expectations of Emotional and Bidirectional Communication in Families.** Interviewees raised concerns that *expressing emotional distress* related to suicide risk, as well as Eurocentric norms around open discussion of feelings, may be incompatible with cultural norms of emotion communication in AA and other immigrant families. Similarly, interviewees suggested that *bidirectional communication* (e.g., youth being asked to tell their caregivers how they prefer to be supported during crises) may be incongruent with their family dynamic and hierarchy. We saw this misalignment as situated in the context of *intergenerational acculturation gaps*. Immigrant caregivers and their children raised in different cultural contexts can hold different values and expectations that impact their communication, and in turn, youths' openness to sharing their emotions with their families.

   The SAFETY-A manual was augmented with a **module on navigating intergenerational acculturation gaps** to guide providers on being cultural "brokers" for families between two cultures to enhance protective support (Bernal et al., 1995). The research team added content on listening for possible acculturation gaps, normalizing and validating them, and exploring ways caregivers do show care. For example, in the youth session, providers might say: "*Some students have shared that their parents have other ways of showing they care, even when they don't say it with words. Do you think this might be happening in your family, or not?*" In the caregiver session, providers might say: "*In your family, what are the ways you try to show your child you care about them?*" Optional content was added to the family session to facilitate finding a shared language to express needs/support within the family for the safety plan. For example, AA caregivers may offer instrumental support or food as a way to express care whereas verbal or physical affection may be less culturally familiar (Cheah et al., 2015; Wong et al., 2012; Wu, 2012). Finally, for families where bidirectional communication may be less familiar, the research team added a recommendation to spend extra time with the youth and caregiver to role play and practice how youth might express and caregivers might listen to their child's needs.

3. **Stigma Toward Mental Health.** Interviews identified *mental health stigma* among caregivers as possibly hindering engagement in suicide risk management. This included concerns that caregivers may deny mental health problems or discourage youth from disclosing them outside of the family. Interviewees acknowledged that concerns of being stigmatized may be driven by caregivers' fears that disclosure could impact their child's school record and future academic opportunities. The manual was adapted to use **alternative terms to describe mental health,** such as "stress," "mood," and "Personal Plan" instead of "Safety Plan."

4. **Linguistic Barriers.** Interviews highlighted linguistic barriers to having conversations consistent with SAFETY-A. These included *lacking enough linguistically-responsive providers* to

4 (L)earned mistrust was also addressed iteratively in later stages of the SAFETY-A roll-out through implementation strategies tailored by district. These mainly involved educational strategies to help providers learn and adopt collaborative practices, along with organizational changes to de-implement policies and practices that undermine trust. Some examples included enhancing buy-in of SAFETY-A's utility in "high-risk" and "medium-risk" cases to de-implement unnecessary emergency transport; providing booster training to replace coercive strategies with more supportive ones; and providing didactic material on links between systems' overinvolvement and racial trauma to reduce provider reliance on invoking child protective services. Given that this chapter focuses on intervention adaptations, further details on these implementation strategies can be found at Vargas et al. (under review).

fully meet the school community's needs, as well as navigating *intergenerational language barriers* between caregivers and their children. The research team asked how schools presently navigated risk assessments with linguistic barriers and learned that schools often relied on informal interpreters, such as bilingual bicultural administrative staff. Mindful of limited school resources, the team employed strategies to build on existing resources for interpretation. These included **encouraging schools to hire bilingual staff, providing translated SAFETY-A handouts, providing introductory training in SAFETY-A to staff who provide interpretation, and building in comprehension checks to assess second-language English-speaking caregivers' understanding**.

Implementation of Adapted SAFETY-A

SAFETY-A implementation was rolled out over two years, with training and consultation staggered across the four school districts. Providers involved in suicide risk assessments were trained in the adapted SAFETY-A in a full-day workshop and then received weekly, one-hour technical assistance consultation from expert SAFETY-A trainers for one semester (4–5 months). Quantitative and qualitative data about the acceptability and effectiveness of adapted SAFETY-A are forthcoming.

Clinical Case Study 2

Run-time Adaptation Case Study

Even spontaneous run-time adaptations can take a selective and directed approach through cultural responsiveness and humility. Cultural responsiveness attends to the cultural identities, values, and belief systems of both the client and provider, along with their dynamic interplay in treatment (Cabassa & Baumann, 2013; Kim-Goh et al., 2015). Culturally humble providers engage with curiosity and collaboration throughout treatment, asking questions and learning from clients and families as the experts in their own cultures and experiences. Together, a culturally responsive and humble approach can foster understanding of contexts that shape clients' presenting concerns alongside strengths that can be leveraged during treatment. They are ongoing processes to continuously strive for rather than static goals to achieve. We present a fictionalized case study that illustrates culturally responsive, selective and directed run-time adaptation. It draws *broad themes and patterns* from intervention approaches and adaptations made in real cases, but with details altered so that the case study does not represent any real-life clients.

"Daniel" is a second-generation Filipino American college-age young adult man presenting with social anxiety and depression, resulting in avoidance of social interactions and difficulty carrying out daily activities. These symptoms worsened after he was harassed and threatened by law enforcement while walking his dog.

Relationship-Building and Information-Gathering

Therapy began with relationship-building, positioning Daniel as the expert of his own experiences. The therapist asked open-ended questions about his strengths, values, and salient identities (e.g., "*What identities and values are important to you?*"). Daniel described skill in online video games, strong familial values within his Filipino culture, and a desire to help more around his parents' house, where he resided.

As information-gathering unfolded, the therapist inquired about possible experiences of "othering" that may have influenced his social anxiety (e.g., *"I know we're both Asian, and I don't want to assume this applies to you, but some of my Asian American clients have shared that it was difficult to fit in growing up. Would you say that's relevant here, or not?"*).[5] Daniel shared how a history of social rejection and discrimination in predominantly White elementary and high schools resulted in difficulty fitting in, fear of negative evaluation, and low self-worth. Over time, Daniel grew to believe that he didn't belong and would never be accepted, which was reinforced by his negative experience with law enforcement.

Treatment Plan

Daniel's treatment began from a cognitive-behavioral approach with psychoeducation, mindfulness, and relaxation skills to help him self-regulate when experiencing anxious thoughts and physiological symptoms about social interactions. Social anxiety and depression measures were administered weekly to monitor progress. The therapist conducted in-session and assigned out-of-session exposures to help Daniel face social situations. Daniel initially struggled with low-stakes exposures involving minimal social interactions to carry out routine activities. Collaboratively, they decided to shift the *goals* of Daniel's exposures to leverage his familial values.[6] For example, exposures shifted focus to assisting his parents by picking up their medication (requiring interaction with pharmacy staff), or making phone calls to schedule their medical appointments, which improved Daniel's motivation. Gradually, Daniel was able to engage in increasingly complex social exposures—first through his online gaming communities and eventually in-person through his college courses. While Daniel's social anxiety scores improved, his depression scores continued to suggest low self-worth and mood difficulties.

Adaptation Design

Daniel's history indicated that discrimination experiences heavily shaped his negative beliefs about belongingness. After consulting the literature on interventions for race-related stress in youth (e.g., DeLapp & Gallo, 2022), the therapist selectively designed adaptations directed toward: (1) providing psychoeducation and processing how interpersonal and systemic racism have impacted Daniel's feelings of self-worth and belongingness, (2) making meaning of rather than challenging experiences of racism, and (3) identifying culturally-resonant coping skills and activities.

Process-based discussions about Daniel's identity uncovered dialectic feelings of pride (associated with family) and shame (associated with lifelong experiences of being "othered"). The therapist employed Socratic Questioning[7] focused on meaning-making, which guided Daniel to externalize social rejection as a deficit of others' biases rather than an inherent deficiency in himself. These discussions situated Daniel's experience with law enforcement in the context of disproportionate targeting of men of color by police, enabling him to narratively reframe the event as a systemic failure rather than an internal fault.

---

5 A culturally nonresponsive approach might be to avoid the topic of identity altogether, or assume experiences based on the client's race or ethnicity.

6 A culturally nonresponsive approach might be to validate the difficulty of exposure, but continue with the treatment plan unaltered.

7 A form of guided discovery where questions are posed to help the client explore their thoughts and beliefs.

Daniel further recognized his disconnect from the Filipino/a/x community, particularly among same-age peers with similar acculturative experiences. Adaptations were collaboratively made, including assigning Daniel homework of researching Filipino/a/x campus organizations, and scheduling activities and exposures to help him engage with them. Through increased involvement in affinity groups, Daniel cultivated more positive regard of his cultural identity along with greater sense of belongingness, resulting in gradual reduction in his depression scores.

Summary and Recommendations

We conclude with a summary of our main points and recommendations:

- AAPI youth, families, and communities are widely heterogeneous, not only considering the distinct ethnic groups within the "AAPI" umbrella, but also the complex, intersectional cultural and contextual dimensions that make up one's identity. We urge those seeking to adapt to use intentional language and disaggregate data whenever possible to avoid contributing to further erasure of these groups when invoking the "AAPI" term.
- Cultural adaptations should be made through a selective and directed approach that relies on theory, empirical research, and the lived experience expertise of the AAPI individuals and local communities involved.
- Knowing the function or "why" of your adaptation can assist with the "what" and "how" of your adaptation. Specific frameworks can help with each step to ensure that the adaptation is tied to its intended purpose. Once adaptations are implemented, it is recommended to evaluate their effectiveness on that intended purpose.
- Cultural responsiveness and humility are reflective processes to continuously strive for rather than concrete goals to achieve. They involve curiosity, collaboration, and ongoing attention to the dynamic roles that youths'/families' and providers' cultures and identities play in treatment.
- Those seeking to adapt should aim to collaborate with and center the voices of the AAPI youth, families, and local communities they are adapting for.

References

Adames, H. Y., Chavez-Dueñas, N. Y., Lewis, J. A., Neville, H. A., French, B. H., Chen, G. A., & Mosley, D. V. (2023). Radical healing in psychotherapy: addressing the wounds of racism-related stress and trauma. *Psychotherapy*, *60*(1), 39–50. https://doi.org/10.1037/pst0000435

Alvidrez, J., Nápoles, A. M., Bernal, G., Lloyd, J., Cargill, V., Godette, D., ... Farhat, T. (2019). Building the evidence base to inform planned intervention adaptations by practitioners serving health disparity populations. *American Journal of Public Health*, *109*(Supplement 1), S94–S101. https://doi.org/10.2105/AJPH.2018.304915

Arora, P. G., & Khoo, O. (2020). Sources of stress and barriers to mental health service use among Asian immigrant-origin youth: a qualitative exploration. *Journal of Child and Family Studies*, *29*, 2590–2601. https://doi.org/10.1007/s10826-020-01765-7

Asarnow, J. R., Baraf, L. J., Berk, M., Grob, C. S., Devich-Navarro, M., Suddath, R., ... Tang, L. (2011). An emergency department intervention for linking pediatric suicidal patients to follow-up mental health treatment. *Psychiatric Services*, *62*(11), 1303–1309. https://doi.org/10.1176/ps.62.11.pss6211_1303

Asarnow, J. R., Goldston, D. B., Tunno, A. M., Inscoe, A. B., & Pynoos, R. (2020). Suicide, self-harm, & traumatic stress exposure: a trauma-informed approach to the evaluation and management of suicide risk. *Evidence-Based Practice in Child and Adolescent Mental Health*, *5*(4), 483–500. https://doi.org/10.1080/23794925.2020.1796547

Augsberger, A., Yeung, A., Dougher, M., & Hahm, H. C. (2015). Factors influencing the underutilization of mental health services among Asian American women with a history of depression and suicide. *BMC Health Services Research*, *15*, 542. https://doi.org/10.1186/s12913-015-1191-7

Barrera, M., Jr., Berkel, C., & Castro, F. G. (2017). Directions for the advancement of culturally adapted preventive interventions: local adaptations, engagement and sustainability. *Prevention Science*, *18*(6), 640–648. https://doi.org/10.1007/s11121-016-0705-9

Barrera, M., Jr., & Castro, F. G. (2006). A heuristic framework for the cultural adaptation of interventions. *Clinical Psychology: Science and Practice*, *13*(4), 311–316. https://doi.org/10.1111/j.1468-2850.2006.00043.x

Bear, L., Finer, R., Guo, S., & Lau, A. S. (2014). Building the gateway to success: an appraisal of progress in reaching underserved families and reducing racial disparities in school-based mental health. *Psychological Services*, *11*(4), 388–397. https://doi.org/10.1037/a0037969

Bernal, G., Bonilla, J., & Bellido, C. (1995). Ecological validity and cultural sensitivity for outcome research: issues for the cultural adaptation and development of psychosocial treatments with Hispanics. *Journal of Abnormal Child Psychology*, *23*(1), 67–82. https://doi.org/10.1007/BF01447045

Bernal, G., Jiménez-Chafey, M. I., & Domenech Rodríguez, M. M. (2009). Cultural adaptation of treatments: a resource for considering culture in evidence-based practice. *Professional Psychology: Research and Practice*, *40*(4), 361–368. https://doi.org/10.1037/a0016401

Bo, A., Durand, B., & Wang, Y. (2023). A scoping review of parent-involved ethnic and racial socialization programs. *Children and Youth Services Review*, *144*, 106750. https://doi.org/10.1016/j.childyouth.2022.106750

Cabassa, L. J., & Baumann, A. A. (2013). A two-way street: bridging implementation science and cultural adaptations of mental health treatments. *Implementation Science*, *8*(1), 90. https://doi.org/10.1186/1748-5908-8-90

Cahill, H., & Dadvand, B. (2018). Re-conceptualising youth participation: a framework to inform action. *Children and Youth Services Review*, *95*, 243–253. https://doi.org/10.1016/j.childyouth.2018.11.001

Carter, R. T. (2007). Racism and psychological and emotional injury: recognizing and assessing race-based traumatic stress. *The Counseling Psychologist*, *35*(1), 13–105. https://doi.org/10.1177/0011000006292033

Castro, F. G., Barrera, M., Jr., & Martinez, C. R., Jr. (2004). The cultural adaptation of prevention interventions: resolving tensions between fidelity and fit. *Prevention Science*, *5*(1), 41–45. https://doi.org/10.1023/b:prev.0000013980.12412.cd

Cénat, J. M., Haeny, A. M., & Williams, M. T. (2024). Providing antiracist cognitive-behavioral therapy: guidelines, tools, and tips. *Psychiatry Research*, *339*, 116054. https://doi.org/10.1016/j.psychres.2024.116054

Cheah, C. S. L., Li, J., Zhou, N., Yamamoto, Y., & Leung, C. Y. Y. (2015). Understanding Chinese immigrant and European American mothers' expressions of warmth. *Developmental Psychology*, *51*(12), 1802–1811. https://doi.org/10.1037/a0039855

Chen, B. C., Lui, J. H. L., Liu, V., Wright, B. A., Benson, L. A., Yen-Jui, L. R., & Lau, A. S. (2022). Mapping racial/ethnic disparities in youth psychiatric emergencies and associations with neighborhood racial composition, child opportunity, and inequality. *Clinical Psychological Science*, *12*(2), 203–219. https://doi.org/10.1177/21677026221121762

Cheng, J., Tsoh, J. Y., Guan, A., Luu, M., Nguyen, I. V., Tan, R., ... Burke, N. J. (2022). Engaging Asian American communities during the COVID-19 era tainted with anti-Asian hate and distrust. *American Journal of Public Health, 11*(S9), S864–S868. https://doi.org/10.2105/AJPH.2022.306952

The Children's Partnership. (2023a). Asian American Children's Health. A Child is a Child, 2023 Snapshot: California Children's Health. https://childrenspartnership.org/wp-content/uploads/2023/05/ChildIsaChild_ACIAC-AA_2023-0522.pdf

The Children's Partnership. (2023b). Native Hawaiian and Pacific Islander Children's Health. A Child is a Child, 2023 Snapshot: California Children's Health. https://childrenspartnership.org/wp-content/uploads/2023/05/FINAL_ACIAC-NHPI_2023.pdf

Chorpita, B. F., & Daleiden, E. L. (2014). Structuring the collaboration of science and service in pursuit of a shared vision. *Journal of Clinical Child and Adolescent Psychology, 43*(2), 323–338. https://doi.org/10.1080/15374416.2013.828297

Chu, J., & Leino, A. (2017). Advancement in the maturing science of cultural adaptations of evidence-based interventions. *Journal of Consulting and Clinical Psychology, 85*(1), 45–57. https://doi.org/10.1037/ccp0000145

Collins, S. E., Clifasefi, S. L., Stanton, J., The LEAP Advisory Board, Straits, K. J. E., Gil-Kashiwabara, E., ... Wallerstein, N. (2018). Community-based participatory research (CBPR): towards equitable involvement of community in psychology research. *The American Psychologist, 73*(7), 884–898. https://doi.org/10.1037/amp0000167

d'Abreu, A., Castro-Olivo, S., & Ura, S. K. (2019). Understanding the role of acculturative stress on refugee youth mental health: a systematic review and ecological approach to assessment and intervention. *School Psychology International, 40*(2), 107–127. https://doi.org/10.1177/0143034318822688

DeLapp, R. C. T., & Gallo, L. (2022). A flexible treatment planning model for racism-related stress in adolescents and young adults. *Journal of Health Service Psychology, 48*(4). https://doi.org/10.1007/s42843-022-00073-6

Doan, S. N., Yu, S. H., Wright, B., Fung, J., Saleem, F., & Lau, A. S. (2022). Resilience and family socialization processes in ethnic minority youth: illuminating the achievement-health paradox. *Clinical Child and Family Psychology Review, 25*, 75–92. https://doi.org/10.1007/s10567-022-00389-1

Domenech Rodríguez, M. M., & Bernal, G. (2012). Frameworks, models, and guidelines for cultural adaptation. In G. Bernal, & M. M. Domenech Rodríguez (Eds.), *Cultural Adaptations: Tools for Evidence-Based Practice with Diverse Populations* (pp. 23–44). American Psychological Association. https://doi.org/10.1037/13752-002

Fancher, T. L., Ton, H., Le Meyer, O., Ho, T., & Paterniti, D. A. (2010) Discussing depression with Vietnamese American patients. *Journal of Immigrant and Minority Health, 12*(2), 263–266. https://doi.org/10.1007/s10903-009-9234-y

French, B. H., Lewis, J. A., Mosley, D. V., Adames, H. Y., Chavez-Dueñas, N. Y., Chen, G. A., & Neville, H. A. (2020). Toward a psychological framework of radical healing in communities of color. *The Counseling Psychologist, 48*(1), 14–46. https://doi.org/10.1177/0011000019843506

Garrett, M. F., Cutrer-Párraga, E. A., Allen, G. E. K., Young, E. L., Urbina, K. J., & Hull, I. M. (2025). "It would ruin my life": Pacific Islander male adolescents' perceptions of mental health help-seeking—an interpretative phenomenological analysis focus group study. *International Journal of Environmental Research and Public Health, 22*(1), 62. https://doi.org/10.3390/ijerph22010062

George, N., Lee, A. H., Gonzalez-Gaspar, J., & Kwan, M. Y. (2024). A systematic review of barriers and facilitators impacting the utilization of mental health services among Asian American youth. *Evidence-Based Practice in Child and Adolescent Mental Health, 10*(1), 187–201. https://doi.org/10.1080/23794925.2024.2392250

Guan, A., Talingdan, A. C. S., Tanjasiri, S. P., Kanaya, A. M., & Gomez, S. L. (2024). Lessons learned from immigrant health cohorts: a review of the evidence and implications for policy and practice in addressing health inequities among Asian Americans, Native Hawaiians, and Pacific Islanders. *Annual Review of Public Health, 45*, 401–424. https://doi.org/10.1146/annurev-publhealth-060922-040413

Gudiño, O. G., Lau, A. S., & Hough, R. L. (2008). Immigrant status, mental health need, and mental health service utilization among high-risk Hispanic and Asian Pacific Islander youth. *Child & Youth Care Forum, 37*, 139–152.

Hahm, H. C., Ha, Y., Scott, J. C., Wongchai, V., Chen, J. A., & Liu, C. H. (2021). Perceived COVID-19-related anti-Asian discrimination predicts post traumatic stress disorder symptoms among Asian and Asian American young adults. *Psychiatry Research, 303*, 114084. https://doi.org/10.1016/j.psychres.2021.114084

Hall, G. C. N., Ibaraki, A. Y., Huang, E. R., Marti, C. N., & Stice, E. (2016). A meta-analysis of cultural adaptations of psychological interventions. *Behavior Therapy, 47*(6), 993–1014. https://doi.org/10.1016/j.beth.2016.09.005

Han, M., Cao, L., & Anton, K. (2015). Exploring the role of ethnic media and the community readiness to combat stigma attached to mental illness among Vietnamese immigrants: the pilot project Tam An (Inner Peace in Vietnamese). *Community Mental Health Journal, 51*, 63–70. https://doi.org/10.1007/s10597-014-9745-4

Henrich, J., Heine, S. J., & Norenzayan A. (2010). The weirdest people in the world? *Behavioral and Brain Sciences, 33*, 2. https://doi.org/10.1017/S0140525X0999152X

Huey, Jr., Stanley J., Park, A. L., Galán. C., & Wang, C. X. (2023). Culturally responsive cognitive behavioral therapy for ethnically diverse populations. *Annual Review of Clinical Psychology, 19*, 51–78. https://doi.org/10.1146/annurev-clinpsy-080921-072750

Huey, Jr., Stanley J., & Tilley, J. L. (2018). Effects of mental health interventions with Asian Americans: a review and meta-analysis. *Journal of Consulting & Clinical Psychology, 86*(11), 915–930. https://doi.org/10.1037/ccp0000346

Hwang, W.-C. (2006). Acculturative family distancing: theory, research, and clinical practice. *Psychotherapy, 43*(4), 397–409. https://doi.org/10.1037/0033-3204.43.4.397

Hwang, W.-C. (2016). Culturally adapting evidence-based practices for ethnic minority and immigrant families. In N. Zane, G. Bernal, & F. T. L. Leong (Eds.), *Evidence-Based Psychological Practice with Ethnic Minorities: Culturally Informed Research and Clinical Strategies* (pp. 289–308). American Psychological Association. https://doi.org/10.1037/14940-014

Hwang, W.-C., & Chan, C. P. (2019). Compassionate meditation to heal from race-related stress: a pilot study with Asian Americans. *American Journal of Orthopsychiatry, 89*(4), 482–492. https://doi.org/10.1037/ort0000372

Hwang, W.-C., & Ting, J. Y. (2008). Disaggregating the effects of acculturation and acculturative stress on the mental health of Asian Americans. *Cultural Diversity & Ethnic Minority Psychology, 14*(2), 147–154. https://doi.org/10.1037/1099-9809.14.2.147

Islam, N. S., Zanowiak, J. M., Riley, L., Nadkarni, S. K., Kwon, S. C., & Trinh-Shevrin, C. (2015). Characteristics of Asian American, Native Hawaiian, and Pacific Islander community health worker programs: a systematic review. *Journal of Health Care for the Poor and Underserved, 26*(2 Suppl), 238–268. https://doi.org/10.1353/hpu.2015.0062

Kazdin, A. E. (2005). *Parent Management Training: Treatment for Oppositional, Aggressive, and Antisocial Behavior in Children and Adolescents*. Oxford University Press.

Kiang, L., Huynh, V. W., Cheah, C. S. L., Wang, Y., & Yoshikawa, H. (2017). Moving beyond the model minority. *Asian American Journal of Psychology, 8*(1), 1–6. https://doi.org/10.1037/aap0000070

Kim, J. H., Lu, Q., & Stanton, A. L. (2021). Overcoming constraints of the model minority stereotype to advance Asian American health. *American Psychologist, 76*(4), 611–626. https://doi.org/10.1037/amp0000799

Kim, J. J., Kodish, T., Bear, L., El-Hendi, T., Duong, J., & Lau, A. S. (2018). Disparities in follow-up care for Asian American youth assessed for suicide risk in schools. *Asian American Journal of Psychology, 9*(4), 308–317. https://doi.org/10.1037/aap0000136

Kim, S. B., & Lee, Y. J. (2022). Factors associated with mental health help-seeking among Asian Americans: a systematic review. *Journal of Racial and Ethnic Health Disparities, 98*(4), 1276–1297. https://doi.org/10.1007/s40615-021-01068-7

Kim-Goh, M., Choi, H., & Yoon, M. S. (2015). Culturally responsive counseling for Asian Americans: clinician perspectives. *International Journal for the Advancement of Counselling, 37*, 63–76. https://doi.org/10.1007/s10447-014-9226-z

Kodish, T., Kim, J. J., Le, K., Yu, S. H., Bear, L., & Lau, A. S. (2020). Multiple stakeholder perspectives on school-based responses to student suicide risk in a diverse public school district. *School Mental Health, 12*(2), 336–352. https://doi.org/10.1007/s12310-019-09354-w

Kodish, T., Lau, A. S., Belin, T. R., Berk, M. S., & Asarnow, J. R. (2023). Improving care linkage for racial-ethnic minority youths receiving emergency department treatment for suicidality: SAFETY-A. *Psychiatric Services, 74*(4), 419–422. https://doi.org/10.1176/appi.ps.20220129

Lau, A. S. (2006). Making the case for selective and directed cultural adaptations of evidence-based treatments: examples from parent training. *Clinical Psychology: Science and Practice, 13*(4), 295–310. https://doi.org/10.1111/j.1468-2850.2006.00042.x

Lau, A. S. (2012). Reflections on adapting parent training for Chinese immigrants: blind alleys, thoroughfares, and test drives. In G. Bernal, & M. M. Domenech Rodríguez (Eds.), *Cultural Adaptations: Tools for Evidence-Based Practice with Diverse Populations* (pp. 133–156). American Psychological Association. https://doi.org/10.1037/13752-007

Lau, A. S., Fung, J. J., Ho., L. Y., Liu, L., & Gudiño, O. G. (2011). Parent training with high-risk immigrant Chinese families: a pilot trial yielding practice-based evidence. *Behavior Therapy, 42*, 413–426. https://doi.org/10.1016/j.beth.2010.11.001

Lau, A. S., Fung, J. J., & Yung, V. (2010). Group parent training with immigrant Chinese families: enhancing engagement and augmenting skills training. *Journal of Clinical Psychology: In Session, 66*, 880–894.

Lau Johnson, W. F. K., Saleem, F. T., Sanders, E. A., & Langley, A. K. (2024). TRANSFORMing theory to practice: developing and implementing an anti-racist, community-based racial stress and trauma group intervention for BIPOC youth. *Journal of Prevention & Intervention in the Community, 52*(2), 272–299. https://doi.org/10.1080/10852352.2024.2408503

Lin, J. L. L., Chan, M., Kwong, K., & Au, L. (2018). Promoting positive youth development for Asian American youth in a Teen Resource Center: key components, outcomes, and lessons learned. *Children and Youth Services Review, 91*, 413–423. https://doi.org/10.1016/j.childyouth.2018.06.040

López-Hinojosa, I., Zhang, J., López-Hinojosa, K., Baig, A. A., Tung, E. L., & Martinez-Cardoso, A. (2024). "We have to lie low ... that sort of poisons me more and more": a qualitative study of violent political rhetoric and health implications for Spanish and Chinese speaking immigrants. *Social Science & Medicine, 341*, 116504. https://doi.org/10.1016/j.socscimed.2023.116504

Lui, C. K., Ye, Y., Gee, J., Cook, W. K., Tam, C. C., Sun, S., ... Mulia, N. (2024). Unmasking suicidal ideation for Asian American, Native Hawaiian, and Pacific Islander youths via data disaggregation. *JAMA Network Open, 7*(11), e2446832. https://10.1001/jamanetworkopen.2024.46832

McDonald, L., Coover, G., Sandler, J., Thao, T., & Shalhoub, H. (2012). Cultural adaptation of an evidence-based parenting programme with elders from South East Asia in the US: co-producing Families and Schools Together – FAST. *Journal of Children's Services*, *7*(2), 113–127. https://doi.org/10.1108/17466661211238673

McGrath, B. B., & Ka'ili, T. O. (2010). Creating Project Talanoa: a culturally based community health program for U.S. Pacific Islander adolescents. *Public Health Nursing*, *27*(1), 17–24. https://doi.org/10.1111/j.1525-1446.2009.00822.x

Millner, U. C., Maru, M., Ismail, A., & Chakrabarti, U. (2021). Decolonizing mental health practice: reconstructing an Asian-centric framework through a social justice lens. *Asian American Journal of Psychology*, *12*(4), 333–345. https://doi.org/10.1037/aap0000268

Misra, S., Jackson, V. W., Chong, J., Choe, K., Tay, C., Wong, J., & Yang, L. H. (2021). Systematic review of cultural aspects of stigma and mental illness among racial and ethnic minority groups in the United States: implications for interventions. *American Journal of Community Psychology*, *68*(3–4), 486–512. https://doi.org/10.1002/ajcp.12516

Morey, B. N., Tulua, 'A., Tanjasiri, S. P., Subica, A. M, Kaholokula, J. K., Penaia, C., ... Ong, E. (2020). Structural racism and its effects on Native Hawaiians and Pacific Islanders in the US: issues of health equity, census undercounting, and voter disenfranchisement. *AAPI Nexus*, *17*(1–2). https://escholarship.org/uc/item/1gs2t6mk

Nguyen, J. D., Kim, J., Ngo, V., Weiss, B., & Lau, A. S. (2018). Prospective relations between parent-adolescent acculturation conflict and adolescent mental health symptoms among Vietnamese American adolescents. *Cultural Diversity and Ethnic Minority Psychology*, *24*(2), 151–161. https://doi.org/10.1037/cdp0000157

Nieri, T., Yoo, M., & Tam, C. (2024). Ethnic-racial socialization in mono-racial Asian American and Pacific Islander families: a 21-year systematic literature review. *Sociology Compass*, *18*(2), e13185. https://doi.org/10.1111/soc4.13185

O'Neill, J. C., Goldston, D. B., Kodish, T., Yu, S. H., Lau, A. S., & Asarnow, J. R. (2021). Implementing trauma informed suicide prevention care in schools: responding to acute suicide risk. *Evidence-Based Practice in Child and Adolescent Mental Health*, *6*(3), 379–392. https://doi.org/10.1080/23794925.2021.1917019

Park, A. L., Rith-Najarian, L. R., Saifan, D., Gellatly, R., Huey, S. J., & Chorpita, B. F. (2023). Strategies for incorporating culture into psychosocial interventions for youth of color. *Evidence-Based Practice in Child and Adolescent Mental Health*, *8*(2), 181–193. https://doi.org/10.1080/23794925.2022.2025629

Park, M., Choi, Y., Yasui, M., & Hedeker, D. (2021). Racial discrimination and the moderating effects of racial and ethnic socialization on the mental health of Asian American youth. *Child Development*, *92*(6), 2284–2298. https://doi.org/10.1111/cdev.13638

Pérez, D., van der Stuyft, P., Zabala, M. C., Castro, M., & Lefèvre, P. (2016). A modified theoretical framework to assess implementation fidelity of adaptive public health interventions. *Implementation Science*, *11*, 91. https://doi.org/10.1186/s13012-016-0457-8

Rastogi, R., Raval, V. V., Yip, T., Chen, J. A., & Liu, C. L. (2025). The effects of racial exclusion and racial othering on South Asian American identity and population health. *American Journal of Public Health*, *115*(3), 274–278. https://doi.org/10.2105/AJPH.2024.307938

Rathod, S., Gega, L., Degnan, A., Pikard, J., Khan, T., Husain, N., Munshi, T., & Naeem, F. (2018). The current status of culturally adapted mental health interventions: a practice-focused review of meta-analyses. *Neuropsychiatric Disease and Treatment*, *14*, 165–178. https://doi.org/10.2147/NDT.S138430

Resnicow, K., Soler, R., Braithwaite, R. L., Ahluwalia, J. S., & Butler, J. (2000). Cultural sensitivity in substance use prevention. *Journal of Community Psychology, 28*(3), 271–290. https://doi.org/10.1002/(SICI)1520-6629(200005)28:3<271::AID-JCOP4>3.0.CO;2-I

Rodriguez Espinosa, P., & Verney, S. P. (2021). The underutilization of community-based participatory research in psychology: a systematic review. *American Journal of Community Psychology, 67*(3–4), 312–326. https://doi.org/10.1002/ajcp.12469

Sangalang, C. C., Becerra, D., Mitchell, F. M., Lechuga- Peña, S., Lopez, K., & Kim, I. (2019). Trauma, post-migration stress, and mental health: a comparative analysis of refugees and immigrants in the United States. *Journal of Immigrant Minority Health, 21*, 909–919. https://doi.org/10.1007/s10903-018-0826-2

Sharma, N., Shaligram, D., & Yoon, G. H. (2020). Engaging South Asian youth and families: a clinical review. *International Journal of Social Psychiatry, 66*(6), 584–592. https://doi.org/10.1177/0020764020922881

Singh, S., McBride, K., & Kak, V. (2015). Role of social support in examining acculturative stress and psychological distress among Asian American immigrants and three sub-groups: results from NLAAS. *Journal of Immigrant Minority Health, 17*, 1597–1606. https://doi.org/10.1007/s10903-015-0213-1

Sit, H. F., Ling, R., Lam, A. I. F., Chen, W., Latkin, C. A., & Hall, B. J. (2020). The cultural adaptation of step-by-step: an intervention to address depression among Chinese young adults. *Frontiers in Psychiatry, 11*, 650. https://doi.org/10.3389/fpsyt.2020.00650

Skopp, N. A., Smolenski, D. J., Bush, N. E., Beech, E. H., Workman, D. E., Edwards-Stewart, A., & Belsher, B. E. (2023). Caring contacts for suicide prevention: a systematic review and meta-analysis. *Psychological Services, 20*(1), 74–83. https://doi.org/10.1037/ser0000645

Song, J., Ngo, N. T., Vigneron, J. G., Lee, A., Sust, S., Martin, A., & Yuen, E. Y. (2022). *CHATogether*: a novel digital program to promote Asian American Pacific Islander mental health in response to the COVID-19 pandemic. *Child and Adolescent Psychiatry and Mental Health, 16*, 76. https://doi.org/10.1186/s13034-022-00508-4

Stein, G. L., Coard, S. I., Gonzalez, L. M., Kiang, L., & Sircar, J. K. (2021). One talk at a time: developing an ethnic-racial socialization intervention for Black, Latinx, and Asian American families. *Journal of Social Issues, 77*(4), 1014–1036. https://doi.org/10.1111/josi.12482

Steinka-Fry, K. T., Tanner-Smith, E. E., Dakof, G. A., & Henderson, C. (2017). Culturally sensitive substance use treatment for racial/ethnic minority youth: a meta-analytic review. *Journal of Substance Abuse Treatment, 75*, 22–37. https://doi.org/10.1016/j.jsat.2017.01.006

Stirman, S., Baumann, A. A., & Miller, C. J. (2019). The FRAME: an expanded framework for reporting adaptations and modifications to evidence-based interventions. *Implementation Science, 14*(1), 58. https://doi.org/10.1186/s13012-019-0898-y

Sung, J., Mayo, N., Ko, M. J., & Lasley, C. (2013). Characteristics of collaborative care in increasing access to mental health service in the Asian community. *Families, Systems, & Health, 31*(3), 307–318. https://doi.org/10.1037/a0033773

Ta Park, V. M., Olaisen, R. H., Vuong, Q., Rosas, L. G., & Cho, M. K. (2019). Using Korean dramas as a precision mental health education tool for Asian Americans: a pilot study. *International Journal of Environmental Research and Public Health, 16*(12), 2151. https://doi.org/10.3390/ijerph16122151

Ta Park, V. M., Park, C. J., Kim, C., Nguyen, N. C. Y., Tran, A. T., Chiang, A., ... Cho, M. K. (2021). Use of Korean dramas to facilitate precision mental health understanding and discussion for Asian Americans. *Health Promotion International, 36*(5), 1425–1438. https://doi.org/10.1093/heapro/daab012

Ta Park, V. M., Suen Diwata, J., Win, N., Ton, V., Nam, B., Rajabally, W., & Jones, V. C. (2020). Promising results from the use of a Korean drama to address knowledge, attitudes, and behaviors on school bullying and mental health among Asian American college-aged students. *International Journal of Environmental Research and Public Health*, *17*(5), 1637. https://doi.org/10.3390/ijerph17051637

Telzer, E. H. (2011). Expanding the acculturation gap-distress model: an integrative review of research. *Human Development*, *53*(6), 313–340. https://doi.org/10.1159/000322476

Tsong, Y., Chopra, S. B., & Cheng, H.-L. (2022). Racial healing during the COVID-19 and anti-Asian pandemics through critical consciousness informed antiracist parenting practices (CCIARP). *Asian American Journal of Psychology*, *13*(4), 385–393. https://doi.org/10.1037/aap0000305

Tummala-Narra, P., Deshpande, A., & Kaur, J. (2016). South Asian adolescents' experiences of acculturative stress and coping. *American Journal of Orthopsychiatry*, *86*(2), 194–211. https://doi.org/10.1037/ort0000147

Vargas, S. M., Martin, P., Bear, L., Yu, S. H., Goldston, D., Asarnow, J., & Lau, A. S. (under review). Applying a Roll Out Implementation Optimization (ROIO) design to implement a trauma-informed suicide prevention intervention in schools. [Manuscript in preparation].

Vargas, S.M., Yu, S.H., Onipede, Z.A., Flores, A., Martin, P., Bear, L., Goldston, D., Asarnow, J.R., & Lau, A.S. (in press). Community partner perspectives on implementation determinants of a strengths-based, trauma-informed school suicide prevention intervention. *Implementation Research and Practice.*

von Thiele Schwarz, U., Aarons, G. A., & Hasson, H. (2019). The value equation: three complementary propositions for reconciling fidelity and adaptation in evidence-based practice implementation. *BMC Health Services Research*, *19*(1), 868. https://doi.org/10.1186/s12913-019-4668-y

Wang, C., Do, K. A., Frese, K., & Zheng, L. (2019). Asian immigrant parents' perception of barriers preventing adolescents from seeking school-based mental health services. *School Mental Health*, *11*(2), 364–377. https://doi.org/10.1007/s12310-018-9285-0

Wang, C., Havewala, M., Bali, D., Hui, J., Stancofski, R. M., & Patel, A. (2024). Parent and youth interventions for Chinese American families to address COVID-19 related discrimination and promote youth mental health. *School Psychology Review*, 1–17. https://doi.org/10.1080/2372966X.2024.2441648

Wang, C., Liu, J. L., Do, K. A., Shao, X., & Lu, H. (2020). Engaging parents to promote mental health among Chinese American youth. In A. M. Breland-Noble (Ed.), *Community Mental Health Engagement with Racially Diverse Populations* (pp. 49–82). Elsevier Academic Press. https://doi.org/10.1016/B978-0-12-818012-9.00003-4

Wang, C., Liu, J. L., Havewala, M., Zhu, Q., Do, K. A., & Shao, X. (2021). Parent–child connect: a culturally responsive parent training for Asian American parents at school. *Psychology in the Schools*, *58*(8), 1624–1641. https://doi.org/10.1002/pits.22520

Wang, C., Liu, J. L., Marsico, K. F., & Zhu, Q. (2022). Culturally adapting youth mental health first aid training for Asian Americans. *Psychological Services*, *19*(3), 551–561. https://doi.org/10.1037/ser0000574

Weng, S. S., & Spaulding-Givens, J. (2016). Informal mental health support in the Asian American community and culturally appropriate strategies for community-based mental health organizations. *Human Service Organizations: Management, Leadership & Governance*, *41*(2), 119–132. https://doi.org/10.1080/23303131.2016.1218810

Williams, M. T., Holmes, S., Zare, M., Haeny, A., & Faber, S. (2023). An evidence-based approach for treating stress and trauma due to racism. *Cognitive and Behavioral Practice*, *30*(4), 565–588. https://doi.org/10.1016/j.cbpra.2022.07.001

Wong, A., Wong, Y. J., & Obeng, C. S. (2012). An untold story: a qualitative study of Asian American family strengths. *Asian American Journal of Psychology*, *3*(4), 286–298. https://doi.org/10.1037/a0025553

Wong, P. O., Deng, S. Z., Benhayoun, A., Leong, A. W., Lee, A., Beck, K., & Yuen, E. Y. (2024). *CHATogether* skit development and healing of Asian American Generation Z's unspoken agonies: a qualitative study. *Journal of Creativity in Mental Health*, *20*, 1–17.

Woo, B. K. P. (2012). Using a Chinese radio station to disseminate dementia knowledge to Chinese Americans. *Journal of American Geriatrics Society*, *60*(11), 2175–2176. https://doi.org/10.1111/j.1532-5415.2012.04230.x

Wright, B., Chen, B. C., Kodish, T., Meza Lazaro, Y., & Lau, A. S. (2024). Immigration stress and internalizing symptoms among Latinx and Asian American students: the roles of school climate and community violence. *Journal of School Psychology*, *104*, 101286. https://doi.org/10.1016/j.jsp.2024.101286.

Wu, M. Y. (2012). The concept of *guan* in the Chinese parent-child relationship. In C. C. Yi (Ed.), *The Psychological Well-being of East Asian Youth. Quality of Life in Asia* (Vol. 2). Dordrecht: Springer. https://doi.org/10.1007/978-94-007-4081-5_2

Xin, R., Fitzpatrick, O. M., Lai, P. H. L., Weisz, J. R., & Price, M. A. (2022). A systematic narrative review of cognitive-behavioral therapies with Asian American youth. *Evidence-Based Practice in Child and Adolescent Mental Health*, *7*, 198–212. https://doi.org/10.1080/23794925.2022.2042872

Yu, S. H., Kodish, T., Bear, L., O'Neill, J. C., Asarnow, J. R., Goldston, D., ... Lau, A. S. (2023). Leader and provider perspectives on implementing safe alternatives for teens and youth - acute (SAFETY-A) in public school districts serving racial/ethnic minoritized youth. *School Mental Health*, *15*(2), 583–599. https://doi.org/10.1007/s12310-023-09572-3

Yu, S. H., Wright, B., Aguirre, D., Lazaro, Y. M., Kodish, T., & Lau, A. S. (2025). Determinants of stigma against help-seeking in schools and help-seeking behaviors of Asian American and Latinx youth experiencing internalizing problems. *Cultural Diversity & Ethnic Minority Psychology*. https://doi.org/10.1037/cdp0000736

Zhang, E., Hyun, S., Yip, T., Hahm, H. C., & Liu, C. H. (2022). Learning about discrimination during childhood: implications for racial trauma among Asians and Asian Americans during the pandemic. *Asian Journal of Psychiatry*, *77*, 103250. https://doi.org/10.1016/j.ajp.2022.103250

6

Bullying and Beyond

Cixin Wang, John W. Seipp, and Ami Patel*

Department of Counseling, Higher Education, & Special Education, University of Maryland, College Park, MD, USA

*Corresponding author: cxwang@umd.edu

Bullying remains a pervasive issue that significantly impacts the mental health and well-being of Asian American and Pacific Islander (AAPI) youth. Guided by an ecological framework, this chapter examines the prevalence of discrimination and bullying and their effects on AAPI youth across developmental stages. It then highlights innovative and practical strategies that schools, educators, and parents can adopt to create safer, more inclusive environments and promote positive youth mental health. Looking beyond, the development of novel antibullying approaches and interventions will be essential to ensuring that AAPI youth receive the support they need to navigate, and thrive, in a postpandemic world.

Discrimination Experiences of AAPI Youth

Research consistently shows that AAPI youth experience a range of victimization (e.g., verbal, relational, and cyberbullying), with verbal harassment being the most prevalent form (Robers et al., 2010). Racial identity and immigrant status often contribute to bullying experiences. For instance, Asian American first-generation immigrants (individuals born in foreign countries with both parents also born abroad) and second-generation immigrants (individuals born in the United States with at least one parent born abroad) are more likely to experience victimization compared to third-generation or later Asian Americans (individuals born in the United States with both parents also born in the United States) (Peguero, 2009). This phenomenon may be explained in part by the similarity hypothesis, which suggests individuals that fall outside the perceived majority are more likely to face discrimination (Goto et al., 2002). At the same time, the perpetual foreigner stereotype casts AAPI youth as forever outsiders, perpetuating exclusion and victimization based on cultural and linguistic differences (Lee et al., 2017; Park et al., 2021).

Model Minority Stereotype. For AAPI youth, these experiences can be exacerbated by harmful stereotypes, such as the model minority myth (MMM), which increase their vulnerability to bullying (Qin et al., 2008). The term is often used to portray the success of marginalized communities, particularly Asian Americans, as embodying the American Dream in contrast to other racial groups (Peterson, 1966). This stereotype suggests that Asian Americans have successfully overcome structural barriers, achieved socioeconomic success, and no longer face discrimination in the United States (Wang et al., 2020). However, the MMM overlooks the ongoing challenges experienced by this historically marginalized group (Yip et al., 2021). In reality, Asian Americans represent a highly diverse population with unique migration histories, languages, and educational backgrounds (Sue et al., 1995). Applying the "model minority" label to Asian American students not only ignores these differences but also minimizes their individual academic and behavioral needs, ultimately limiting opportunities for AAPI youth to participate and thrive in classrooms (Suzuki, 2002).

COVID-19. The rise in anti-Asian sentiment during the COVID-19 pandemic further compounded the challenges faced by Asian American communities. In 2021, a Pew Research Center survey found that approximately 81% of Asian American adults reported violence against them had been increasing, and 32% expressed fearing that "someone might threaten or physically attack them" (Ruiz et al., 2021). As noted in Chapter 11, research has also documented widespread xenophobia fueled by political rhetoric and stigmatizing terms such as "Chinese virus" and "Kung Flu" (Stop AAPI Hate, 2020; Rogers et al., 2020). Police data from 2020 indicated that hate crimes against Asian Americans in 16 of the largest US cities rose nearly 150% (Beers et al., 2021). Although the federal government declared the official end of the COVID-19 pandemic in 2023, anti-Asian bias remains prevalent. For example, a 2024 report from the Asian American Foundation found that one in five Asian Americans in New York City reported experiencing physical attacks or assaults, with 54% of hate incidents going unreported (The Asian American Foundation, 2024).

In addition to its effects on the broader Asian American community, numerous studies have highlighted the deleterious impact of COVID-19-related racism and discrimination on the mental health and well-being of AAPI youth. A study of adolescents' experiences of anti-Chinese discrimination found that vicarious experiences of discrimination led to increased anxiousness, depression, and stress during the pandemic (Benner et al., 2023). Similarly, a survey of 543 Chinese American parents and their children found that higher levels of both parent- and youth-perceived Sinophobia were associated with poorer mental health outcomes (Cheah et al., 2020).

Prevalence of Bullying Among AAPI Youth

Adolescence is a pivotal stage of development when racial identity begins to take shape (Erikson, 1963) and the likelihood of experiencing bullying victimization is at its highest (Espelage & Swearer, 2003). During this time, adolescents' mental health is particularly sensitive to the physical, emotional, and social transitions they face (Blakemore & Mills, 2014). Bullying remains a pervasive issue in schools, with significant consequences for AAPI youth. During the COVID-19 pandemic, cyberbullying rates increased among youth overall, with AAPI students reporting the highest levels of victimization during this time (Patchin & Hinduja, 2022). Specifically, AAPI youth who reported being cyberbullied because of their race more than tripled, increasing from 7.4% in 2019 to 23.5% in 2021 (Patchin & Hinduja, 2022).

In addition, the AAPI youth advocacy organization Act to Change found that while nearly 80% of AAPI students reported experiencing online or in-person bullying, just 38% disclosed the incident to an adult, compared with 63% of their non-Asian peers (Act to Change, 2021). Similarly, findings from the *Stop Stop AAPI Hate Youth Campaign (2020)* indicate that AAPI youth were more likely to face harassment at school, parks, and online. Although adults were present in nearly half of these cases, bystanders intervened in only 10% of incidents (Stop AAPI Hate, 2020). Taken altogether, the prevalence of underreporting and low bystander intervention suggest national survey data may significantly underestimate the true scale of bullying of AAPI youth.

Relationship Between Bullying and Mental Health. Bullying victimization has been consistently associated with a range of negative mental health and well-being outcomes, including depression, anxiety, low self-esteem, poor academic performance, substance use, involvement in violence, and suicidal ideation and planning among middle and high school students (Huang & Vidourek, 2019). The adverse effects of bullying can persist into adulthood, where victims face higher risks of psychiatric disorders, unemployment, and unstable social relationships (Huang & Vidourek, 2019). Chronic exposure to bullying has the potential to disrupt cognitive schemas and contribute to the development of posttraumatic stress disorder (PTSD) (American Psychiatric Association, 2013).

Bullying represents a significant risk factor for negative mental health outcomes among AAPI youth in particular (Shea et al., 2016). Indeed, previous research has found that AAPI youth face a greater risk of depression, self-harm, and suicide than their White or African American peers (Sen, 2004). For example, physical and relational victimization among Chinese immigrant high school students were positively related to heightened levels of anxiety and depression (Yeh et al., 2014). Similarly, Korean American students who reported being bullied experienced significantly higher rates of depression compared to their nonbullied peers (Shin et al., 2011).

Although Asian American students report elevated levels of stress and mental health challenges, they remain less likely than their White peers to utilize mental health services (Gudiño et al., 2008; Wang et al., 2020). Further, given that more than half of Asian Americans are immigrants (Ruiz et al., 2023), many Asian immigrant parents may have limited familiarity with the US educational system (Crosnoe & Ansari, 2015), which can hinder their ability to advocate for the support their children need at school.

Protective Factors

School connectedness, support from family and peers, and living in a dual-parent household are protective factors commonly associated with positive mental health among adolescents (Costello et al., 1990). For AAPI youth in particular, prior research also suggests that maintenance of cultural practices, bilingualism, and a sense of ethnic community are culturally unique factors that may be protective against depression (Zhou et al., 2012).

To further investigate risk and protective factors among racially and ethnically marginalized groups, Anyon et al. (2014) evaluated a school-based mental health prevention initiative across 15 urban high schools, with a focus on Asian American youth. Using data from the California Healthy Kids Survey (CHKS) collected in 2008–2009, the study analyzed responses from 8,466 students, 58% of whom identified as Asian (e.g., Chinese, Cambodian, Filipino, and Vietnamese) (Anyon et al., 2014). The researchers assessed universal risk factors, such as depressive symptoms, substance use, externalizing behavior, failing grades, truancy, and experiences of racial discrimination, alongside protective factors including school, home, peer, and internal assets.

Protective factors were operationalized as strengths and support systems that buffer the negative effects of risk exposure. For example, school assets (e.g., positive teacher–student relationships, supportive environments, and inclusive policies) not only promoted overall well-being but also facilitated referrals to mental health services. Home assets reflected the stability, care, and support provided by families, while peer assets encompassed friendships and social networks that supported youth resilience. Internal assets were defined as the personal qualities (e.g., self-efficacy and problem-solving skills) that help youth cope with stress and navigate challenges. Overall, the study found that *school assets* were the most influential protective factor in promoting AAPI youth's engagement with mental health services. By providing social support and institutional access, schools functioned as an important bridge to prevention programs (Anyon et al., 2014).

Another study examined how protective factors among AAPI youth during the pandemic's unique context (e.g., reduced social interactions and distance learning) interacted with prior bullying experiences and current peer discrimination to influence mental health adjustment among Chinese American adolescents (Yang, 2024). Although internalizing problems such as anxiety and depression were associated with both earlier victimization and ongoing racial discrimination, some adolescents reported increased resilience, likely reflecting coping strategies developed from previous adversity (Yang, 2024). Interestingly, prepandemic cyberbullying appeared to act as a protective factor, buffering the negative impact of pandemic-related peer discrimination on mental well-being. One reason for this may be due to Chinese American adolescents' heightened awareness and adaptability in response to earlier victimization. It could also be due to improved coping skills. In such cases, Chinese American adolescents' prior exposure to multiple forms of victimization (e.g., race, gender identity, sexual orientation, immigration status) may have led them to perceive COVID-19-related peer discrimination as less distressing than other forms of victimization (Yang, 2024).

Positive school climates can also serve as a protective factor and are associated with less peer victimization and fewer internalizing symptoms (Leadbeater & Hoglund, 2006; Waasdorp et al., 2011). Prior research has demonstrated that a positive school climate contributes to higher student achievement, school completion, and greater school connectedness (Haynes et al., 1997; Worrell & Hale, 2001; McNeely et al., 2002). Conversely, negative perceptions of school climate are linked to higher rates of risk-taking behaviors and delinquency (Bao et al., 2015). For racially minoritized students, perceptions of school climate are an indicator of school diversity and inclusivity (Parris et al., 2018). Bellmore et al. (2012) found that students reported lower levels of high school peer-ethnic discrimination when they perceived both a positive interracial climate and when they were part of the ethnic majority within their schools.

On the other hand, more recent research has found connections between positive perceptions of school climate and internalizing symptoms as it relates to cybervictimization (Holfeld & Baitz, 2020). Specifically, when students reported increased levels of safety and caring from teachers, they were vulnerable to higher levels of internalizing symptoms when they experienced high levels of cybervictimization (Holfeld & Baitz, 2020). This unexpected finding may be attributed to the "healthy context paradox," which posits that students who experience victimization in low bullying environments may experience worse mental health by internalizing the victimization (e.g., "it must be me") (Salmivalli, 2018, p. 70; Huitsing et al., 2012).

Similarly, Wang et al. (2023) observed that in schools where students perceive the climate negatively (e.g., poor peer–teacher relationships, unclear or unfair rules), peer victimization was more common and inconsistently addressed. As such, students' internalizing symptoms may be less severe because students were accustomed to victimization. Extending this work, Seipp et al. (2025)

found that democratic school climates (e.g., fair classroom rules) exacerbated the negative effects of racial-ethnic microaggressions on psychological well-being. In classrooms that are perceived as fairer, experiencing victimization or microaggressions could be especially harmful to student well-being, as such behavior paradoxically goes against core classroom values.

Developmental Specific Considerations

While bullying is a concern across all ages, the stage of development plays an important role in shaping both the nature of bullying and the protective factors that buffer its effects. Understanding these differences can help schools and educators adapt prevention and intervention strategies to meet the evolving needs of AAPI students throughout childhood, adolescence, and into adulthood.

Preschool to Elementary School. At younger ages, bullying often takes the form of physical aggression, and increasingly, cyberbullying (Broidy et al., 2003). Some research shows that bullying can begin as early as preschool, with children as young as four being victimized or bullying perpetrators (Vlachou et al., 2011). Approximately 21% of primary school educators reported bullying occurs in their schools on a daily or weekly basis (Bauer et al., 2008). Notably, childhood bullying victimization has been linked to higher rates of depression, peer rejection, and internalizing symptoms later in life (Ttofi et al., 2011; Kochenderfer & Ladd, 1996). Protective factors at this stage include strong family and peer relationships, consistent educator intervention, and early implementation of social-emotional learning (SEL) programs (e.g., *Merrell's Strong Start, Grades K-2;* Whitcomb & Parisi Damico, 2016) within schools (Garner et al., 2014; Durlak et al., 2011). Given the evidence that bullying emerges as early as preschool, early implementation of prevention and intervention programs is important for building safe and supportive school environments, particularly for culturally and ethnically diverse children.

Transition from Elementary School to Middle School. Bullying peaks in middle school, as this marks a transitionary period in youth's development (Felix et al., 2011; Hamstra & Fitzgerald, 2022). Alongside physical and cognitive changes, youth must adjust to larger schools with older students, new teachers with greater academic demands, and familiar and unfamiliar peers, compared to elementary school (Eccles & Wigfield, 1997). Bullying prevalence increases during this time, often in the form of relational aggression as youth attempt to gain social influence and dominance in peer groups (Wang et al., 2016). Significant associations between externalizing and bullying behaviors have also been documented during this transitional period. For example, Farmer et al. (2015) found that teacher- and peer-rated externalizing in fifth graders was positively associated with bullying, while it was negatively associated with victimization in older, sixth-grade students. Further, youth who experienced both internalizing and externalizing symptoms were more likely to be both a bully *and* a victim (Cook et al., 2010).

Given the link between bullying victimization and negative mental health before and during middle school, such a transition is an important time for school-based bullying prevention programs, youth mental health promotion, and increased mental health screenings. Combining school-wide positive behavioral interventions and supports (SW-PBIS; Sugai & Horner, 2020) with social-emotional learning (SEL) lessons (Espelage, 2014) can strengthen prosocial skill building and reduce biases that contribute to racial and ethnic bullying. Teaching youth bystander intervention strategies, as discussed later in this chapter, is also a key component of addressing bullying in middle school.

High School. Bullying often declines once adolescents reach high school (Nylund et al., 2007). Indeed, some evidence suggests that bullying interventions are less effective with high schoolers compared to middle school students (Yeager et al., 2015). Part of this decline may be due to underreporting, however, as changes with relationships with teachers, parents, and peers in high school may discourage adolescents from disclosing bullying incidents. With parents, for example, adolescents may be reluctant to share personal experiences with parents out of fear of disapproval or victim-blaming (Smetana et al., 2009; Harcourt et al., 2014).

Bullying within peer relationships may also decline in high school as factors of bullying (e.g., repetition, intentionality, and power differential; Hellström et al., 2015) become less relevant and social hierarchies are already established. Developmental changes also play a role; increased intimacy and trust in peer relationships, as well as increased cognitive and social skills, help adolescents better distinguish between bullying and teasing (Andrews & Dawes, 2024). On the other hand, being a victim of bullying in high school is associated with a range of physical and mental health risk behaviors, including depression, substance use, poor sleep, and anxiety (Hertz et al., 2015).

While researchers continue to debate the effectiveness of antibullying programs on adolescents compared to younger, elementary school children (Smith, 2010; Kärnä et al., 2013), other studies highlight the role of parent and peer involvement. Huang et al. (2019) found that prevention programs with parent components (e.g., workshops, school–home communication) were effective in reducing bullying and victimization. Similarly, Gaffney et al. (2021) reported that providing parents with information was more effective than parent meetings or discussion. In the same study, the authors found "informal peer involvement" involving small group or whole-class discussions around bullying experiences significantly reduced bullying perpetration and victimization, compared to more formal peer involvement (e.g., peer-led antibullying activities, peer-mentoring).

Taken together, these findings highlight the importance of school-based bullying prevention and SEL programs that address the needs of students across age groups. Examining risk and protective factors at each stage of development helps ensure that strategies are developmentally responsive and effective in supporting AAPI students of all ages.

Bullying Prevention Strategies and Techniques

While protective factors can buffer the effects of bullying, effective prevention requires intentional efforts from schools, educators, and families. Recent years have seen progress in developing prevention and intervention programs to prevent bullying within schools and communities serving AAPI youth. The following section adopts an ecological perspective—encompassing schools, families, and students—to highlight strategies and interventions that educators and mental health providers can use to support and advocate for AAPI students and families.

School-based Strategies to Reduce Bullying

In school-based settings, both well-established and novel approaches to bullying and cyberbullying prevention have become increasingly relevant for AAPI youth postpandemic, offering practical strategies to promote mental health. Many of these approaches emphasize cultural responsiveness by reducing educator bias, celebrating student identities, and improving digital citizenship. School-wide initiatives that explicitly address AAPI bullying, including discussions of stereotypes such as the model minority myth and the pandemic's impact on AAPI families, can promote more inclusive school climates and create a space for Asian American perspectives.

Educator Bias. Educators must be aware of and critically examine their own biases, particularly when working with marginalized students (National Association of School Psychologists [NASP], 2012). School leaders, teachers, and staff should assess stereotypes and assumptions about Asian American students (e.g., model minority myth) that may act as a barrier to providing individual students or families with necessary support (Sue et al., 2007). One effective strategy is structured reflection. For example, the ABC-Diversity Iceberg Framework (ABC-DI; Aspy & Grossman, 2011) was originally developed within a behavior-analytic approach to support autistic students. The model emphasizes that observable patterns of behaviors (i.e., antecedents, behaviors, and consequences) are just "tip of the iceberg." In other words, self-reflection of bias requires a below-the-surface look. Thus, the model encourages professionals to examine personal, systemic, and student-level factors related to implicit bias. Educators working with marginalized students, for example, could ask themselves, "*How might differences in cultural and social identity influence my interpretation of the student's behavior?*" or "*Am I blending my own experiences with the student's, or am I viewing their behavior independently?*"

Cultural Responsiveness. Educators should always strive to learn and grow alongside students and their culture. Culturally responsive teaching involves using cultural experiences and perspectives of ethnically diverse students as tools for effective teaching (Gay, 2018). In the context of working with AAPI students, this means understanding families and parents, the culture both at home and in school, and recognizing how experiences of racial and ethnic discrimination can impact student mental health (Tormala et al., 2015). For example, educators should be mindful of the misconception of an Asian monolith, as this perspective obscures the heterogeneity, strengths, and challenges faced by Asian American communities (Poon et al., 2016). Moreover, culturally responsive educators should assess acculturative risk factors such as stress related to academics, trauma, language barriers, and the stigma associated with help-seeking. These factors can worsen the effects of peer victimization, especially for AAPI immigrant students (Goldston et al., 2008).

Increasing Discrimination Awareness. Earlier sections of this chapter highlighted the pervasiveness of AAPI bullying and presented research on racial-ethnic discrimination (Patchin & Hinduja, 2022; Huang & Vidourek, 2019; Robers et al., 2010). Within school settings, it is essential for educators, school leaders, and mental health professionals to take steps to address and prevent bullying involving AAPI students. Strategies may include sharing current data on AAPI discrimination with colleagues, using class time to discuss the impact of Asian American stereotypes and assumptions other students may have, and showing culturally relevant materials (e.g., *Fresh Off the Boat*; Khan, 2015) that illustrate immigrant students' lived experiences with bias and discrimination.

Celebrating AAPI Identity. While raising awareness of ethnic-racial discrimination in schools can help AAPI students cope with adversity, inclusive classrooms that highlight AAPI representation also empower students to take pride in their heritage. Such practices might include inviting AAPI students to share their cultural traditions during community circles or morning meetings. To emphasize Asian and Asian American holidays, including Lunar New Year, Diwali, and AAPI Heritage Month, educators can promote collaborative student-led activities such as creating artwork, sharing music, or bringing traditional foods from home. Further, by intentionally integrating prosocial and social and emotional learning (SEL) skills into these activities, educators can strengthen student engagement, build a sense of community, and celebrate the diverse identities represented in the classroom.

Teaching Asian American History. As a part of implementing culturally responsive practices, educators must also recognize that anti-AAPI racism is deeply rooted in US history. Acts of racism and violence against people of Asian descent, especially Asian American immigrants, have persisted for more than a century. Educating students about Asian American history is important to promoting ethnic pride, raising awareness of Asian American discrimination, and understanding the historical context of Asian Americans in this country. At present, only 13 states require a K-12 curriculum that references Asian American history (Committee of 100, 2025). For example, the first Asians to arrive in North America were Filipinos who landed at Morro Bay, California, in October 1587 (Gomez Borah, 1995). This early history, along with key sociopolitical events (e.g., COVID-19 pandemic) and anti-Asian legislation (e.g., the 1882 Chinese Exclusion Act and the internment of Japanese Americans during World War II), highlights the longstanding and systemic nature of anti-Asian discrimination and its continued impact on AAPI students.

Cyberbullying and Digital Citizenship. In response to cyberbullying, digital citizenship education (DCE) offers a promising avenue for preventing cyberbullying and aggressive online behavior, particularly those targeting AAPI students in the United States and abroad (Yang, 2021). Schools can play an essential role in addressing cyberbullying across three major areas (Kowalski et al., 2019; Llorent et al., 2021). First, they can promote a positive school climate that emphasizes respect, empathy, and inclusion, thus mitigating risk factors that contribute to cyberbullying. Second, schools can establish and enforce anticyberbullying policies and procedures to protect students online. Third, educators can monitor student behaviors for early warning signs of cyberbullying and then intervene (Yang, 2021).

DCE equips children with the skills to access online spaces safely and responsibly. Several Asian countries have taken the lead in embedding digital literacy within their education systems. In Japan and South Korea, for example, national initiatives emphasize digital skill development, responsible online behavior, and effective online strategies (Shin et al., 2019). Japan's Ministry of Education, Culture, Sports, Science, and Technology (2017) has also developed resources for parents to recognize signs of cyberbullying in their children and intervene effectively.

AAPI youth in the United States could benefit from similar school-based DCE frameworks, given that federal regulations on children's online safety are less stringent and slower to develop compared to those in other countries (Kelly, 2024). Such frameworks may involve teaching students on the ethical use of technology, strategies for safe internet use, and awareness of the consequences of online actions. By guiding youth on online etiquette, critical thinking, and empathy, DCE represents a practical and culturally responsive approach to preventing cyberbullying of AAPI youth that American schools are well positioned to implement.

Bullying Reporting. The National Association of School Psychologists (NASP) emphasizes the importance of schools establishing effective systems that allow students and families to report racial and ethnic bullying or discrimination, with clear and consistently enforced consequences for such behavior (Rossen & Cowen, 2012). This might include the early identification of ethnic and racial peer victimization through school climate assessments and the continual monitoring of risk factors for bullying (Rossen & Cowen, 2012) by school leaders.

Utilizing systematic data collection and tracking can highlight the prevalence of bullying among AAPI students and help school leaders in addressing the underlying cause. Yet, many Asian American families are immigrants who may be unfamiliar with school procedures or hesitant to report concerns due to fears of repercussions (Wang et al., 2020). To address these barriers, schools should develop culturally responsive reporting systems by engaging AAPI communities about bullying policies and supports for victimized students. Closing this reporting gap not only helps reduce racial-ethnic bullying but also provides school leaders with an important indicator of overall climate and inclusivity.

Empowering AAPI Families Through SEL and Parenting Programs

Parents and families are essential in guiding children through conversations about current events, experiences of discrimination, and mental health. In fact, discussions about race became more common in Asian American households during the pandemic, influenced by movements like Black Lives Matter (Sullivan et al., 2021) and rising anti-Asian sentiment, including incidents such as the Atlanta spa shootings (Associated Press, 2021). In response to these events, Chinese American parents became more actively involved in racial socialization, helping their children recognize potential barriers and instances of discrimination in US society (Kiang et al., 2023). Such highlights the importance of involving parents in training programs aimed at supporting youth mental health (e.g., Connell & Dishion, 2017; Hanisch et al., 2014). Similarly, in Chapter 1, Yip and colleagues expand on the importance of ethnic-racial identity (ERI) and ethnic-racial socialization (ERS) as protective factors that can prepare youth and families to address bias and discrimination.

Parenting Workshops. Mental health professionals can teach AAPI parents effective bullying prevention strategies through parenting workshops. In one such intervention, school psychologists openly discussed racism and Asian American history with parents to raise awareness, focusing on how parents can engage in ERS with youth. They explored community-based strategies, such as civic engagement, learning about Asian American history, and advocacy through parent teacher associations and community organizations. Additionally, they also connected parents to relevant resources and support systems at school and in the community (Wang et al., 2025; 2026). Wang et al. (2021; 2025; 2026) found that these parenting workshops promoted positive parenting behaviors (e.g., autonomy-granting, parental warmth) while reducing negative parenting behaviors (e.g., verbal hostility, punitive parenting, and shaming). The intervention also improved parents' sense of competence, parent-child communication, and parent self-efficacy to support youth who experienced discrimination (Wang et al., 2021; 2025; 2026).

One effective strategy for educating AAPI parents and families on preventing racial and ethnic discrimination is to introduce the WITS skills: Walk away, Ignore the perpetrator, Talk it out, and Seek help (Wang et al., 2015; 2021) and micro-intervention skills (Sue et al., 2020). For example, if a child is teased with "*Four eyes!*" a constructive WITS response might be: "*Thank you for noticing my glasses; yes, I see very well.*" Similarly, when a student is told to "*go back to China*," parents can encourage youth to create a calm and assertive reply, such as: "*This is my country. America is a nation of immigrants*" (Wang et al., 2021).

In addition, when AAPI youth witness bullying or discrimination as bystanders, parents can equip them with strategies like interruption and redirection, for example, "*This isn't acceptable. Please stop.*" Youth can also be encouraged to express their values, set clear boundaries, and address bullying behavior directly. For instance, if a student hears someone being told to "*go back to their country*," they might respond using an I-statement to clearly express feelings, needs, and expectations: "*Not all Asians are foreigners. I was born here, and I feel hurt when you say that. We should respect each other in school.*" Teaching WITS skills to parents is important for helping their AAPI youth respond to bullying safely and effectively, reduce the risk of further victimization, and advocate for themselves and peers.

Social and Emotional Learning (SEL). SEL is the systematic process by which youth acquire the knowledge, skills, and attitudes needed to navigate the complexities of life. It includes five core areas: self-awareness, self-management, responsible decision-making, relationship skills, and social awareness (Collaborative for Academic, Social, and Emotional Learning, 2021). Research consistently shows that SEL interventions are linked to positive outcomes for children, including better social skills, self-image, academic achievement, coping, and mental health, as well as reduced antisocial behavior and substance abuse (Durlak et al., 2011; Sklad et al., 2012).

Although still emerging, recent studies suggest that SEL interventions may be particularly beneficial for youth from diverse racial-ethnic backgrounds by building prosocial skills and equipping them to cope with stress related to bullying (Yang & Golshirazi, 2023). For example, a universal school-based SEL intervention over a year led to significant growth in SEL skills among K-2 Black students, whereas Black students in the control group showed lower skill growth compared to White students (Lee et al., 2023).

Another example of an SEL intervention is Merrell's *Strong Kids* curriculum, a widely recognized and well-researched SEL intervention for elementary and middle school students (Carrizales-Engelmann, 2016). Grounded in cognitive-behavioral theory, the 12-lesson curriculum covers topics such as understanding and managing emotions, recognizing the emotions of others, coping with stress, and goal setting. Research has shown that *Strong Kids* can enhance social and emotional skills and reduce internalizing symptoms (Harlacher & Merrell, 2010). However, most studies of this curriculum have focused primarily on White youth, producing mixed results for racial and ethnic minority students (Ryan et al., 2016).

In a recent study, Wang et al. (2026) culturally adapted the *Strong Kids* curriculum for Chinese American youth by discussing Asian American history and experiences, as well as strategies for responding to racial discrimination and bullying. The program included activities celebrating Asian American culture (e.g., Lunar New Year) and facilitated discussions on culture-specific topics such as the model minority stereotype, academic pressure, and high parental expectations. Findings indicated that after participating in the culturally adapted *Strong Kids* program, youth reported significant improvements in SEL knowledge and resilience, as well as greater positive coping, emotional regulation, and overall mental health (Wang et al., 2026). Developing and evaluating culturally tailored SEL lessons represents a promising direction for advancing SEL skill acquisition among AAPI youth, with the potential to reduce bullying behaviors and improve school-based mental health (Tables 6.1 and 6.2).

Table 6.1 Practical school-based bullying prevention and intervention strategies for AAPI youth.

Strategy	Why it matters	How to implement
Engage in Self-reflection	Biases can reinforce stereotypes, prevent recognition of discrimination, and limit behavioral and academic supports	Participate in implicit bias training, engage in professional development on bias, and protect time for self-reflection
Practice Culturally Responsive Communication and Teaching	Lack of awareness of acculturative risk factors (e.g., stress, trauma, language barriers, stigma) can weaken trust and create barriers for families	Recognize cultural norms (e.g., eye contact, silence) in family communication, and incorporate culturally relevant materials and classroom discussions (e.g., *Fresh Off the Boat*; Khan, 2015) to illustrate immigrant students' lived experiences
Increase Awareness of Bullying and Discrimination	AAPI bullying and racial-ethnic discrimination are pervasive in schools, yet often underreported	Share current data on AAPI discrimination with colleagues, use class time to discuss stereotypes and assumptions, and incorporate culturally relevant materials (e.g., *Young, Proud, and Sung-Jee*) to discuss students' experiences with discrimination

(*Continued*)

Table 6.1 (Continued)

Strategy	Why it matters	How to implement
Celebrate and Affirm AAPI Identities	Inclusive classrooms that highlight AAPI representation empower students to take pride in their cultural heritage and foster resilience against discrimination	Invite AAPI students to share cultural traditions in community circles, celebrate holidays (e.g., Lunar New Year, Diwali, and AAPI Heritage Month) and integrate SEL skills into student-led activities (e.g., sharing artwork, music, and food)
Teach AAPI History	Anti-AAPI racism is deeply rooted in US history, and teaching Asian American history promotes ethnic pride, raises awareness of discrimination, and provides important historical context for understanding students' experiences	Incorporate key events (e.g., Chinese Exclusion Act, Japanese American internment, COVID-19 pandemic), highlight early immigration histories (e.g., Filipino arrived in North America in 1587), and highlight Asian American contributions in classrooms
Prevent and Respond to Cyberbullying	AAPI youth face increased online harassment	Implement digital citizenship education (DCE), enforce cyberbullying policies, and equip parents and educators to recognize and intervene in cyberbullying
Strengthen Bullying Reporting Systems	Many AAPI students and families are unfamiliar with school procedures to report bullying, leaving racial-ethnic bullying unaddressed and underreported	Establish culturally responsive reporting systems, engage AAPI communities in clarifying policies, and use data from school climate assessments and incident reports to monitor and respond to bullying

Table 6.2 Practical at-home bullying prevention and intervention strategies for AAPI youth.

Strategy	Why it matters	How to implement
Equip Parents Through Workshops	Parent workshops are effective, and their understanding of SEL and youth mental health can help their children manage stress, anxiety, and discrimination	Partner with trusted community organizations. Use culturally relevant examples and interactive activities in the workshops.
Teach WITS Skills to Families	By teaching their children to use WITS skills (Walk away, Ignore, Talk it out, Seek help), parents can empower youth to respond to bullying effectively	Model skills during workshops. Encourage parents to role play with youth. Encourage families to have conversations around bullying and discrimination
Engage in Ethnic Racial Socialization at Home	Ethnic-racial socialization can strengthen cultural pride and identity, which are protective factors against bullying and mental health challenges	Encourage families to share cultural traditions, stories, and promote cultural identity
Implement SEL to Build Coping Skills	SEL helps children develop emotional regulation, problem-solving, and prosocial skills. These skills can help youth better cope with stress, bullying, and acculturation challenges faced by immigrant youth	Integrate evidence-based SEL lessons (e.g., *Strong Kids*) with culturally relevant examples

Clinical Case Study

To demonstrate effective strategies for addressing racial and ethnic bullying in schools, we share a brief case study that outlines practical recommendations, actionable steps, and approaches for creating a safer, more inclusive school environment for Asian American youth.

At Willow Brook Elementary, a suburban school reflecting the local community demographics (59% White, 14% Asian, 13% Latinx, 9% multiracial, and 5% Black, with 5% of students qualifying for free or reduced-price lunch), the school psychologist (you) was notified of a bullying incident by the school principal. The bullying report included an email from Ms. Wong, a Chinese immigrant mother, who described how her second-grade son, Ryan, was targeted during recess. Two classmates had told him, "Chinese people brought the coronavirus here. You should go back to China." According to Ms. Wong, the bullying continued in class, with peers making fun of Ryan's eyes and perpetuating the model minority stereotype by claiming, "Asian people have tiny eyes and always squint. How are they good at math?" Upset by the teasing and blame for COVID-19, Ryan refused to attend school the next day. Ms. Wong also reported that a school staff member overheard the comments but did not intervene on Ryan's behalf. Consequently, she expressed her concerns about the lack of action provided by the school and filed an official bullying report.

You and the principal first met Ms. Wong to better understand her concerns and gather more details about Ryan's experience. During the discussion, Ms. Wong shared that other Asian American parents had reported incidents of racial and ethnic bullying directed at their children, but they were unsure how to report it. In response, you organized a discussion session with Asian American parents to reduce barriers to reporting and to clarify school antibullying policies.

Recognizing a gap in bullying reporting, you collaborated with school leaders to implement a student climate survey on bullying. The results revealed that nearly one-third of students felt unsafe at school, and many did not report bullying to parents or other trusted adults. You shared these findings, along with the parent concerns, during a staff training. Building on this, you facilitated a school-wide professional development session that presented current data on AAPI bullying. The training also emphasized the importance of cultural responsiveness by discussing the history of AAPI discrimination and by collaboratively examining educator biases.

Additional steps were taken at the school level. The principal requested the school library purchase children's books featuring Asian American characters (e.g., Eyes That Kiss in the Corners) to facilitate classroom discussions around diversity and inclusion during morning meetings. Teachers were encouraged to have students read Young, Proud and Sung-Jee by Joyce Y. Lee and Emily Ku. The book tells the story of Sung-Jee, a young girl whose family runs a Korean restaurant during the COVID-19 pandemic. Targeted with bullying and blamed for the virus because of her race, Sung-Jee navigates these challenges with the supportive guidance of her parents. Eventually, with her parent's encouragement, Sung-Jee learns to confront and overcome hurtful stereotypes and racism, ultimately developing pride in her Asian heritage.

To celebrate AAPI Heritage month in May, teachers incorporated lessons on AAPI history and engaged students in art, music, and media that celebrated diverse Asian cultures. Finally, the school counselor led a bystander intervention session that taught students how to be a positive bystander through WITS (Walk away, Ignore the perpetrator, Talk it out, and Seek help).

In summary, this case study illustrates how educators, working collaboratively with school leaders, parents, and staff, can effectively address and prevent racial and ethnic bullying while creating a climate in which all students feel safe, included, and celebrated. The following section outlines practical recommendations from the case study to guide schools in addressing racial and ethnic bullying.

Practical Recommendations for Educators in Addressing Racial and Ethnic Bullying in Schools

- **Promote Cultural Responsiveness**. Because many students are reluctant to report bullying incidents and parents are often unaware of school policies, engaging Asian American families was important to understanding youths' experiences of racial-ethnic bullying at school, clarifying school antibullying policies, and removing potential cultural or linguistic barriers to bullying reporting.
- **Engage in Self-reflection**. Adults in schools serve as the first line of defense in preventing bullying. To do so effectively, it is important to engage in ongoing self-reflection and critically reflect on biases.
- **Adopt a Data-based Approach**. Collecting and analyzing school climate data provides a clearer picture of bullying prevalence and overall climate, which in turn informs effective school-based interventions.
- **Develop Prosocial Skills**. Educators can teach students prosocial skills, such as WITS (Walk away, Ignore the perpetrator, Talk it out, and Seek help) to help AAPI youth assertively stand up for themselves, reduce future discrimination incidents, and report bullying.
- **Celebrate Diversity**. Adapting SEL curriculum to include AAPI culture and heritage both celebrates diversity and creates a more inclusive classroom climate. Additionally, incorporating culturally relevant books and media into classroom discussions allows for conversations around challenging stereotypes (e.g., model minority myth), while also serving as an opportunity to collaboratively establish classroom norms around bullying and to encourage students to report racial-ethnic bullying incidents.

References

Act to Change. (2021). *2021 Asian American bullying survey report*. https://acttochange.org/press-release-bullying-report/

American Psychiatric Association. (2013). *Diagnostic and Statistical Manual of Mental Disorders* (Fifth Edition). American Psychiatric Publishing.

Andrews, N. C. Z., & Dawes, M. (2024). Using retrospective reports to develop profiles of harmful versus playful teasing experiences. *Journal of Adolescence*, *96*, 1512–1526. https://doi.org/10.1002/jad.12359

Anyon, Y., Ong, S. L., & Whitaker, K. (2014). School-based mental health prevention for Asian American adolescents: risk behaviors, protective factors, and service use. *Asian American Journal of Psychology*, *5*(2), 134–144. https://doi.org/10.1037/a0035300

Aspy, R., & Grossman, B. G. (2011). *The Ziggurat Model: A Framework for Designing Comprehensive Interventions for High-Functioning Individuals with Autism Spectrum Disorders* (Second Edition). Autism Asperger Publishing Company.

Associated Press. (2021). Prosecutor to seek hate crime charges, death penalty for spa shooting suspect. *NPR*. https://www.npr.org/2021/05/11/995915454/prosecutor-plans-to-seek-death-penalty-in-spa-shootings

Bao, Z., Li, D., Zhang, W., & Wang, Y. (2015). School climate and delinquency among Chinese adolescents: analyses of effortful control as a moderator and deviant peer affiliation as a mediator. *Journal of Abnormal Child Psychology*, *43*(1), 81–93. https://doi.org/10.1007/s10802-014-9903-8

Bauer, A. M., Lozano, P., & Rivara, F. P. (2008). The effectiveness of school-based bullying prevention programs. *Pediatrics*, *121*(2), e15–e25. https://doi.org/10.1542/peds.2007-1517

Beers, L. S., Szilagyi, M., Seigel, W. M., Davis, W. S., Fukuda, Y., Joseph, M., ... American Academy of Pediatrics Board of Directors Executive Committee, Board Committee on Equity. (2021). Immunizing against hate: overcoming Asian American and Pacific Islander racism. *Pediatrics*, *148*(1), 1–3. https://doi.org/10.1542/peds.2021-051836

Bellmore, A. D., Nishina, A., You, J.-I., & Ma, T.-L. (2012). School context protective factors against peer ethnic discrimination across the high school years. *American Journal of Community Psychology*, *49*(1–2), 98–111. https://doi.org/10.1007/s10464-011-9443-0

Benner, A. D., Rojas, F. A., Kim, S. Y., Hou, Y., & Coulter, K. M. (2023). COVID-19 anti-Chinese discrimination, current pandemic stress, and adolescents' mental health. *Journal of Racial and Ethnic Health Disparities*, *11*(4), 1946–1955. https://doi.org/10.1007/s40615-023-01663-w

Blakemore, S.-J., & Mills, K. (2014). Is adolescence a sensitive period for sociocultural processing? *Annual Review of Psychology*, *65*, 187–207. https://doi.org/10.1146/annurev-psych-010213-115202

Broidy, L. M., Nagin, D. S., Tremblay, R. E., Bates, J. E., Brame, B., Dodge, K. A., ... Vitaro, F. (2003). Developmental trajectories of childhood disruptive behaviors and adolescent delinquency: a six-site, cross-national study. *Developmental Psychology*, *39*(2), 222–245. https://doi.org/10.1037/0012-1649.39.2.222

Carrizales-Engelmann, D., Feuerborn, L. L., Gueldner, B. A., & Tran, O. K. (2016). *Merrell's Strong Kids—Grades 6–8: A Social & Emotional Learning Curriculum* (Second Edition). Paul H. Brookes Publishing.

Cheah, C. S. L., Wang, C., Ren, H., Zong, X., Cho, H. S., & Xue, X. (2020). COVID-19 racism and mental health in Chinese American families. *Pediatrics*, *146*(5). https://doi.org/10.1542/peds.2020-021816

Collaborative for Academic, Social, and Emotional Learning. (2021). What is SEL? https://casel.org/what-is-sel/

Committee of 100. (2025, August 28). *More students than ever learning Asian American history as 23 states adhere to Asian American history requirements.* https://www.committee100.org/media-center/more-students-than-ever-learning-asian-american-history-as-23-states-adhere-to-asian-american-history-requirements/

Connell, A. M., & Dishion, T. J. (2017). Long-term effects of the *Family Check-Up* in public secondary school on diagnosed major depressive disorder in adulthood. *Journal of Youth and Adolescence*, *46*(3), 570–581. https://doi.org/10.1007/s10964-016-0482-6

Cook, C. R., Williams, K. R., Guerra, N. G., Kim, T. E., & Sadek, S. (2010). Predictors of bullying and victimization in childhood and adolescence: a meta-analytic investigation. *School Psychology Quarterly*, *25*(2), 65–83. https://doi.org/10.1037/a0020149

Costello, E. J., & Janiszewski, S. (1990). Who gets treated? Factors associated with referral in children with psychiatric disorders. *Acta Psychiatrica Scandinavica*, *81*, 523–529. https://doi.org/10.1111/j.1600-0447.1990.tb05492.x

Crosnoe, R., & Ansari, A. (2015). Latin American immigrant parents and their children's teachers in U.S. early childhood education programmes. *International Journal of Psychology*, *50*(6), 431–439. https://doi.org/10.1002/ijop.12173

Durlak, J. A., Weissberg, R. P., Dymnicki, A. B., Taylor, R. D., & Schellinger, K. B. (2011). The impact of enhancing students' social and emotional learning: a meta-analysis of school-based universal interventions. *Child Development*, *82*(1), 405–432. https://doi.org/10.1111/j.1467-8624.2010.01564.x

Eccles, J. S., & Wigfield, A. (1997). Young adolescent development. In J. L. Irvin (Ed.), *What Current Research Says to the Middle Level Practitioner* (pp. 15–29). National Middle School Association.

Erikson, E. H. (1963). *Childhood and Society*. Norton.

Ermis-Demirtas, H., Luo, Y., & Huang, Y.-J. (2022). The impact of COVID-19-associated discrimination on anxiety and depression symptoms in Asian American adolescents. *International Perspectives in Psychology*, *11*(3), 153–160. https://doi.org/10.1027/2157-3891/a000049

Espelage, D. L., Polanin, J. R., & Low, S. K. (2014). Teacher and staff perceptions of school environment as predictors of student aggression, victimization, and willingness to intervene in bullying situations. *School Psychology Quarterly*, *29*(3), 287–305. https://doi.org/10.1037/spq0000072

Espelage, D. L., & Swearer, S. M. (2003). Research on school bullying and victimization: what have we learned and where do we go from here? *School Psychology Review*, *32*(3), 365–383.

Farmer, T. W., Irvin, M. J., Motoca, L. M., Leung, M. C., Hutchins, B. C., Brooks, D. S., ... Hall, C. M. (2015). Externalizing and internalizing behavior problems, peer affiliations, and bullying involvement across the transition to middle school. *Journal of Emotional and Behavioral Disorders*, *23*(1), 3–16. https://doi.org/10.1177/1063426613491286

Felix, E. D., Sharkey, J. D., Green, J. G., Furlong, M. J., & Tanigawa, D. (2011). Getting precise and pragmatic about the assessment of bullying: the development of the California Bullying Victimization Scale. *Aggressive Behavior*, *37*(3), 234–247. https://doi.org/10.1002/ab.20389

Gaffney, H., Ttofi, M. M., & Farrington, D. P. (2021). Evaluating the effectiveness of school-bullying prevention programs: an updated meta-analytical review. *Aggression and Violent Behavior*, *61*, 101631. https://doi.org/10.1016/j.avb.2021.101631

Garner, P. W., Mahatmya, D., Brown, E. L., & Vesely, C. K. (2014). Promoting desirable outcomes among culturally and ethnically diverse children in social emotional learning programs: a multilevel heuristic model. *Educational Psychology Review*, *26*(2), 165–189. https://doi.org/10.1007/s10648-013-9241-y

Gay, G. (2018). *Culturally Responsive Teaching: Theory, Research, and Practice* (Third Edition). Teachers College Press.

Goldston, D. B., Molock, S. D., Whitbeck, L. B., Murakami, J. L., Zayas, L. H., & Hall, G. N. (2008). Cultural considerations in adolescent suicide prevention and psychosocial treatment. *American Psychologist*, *63*(1), 14–31. https://doi.org/10.1037/0003-066X.63.1.14

Gomez Borah, E. (1995). Filipinos in Unamuno's California expedition of 1587. *Amerasia Journal*, *21*(3), 175–184. https://doi.org/10.17953/amer.21.3.q050756h25525n72

Goto, S. G., Gee, G. C., & Takeuchi, D. T. (2002). Strangers still? The experience of discrimination among Chinese Americans. *Journal of Community Psychology*, *30*(2), 211–224. https://doi.org/10.1002/jcop.9998

Gudiño, O. G., Lau, A. S., Yeh, M., McCabe, K. M., & Hough, R. L. (2008). Understanding racial/ethnic disparities in youth mental health services: do disparities vary by problem type? *Journal of Emotional and Behavioral Disorders*, *17*(1), 3–16. https://doi.org/10.1177/1063426608317710

Hanisch, C., Hautmann, C., Plück, J., Eichelberger, I., & Döpfner, M. (2014). The prevention program for externalizing problem behavior (PEP) improves child behavior by reducing negative parenting: analysis of mediating processes in a randomized controlled trial. *Journal of Child Psychology and Psychiatry*, *55*(5), 473–484. https://doi.org/10.1111/jcpp.12177

Hamstra, C., & Fitzgerald, M. (2022). Longitudinal effects from childhood abuse to bullying perpetration in adolescence: the role of mental health and social problems. *Journal of Child & Adolescent Trauma*, *15*(3), 869–881. https://doi.org/10.1007/s40653-021-00409-2

Harcourt, S., Jasperse, M., & Green, V. A. (2014). "We were sad and we were angry": a systematic review of parents' perspectives on bullying. *Child & Youth Care Forum*, *43*(3), 373–391. https://doi.org/10.1007/s10566-014-9243-4

Harlacher, J. E., & Merrell, K. W. (2010). Social and emotional learning as a universal level of student support: evaluating the follow-up effect of Strong Kids on social and emotional outcomes. *Journal of Applied School Psychology*, *26*(3), 212–229. https://doi.org/10.1080/15377903.2010.495903

Haynes, N. M., Emmons, C., & Ben-Avie, M. (1997). School climate as a factor in student adjustment and achievement. *Journal of Educational and Psychological Consultation*, *8*(3), 321–329. https://doi.org/10.1207/s1532768xjepc0803_4

Hellström, L., Persson, L., & Hagquist, C. (2015). Understanding and defining bullying—adolescents' own views. *Archives of Public Health*, *73*(1), 4. https://doi.org/10.1186/2049-3258-73-4

Hertz, M. F., Everett Jones, S., Barrios, L. C., David-Ferdon, C., & Holt, M. (2015). Association between bullying victimization and health risk behaviors among high school students in the United States. *Journal of School Health*, *85*(12), 833–842. https://doi.org/10.1111/josh.12339

Holfeld, B., & Baitz, R. (2020). The mediating and moderating effects of social support and school climate on the association between cyber victimization and internalizing symptoms. *Journal of Youth and Adolescence*, *49*(11), 2214–2228. https://doi.org/10.1007/s10964-020-01292-0

Huang, S. T., & Vidourek, R. A. (2019). Bullying victimization among Asian American youth: a review of the literature. *International Journal of Bullying Prevention*, *1*(2), 187–204. https://doi.org/10.1007/s42380-019-00029-3

Huang, Y., Espelage, D. L., Polanin, J. R., & Hong, J. S. (2019). A meta-analytic review of school-based anti-bullying programs with a parent component. *International Journal of Bullying Prevention*, *1*(1), 32–44. https://doi.org/10.1007/s42380-018-0002-1

Huitsing, G., & Veenstra, R. (2012). Bullying in classrooms: participant roles from a social network perspective. *Aggressive Behavior*, *38*(6), 494–509. https://doi.org/10.1002/ab.21438

Kärnä, A., Voeten, M., Little, T. D., Poskiparta, E., Kaljonen, A., & Salmivalli, C. (2013). Effectiveness of the KiVa antibullying program: grades 1–3 and 7–9. *Journal of Educational Psychology*, *105*(2), 535–551. https://doi.org/10.1037/a0030417

Kelly, S. M. (2024). Outside the US, teens' social media experiences are more tightly controlled. *CNN*. https://www.cnn.com/2024/02/13/tech/social-media-regulation-outside-us/index.html

Khan, N. (Creator & Executive Producer). (2015–2020). Fresh off the boat [TV series]. ABC Studios.

Kiang, L., Christophe, N. K., Stein, G. L., Stevenson, H. C., Jones, S. C. T., Chan, M., & Anderson, R. E. (2023). Ethnic-racial identity and ethnic-racial socialization competency: how minoritized parents "walk the talk." *Cultural Diversity & Ethnic Minority Psychology*, *29*(4), 493–502. https://doi.org/10.1037/cdp0000605

Kochenderfer, B. J., & Ladd, G. W. (1996). Peer victimization: manifestations and relations to school adjustment in kindergarten. *Journal of School Psychology*, *34*(3), 267–283. https://doi.org/10.1016/0022-4405(96)00015-5

Kowalski, R. M., Limber, S. P., & McCord, A. (2019). A developmental approach to cyberbullying: prevalence and protective factors. *Aggression and Violent Behavior*, *45*, 20–32. https://doi.org/10.1016/j.avb.2018.02.009

Lee, J., Shapiro, V. B., & Kim, B. E. (2023). Universal school-based social and emotional learning (SEL) for diverse student subgroups: implications for enhancing equity through SEL. *Prevention Science*, *24*(5), 1011–1022. https://doi.org/10.1007/s11121-023-01552-y

Lee, J. P., Lee, R. M., & Tran, A. G. T. T. (2017). Theory and measurement of foreigner objectification. In S. J. Schwartz, & J. Unger (Eds.), *The Oxford Handbook of Acculturation and Health* (pp. 143–156). Oxford University Press. https://doi.org/10.1093/oxfordhb/9780190215217.013.9

Leadbeater, B. J., & Hoglund, W. L. (2006). Changing the social contexts of peer victimization. *Journal of the Canadian Academy of Child and Adolescent Psychiatry*, *15*(1), 21–26.

Llorent, V. J., Farrington, D. P., & Zych, I. (2021). School climate policy and its relations with social and emotional competencies, bullying and cyberbullying in secondary education. *Revista de Psicodidáctica (English Ed.), 26*(1), 35–44. https://doi.org/10.1016/j.psicoe.2020.11.002

McNeely, C. A., Nonnemaker, J. M., & Blum, R. W. (2002). Promoting school connectedness: evidence from the National Longitudinal Study of Adolescent Health. *Journal of School Health, 72*(4), 138–146. https://doi.org/10.1111/j.1746-1561.2002.tb06533.x

Ministry of Education, Culture, Sports, Science and Technology. (2017). Guidelines for investigations into serious situations of bullying. https://www.mext.go.jp/en/policy/education/elsec/title02/detail02/__icsFiles/afieldfile/2020/06/05/20200605-mxt_kouhou02-02.pdf

National Association of School Psychologists. (2012). Racism, prejudice, and discrimination [Position statement]. Bethesda, MD.

Nylund, K., Bellmore, A., Nishina, A., & Graham, S. (2007). Subtypes, severity, and structural stability of peer victimization: what does latent class analysis say? *Child Development, 78*(6), 1706–1722. https://doi.org/10.1111/j.1467-8624.2007.01097.x

Park, M., Choi, Y., Yoo, H. C., Yasui, M., & Takeuchi, D. (2021). Racial stereotypes and Asian American youth paradox. *Journal of Youth and Adolescence, 50*(12), 2374–2393. https://doi.org/10.1007/s10964-021-01519-8

Parris, L., Neves, J. R., & La Salle, T. P. (2018). School climate perceptions of ethnically diverse students: does school diversity matter? *School Psychology International, 39*(6), 625–645. https://doi.org/10.1177/0143034318798419

Patchin, J. W., & Hinduja, S. (2022). Cyberbullying among Asian American youth before and during the COVID-19 pandemic. *Journal of School Health, 93*(1), 82–87. https://doi.org/10.1111/josh.13249

Peguero, A. A. (2009). Victimizing the children of immigrants: Latino and Asian American student victimization. *Youth & Society, 41*(2), 186–208. https://doi.org/10.1177/0044118X09333646

Peterson, W. (1966). Success story, Japanese American style. *New York Times Magazine*, 20–21.

Poon, O., Squire, D., Kodama, C., Byrd, A., Chan, J., Manzano, L., ... Bishundat, D. (2016). A critical review of the model minority myth in selected literature on Asian Americans and Pacific Islanders in higher education. *Review of Educational Research, 86*(2), 469–502. https://doi.org/10.3102/0034654315612205

Qin, D. B., Way, N., & Rana, M. (2008). The "model minority" and their discontent: examining peer discrimination and harassment of Chinese American immigrant youth. *New Directions for Child and Adolescent Development, 121*, 27–42. https://doi.org/10.1002/cd.225

Robers, S., Zhang, J., & Truman, J. (2010). Indicators of school crime and safety: 2010 (NCES 2011-002/NCJ 230812). National Center for Education Statistics, U.S. Department of Education, and Bureau of Justice Statistics, U.S. Department of Justice.

Rogers, K., Jakes, L., & Swanson, A. (2020). Trump defends using the 'Chinese virus' label, ignoring growing criticism. *The New York Times*. https://www.nytimes.com/2020/03/18/us/politics/china-virus.html

Rossen, E., & Cowan, K. C. (2012). A framework for schoolwide bullying prevention and safety [Brief]. National Association of School Psychologists.

Ruiz, N. G., Edwards, K., & Lopez, M. H. (2021). One-third of Asian Americans fear threats, physical attacks and most say violence against them is rising. Pew Research Center. https://www.pewresearch.org/short-reads/2021/04/21/one-third-of-asian-americans-fear-threats-physical-attacks-and-most-say-violence-against-them-is-rising/

Ruiz, N. G., Noe-Bustamante, L., & Shah, S. (2023). Diverse cultures and shared experiences shape Asian American identities. Pew Research Center. https://www.pewresearch.org/race-and-ethnicity/2023/05/08/diverse-cultures-and-shared-experiences-shape-asian-american-identities/

Ryan, A., Graves, S., Jr., Sobalvarro, A., Nichols, K., Schutte, K., Aston, C., & Griffin, A. (2016). An evaluation of Strong Kids in an urban African American female sample: the need for gender-specific and culturally focused interventions. *School Psychology Forum*, *10*(2), 157–164.

Salmivalli, C. (2018). Peer victimization and adjustment in young adulthood: commentary on the special section. *Journal of Abnormal Child Psychology*, *46*(1), 67–72. https://doi.org/10.1007/s10802-017-0372-8

Seipp, J. W., Sun, P. L., & Wang, C. W. (2025). Impact of discrimination and school climate on Asian American youth mental health [Paper presentation]. *American Psychological Association Annual Convention*, Denver, CO.

Sen, B. (2004). Adolescent propensity for depressed mood and help seeking: race and gender differences. *Journal of Mental Health Policy and Economics*, *7*, 133–145.

Shea, M., Wang, C., Shi, W., Gonzalez, V., & Espelage, D. (2016). Parents and teachers' perspectives on school bullying among elementary school-aged Asian and Latino immigrant children. *Asian American Journal of Psychology*, *7*(2), 83–96. https://doi.org/10.1037/aap0000042

Shin, J. Y., D'Antonio, E., Son, H., Kim, S. A., & Park, Y. (2011). Bullying and discrimination experiences among Korean American adolescents. *Journal of Adolescence*, *34*(5), 873–883. https://doi.org/10.1016/j.adolescence.2011.01.004

Shin, T. S., Hwang, H., Park, J., Teng, J. X., & Dang, T. (2019). *Digital Kids Asia-Pacific: Insights into Children's Digital Citizenship*. UNESCO Office Bangkok and Regional Bureau for Education in Asia and the Pacific.

Sklad, M., Diekstra, R., De Rieter, M., Ben, J., & Gravesteijn, C. (2012). Effectiveness of school-based universal social, emotional, and behavioral programs: do they enhance students' development in the area of skill, behavior, and adjustment? *Psychology in the Schools*, *49*(9), 892–909. https://doi.org/10.1002/pits.21641

Smetana, J. G., Villalobos, M., Tasopoulos-Chan, M., Gettman, D. C., & Campione-Barr, N. (2009). Early and middle adolescents' disclosure to parents about activities in different domains. *Journal of Adolescence*, *32*(3), 693–713. https://doi.org/10.1016/j.adolescence.2008.06.010

Smith, P. K. (2010). Bullying in primary and secondary schools: psychological and organizational comparisons. In R. Shute, & P. Slee (Eds.), *School Bullying and Mental Health: Risks, Intervention and Prevention* (pp. 11–27). Routledge.

The Asian American Foundation. (2024). *Asian American perspectives: NYC safety study*. https://www.taaf.org/projects/asian-american-perspectives-nyc-safety-study

Stop AAPI Hate. (2020). Stop AAPI hate youth campaign report. https://stopaapihate.org/wp-content/uploads/2021/04/Stop-AAPI-Hate-Report-Youth-Incidents-200917.pdf

Sue, D. W., Calle, C. Z., Mendez, N., Alsaidi, S., & Glaeser, E. (2020). *Micro Intervention Strategies: What You Can Do to Disarm and Dismantle Individual and Systemic Racism and Bias*. Wiley.

Sue, D. W., Capodilupo, C. M., Torino, G. C., Bucceri, J. M., Holder, A. M. B., Nadal, K. L., & Esquilin, M. (2007). Racial microaggressions in everyday life: implications for clinical practice. *American Psychologist*, *62*(4), 271–286. https://doi.org/10.1037/0003-066X.62.4.271

Sue, S., Sue, D. W., Sue, L., & Takeuchi, D. T. (1995). Psychopathology among Asian Americans: a model minority? *Cultural Diversity and Mental Health*, *1*(1), 39–51. https://doi.org/10.1037/1099-9809.1.1.39

Sugai, G., & Horner, R. H. (2020). Sustaining and scaling positive behavioral interventions and supports: implementation drivers, outcomes, and considerations. *Exceptional Children*, *86*(2), 120–136. https://doi.org/10.1177/0014402919855331

Sullivan, J. N., Eberhardt, J. L., & Roberts, S. O. (2021). Conversations about race in Black and White US families: before and after George Floyd's death. *Proceedings of the National Academy of Sciences, 118*(38), e2106366118. https://doi.org/10.1073/pnas.2106366118

Suzuki, B. H. (2002). Revisiting the model minority stereotype: implications for student affairs practice and higher education. *New Directions for Student Services, 97*, 21–32. https://doi.org/10.1002/ss.35

Tormala, T. T., Ivan, I. I., Floyd, R., & Beckum, L. C. (2015). The connection between bullying and suicide in ethnic minority populations. In P. Goldblum, D. L. Espelage, J. Chu, & B. Bongar (Eds.), *Youth Suicide and Bullying: Challenges and Strategies for Prevention and Intervention* (pp. 93–102). Oxford University Press.

Ttofi, M. M., Farrington, D. P., Lösel, F., & Loeber, R. (2011). Do the victims of school bullies tend to become depressed later in life? A systematic review and meta analysis of longitudinal studies. *Journal of Aggression, Conflict and Peace Research, 3*(2), 63–73.

Vlachou, M., Andreou, E., Botsoglou, K., & Didaskalou, E. (2011). Bully/victim problems among preschool children: a review of current research evidence. *Educational Psychology Review, 23*(3), 329–358. https://doi.org/10.1007/s10648-011-9153-z

Waasdorp, T. E., Bradshaw, C. P., & Duong, J. (2011). The link between parents' perceptions of the school and their responses to school bullying: variation by child characteristics and the forms of victimization. *Journal of Educational Psychology, 103*(2), 324–335. https://doi.org/10.1037/a0022748

Wang, C., Barlis, J., Do, K. A., Chen, J., & Alami, S. (2020). Barriers to mental health help-seeking at school for Asian- and Latino-American adolescents. *School Mental Health, 12*, 182–194. https://doi.org/10.1007/s12310-019-09344-y

Wang, C., Couch, L., Rodriguez, G. R., & Lee, C. (2015). The bullying literature project: using children's literature to promote prosocial behavior and social-emotional outcomes among elementary school students. *Contemporary School Psychology, 19*, 320–329. https://doi.org/10.1007/s40688-015-0064-8

Wang, C., Havewala, M., Bali, D., Hui, J., Stancofski, R. M., & Patel, A. (2026). Parent and youth interventions for Chinese American families to address COVID-19 related discrimination and promote youth mental health. *School Psychology Review, 5*(2), 224-240. https://doi.org/10.1080/2372966X.2024.2441648

Wang, C., Hui, J., Sun, P., & Patel, A. (2025). Evaluating parent-child connect: a culturally responsive parent training program for Chinese American parents with adolescents. *School Psychology Review*. https://doi.org/10.1080/2372966X.2025.2592297.

Wang, C., Liu, J., Havewala, M., Zhu, Q., Do, K. A., & Shao, X. (2021). Parent-Child connect: a culturally responsive parent training for Asian American parents at school. *Psychology in the Schools, 58*(8), 1624–1641. https://doi.org/10.1002/pits.22520

Wang, C., Yao, J., Patel, A., & Li, B. (2023). Can school climate or peer preference moderate the adjustment difficulties associated with peer victimization among Chinese middle school students? *School Psychology International, 44*(1), 5–22. https://doi.org/10.1177/01430343221108345

Whitcomb, S. A., & Parisi Damico, D. M. (2016). *Merrell's Strong Start—Grades K–2: A Social and Emotional Learning Curriculum* (Second Edition). Brookes Publishing.

Worrell, F. C., & Hale, R. L. (2001). The relationship of hope in the future and perceived school climate to school completion. *School Psychology Quarterly, 16*(4), 370–388. https://doi.org/10.1521/scpq.16.4.370.19896

Yang, C. (2024). Influences of pre-pandemic bullying victimization and COVID-19 peer discrimination on Chinese American adolescents' mental health during the COVID-19 pandemic. *School Psychology, 39*(1), 20–30. https://doi.org/10.1037/spq0000554

Yang, C., Chen, C., Lin, X., & Chan, M.-K. (2021). School-wide social emotional learning and cyberbullying victimization among middle and high school students: moderating role of school climate. *School Psychology*, *36*(2), 75–85. https://doi.org/10.1037/spq0000423

Yang, C., & Golshirazi, M. (2023). Association between school victimization and substance use among Hispanic/Latinx adolescents: An intersectionality analysis of social–emotional learning (SEL) competencies, immigration status, and gender in predominantly Hispanic/Latinx high schools. *School Psychology Review*, *52*(5), 552–564. https://doi.org/10.1080/2372966X.2022.2158368

Yeager, D. S., Fong, C. J., Lee, H. Y., & Espelage, D. L. (2015). Declines in efficacy of anti-bullying programs among older adolescents: theory and a three-level meta-analysis. *Journal of Applied Developmental Psychology*, *37*(1), 36–51. https://doi.org/10.1016/j.appdev.2014.11.005

Yeh, C. J., Liao, H. Y., Ma, P. W. W., Shea, M., Okubo, Y., Kim, A. B., & Atkins, M. S. (2014). Ecological risk and protective factors of depressive and anxiety symptoms among low-income, Chinese immigrant youth. *Asian American Journal of Psychology*, *5*(3), 190–199. https://doi.org/10.1037/a0035027

Yip, T., Cheah, C. S. L., Kiang, L., & Hall, G. C. N. (2021). Rendered invisible: are Asian Americans a model or a marginalized minority? *American Psychologist*, *76*(4), 575–581. https://doi.org/10.1037/amp0000857

Zhou, Q., Tao, A., Chen, S. H., Main, A., Lee, E., Ly, J., & Li, X. (2012). Asset and protective factors for Asian American children's mental health adjustment. *Child Development Perspectives*, *6*, 312–319. https://doi.org/10.1111/j.1750-8606.2012.00251.x

7

Guidance for Culturally Infused Suicide Prevention in Asian American and Pacific Islander Youth Communities

Fatima Z. Hussain[1], Rainer Schmitz[2], Richard T. Liu[3,4], and Joyce Chu[1]

[1]*Palo Alto University, Palo Alto, CA, USA*
[2]*Dwight Schools, New York, NY, USA*
[3]*Massachusetts General Hospital, Boston, MA, USA*
[4]*Harvard Medical School, Boston, Massachusetts, USA*

Suicide rates among Asian American and Pacific Islander (AAPI) youth have risen over the past decade, underscoring the need for traditional suicide prevention efforts to better address the cultural needs of AAPI communities. In 2021, suicide was the leading cause of death for Asian American and Pacific Islander (AAPI) youth in the United States, with rates doubling from 1999 to 2021 (from 3.6 to 7.1 deaths per 100,000) (Reyes et al., 2024). This concerning increase in suicide rates highlights the need to better serve AAPI youth and tailor suicide prevention efforts to unique stressors that may contribute to increased suicide rates in this population (The Asian American Foundation, 2024; Reyes et al., 2024; Wyatt et al., 2015). This chapter presents the Cultural Theory and Model of Suicide for Youth as a theoretical and evidence-based framework to guide the cultural infusion of suicide prevention efforts for AAPI youth with the goal of providing a practical guide to help clinicians, school leaders, community organizations, community members, suicide prevention programs, and other stakeholders understand the challenges that AAPI youth face, to inform how suicide prevention efforts can be tailored to their needs. It illustrates how the model's core constructs—Minority Stress, Idioms of Suicidal Distress, Social Discord, Cultural Sanctions, and culturally informed help-seeking preferences and behaviors—can be used as a foundation for both upstream prevention programming and downstream clinical management. Case examples for a county suicide prevention program and a clinical setting are discussed to demonstrate how cultural theory and scientific principles can be translated into application. Together, this chapter provides guidance for the transformation of upstream and downstream suicide prevention efforts to better meet the needs of AAPI youth.

Suicide Among AAPI Youth

A recent study by Reyes et al. (2024) analyzed data from the CDC and found that 4,747 AAPI youth between ages 5 and 24 died by suicide from 1999 through 2021. The data also indicated that rates of suicide deaths among AAPI youth have been increasing since 2014, doubling from 1999 to 2021.

Analysis of these suicide deaths suggests that the most common methods of death were suffocation, firearms, and poisoning (Reyes et al., 2024). Concerningly, the 2023 Youth Risk Behavior Survey, a nationally representative study of risky behaviors in youth, found past-year prevalence of 16.0% for suicidal ideation, 13.4% for suicide plans, and 8.9% for suicide attempts among Asian American adolescents (CDC, 2024). Researchers have theorized that suicide rates among Asian Americans may be related to racialized stress (e.g., bullying, hate crimes, xenophobia), increased gun ownership among AAPI households, and increased societal pressure on youth to achieve because of the model minority myth (Bui & Lau, 2024).

Suicide death rates and the prevalence of suicidal ideation also vary between AAPI subgroups. Researchers have recently noted that combining data for all AAPI ethnic groups hides disparities in death rates. For example, Bui and colleagues (2024) analyzed AAPI youth suicides from 2018 to 2021 between five AAPI ethnic subgroups: Vietnamese, Chinese, Korean, Filipinos, Indian, and an "Other" category which included Bangladeshi, Bhutanese, Burmese, Cambodians, Hmong, Indonesian, Japanese, Laotian, Malaysian, Mongolian, Nepalese, Pakistani, Sri Lankan, Taiwanese and Thai youth (Bui et al., 2024). For youth in the 15 to 19 age group, Bui and colleagues' study found that the "Other" category had the highest suicide rate (13.37 per 100,000), followed by Vietnamese American youth (10.57 per 100,000), and with Asian Indian American youth having the lowest suicide death rate (6.91 per 100,000). When examining the 20 to 24 age group, Vietnamese Americans had the highest suicide rate (17.66 per 100,000), followed by the "Other" category (16.79 per 100,000), and Chinese Americans had the lowest suicide rates (9.24 per 100,000). It is important to note that while overall AAPI youth tend to have lower suicide rates than other ethnicities, Vietnamese Americans between ages 20 and 24 had a similar suicide rate to non-Asian American individuals (18.32 per 100,000). Aggregation of AAPI data may lead public health officials and clinicians to underestimate suicide risk among Asian subethnic group populations.

Another recent study looked at data between 2017 and 2018 from California's Healthy Kids Survey and disaggregated the category of AAPI youth to determine frequency of suicidal ideation among specific AAPI ethnic subgroups (Lui et al., 2024). This study found that multiethnic youth reported the highest rates of suicidal ideation (27.3%), pointing to the need for more disaggregated data on different multiethnic subgroups of Asian youth. Lui et al. (2024) also identified that among monoethnic AAPI youth, Filipino American youth had the highest (21.8%) and Asian Indian American youth the lowest frequencies of suicidal ideation (13.6%). Together, this research points to potentially high elevations in suicidal thoughts or behaviors for Vietnamese American, Filipino American, and multiethnic youth. However, further research is needed to further investigate AAPI subethnic disparities in larger samples.

Models of Culturally Responsive Suicide Prevention

Recent scholars have called attention to existing gaps in suicide prevention programs and interventions along the upstream (i.e., efforts to prevent suicide within the community) and downstream (i.e., suicide management within clinical care systems) levels of the crisis continuum (Cwik et al., 2016; Wong et al., 2014). Traditional approaches to suicide prevention have neglected cultural considerations in suicide prevention and management, asking standard suicide questions and implementing safety plans and interventions for suicide without cultural adaptation, or accounting for suicide risk and resilience factors without inclusion of culturally specific factors that may be more salient for cultural minority youth. Recent trends in suicide rates showcase these issues, with suicide rates among minority youth increasing at higher rates than their White counterparts (Keum et al., 2024; Ramchand et al., 2021).

In response, researchers have created several frameworks of culturally responsive suicide prevention, such as the Racial Cultural Framework for Suicide (Wong et al., 2014) and the Structural Racism and Suicide Prevention Systems Framework (Alvarez et al., 2022), to better address the needs of cultural minority groups. Wong and colleague's (2014) Racial Cultural Framework for Suicide focuses on a cultural approach as an important alternative to traditional, individualistic models of suicide by emphasizing how racial identity, cultural values, historical oppression, discrimination, and cultural norms about help-seeking influence suicidal thoughts and behaviors for racial and ethnic minorities. Alvarez and colleagues' (2022) Structural Racism and Suicide Prevention Systems Framework expands the cultural lens of Wong et al.'s work to a systems lens, recognizing to the need to address social determinants of health and the systemic structural racism within policies and organizations that create suicide-related disparities.

The Cultural Theory and Model of Suicide

One particular model—the Cultural Theory and Model of Suicide (Chu et al., 2010)—encompasses the individual and systemic level factors of previous frameworks and expands its applicability beyond race and ethnicity to multiple intersecting identities (i.e., the intersection of LGBTQ+, age, ethnic minority identities, and others). As such, the cultural factors and core concepts of the Cultural Theory and Model of Suicide allow for flexible application with multiple intersecting identities in suicide prevention efforts with diverse communities. This chapter will focus on guidance provided by the Cultural Theory and Model of Suicide (Chu et al., 2010), to demonstrate how key cultural considerations can be infused in both downstream clinical suicide practice and upstream suicide prevention programming, specifically for AAPI youth.

The Cultural Theory and Model of Suicide was created by qualitative coding of 20 years of empirical research on culturally specific suicide risk factors. Chu and colleagues (2010) found that four factors account for 95% of existing culturally specific risk data, forming the acronym of "MISC": Minority Stress, Idioms of Suicidal Distress, Social Discord, and Cultural Sanctions (defined in Table 7.1). Further research by Yang et al. (2018) expanded the Cultural Theory and Model of Suicide by adding cultural considerations in help-seeking as an important cultural factor in suicide. Altogether, the four "MISC" cultural factors influence one's experience and expression of suicidality through four main concepts:

1. Culture affects the types of stressors (i.e., Minority Stress and Social Discord) that lead to suicide.
2. Cultural meanings associated with stressors and suicide (i.e., Cultural Sanctions) affect the development of suicidal tendencies, one's threshold of tolerance for psychological pain, and subsequent suicidal acts.
3. Culture affects how suicidal thoughts, intent, plans, and attempts are expressed (i.e., Idioms of Suicidal Distress).
4. Cultural considerations in the help-seeking process and cultural barriers in service systems can exacerbate suicide risk and impact one's ability to connect with resources, referrals, and services.

Figure 7.1 displays this model, with asterisks (*) denoting youth-specific factors. The main "MISC" and help-seeking factors of the Cultural Theory and Model of Suicide are described below.

Table 7.1 Definition of the four factors of the cultural theory and model of suicide, with youth- and AAPI-specific considerations and examples.

Cultural Theory and Model of Suicide Factor ("MISC")	Youth-specific consideration	Description and AAPI youth example
Minority Stress	• Peer rejection, victimization, or bullying	Stressors experienced due to one's cultural identity(ies) • *Example*: An AAPI youth experiences bullying related to having an accent while speaking
Idioms of Distress	N/A	Cultural variations in one's experience and expression of suicidal thoughts, feelings, or behaviors • *Example:* An AAPI youth states they are tired and nauseous instead of depressed and anxious
Social Discord	• Peer rejection, victimization, or bullying • Family rejection • Intergenerational Cultural Conflict	Conflict with or detachment from family, friends, or community • *Example:* An LGBTQ+ identifying AAPI youth's parents forbid them from dating a same-sex partner
Cultural Sanctions	• Expectations, pressure, and/or meanings associated with academic stress	The acceptability or meaning associated with life events or suicide in one's culture • *Example:* An AAPI youth is extremely stressed after receiving a B in a class. • *Example:* An AAPI youth believes suicide is a way to relieve their family of the burden of caring for them.

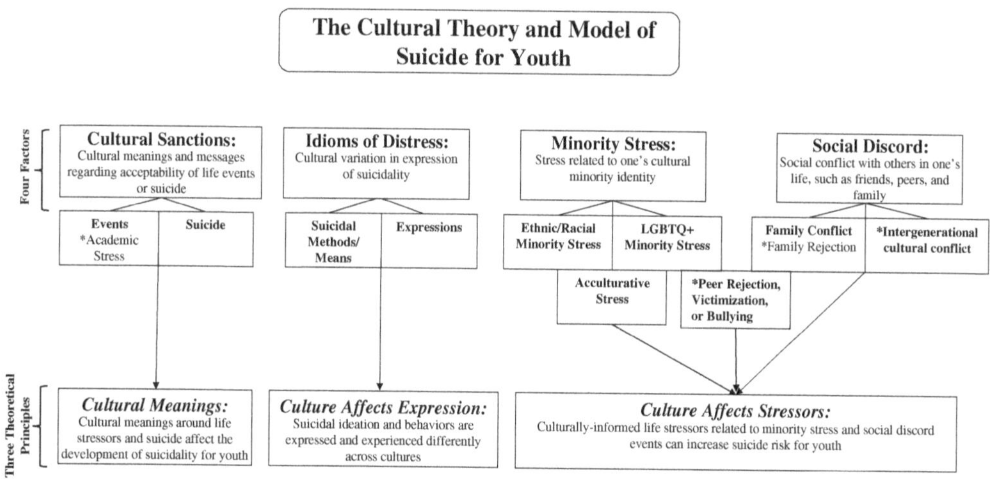

Figure 7.1 The cultural theory and model of suicide for youth. *Note:* *Considerations that are particularly salient for youth. *Source:* Chu et al. (2022)/Springer Nature/CC BY 4.0.

Minority Stress from the Cultural Theory and Model of Suicide

Minority stress refers to stressors experienced due to one's cultural identity(ies) (Chu et al., 2010). These stresses can affect one's sense of hope, desire to live, belief in a just world, and thus suicide risk. Minority stress may stem from the external environment, such as experiences of discrimination, social inequities, and acculturative stress. For example, a 2024 survey found that 93% of 1,400 AAPI youth participants reported experiencing discrimination because of their race in the past year, including microaggressions (i.e., jokes, asking where one is from, confusing ones ethnicity for another) (The Asian American Foundation, 2024). These minority stress experiences may include peer rejection, victimization, or bullying tied to one's racial identity(ies), such as racial slurs, ridicule based on race/culture, or hate crimes. Acculturative stress, defined as stress related to adapting to and negotiating differences between two cultures, has also been linked to depression and suicide risk in AAPI youth (Gomez et al., 2011; Wyatt et al., 2015). Negative views, beliefs, and experiences toward one's cultural identity(ies) can also become internalized into bias or stigma that may affect one's self-concept or sense of self-worth. Indeed, one study found that Asian values was related to more higher rates of internalized sexual stigma among a sample of Asian American lesbian, gay, bisexual, and questioning individuals (Szymanski & Sung, 2013).

Idioms of Suicidal Distress from the Cultural Theory and Model of Suicide

Cultural Idioms of Suicidal Distress are defined as cultural variations in one's experience and expression of suicidal thoughts, feelings, or behaviors, which often vary depending on cultural context, values, and practices. For example, previous research has found that ethnic minority college students are less likely than White peers to self-disclose suicidal ideation and are more likely to disclose suicidal ideation when asked via face-to-face interview inquiry rather than written survey (Morrison & Downey, 2000). Similarly, ethnic minority youth were more likely than White youth to skip or provide a nonresponse to items about suicidal behavior on the Youth Risk Behavior Survey (Anderson et al., 2015). This phenomenon is referred to as "hidden suicidal ideation" and defined as concealment or nondisclosure of suicidal distress. One study specific to AAPI individuals with active suicidal ideation found that the majority (60.30%) of participants displayed hidden suicidal ideation, as measured by reporting "I have held back telling people about wanting to kill myself" or "I have attempted to hide, conceal, or lie about wanting to commit suicide" on the Beck Scale for Suicide Ideation (Chu et al., 2018). This nondisclosure of suicidal ideation was associated with greater experience of cultural risk factors and higher severity of suicidal distress compared to individuals without hidden suicidal ideation.

Suicidal distress may also present in different forms based on presence of stigma about suicide and cultural practices that value different methods of coping (e.g., emphasis on emotional self-control rather than expression) (e.g., Tsai et al., 2002). Indeed, researchers have also found that some AAPI individuals find it more acceptable to report physical symptoms than emotional symptoms (Chen 2005; Yeung et al., 2004), verbalizing "I have been feeling tired and nauseous," rather than "I have been depressed and anxious." Additional research is needed to identify other emotional, cognitive, behavioral, or physical ways in which AAPI youth express their suicidal distress.

Social Discord from the Cultural Theory and Model of Suicide

Social Discord refers to conflict with or detachment from family, friends, or community, which can be more strongly related to suicide risk in collectivistic communities such as AAPI youth. For example, research has shown that perceived burdensomeness and family conflict are predictors of suicide risk among AAPI youth (Lau et al., 2002; Walker et al., 2025). Additionally, intergenerational cultural conflict, defined as differences in acculturation levels and values between parents and youth, can be a salient risk factor for AAPI youth. Research suggests intergenerational cultural conflict plays a higher role in suicidal behavior for AAPI youth than White youth (Lau et al., 2002).

Cultural Sanctions from the Cultural Theory and Model of Suicide

Cultural Sanctions are defined as the acceptability or meaning associated with life events or suicide in one's culture (Chu et al., 2010). When life events are considered unacceptable, met with negative judgment, or are shameful, suicide risk can increase. For AAPI youth, academic stress may be magnified by cultural sanctions and heightened cultural expectations around academic achievement, along with intense feelings of shame related to failure (Wong et al., 2011). A recent study by the Asian American Foundation (2024) found that 43% of AAPI youth participants reported that pressure to excel in school, extracurriculars, and work has a "very" or "extremely" negative impact on their mental health.

Similarly, when suicide itself is considered a sanctioned or acceptable option, suicide risk may increase, whereas cultural or religious beliefs about suicide as unacceptable or a sin may be associated with decreased suicide risk. For example, research has suggested that some AAPI youth may view suicide as an acceptable way of dealing with a problem that could bring shame to their family (Thapa et al., 2015).

Cultural Considerations in Help-seeking from the Cultural Theory and Model of Suicide

Cultural considerations in help-seeking refer to cultural differences, barriers, and preferences at multiple points of the help-seeking process from perceived need for help, to the decision to seek help, to one's preference for help sources (Chu et al., 2011; Yang et al., 2018). One study found that Asian Americans with a history of suicide attempts had lower perceived need for help and lower help-seeking behaviors compared to their Latine counterparts (Chu et al., 2011). These disparities exist within a larger context of research that has consistently found AAPI communities to have some of the lowest rates of mental health utilization in the United States (Lu et al., 2024; Sue et al., 2012). AAPI youth with intersectional identities also experience low rates of service connection; about 50% of AAPI LGBTQ+ identifying youth wanted mental health services but did not receive them (Nath et al., 2022).

The Cultural Theory and Model of Suicide states that barriers like insufficient access to culturally and linguistically responsive services and higher stigma/lower willingness to express distress and/or seek help, can exacerbate one's level of suicide risk (Yang et al., 2018). Indeed, among AAPI individuals, low rates of service utilization may be due to barriers such as insufficient availability of language-matched services, lack of health insurance, perceived discrimination, and stigma toward mental health (Cho & Velez-Ortiz, 2014). Clearly, it will be important to account for cultural considerations in help-seeking to provide culturally infused suicide prevention services.

Altogether, the framework of the Cultural Theory and Model of Suicide offers guidance on how culture impacts suicidality and provides evidence-based cultural factors and concepts that can guide the infusion of cultural considerations into suicide prevention for AAPI youth. The remaining portions of this chapter provide specific examples and recommendations on how to incorporate the Cultural Theory and Model of Suicide factors into upstream and downstream suicide prevention efforts for AAPI youth.

Case Study 1: Upstream Suicide Prevention Programming

Culturally Infused Upstream Suicide Prevention Programming for AAPI Youth, Guided by the Cultural Theory and Model of Suicide

The following hypothetical county suicide prevention case description is provided to illustrate use of the Cultural Theory and Model of Suicide framework to culturally infuse upstream suicide prevention efforts.

Sunridge County is a medium-sized county with a population of 300,000. The population has grown dramatically over the last few decades due to an influx of immigration from Asian countries and the Pacific Islands. In response to several recent high-profile youth suicides in the area, county public health officials commissioned a report to investigate youth mental health concerns in the area. Several findings of the report indicated that AAPI youth are underserved by existing suicide prevention program efforts.

The report found that there has been a 60% increase in the number of AAPI youth deaths by suicide from 2014 to 2024. Despite AAPI youth making up 25% of the youth in the area, only 7% AAPI youth utilize mental health services. Based on survey data from several high schools in the county, about 45% of AAPI youth reported experiencing at least one instance of discrimination. Almost 35% of AAPI youth report experiencing conflict with their families at home.

Current youth suicide prevention programs in the county include monthly community helper trainings, school-based mental health services, and a youth-focused social media campaign that points to 988 as a resource. Community helper trainings teach nonmental health professionals (including teachers, parents, principals, and community members at the local public libraries) to identify and intervene when someone is at risk for suicide. The school-based mental health services include staffing each school with at least one mental health counselor, and teachers are encouraged to refer students with suicidal thoughts to the counselors. The school counselors are also responsible for holding mental health promotion events at schools and giving monthly psychoeducational presentations to the students. The suicide prevention youth-focused social media campaign has been running for the last two years; the campaign content was created by a graphic designer contracted by the behavioral health department to mirror many of the well-known warning signs for suicide from national suicide prevention resources and websites. Currently, there is no mention of cultural differences or stressors for different populations in any of the materials for the training, psychoeducational presentations, or social media campaign.

Exercise. You have been recently hired to lead the youth suicide prevention task force for the county. Brainstorm how the four factors of the Cultural Theory and Model of Suicide (Minority Stress, Idioms of Suicidal Distress, Social Discord, and Cultural Sanctions) and AAPI-specific considerations for help-seeking can be addressed in this county. Sample responses are described in detail below.

Minority Stress with Cultural Sanctions for Upstream Efforts. The high frequencies of discrimination experiences point to the salience of minority stress among AAPI youth in this county. Minority stress (i.e., "feeling treated differently because of your cultural identities") should be listed as a warning sign of suicide in media campaigns and counselors' educational sessions. Community helper trainings should be culturally infused to have minority stress integrated throughout their curriculum as a culturally specific warning sign for suicide, alongside emphasis on how Cultural Sanctions and meaning surrounding Minority Stress can exacerbate suicide risk. The school counselors can also organize events to increase cultural awareness and discourage bullying and discrimination at schools. Schools can organize peer ally and support programs to empower youth to speak out against bullying and discourage discrimination. Social media content can also include posts about the negative impacts of discrimination and resources for support. Social media outreach should be grounded in culturally congruent imagery, posted on AAPI holidays, and built around AAPI specific minority and social discord stressors.

Idioms of Distress for Upstream Efforts. It will be important to note the juxtaposition between growing rates of suicide and low rates of mental health service utilization; this pattern highlights the potential importance of looking out for hidden suicidal ideation. The county should ensure that the community helper programs they offer are culturally infused evidence-based trainings that highlight culturally specific idioms of distress in their education about warning signs, and train community members to ask about suicide in alternative ways that may identify Cultural Idioms of Suicidal Distress. These culturally infused community helper trainings can be extended to local volunteers for the 988 hotline and teachers, to ensure that such community leaders are able to detect cultural idioms of suicidal distress and ask about suicide in culturally responsive ways. Additionally, research can be conducted to identify differences in methods of suicide attempts among AAPI youth, including AAPI LGBTQ+ identifying youth, to tailor any means safety efforts to methods commonly utilized by AAPI youth communities.

Social Discord with Cultural Sanctions for Upstream Efforts. Data from this county suggests that AAPI youth may be experiencing social discord in the form of family conflict, which can increase risk for suicide. Community helper trainings can include family conflict as a culturally specific warning sign for suicide, and work with families on ways to communicate and work through difficult situations. These trainings should address Cultural Sanctions and meaning around family conflict that can bring shame and exacerbate suicide risk. School counselors can promote healthy family support at home by holding community events for parents and/or their children that educate about common intergenerational points of conflict and ways to navigate such differing expectations and communication styles. Social media messaging can also cover topics related to culturally congruent communication and conflict resolution approaches for AAPI families, grounded in culturally congruent images and dissemination.

Cultural Considerations for Help-seeking in Upstream Efforts. Suicide prevention programs should adopt a culturally infused lens when connecting AAPI youth to resources and professional services, engaging all relevant stakeholders for service connection such as community helpers, 988 volunteers, school staff and counselors, mobile crisis, and behavioral

(Continued)

Case Study 1: Upstream Suicide Prevention Programming (Continued)

health providers. All stakeholders should assess the availability of Asian language services at each step of the help-seeking pathway, and advocate for resources accordingly. Stakeholders engaged in service connection efforts should all be trained on how to discuss highly stigmatized topics, answer questions about privacy and safety, and ways to approach interactions in a culturally responsive manner; goals of these efforts would be to ensure that AAPI youth and families encounter culturally congruent services whenever they make the difficult decision to reach out for support. Family, psychoeducation and outreach efforts can similarly focus on culturally responsive messaging to ensure a smooth transition to service connection when needed.

Recommendations for Upstream Prevention

- **Incorporate Understanding About AAPI Youths' Culturally Informed Suicide-related Experience in All Upstream Efforts**. Ensure that all upstream programs and stakeholders look for culturally influenced signs (i.e., Cultural Idioms of Distress) that AAPI youth are struggling. This can include changes in behavior, mood, social interactions, and school performance. Encourage stakeholders to provide emotional support even if suicidal thoughts have not been explicitly stated. Be aware that the model minority myth and cultural norms around emotional self-control and hidden suicidal ideation may cause AAPI youth to appear "fine" until they suddenly are not.
- **Public Data Monitoring of Disparities, and Incorporation of Cultural Sanctions to Identify Community Risk**. At a public health level, data monitoring and surveillance should build AAPI ethnic subgroup analysis of suicidal thoughts and behaviors into their standard annual analytic reports to identify disparities. These data efforts should also analyze any available community survey data that attends to cultural meanings, to identify time periods and specific communities where AAPI youth might be at risk. For example, spikes in xenophobic rhetoric in the media may increase minority stress and by extension suicide risk among AAPI youth. Time periods related to college acceptances and rejections should be targeted for community messaging efforts that counter messages of shame surrounding college acceptance results. Once risk is identified, outreach and support should incorporate culturally relevant imagery, values, ideas, and skills.
- **Culturally Infused Community Helper Trainings**. Provide culturally infused evidence-based community helper trainings that include education about all of the "MISC" factors and cultural considerations for help-seeking. Recognize that the AAPI community may know less about how to refer a distressed loved one to resources. Prepare community helpers for the possibility that recognizing distress, perceiving the need for help, and initiating action for help may take longer or may need more persistent messaging and outreach for the AAPI community. Collaborate with faith or other cultural community leaders to increase awareness about mental health and suicide.
- **Culturally Infused Social Media Campaigns**. Public awareness campaigns should build community strength and awareness around minority stressors such as anti-Asian hate (e.g., Stop AAPI Hate, n.d.). These efforts can include outreach programs that are antibullying in nature and build community around cultural identity. Use inclusive media messaging that includes images, values, stressors, and signs of distress that are specific to AAPI youth.

- **Culturally Tailored School Programming**. Collaborate with school staff and counselors to provide culturally tailored support to AAPI youth and their families. Consider community building and psychoeducation events that educate parents and families about effective ways to communicate across intergenerational divides. Work with school staff to initiate programming that counters bullying of AAPI youth and builds peer allies and support that build social resilience rather than facilitate peer victimization. See Chapter 6 for further information about bullying among AAPI youth.
- **Trainings and Resources for Service Connection Stakeholders**. Ensure that service connection stakeholders (community helpers, 988 volunteers, school staff, crisis workers) are trained to recognize Cultural Idioms of Distress for AAPI youth and use culturally congruent ways to ask about suicide. Support these stakeholders in learning how to decrease stigma and answer AAPI families' questions and concerns about suicide prevention resources and professional services.
- **Building AAPI Community Resilience and LGBTQ+ Safe Spaces**. Reach out to communities to build community resilience as a protective factor. Collaborate with community leaders, such as faith leaders, to increase awareness about suicide and other distress. Build safe and affirming spaces for LGBTQ+ identifying AAPI youth.

Case Study 2: A Downstream Clinical Case

Culturally Infused Downstream Suicide Prevention Clinical Practice for AAPI Youth, Guided by the Cultural Theory and Model of Suicide

This section provides a hypothetical case vignette to illustrate how the cultural factors of the Cultural Theory and Model of Suicide can inform downstream individualized clinical care.

"Mira" (she/her) identifies a 14-year-old Indian American bisexual girl who presented to outpatient therapy following a recent suicide attempt that led to an inpatient psychiatric hospitalization. Two weeks ago, while her father and stepmother were driving her home from school, Mira jumped out of the car. Concerned that she was injured, her parents called 911 for medical assistance. When emergency medical services (EMS) arrived, Mira disclosed that she no longer wanted to live, prompting EMS to initiate hospitalization.

Hospital records indicate that upon admission, Mira initially claimed her stepmother had pushed her out of the moving car and expressed reluctance to return home. However, after several days in the hospital, she acknowledged that the incident was a suicide attempt and reported ongoing conflict at home. Before discharge, a family conference call was held with Mira's father, stepmother, and the unit social worker to coordinate discharge planning and aftercare. Following this discussion, Mira agreed to return home.

During her therapy intake assessment, Mira described persistent feelings of sadness, hopelessness about the future, and frequent irritability. She also reported ongoing fatigue, nausea, and headaches, which often followed arguments with her parents. She identified several stressors at home and school that were contributing to her distress.

(Continued)

Case Study 2: A Downstream Clinical Case (Continued)

Mira shared that her biological mother passed away several years ago and that her father had recently remarried. She was struggling to adjust to her father's new marriage and her relationship with her stepmother. Recently, she had frequent verbal arguments with her father and admitted to disliking her stepmother. She also reported that her father occasionally hit her during arguments when she was disobedient, which made her angry, though she considered it "normal" in her culture.

Mira and her parents frequently clashed over various issues. Her father, who held conservative values, expected her to dress modestly, while Mira wanted to wear clothing similar to her classmates. Fitting in was important to her, as she had been bullied in middle school for her more conservative attire and cultural food, with some students even directing racial slurs at her. Both her middle and high schools had predominantly White students and teachers, making her experiences of cultural difference more pronounced.

Another source of conflict was her father's emphasis on academics. Mira, a B-average student, felt she was doing her best, but her father believed she could achieve higher grades if she put in more effort and spent less time on her phone.

In addition, Mira was hiding her relationship with her girlfriend. They had been dating for a year, but she kept it a secret because her father often expressed negative views about same-sex relationships, calling them unnatural—an opinion echoed by others in their community. Despite these challenges, Mira found significant emotional support in her girlfriend, often turning to her after arguments with her parents to help calm down. However, before her suicide attempt, she had been unable to reach out to her girlfriend because her parents had taken away her phone as punishment for what they considered a disrespectful tone during an argument.

Despite the ongoing conflicts, Mira expressed love for her father and a desire to improve their relationship. Prior to her suicide attempt, she had told him she was feeling sad and stressed but concealed her suicidal thoughts and nonsuicidal self-injury (scratches and cuts on her arms). Her father, distrustful of doctors and believing that family matters should be handled privately, initially refused to seek professional help for her. However, after her suicide attempt and conversations with the hospital social worker, he agreed to bring her to therapy.

Exercise. Imagine you are Mira's therapist. How do the cultural factors of the Cultural Theory and Model of Suicide—Minority Stress, Idioms of Distress, Social Discord, and Cultural Sanctions, along with cultural considerations for help-seeking—impact your suicide-specific case conceptualization for Mira? How can you use your knowledge of these factors to improve her suicide-related screening, assessment, and management clinical care? Sample responses are provided below.

Culturally Infused Suicide-specific Case Conceptualization for Mira

Minority Stress. Mira experiences Minority Stress related to both her Indian American identity and her bisexuality. At school, she has been bullied for her cultural food and clothing, which has contributed to feelings of exclusion and suicidal distress. Her past experiences of being ridiculed for her clothing choices have also led to conflict at home; her efforts to change her wardrobe to avoid further bullying created increased tension with her father, who expects her to dress more conservatively. Additionally, Mira faces minority stress related to her sexual identity, as she fears her father's disapproval of her bisexuality and feels compelled to keep her relationship hidden.

Idioms of Distress. Mira reports numerous somatic complaints, including feeling constantly tired and having nausea and headaches after conflict with her parents. These experiences of distress in physical form are consistent with research showing that AAPI individuals may experience psychological distress in the form of somatic symptoms, as a more acceptable and less stigmatized expression of pain (Grover & Ghosh, 2014). Also consistent with literature suggesting that AAPI individuals may underreport their suicidal thoughts ("hidden ideation"), particularly in the midst of experiencing cultural stress like Minority Stress (Chu et al., 2018), Mira chose not to disclose her suicidal thoughts directly before her recent suicide attempt.

Social Discord. Mira is experiencing social discord in her home and school environments. She has frequent arguments with her parents and experiences intergenerational conflict related to acculturation stress, especially differing opinions about appropriate clothing and different expectations about grades. Mira has also experienced peer rejection and bullying in the past which continues to impact her as she fears being bullied again.

Cultural Sanctions. Mira experiences heightened suicidal distress because of cultural sanctions, expectations, or meanings related to her academic performance and sexual identity. She faces significant pressure from her father to achieve higher grades, as academic excellence is highly valued in her cultural background, where a "B" is perceived as inadequate. Additionally, her bisexual identity is not supported by her family or community. Mira is acutely aware of the negative messages surrounding same-sex relationships, which she frequently hears from her father and others in her cultural environment, reinforcing feelings of unacceptability and hopelessness.

Cultural Preferences for Help-seeking. Mira's mental health journey is influenced by her cultural preferences regarding help-seeking. Although she expressed her depressive feelings to her father, she did not receive professional support. His initial reluctance to seek mental health services was influenced by a cultural mistrust of providers, a sentiment often found in ethnic minority communities (Cheng & Mallinckrodt, 2015). Additionally, he prefers to manage family conflicts privately, which may stem from cultural beliefs about how families should function.

Culturally Infused Suicide Care: Clinical Implications for Mira

The above cultural considerations impact each component of Mira's suicide care, from service connection to screening, assessment, safety planning, crisis response, and treatment.

Culturally Infused Screening. First, screening would be affected by cultural considerations of the Cultural Theory and Model of Suicide's Idioms of Suicidal Distress factor. When screening for suicide risk, her therapist should be flexible in their conceptualization of what Mira's suicidal distress may look like as her suicidal thoughts build from mild to severe. It will be important to recognize that Mira may choose not to disclose suicidal thoughts, particularly in earlier stages of distress or to certain individuals, e.g., family members. As such, her suicidal distress may not show up on standard, traditional screeners like the Columbia Suicide Severity Rating Scale (C-SSRS; Posner et al., 2011). Additionally, when asking questions about suicidal thoughts and behaviors, her therapist may consider being flexible in her wording choice to fit cultural conceptualizations of suicide and worldviews. For example, other-oriented questions

(Continued)

Case Study 2: A Downstream Clinical Case (Continued)

from the Cultural Assessment of Risk for Suicide for Adolescents measure (Khoury, 2018) such as "Recent conflict with my family or friends makes me think that they are better off without me" may help to initially identify Mira's level of suicidal distress without triggering concerns about stigma or rehospitalization. Once trust is built, the clinician could follow-up this other-oriented question with more direct questions about suicide. Additionally, her more readily reported signs of irritability and somatic distress (fatigue, nausea, and headaches) may be considered as potential early signs of suicidal distress that are more acceptable for her to report and allow for the potential opportunity to intervene with her suicidal distress earlier on before she considers a suicide attempt.

Culturally Infused Assessment. Comprehensive assessment would be affected by considerations of the Cultural Theory and Model of Suicide's Minority Stress, Social Discord, and Cultural Sanctions factors. include Mira's experiences of minority stress (from both the peer experiences of bullying about her race and ethnicity, as well as her family's messages that bisexuality is unacceptable) and family intergenerational conflict as risk factors that increase her suicide risk level. These risk factors would be both magnified as more concerning with regards to increased risk level, by cultural meanings surrounding her academic performance and sexual identity.

Culturally Infused Safety Planning. Culturally infused safety planning for Mira would require integration of all help-seeking preference and "MISC" factors of her Cultural Theory and Model of Suicide-informed suicide case conceptualization. For example, Mira's safety plan may include her cultural Idioms of Distress of irritability and somatic complaints, and Social Discord factors of family arguments and peer bullying as warning signs or triggers of her suicidal distress. The therapist can work with Mira to identify coping skills that she is comfortable using, given the sensitive nature of to whom, where, and how she is able to talk about some of her minority and social stressors.

People whom she can turn to for distraction and support should be carefully chosen, including how she can access those supports during a time of crisis. For example, the therapist may want to facilitate collaboration with her parents to ensure they support Mira in using her safety plan, including providing access to alternative technology or creating alternative disciplinary actions to taking her phone, so that she is able to reach out to her preferred supports (i.e., her girlfriend) during times of heightened suicidal risk. In addition, it would be prudent to assess Mira's recent experiences with hospitalization for difficult or traumatic experiences that would affect her willingness to disclose suicidal distress in the future or affect her willingness to engage with crisis services. When integrating calling or texting 988 as a resource, a similar conversation about the fit of 988 with her help-seeking preferences would help to ensure that the safety plan is feasible and usable for Mira. Finally, the therapist would need to think flexibly and creatively about how to involve her family in restricting any access to lethal means, given their history of family conflict.

Culturally Infused Treatment. Mira's treatment plan would be affected by all help-seeking and "MISC" factors of her culturally infused suicide-specific case conceptualization. For example, Mira's Minority Stressors and Social Discord (family arguments) may be "prompting events" in a suicidal behavior chain analysis, exacerbated by the Cultural Sanctions of disapproval by her family and peers, and followed by her self-injurious behaviors and Idioms of Distress of fatigue, nausea, headaches, and irritability. Hopelessness and thoughts of despair about her family situation may follow, and without intervention at these earlier points of her suicidal behavior chain analysis, Mira may quickly escalate to a suicide attempt (i.e., jumping out of a moving car). This culturally infused understanding of Mira's case could help the therapist to identify specific skills to intervene and stop this cascade of events, specific to her MISC and help-seeking preference factors.

Recommendations for Culturally Infused Downstream Suicide Care

- **Account for Minority Stress as a Risk Consideration, and the Opposite of Minority Stress (i.e., Identity Pride) as a Resilience Consideration**. Incorporate minority stress into your comprehensive assessment, safety planning and treatment as both a risk factor (i.e., identity based bullying, acculturative stress) and a protective factor (i.e., ethnic pride, or resilience built up from conquering minority stressors in life).
- **Be Flexible in Looking for Alternative Signs or Idioms of Suicidal Distress**. When screening for suicide, account for cultural Idioms of Suicidal Distress by practicing flexibility in noticing signs of suicidal distress that may not show up traditional reports of explicit suicidal thoughts. Examples may include shame, somatic symptoms, anger or irritability, reckless behavior, fatigue, functioning difficulties (e.g., having a hard time at school or not wanting to go to school), and others. Recognize that traditional screeners may not capture these culturally influenced and/or alternative Idioms of Suicidal Distress.
- **Look for Underreporting or Hidden Suicidal Ideation**. Look for signs that your AAPI youth and family clients may not be comfortable disclosing suicidal thoughts. Examples might include changes in eye contact, pauses or hesitations when answering questions about suicide, difference in tone, or body language that seems tense or nervous. Pay attention to any stigma, cultural mistrust of systems, history of experiencing systemic discrimination, or lower mental health and suicide literacy that may contribute to a reluctance to disclose suicidal distress. Take care not to underestimate risk in these situations, and consider the need for alternative screeners or other ways to detect suicidal distress. Consider normalizing suicidal thoughts as commonplace to counter any stigma families may experience, and explore alternative ways to ask about suicide such as "Do you ever think your family would be better off if you weren't around anymore?" Additionally, it may be helpful to revisit suicidal ideation after you have built additional rapport in case a client may not be ready to disclose yet during an intake.
- **Track Progress and Symptom Progression Using Culturally Tailored Screeners**. Consider utilizing qualitative items from the Culturally Assessment of Risk for Suicide for Adolescents (CARS-A) measure (Khoury, 2018), other measures that fit your client's experience of distress, or your own tailored indicators of distress if needed. Note that though the CARS measure for adults is a psychometrically validated instrument (Chu et al., 2013, 2017), the CARS-A is still undergoing its psychometrically validation process; thus, only individual items can be used qualitatively in a clinical interview or session. Some examples of items in the CARS-A are: "Others treatment me unfairly because of my ethnic/sexual/gender identity" and "Sometimes I feel so tired of life that I don't want to get up/wake up."

(Continued)

Case Study 2: A Downstream Clinical Case (Continued)

- **Incorporate Social Discord (Including Family Conflict) as a Risk Consideration, and Its Opposite of Social Support as a Resilience Consideration**. Incorporate social discord (as a cultural risk factor) and social support (as a protective or resilience factor) into your comprehensive assessment, safety planning, and treatment. Examples may include looking out for intergenerational conflicts around differing expectations, involving family in culturally responsive systems-based treatments, including family as reasons for living, and involving family as appropriate in safety efforts.
- **Cultural Sanctions: Assess for Culturally Meaningful or Unacceptable Stressors and Experiences.** Ask about the cultural script and meanings related to the stressors someone is experiencing (i.e., Does failing mean shaming the whole family?). Pay particular attention to any stressors that may trigger experiences of shame.
- **Cultural Sanctions: Ask About the Meaning of Suicide for the Client**. Ascertain whether suicide is an acceptable versus unacceptable option, or whether it would be associated with shame, a sin, or other consequences (e.g., Will suicide make them more popular posthumously? Will it relieve any burden or shame experienced by their family? Is suicide considered a sin?). Be sure to incorporate this information into your clinical risk assessment and treatment planning.
- **Culturally Infused Case Conceptualization**. Integrate an analysis of cultural help-seeking considerations and "MISC" Cultural Theory and Model of Suicide factors into your culturally infused suicide-specific case conceptualization. Doing so will prepare you for culturally infused screening, assessment, safety planning, crisis response, and treatment planning.
- **Culturally Responsive Approach to Initial Engagement**. Provide thorough initial psychoeducation with your client and stay informed about issues that are relevant for AAPI youth to develop rapport and prevent dropout. Think carefully about what is needed in initial phases of treatment to engender trust and comfort (i.e., addressing concerns about privacy, extra time on psychoeducation, creating a safe space to discuss identities between the therapist and client, creating a therapeutic space and relationship that fits your client's expectations, or others).
- **Thinking Carefully About the Role of Family in Treatment**. It will be important to understand family's preferences for care and conceptualizations of illness when trying to involve families who may be reluctant to have their youth seek help. Think carefully about enhancing or creating appropriate boundaries around involvement of families in treatment based on family dynamics (and any Social Discord). Assess whether the family is a facilitator of suicide recovery, or a trigger for increased risk, and approach family collaboration accordingly. Discuss the best way to navigate complex family situations in crisis situations. It may be important to provide psychoeducation for the family to mitigate potential shame around suicide or mental health, or related stressors. It may be helpful to discuss in advance, preferred options for involvement of adults and how family will be involved in emergencies (be clear about limits of confidentiality).

Summary

AAPI youth suicides have been increasing for the last decade, and there is a need for traditional suicide prevention practices to pay increased attention and dedicate resources to addressing cultural needs specific to AAPI communities. AAPI youth live with unique challenges that can lead to suicidal thoughts and behaviors, including xenophobic rhetoric, discrimination, acculturative stress, and high academic expectations. These stressors may be compounded for AAPI youth with multiple intersecting minoritized identities, such as AAPI youth who also identify as LGBTQ+. Addressing culturally influenced suicide risk requires a culturally infused suicide prevention approach. The Cultural Model and Theory of Suicide provides a framework of four factors that are essential to addressing AAPI youth suicide: cultural sanctions, idioms of distress, minority stress, and social discord. Culturally informed help-seeking preferences and behaviors are also a key factor that must be integrated into suicide prevention practices. This chapter translated theory and research findings into practical recommendations for addressing each of these factors to foster culturally infused suicide prevention practices and programs, upstream and downstream.

References

Alvarez, K., Polanco-Roman, L., Duarte, C. S., & Cha, C. B. (2022). Structural racism and suicide prevention for ethnoracially minoritized youth: a conceptual framework and illustration across systems. *American Journal of Psychiatry*, *179*(6), 408–417. https://doi.org/10.1176/appi.ajp.21101001

Anderson, L. M., Lowry, L. S., & Wuensch, K. L. (2015). Racial differences in adolescents' answering questions about suicide. *Death Studies*, *39*, 600–604. http://dx.doi.org/10.1080/07481187.2015.1047058

The Asian American Foundation. (2024). Beyond the surface: understanding mental health among Asian American, Native Hawaiian, and Pacific Islander youth. https://www.taaf.org/youthmentalhealth

Bui, A. L., & Lau, A. S. (2024). Suicide rates among Asian American and Pacific Islander youths—a cause for alarm. *JAMA Network Open*, *7*(7), e2422694. https://doi.org/10.1001/jamanetworkopen.2024.22694

Bui, A. L., Rhew, I. C., Rivara, F. P., & Coker, T. R. (2024). Disaggregated suicide mortality rates among Asian American youths and young adults by ethnic subgroup. *JAMA Pediatrics*, *178*(10), 1076–1078. https://doi.org/10.1001/jamapediatrics.2024.2686

Centers for Disease Control and Prevention. (2024). Youth Risk Behavior Survey data summary & trends report: 2013–2023. U.S. Department of Health and Human Services.

Chen, H. J. (2005). Mental illness and principal physical diagnoses among Asian American and Pacific Islander users of emergency services. *Issues in Mental Health Nursing*, *26*(10), 1061–1079. https://doi.org/10.1080/01612840500280729

Cheng, H. L., & Mallinckrodt, B. (2015). Racial microaggressions, cultural mistrust, and mental health outcomes among Asian American college students. *Journal of Counseling Psychology*, *62*(3), 363–370. https://doi.org/10.1037/cou0000084

Cho, H., Kim, I., & Velez-Ortiz, D. (2014). Factors associated with mental health service use among Latino and Asian Americans. *Community Mental Health Journal*, *50*, 960–967. https://doi.org/10.1007/s10597-014-9719-6

Chu, J., Goldblum, P., Floyd, R., & Bongar, B. (2010). The cultural theory and model of suicide. *Cognitive and Behavioral Practice*, *17*(2), 236–254. https://doi.org/10.1016/j.cbpra.2009.11.001

Chu, J., Hoeflein, B., Goldblum, P., Espelage, D., Davis, J., & Bongar, B. (2017). A shortened screener version of the Cultural Assessment of Risk for Suicide. *Archives of Suicide Research*, *22*(4), 679–687.

Chu, J., Lin, M., Akutsu, P., Joshi, S., & Yang, L. (2018). Hidden suicidal ideation or intent among Asian American Pacific Islanders: a cultural phenomenon associated with greater suicide severity. *Asian American Journal of Psychology*, *9*(4), 262–269. https://doi.org/10.1037/aap0000134

Chu, J., O'Neill, S. E., Ng, J. F., & Khoury, O. (2022). The cultural theory and model of suicide for youth. In J. P. Ackerman, & L. M. Horowitz (Eds.), *Youth Suicide Prevention and Intervention* (pp. 159–174). Springer. https://doi.org/10.1007/978-3-031-06127-1_11

Chu, J. P., Floyd, R., Diep, H., Pardo, S., Goldblum, P., & Bongar, B. (2013). A tool for the culturally competent assessment of suicide: the Cultural Assessment of Risk for Suicide (CARS) measure. *Psychological Assessment*, *25*(2), 424–434.

Chu, J. P., Hsieh, K., & Tokars, D. (2011). Help-seeking tendencies in Asian Americans with suicidal ideation and attempts. *Asian American Journal of Psychology*, *2*(1), 25–38.

Cwik, M. F., Tingey, L., Wilkinson, R., Goklish, N., Larzelere-Hinton, F., & Barlow, A. (2016). Suicide prevention gatekeeper training: can they advance prevention in Indian country? *Archives of Suicide Research*, *20*(3), 402–411. https://doi.org/10.1080/13811118.2015.1033122

Gomez, J., Miranda, R., & Polanco, L. (2011). Acculturative stress, perceived discrimination, and vulnerability to suicide attempts among emerging adults. *Journal of Youth and Adolescence*, *40*(11), 1465–1476. https://doi.org/10.1007/s10964-011-9688-9

Grover, S., & Ghosh, A. (2014). Somatic symptom and related disorders in Asians and Asian Americans. *Asian Journal of Psychiatry*, *7*, 77–79.

Keum, B. T., Oh, S., & Sheftall, A. H. (2024). National trends in suicide among Asian American or Pacific Islander youth. *JAMA Network Open*, *7*(7), e2422744. https://doi.org/10.1001/jamanetworkopen.2024.22744

Khoury, O. (2018). Adaptation of the Cultural Assessment of Risk for Suicide measure for adolescents. [Doctoral Dissertation, Palo Alto University]. ProQuest Dissertations and Theses Global.

Lau, A. S., Jernewall, N. M., Zane, N., & Myers, H. F. (2002). Correlates of suicidal behaviors among Asian American outpatient youths. *Cultural Diversity & Ethnic Minority Psychology*, *8*(3), 199–213. https://doi.org/10.1037/1099-9809.8.3.199

Lu, F. Q., Flores, M. W., Carson, N. J., Le, T., & Cook, B. L. (2024). Trends and disparities in mental health use among Asian American sub-groups, 2013-2019. *Journal of Racial and Ethnic Health Disparities*. https://doi.org/10.1007/s40615-024-02177-9

Lui, C. K., Ye, Y., Gee, J., Subica, A. M., Chung, P. J., & Takeuchi, D. T. (2024). Unmasking suicidal ideation for Asian American, Native Hawaiian, and Pacific Islander youths via data disaggregation. *JAMA Network Open*, *7*(11), e2446832. https://doi.org/10.1001/jamanetworkopen.2024.46832

Morrison, L. L., & Downey, D. L. (2000). Racial differences in self-disclosure of suicidal ideation and reasons for living: implications for training. *Cultural Diversity and Ethnic Minority Psychology*, *6*(4), 374–386. https://doi.org/10.1037/1099-9809.6.4.374

Nath, R., Price, M., DeChants, J. P., Hobaica, S., & Clark, C. M. (2022). The mental health and well-being of Asian American and Pacific Islander (AAPI) LGBTQ youth. The Trevor Project.

Posner, K., Brown, G. K., Stanley, B., Brent, D. A., Yershova, K. V., Oquendo, M. A., ... Mann, J. J. (2011). The Columbia–suicide severity rating scale: initial validity and internal consistency findings from three multisite studies with adolescents and adults. *American Journal of Psychiatry*, *168*(12), 1266–1277. https://doi.org/10.1176/appi.ajp.2011.10111704

Ramchand, R., Gordon, J. A., & Pearson, J. L. (2021). Trends in suicide rates by race and ethnicity in the United States. *JAMA Network Open*, *4*(5), e2111563. https://doi.org/10.1001/jamanetworkopen.2021.11563

Reyes, M. P., Song, I., & Bhatt, A. (2024). Breaking the silence: an epidemiological report on Asian American and Pacific Islander youth mental health and suicide (1999-2021). *Child and Adolescent Mental Health*, *29*(2), 136–144. https://doi.org/10.1111/camh.12708

Stop AAPI Hate. (n.d.). Stop AAPI hate. https://stopaapihate.org/

Sue, S., Cheng, J. K. Y., Saad, C., & Chu, J. P. (2012). Asian American mental health: a call to action. *American Psychologist*, *67*(7), 532–544.

Szymanski, D. M., & Sung, M. R. (2013). Asian cultural values, internalized heterosexism, and sexual orientation disclosure among Asian American sexual minority persons. *Journal of LGBT Issues in Counseling*, *7*(3), 257–273.

Thapa, P., Sung, Y., Klingbeil, D. A., Lee, C. Y., & Klimes-Dougan, B. (2015). Attitudes and perceptions of suicide and suicide prevention messages for Asian Americans. *Behavioral Sciences (Basel, Switzerland)*, *5*(4), 547–564. https://doi.org/10.3390/bs5040547

Tsai, J. L., Chentsova-Dutton, Y., Freire-Bebeau, L., & Przymus, D. E. (2002). Emotional expression and physiology in European Americans and Hmong Americans. *Emotion*, *2*, 380–397. http://dx.doi.org/10.1037/1528-3542.2.4.380

Walker, R. L., Odafe, M. O., Hong, J. H., Jewell, R. D., & Gonzalez, I. M. (2025). Burdensomeness, acculturative stress, and suicide ideation among second-generation Asian American and Latinx university students. *American Journal of Orthopsychiatry*, *95*(2), 199–211. https://doi.org/10.1037/ort0000779

Wong, Y. J., Brownson, C., & Schwing, A. E. (2011). Risk and protective factors associated with Asian American students' suicidal ideation: a multicampus, national study. *Journal of College Student Development*, *52*(4), 396–408.

Wong, Y. J., Maffini, C. S., & Shin, M. (2014). The racial-cultural framework: a framework for addressing suicide-related outcomes in communities of color. *The Counseling Psychologist*, *42*(1), 13–54. https://doi.org/10.1177/0011000012470568

Wyatt, L. C., Ung, T., Park, R., Kwon, S. C., & Trinh-Shevrin, C. (2015). Risk factors of suicide and depression among Asian American, Native Hawaiian, and Pacific Islander youth: a systematic literature review. *Journal of Health Care for the Poor and Underserved*, *26*(2 Suppl), 191–237. https://doi.org/10.1353/hpu.2015.0059

Yang, L. H., Lam, J., Vega, E., Martinez, M., Botcheva, L., Hong, J. E., Chu, J., & Lewis, S. E. (2018). Understanding the impact of community on the experience of suicide within the Lao community: an expansion of the cultural model of suicide. *Asian American Journal of Psychology*, *9*(4), 284–295. https://doi.org/10.1037/aap0000131

Yeung, A., Chang, D., Gresham, R. L., Jr., Nierenberg, A. A., & Fava, M. (2004). Illness beliefs of depressed Chinese American patients in primary care. *The Journal of Nervous and Mental Disease*, *192*(4), 324–327. https://doi.org/10.1097/01.nmd.0000120892.96624.00

8

Autism and Neurodiversity in AAPI Youth: Assessment and Treatment Considerations

Janie J. Hong[1] and Surina Bothra[2]

[1]*Stanford University School of Medicine and Redwood Center for CBT and Research, Stanford, CA, USA*
[2]*PAU-Stanford PsyD Consortium Palo Alto, CA, USA*

Clinical Case Study[1]

Both Lily and Minh immigrated to California from Vietnam in their early 20s. They met in their early 30s through a dating app and connected over similar paths to immigration and the challenges they experienced adjusting to the new cultural context. Once married, they spent years trying to start a family. After multiple failed rounds of fertility treatments, they finally gave birth to a healthy baby girl, Tina. As Tina grew into her toddler years, her pediatrician expressed concerns about Tina's limited language and interest in communicating with others. Tina's parents dismissed the concern as a function of growing up in a primarily Vietnamese-speaking home, and referenced how "smart Tina was" because of her fascination with numbers. At age 4, for example, her favorite toy was a calculator; she would spend hours daily reciting the numbers and predicting the calculations she produced.

When Tina entered kindergarten, she remained shy and showed little interest in participating in most group activities. She learned to read at an early age and spent most of her time away from the class activities, reading books or writing out math equations. Her struggle with school expectations grew as she moved through the grammar school grades. For example, in first grade, she refused to create the crafts led by the teacher or, in second grade, ran out of the classroom if asked to read aloud to the class or, in fourth grade, cried when asked to engage in group projects. She avoided participating in school performances or sports and stayed home on days she knew there were school-wide assemblies. Socially, Tina rarely made eye contact with others, looked at the ground when she spoke, and spoke softly with minimal intonation. Tina, however, did well academically, which led to minimal effort by the teachers or parents to shift Tina's behavior to engage more with her peers or in class. She was just seen as "terribly shy."

---

1 *Case is based on a composite picture of cases, with identifying information included in the vignette portions of the chapter.*

At home, Tina enjoyed spending time in her room rearranging her collection of rocks by size and color and playing the same math games over and over again. She would, on occasion, become emotional when something or someone interrupted her from arranging her rocks or if there was a sudden change in plans. She also became highly dysregulated in loud and/or crowded environments, so she frequently stayed in the car with Minh or Lily while the other parent completed errands. She also could not wear socks with seams or clothes until all tags had been removed. Tina's parents recognized that their daughter had sensitivities, but saw that, overall, she was a healthy, well-developing child. They, themselves, preferred solitary activities, so Tina's social withdrawal at home and school did not concern them.

Fifth grade proved to be a turning point. She transitioned to middle school and found herself managing different social pressures and dynamics. Rather than being ignored, her peers began to tease and impersonate her by exaggerating her difficulties with eye contact and speaking. They assumed her minimal speech came from not knowing the English language. They taunted her with nonsense "Ching Chong Ching" sounds to mimic "Chinese," then would say she should learn to speak English. As the year continued, Tina stopped speaking completely at school, which frustrated the teachers when they asked for a response. It was only when she began hiding in the bathroom instead of eating her lunch and failing her exams did her parents and teachers finally meet to discuss a plan.

In the meeting, Tina's teachers, principal, and school counselor shared their concerns, underscoring Tina's social difficulties and withdrawal. They recommended that Tina meet with her pediatrician and seek a referral for an autism assessment. Her parents felt confused by the recommendation but also deeply worried about a possible illness affecting their daughter's health and ability to engage in school. They dared not tell anyone out of fear of judgment of Tina's mental capabilities and refused to explain to Tina why she was undergoing the assessment. A few months after the initial parent–teacher meeting, Tina received a diagnosis of autism spectrum disorder (ASD) and the diagnosing psychologist recommended a 10-week social skills intervention program.

What Is Autism Spectrum Disorder (ASD)?

When considering clients like Tina, one of the first questions a clinician considers is "what is the best way to understand the problems this person is experiencing?" In the context of mental health, the *Diagnostic and Statistical Manual of Mental Disorders* (5th ed.; DSM–5; American Psychiatric Association, 2013) is often used to answer this question. The DSM-5 outlines a set of criteria by which a provider can diagnose a set of problems as a psychiatric disorder. Widely-used, this rubric offers a way to organize behaviors and patient-reported experiences as identifiable symptoms of a disorder and quickly communicate the areas of interference and likely treatment needs of the patient. For Tina, her difficulties and differences map well with the DSM-5 criteria for autism spectrum disorder (ASD).

According to the DSM-5, ASD is diagnosed when individuals show symptoms of both persistent deficits in social communication and interaction across multiple contexts and restricted (Criterion A), repetitive patterns of behavior, interests or activities (Criterion B). These symptoms must be present in the early developmental period (Criterion C), cause clinically significant impairment in social, occupational, or other important areas of current functioning (Criterion D), and cannot be better explained by intellectual developmental disorder or global developmental delay (Criterion E) (APA, 2013). Table 8.1 shows the diagnostic requirements of both Criterion A and Criterion B and how they relate to Tina's symptoms. Both Criterion A and Criterion B must be present to be diagnosed.

Table 8.1 The diagnostic requirements of both Criterion A and Criterion B and how they relate to Tina's symptoms.

Criterion A: Persistent deficits in social communication and social interaction across multiple contexts.

Evidence of persistent deficits in all three of the following areas is required for a diagnosis.

	Criteria and DSM-5 provided examples	Tina examples
A1	**Deficits in social-emotional reciprocity**, ranging, for example, from abnormal social approach and failure of normal back-and-forth conversation; to reduced sharing of interests, emotions, or affect; to failure to initiate or respond to social interactions	• Does not initiate conversation with others, including parents • Does not respond to teachers when asked questions or engage in class activities • Does not respond to peers questioning of language capabilities
A2	**Deficits in nonverbal communicative behaviors used for social interaction**, ranging, for example, from poorly integrated verbal and nonverbal communication; to abnormalities in eye contact and body language or deficits in understanding and use of gestures; to a total lack of facial expressions and nonverbal communication	• Poor eye contact • Look at ground when speaking • Limited variation in speech volume and tone
A3	**Deficits in developing, maintaining, and understanding relationships**, ranging, for example, from difficulties adjusting behavior to suit various social contexts; to difficulties in sharing imaginative play or in making friends; to absence of interest in peers	• No friends • Minimal interest in friendships or social play

Criterion B: Restricted, repetitive patterns of behavior, interests, or activities.

Evidence of symptoms in at least two of the following categories is required for a diagnosis.

	Criteria and DSM-5 provided examples	Tina examples
B1	**Stereotyped or repetitive motor movements**, use of objects, or speech (e.g., simple motor stereotypes, lining up toys or flipping objects, echolalia, idiosyncratic phrases).	• Repetitive arranging of rocks • Repetitive play of same math computer game
B2	**Insistence on sameness, inflexible adherence to routines, or ritualized patterns of verbal or nonverbal behavior** (e.g., extreme distress at small changes, difficulties with transitions, rigid thinking patterns, greeting rituals, need to take same route or eat same food every day).	• Difficulty with unexpected transitions • Insistence of routine of rearranging rocks
B3	**Highly restricted, fixated interests that are abnormal in intensity or focus** (e.g., strong attachment to or preoccupation with unusual objects, excessively circumscribed or perseverative interests).	• Preoccupation with calculator • Writing out math equations
B4	**Hyper- or hyporeactivity to sensory input or unusual interest in sensory aspects of the environment** (e.g., apparent indifference to pain/temperature, adverse response to specific sounds or textures, excessive smelling or touching of objects, visual fascination with lights or movement).	Unusual sensitivity to • Loud sounds and crowds • Sock seams • Clothing tags

Consistent with the medical model, the DSM-5 takes a deficit-centered approach to understanding ASD. The benefit of this approach is it standardizes criteria for the presence or absence of a diagnosis. Such standardization is helpful in many ways. On a practical level, diagnosis helps identify who may be eligible for externally-funded or insurance-based treatments and resources. Consistency in criteria also allows for the study of ASD-related phenomena and interventions, communication among practitioners, and increases the generalizability of findings. As with any disorder, the goal is to treat the symptoms related to the illness or disease either to the point of recovery or, for more chronic conditions, to the point of symptom maintenance and reduced interference. In other words, treat the problem to achieve normal functioning or as close to normal functioning as possible.

The Neurodiversity Framework for Autism

More recently, there has been a call for an alternate model to understand autism-related difficulties; namely, the neurodiversity framework. The main idea behind this framework is that neurodevelopmental differences are seen as a natural part of human biodiversity (Leadbitter et al., 2021), and these differences can contribute positively to society when recognized and valued. Consistent with this model, the social and behavioral profile of autism—although in the minority—is not indicative of disease, much in the same way as being a racial or sexual minority.

Using this frame, normalcy is seen as a social construction of wellness, with treatments focused on curing or treating autistic individuals to meet majority norms. These treatments parallel historical efforts of assimilation, like residential schools for Indigenous children (e.g., Wilk et al., 2017), conversion therapies for sexual minorities (e.g., Drescher, 2002), or efforts to cure children of being left-handed (e.g., Coren, 1993). The difficulties associated with autism are thus better explained by their minority status and poor fit with behavioral norms and expectations that reflect those of the majority (i.e., neurotypical individuals). Any distress or problems with functioning should be treated by helping neurodivergent patients and their caregivers advocate for the accommodation of their differences, while also developing skills to work in systems not designed for them (e.g., code switching), without internalizing their differences as a sign of weakness, illness, or low self-worth.

The neurodiversity framework offers many strengths when treating neurodivergent individuals and extends well to other diversity-related differences like race and ethnicity. First, it can reduce illness-related stigma and allows neurodivergent individuals to see differences from a strength-based lens and as part of their identity. This shift in perspective helps explain the growing preference for identity-first (e.g., autistic person) over person-first (e.g., person with autism spectrum disorder) language for autism, mirroring the way we say, "Asian woman" instead of "woman with Asian heritage."

The rise of social media and online blogs has helped to catalyze and support the neurodiversity movement, partly by connecting autistic individuals with others with shared lived experiences. For example, individuals who learned about autism through digital platforms and support networks not only preferred identity-first language but also reported lower internalized stigma and more accurate knowledge of autism compared those who learned of the diagnosis from professionals or their caregivers (Bury et al., 2024). In another study with autistic Australian adults, Bury and colleagues (2023) asked participants to rank order various descriptors for an autistic individual. When explaining their choices, study participants brought up themes of autism being central to their identity, the importance of acknowledging the spectrum aspect of autism, and wanting to reject medicalized language.

Second, the neurodiversity framework allows clinicians to individualize care to meet the constellation of differences represented by the person's identities. Together with the patient, the clinician can examine the ways the patient's differences may not be meeting social norms and allows for potential unique problems caused by the intersection of different identities. Once named, the clinician and patient can articulate treatment goals and the interventions that will support these goals. This frame allows the clinician to bring in existing evidence-based interventions to support the goals, without pathologizing the person's differences.

Third, the framework shifts responsibility of treatment outcome from being solely on the patient and their response to the interventions. Treatment also emphasizes the system in which the person is and includes advocating for others to change, specifically by increasing others' understanding and accommodation of the patient's differences. Advocacy to shift others' responses to them includes the treating clinician. The clinician must adjust their interventions and therapy process to accommodate patient differences to, in turn, support patient learning.

Finally, unlike disorder-based treatments, where clinicians develop expertise in treating specific, discrete conditions, those who become skilled in understanding and working with diversity-based differences enhance their ability to work with all individuals. This is because traits that are more pronounced in autism and other neurodivergent profiles exist on a continuum. Clinicians who develop expertise in addressing these traits within a neurodivergent context can apply these skills more broadly to others.

Table 8.2 summarizes the differences between the neurodiversity framework and existing disorder-based models of autism.

In this chapter, we cite prevalence rates and research based on the DSM-5 definition of the autism spectrum disorder (ASD) diagnosis and organize intervention recommendations based on ASD diagnostic criteria. The approach to treating ASD-related differences, however, draws from the neurodiversity framework and affirming these differences to support well-being and improve treatment outcomes. As such, when possible, we will use identity-first language when referring to autistic individuals and the term *neurodivergent* when referring to a broader group of minoritized individuals with neurodevelopmental profiles (e.g., autism, Attention Deficit Hyperactivity Disorder (ADHD), dyslexia) that depart from existing norms.

Table 8.2 Key differences in the neurodiversity framework vs. disorder model.

	Neurodiversity framework	Disorder model
Symptoms	• Signs of normal human variation • Named as "differences"	• Signs of underlying illness or pathology • Named as "deficits"
Treatment goal	• Accommodates patient neurodevelopmental differences	• Treats or cure symptoms, with the goal of achieving "normalcy"
Treatment focus	• Includes advocacy and others' understanding and behavior change	• Limited to patient understanding and behavior change
Interventions	• Strengths-based • Adapted to account for individual differences	• Deficit-based • Specific and targeted to the disorder
Outcomes	• Measured by improved quality of life and well-being	• Measured by reduction or elimination of symptoms

Autism Spectrum Disorder and AAPI Youth

While the rates of ASD diagnoses have, in general, increased over time, in Western contexts like the United States and Canada, the increase in ASD diagnoses among Asian American and Pacific Islander (AAPI) children outpaces that of their White peers. In a 2010 birth cohort, ASD prevalence rates among Black, Hispanic, and AAPI (2.23%, 2.25%, and 2.22%, respectively) surpassed those of White children (2.12%). This trend progressed even further in the 2012 cohort, with AAPI children showing the highest rates of ASD (3.34%) compared to Black, Hispanic, and White children (2.93%, 3.16%, and 2.43%, respectively; Gallin et al., 2025). These findings are in contrast with US studies conducted before 2010, which found White children had the highest ASD prevalence rate among the different racial/ethnic groups.

Interestingly, we do not see higher or even comparable rates of ASD diagnoses in Asian countries, with the overall pooled estimate of ASD prevalence in Asia being 0.36%. The prevalence rates do, however, vary greatly by Asian country; for example, ASD rates range from 0.06% in Iran to 2.64% in Korea (Qiu et al., 2020). The discrepancy in ASD prevalence rates among children in Asia compared to those seen among Asian children in the United States is not only striking but also raises questions about potential cultural explanations for this difference (e.g., 0.36% vs. 3.34%).

Differences in ASD awareness, access to diagnostic services, effectiveness in ASD screening, provision of academic or employment accommodations, and cultural stigma around ASD that prevent parents from seeking diagnoses (such as the belief that a child's diagnosis is the result of bad parenting or karma; Kim et al., 2021) may help explain why some Asian countries have lower ASD rates and why Asian children show significantly lower rates than AAPI children. It remains unclear if there are any genetic factors that predispose children with Asian ancestry to ASD or if the higher rates seen in AAPI youth compared to other American youth are better explained by sociocultural factors. Similar questions have come up in relation to racial disparities identified in the diagnosis of ADHD, with some studies finding that Black individuals have a greater risk of ADHD than the general population (Cénat et al., 2021).

Complicating the discussion further, given cultural and language barriers that can prevent parents from seeking ASD assessments for their children, it could be that rates of ASD are even higher in AAPI populations than currently reported. On the other hand, it is also possible that ASD is being overdiagnosed in AAPI populations. It could be that the higher prevalence rate found in the United States is due a cultural bias is assessment that increases the likelihood of pathologizing social communication behaviors that are seen as culturally normative in Asian contexts, where significantly lower rates are found. For example, common symptom ASD assessments screen for an avoidance of eye contact, which is a socially promoted behavior in Asian contexts, and may unfairly characterize Asian children showing this behavior (Pham & Charles, 2023). Play behavior among AAPI children might also be misinterpreted as a sign of ASD; for example, research has found that Korean American children engage in parallel play more often than social or pretend play compared to White children, which is also seen more frequently among children diagnosed with ASD (Pham & Charles, 2023). The cultural differences can interfere with accurate diagnoses when AAPI children are assessed by clinicians who are not aware of them and, thus, more likely to attribute such behaviors to neurodivergence.

Despite AAPI children now having the highest reported rates of ASD in the United States, they are the least likely to utilize *Individuals with Disabilities Education Act* (IDEA) services and are underrepresented in special education programs (Truong et al., 2022; Cooc, 2018). AAPI youth face several potential barriers to effective care that likely contribute to the underutilization of services. Because of cultural stigma or fears of their children being academically disadvantaged or negatively judged by others, parents may be less likely to seek out resources or feel able to talk with others in their community to learn about resources needed to gain a diagnosis (Kim et al., 2021). Language barriers and lack of clinicians available with cultural understanding of AAPI families may also interfere with the assessment process (Zechella & Raval, 2016).

In addition to stigma associated with autism, AAPI families are also known to struggle with stigma associated with seeking mental health services in general (Kim et al., 2021; Yan et al., 2017). Generally, in Asian contexts there is an emphasis on not disclosing emotional difficulties, particularly to those outside of the family, and preventing *face loss*, which is a common value in many East Asian cultures. Seeking outside help from a mental health provider could be seen as risking face loss and exposing difficulties that are meant to be kept private (DeLambo et al., 2011). Also, given the importance of social conformity and meeting external expectations (e.g., academic achievement), it may be particularly difficult to acknowledge the social difficulties or associated mental health concerns that neurodivergent youth experience (Yan et al., 2017). This is particularly compelling given the high prevalence of mental health concerns among neurodivergent youth. For example, a study examining the data of 42,283 caregivers through the National Survey of Children's Health found that 77% of autistic children aged 3–17 years had at least one comorbid mental health condition, and 49% had multiple (Kerns et al., 2020).

AAPI youth may also be motivated to minimize or hide their difficulties from their parents. Children of immigrant parents often feel a pressure to not add to their parents' stress and support the family by not causing disruption or concern. This stems from an acute awareness of the parents' stress navigating a new cultural context while trying to support their family financially. This stress leaves immigrant parents with less time and mental capacity to support their children's more specific emotional needs (Shorey et al., 2020). The pressure to not contribute to parental stress and meet external expectations at the expense of their own well-being can mask the child's difficulties and consequently delay assessment or services.

Stereotypes may also be contributing to service underutilization, where difficulties indicative of autism are seen as characteristic of AAPI groups. Indeed, several other stereotypes associated with AAPI groups, like being social awkward, focused on math or other STEM (i.e., science, technology, engineering and mathematics) topics, or being shy, have also been associated with autistic individuals. The model minority stereotype, which refers to the perception that members of a group have few problems and are generally successful, may also be obscuring problems experienced by AAPI youth. For example, a study of college students found that participants were more likely to attribute positive mental health functioning to Asian American targets when primed with the model minority stereotype (Cheng et al., 2017). This stereotype may create a sense of pressure for AAPI youth to meet expectations associated with it, but it may also lead others to minimize social struggles and see AAPI individuals as doing "fine," particularly when the individual is succeeding in other domains (e.g., academics).

Given the pressures described, it is not surprising that research indicates Asian American parents of neurodivergent youth have high levels of parental stress, and that the level of stress experienced is significantly higher than that of their non-Asian counterparts (Bothra, 2021; Shorey et al., 2020). As an example, DeLambo and colleagues compared Asian American and non-Asian American parents of neurodivergent children and found that while parents from all ethnic backgrounds demonstrated high parental stress levels, Asian American parents showed higher levels of stress in the context of their child's differences. In addition, while parental stress levels seemed to be negatively correlated with child age for the non-Asian parents, with lower stress as the child aged, this trend did not hold for the Asian American parents. The authors explain this difference as a cultural one. While non-Asian parents are more likely to emphasize their child's independence as they age and, therefore, feel less responsible for their behavior, Asian parents are more likely to hold a more interdependent self-view and continue to see their children and the family as an extension of themselves, regardless of their children's age. Additionally, AAPI immigrant parents may feel a greater sense of responsibility to their children due to distance from extended family who remain in their home countries, and feel unable to rely on others to help their children thrive in the new cultural context (Zechella & Raval, 2016).

Treatment Implications

Let's return to the case of Tina. Using her story, we describe an illustrative composite of AAPI client experiences in treatment with a particular focus on ways competing cultural beliefs and values may influence treatment response and can fuel clinician bias. We then use the case example to highlight ways the neurodiversity framework can inform treatment adaptations, guide caregivers and school staff in decision-making, and enhance outcomes. We end with a summary of practical recommendations.

***

When Tina arrived for her first social skills training session with her parents, she was warmly greeted by a team of providers. Tina and her parents were then led to different rooms—one for the youth, another for the parents. Tina's social skills group included seven other autistic youth, a lead psychologist, and multiple other clinicians. Tina was notably the only Asian but matched the other children well in age and other demographics. Similar to all future sessions, the session started with a short social skill lesson (e.g., initiating conversations, asking questions), then moved to practice of the skill with a partner with feedback from the clinicians, and then ended with free play and structured game time, where staff would reinforce prosocial engagement and behaviors.

At the first session, Tina remained quiet looking at the floor, struggling to make eye contact with others. She shied away from engaging with her peers during the free play and game time, choosing to play with objects on her own. When asked to engage with the group, she spoke minimally and would quietly slip away the minute the staff's attention shifted to children who were being disruptive or asking for their attention. In the other room, her parents sat with the other children's parents and were asked to participate in a discussion facilitated by the lead psychologist. The psychologist shared with the group the goal of answering parents' questions about ASD and helping them process feelings about the diagnosis.

Lily and Minh immediately felt out of place. Everyone else, including the psychologist, seemed to understand each other effortlessly and were taken aback by their comments when they tried to join in. For example, questions about the possibility of a full recovery or the likelihood of Tina going to a good college led to silent pauses and halting responses. Their heavy accents further disrupted the flow of conversation, highlighting yet another way they did not seem to belong. Lily and Minh remained, however, committed to helping Tina. They still could not believe she had this illness, and worried greatly for her future and ability to succeed in a context that felt so foreign.

After Tina and her parents' sessions ended, the three of them met separately with a clinician, Joan, to discuss what Tina had learned and ways the parents could support Tina during the week. The parents' questions about Tina's behavior during group surprised Joan; the parents seemed anxious about whether Tina had behaved appropriately and if she had been disruptive, which was quite the opposite of what the team had observed. The parents also asked questions about the likelihood of Tina's ability to re-engage academically in school and, to Joan, seemed overly concerned about academic success.

When planning for the week, the parents sought guidance on how to support Tina's school work and seemed uncomfortable with suggestions of supporting Tina's social life and feelings.

After the families left, the clinical team met to debrief. Several of them voiced their pity and concern for Tina and named the parents' fixation on academic success and seeming lack of concern for Tina's social-emotional needs. One person commented how the parents showed minimal positive emotion or energy when Tina returned from the group, and how this was a stark contrast to the warmth and enthusiasm of the other parents. The other providers nodded in agreement and questioned the parents' commitment to Tina's care and well-being.

Over the 10 weeks, Tina and her parents did not miss a single session and always were one of the first to arrive. They also were the first to leave and never stayed to converse with the other families. Although Lily and Minh felt uncomfortable with others in the parent group, they appreciated the information on ASD and examples of how others with ASD had been able to go to college and create stable lives for themselves. Tina also benefitted from being part of the social skills group. Most importantly, she made a friend—her first friend. Her friend, Anna, also loved rocks and had an enviable collection and wealth of geological knowledge. The parents saw the positive impact of the friendship, particularly in how it helped Tina reengage with school and feel motivated to learn more about rocks. While it was unclear if the treatment itself had helped Tina change, Tina's parents felt grateful that Tina had a friend and they had learned how to communicate with Tina's teachers about Tina, as well as information about services Tina qualified to receive at school and in the community.

***

Cultural Considerations

One notable theme is a cultural barrier to a sense of belonging. Lily and Minh, clearly felt out of place in the parent group; they looked visibly different (e.g., appearance, accent) and their worries did not match those of the other parents. The clinicians also felt the difference and interpreted Lily and Minh's behaviors as signs of noncommitment and lacking warmth (Wang et al., 2026). A second theme is the seeming difference in treatment goals, which can reduce alignment between the parents and the treatment providers. The treatment program in the vignette, for example, emphasized social engagement and interaction, whereas the parents focused more on Tina meeting social expectations (e.g., not misbehave) to ensure academic achievement. The parental pressure to succeed academically may be explained by more than a cultural difference in values. It may also reflect immigrant parents' struggles to orient to a new cultural context and find (familiar) established paths that will ensure their child's survival, safety, and inclusion in the new culture. Families with established generations of cultural knowledge may be seen as having the resources and space to focus on social and emotional well-being, which is a luxury many immigrant families simply do not have.

Finally, a less explicit cultural tension is the one Tina is managing. As a child of immigrant parents, she is navigating several added tensions that others in her social skills group may not be. This includes competing messages of how success is defined and the barriers that come with parents who are not only being nonnative English speakers and unfamiliar with US systems, but also less able to support her with making friends and responding to the bullying (see Chapter 6).

Hall and colleagues (2021) provide a review of how AAPI individuals may differ in their goals for treatment and preferences for care and highlight how AAPI individuals are more likely to emphasize pragmatic goals and favor observable, concrete changes as evidence of therapeutic gains.

This cultural preference is consistent with the more external orientation of Eastern contexts and may explain why immigrant parents or families may be more likely to focus on academic achievement or behavioral compliance (e.g., not be disruptive in a group) than on emotions or other internal experiences.

Another possible reason for the emphasis on achievement markers may be related to the family's immigration history and minority status in a White majority culture. Individuals with minoritized identities, like being of AAPI origin, who migrate to Western contexts like the United States or Canada, are tasked with integrating into the majority culture and, ideally, thriving in it. The focus is one of survival, not self-actualization. There is less room for elaboration of internal thoughts and feelings when the family needs to be fed and earn an income. In this context, it makes sense that immigrant parents like Minh and Lily would be highly concerned with Tina's ability to succeed academically as it is an understood path to security and cultural integration. They are not afforded the same space as White peers who already have a sense of belonging and can consider the emotional inner world of their children.

Shifting the Treatment Frame

By shifting away from a disorder-driven model, we can include neurodiversity-related differences into the case formulation without assuming these differences are signs of illness needing to be treated to normalcy. Consistent with this, we argue that interventions should move from being illness-centered to one focused on patient learning. By focusing on learning, we no longer ask what behaviors need to be changed or eliminated and, instead, consider ways to *add* to the patient's understanding of their problems, and give them *more* ways to manage difficult situations, rather than fixating on the *right* way to manage the situation.

Although rooted in the medical model, we use DSM-5 criteria for ASD as a starting point for translation, and we highlight areas of clinical focus where taking a patient learning approach can improve care.

Limitations of the Psychotherapy Context

According to the DSM-5, all autistic patients demonstrate difficulties listed in the *Social Communication and Interaction Deficits* category (i.e., Criterion A). This category broadly describes difficulties with the expected back and forth in social interactions and with verbal and nonverbal communication. Underlying this is the assumption that such skills are necessary for developing and maintaining relationships. From a neurodiversity focused lens, this category reflects how autistic individuals do not naturally engage with others in the *expected* ways that fit with majority-centered social norms. This does not mean, however, that they do not want to engage socially, nor does it mean they are unable to respond to others in prosocial ways. Instead, it means that autistic individuals instinctively respond to social cues differently and may be less inclined to respond verbally or outwardly express social interest when approached by others.

This also suggests that the social difficulties experienced by autistic individuals may be better explained by a lack of alignment with majority norms, rather than a disease or disorder. Consistent with this, research indicates that autistic individuals are more likely to prefer and feel connected to other autistic individuals than to neurotypical individuals, citing a greater ease and reduced feelings of misunderstanding (e.g., Crompton et al., 2020; Morrison et al., 2020). The lack of alignment felt by autistic individuals with their neurotypical peers is a significant contributing factor to their distress and feeling a need to hide or mask aspects of themselves to conform to social norms.

This difference holds important implications for the context of psychotherapy itself. Psychotherapy is designed to build a strong relationship between the therapist and the patient through both nonverbal and verbal, back and forth communication. Therapists are also trained to observe patients' nonverbal behaviors and encourage the patient to elaborate and verbalize their internal experiences, with an emphasis on guided discovery. It is through this communication process and developed therapeutic relationship that patients can learn a new understanding of themselves and skills to manage their distress. In other words, AAPI-related cultural barriers notwithstanding, being autistic adds another layer of difficulty with treatment engagement, where the very difficulties that are causing distress are present and seen as an interfering factor to the treatment process itself.

Rather than pressuring the patient to meet existing (neurotypical) norms, the clinician must adapt their approach to psychotherapy and adjust their expectations to better meet the needs of their autistic patient. In the same way, speaking louder to someone who does not speak the language, approaching difficulties with verbalizing internal experiences by simplifying your language, or making assumptions that the person is cognitively limited is simply unhelpful and, at times, insulting. The therapist should start with the assumption that the patient does have an awareness of their thoughts and feelings but may have difficulty articulating them verbally. Those who have experience learning a second language will likely identify with the experience of understanding what others are saying and feeling unable to respond accurately or fully because of their limited vocabulary. Many autistic individuals experience a similar feeling of limitation when expressing their thoughts and feelings, particularly when asked to respond immediately as part of a back and forth conversation, or when they feel a verbal pressure to perform in a certain way, or when there are fears of being judged negatively.

The performative difficulties experienced by autistic patients may also resonate with some AAPI patients, as research indicates Asian Americans show more alexithymic tendencies than their White American counterparts (Dere et al., 2012). Alexithymia is characterized by difficulties identifying and describing emotion states, with the following features associated with it (1) a difficulty identifying feelings and distinguishing them from physical sensations of emotional arousal, (2) a difficulty describing emotions to others, (3) a reduced capacity to imagine or engage in fantasy, and (4) externally-oriented thinking (EOT) style that emphasizes concrete stimuli, rather than inner emotions (Taylor, 2000). This difference appears to be tied to Eastern cultural emphases on being externally oriented (a facet of alexithymia) and on context responsivity to guide decision-making (Dere et al., 2012). Given the cultural emphasis on concrete, external cues over internal ones (e.g., thoughts, feelings), many AAPI individuals may experience a parallel mismatch with autistic individuals, finding the expectations of the psychotherapy context difficult to meet.

Mismatches in verbal and emotional expectations are not limited to psychotherapy. They can extend to other structured contexts with expected patterns of performance, including work, school, sports and other social activities. In the context of school, for example, teachers may find a student's lack of participation in class discussions or inappropriate tone when responding as signs of noncompliance or low motivation to succeed. Peer-to-peer interactions can also be difficult as social norms tend to favor neurotypical patterns of engagement and may conflict with Asian cultural communication styles. Misinterpretation of behaviors as signs of illness, disinterest, or character flaws reinforces beliefs that the individual is solely responsible for their struggles and fails to recognize the broader contextual mismatch in assumptions.

Here, we offer clinical strategies that may alleviate the verbal performative pressures of psychotherapy. These strategies might also be useful to educators, school administrators, and others working with autistic individuals. First, therapists ideally are attuned to signs a patient may be struggling to respond to their questions in session. Some examples of this struggle could include frequent responses of "I don't know," or giving short one-word responses, or changing the topic. Common therapist interpretations of these patient responses fall into categories of emotional avoidance or skill deficits in elaborating on their internal experiences. Consequently, therapists will work to help these patients to become more comfortable with verbalizing their internal experiences by repeatedly exposing them to the same types of questioning or work on teaching skills (e.g., identifying emotions, thought monitoring) to help the patient become more competent with answering their questions. Although these strategies, in and of themselves, are not inappropriate for AAPI youth or for autistic individuals, the approach focuses on patient remediation, and the responsibility is wholly on the patient to change so that they can access the benefits of therapy.

When the goal of psychotherapy shifts from remediation to patient learning, the responsibility of change widens to include the *therapist*. The therapist must adapt their approach to meet the unique learning needs and differences of the patient (i.e., the learner), even when it contradicts the typical therapy process. The therapist must also monitor whether the patient's learning supports the patient's well-being and growth and be open to flexibly adapting their approach if the patient is struggling to engage. Concretely, what does this look like?

Problem 1: Difficulty Responding to Direct Questions

If a patient struggles to answer the therapist's questions, it is helpful, unless there is indication otherwise (e.g., cognitive limitations, language barriers), to assume that the patient understands what is being asked but is unclear how to verbally communicate their experiences. One reason a patient may struggle to answer questions is due to what we call the "spotlight effect." When a clinician asks a patient a question, it is like turning the spotlight onto an actor and asking them to perform without access to a script. All eyes are on the patient to respond, quickly and clearly. If someone is autistic or alexithymic, this already puts them at disadvantage, like having no script, and the pressure of a spotlight only worsens this disadvantage.

There are many ways to reduce the spotlight effect for a patient. For example, patients can be asked to answer questions in written form between sessions; this gives them space to reflect and share their thoughts without the time pressure or spotlight of doing so verbally in session. Some patients also find it helpful to use an AI chatbot to help clarify and organize their thoughts, which can also be done outside of session. Variants of this option can include having patients type their answers in the chat of a video session with their camera turned off, or having patients complete a more structured log where the patient documents behaviors that are observable and in concrete ways (e.g., frequency, duration, etc.). Another benefit of asking patients to write their answers is the therapist and patient can place the spotlight on the written work, rather than directly on the patient.

Another way to reduce the spotlight while also gathering information about the patient's internal world is to ask the patient to speak on topics familiar to them or stories that feel clear. In the context of Tina, this may mean having her share her knowledge of rocks and asking for information that is factual and observable. To help reduce the spotlight effect even more, the clinician can ask the patient in advance of the next session that they would like the patient to share on a topic of interest. In session, the clinician can ask the patient to share on a topic of interest and allow them to lead the story without interruption. Of note, autistic individuals are less likely to seek a back and forth in conversation and when verbally sharing information, it can be more helpful to allow them to talk for an extended period. Clinician efforts to show interest by asking questions or expressing shared understanding can sometimes be received as disruptive to the discussion. This preference may reflect the flow states that autistic individuals are able to access when engaging in their areas of interest and can be seen as a strength that many neurodivergent individuals hold.

With the data on hand, the therapist can describe patterns they notice and their understanding of why the patient may be experiencing problems, and then ask the patient if the ideas resonate. The therapist is, in essence, taking on the verbal burden, while ensuring the patient agrees with what's shared. Patients can further benefit from the therapist modeling and providing of language for their difficulties, which patients can then use with others.

Problem 2: Difficulty Meeting Expected Social Norms

When a patient, particularly when they are holding one (or more) minoritized identities, is experiencing distress, a helpful starting point for the therapist is to identify what changes they feel the patient must make to feel better. The therapist can then reflect on whether the identified changes are based on underlying (Western) majority-based norms about what good mental health (and pathways to it) look like. This type of reflection allows the therapist to consider whether the distress a patient is experiencing is less due to skill deficits and more due to the identities they hold. For example, consider a patient who becomes upset (i.e., crying, yelling) about a last-minute change in plans that a parent makes, the therapist might assume the patient needs to increase flexibility and be more open to unexpected changes. While this may make sense from neurotypical perspective, autistic individuals characteristically show difficulties with psychological flexibility and may feel further pathologized for this difference. Given this, it could be that for the autistic individual increasing use of distress tolerance and sensory soothing skills when triggered is a more helpful approach than trying to increase flexibility.

Once a therapist has identified areas where existing majority norms (like the ones described previously in this chapter) may be a poor fit for the AAPI and neurodivergent aspects of a patient's identity, the therapist can reduce the distress associated with their differences by naming (1) the cultural norms and expectations that are a poor fit for the patient and (2) ways to advocate for others to acknowledge their differences and work with them on accommodating these differences. Websites like *Job Accommodation Network* (https://askjan.org) have a wealth of resources listing different disabilities and types of accommodations to support at work.

Within the framework of an ill-fitting system, the therapist can also work with the patient on identifying the ways they wish to be a part of this system and where accommodations alone are likely insufficient to meet their goals. This allows the therapist and patient to collaboratively decide whether the patient wants to *choose* to develop skills that would reduce the friction caused by their differences, and the therapist can present skills without reinforcing a disorder model. For example, a patient may *choose* to learn assertiveness skills in the workplace, despite such skills feeling inconsistent with their values in other contexts, because they know that such skills are more aligned with the (Western) White majority workplace.

Problem 3: Difficulty with Sensory Sensitivities and Other Restricted, Repetitive Behaviors or Patterns

While the DSM-5 Autism Spectrum Disorder Criterion A describes differences in social interactions and relationships, Criterion B lists ways autistic individuals can differ in how they experience and navigate the external world. One challenge is these differences, by definition, are at odds with behavioral norms and expectations. The therapist is then responsible for disentangling which of the patient's "problem behaviors" are examples of the patient's unique experience of different stimuli and how to best support these differences. For example, autistic individuals can be "hypo- or hyperreactive to sensory input" (Criterion B4). This is not unusual for people to vary in their sensory sensitivities—indeed, a common conversation activity is people sharing their "pet peeves" with sound or smells or different tastes. Imagine, however, a situation where the intensity of this pet peeve is dialed up ten times (or more). How might this shift a person's behavior or ability to tolerate other stressors? It would be understandable, if not likely, for the person to become avoidant or developed other "problematic behaviors" in response to the situation.

For any of the differences listed under Criterion B, the patient has likely received messages that their behaviors are inappropriate and should be changed, if not remain hidden from others. The therapist must be sensitive to the possibility that existing treatments for anxiety and mood disorders may also convey such messages. For example, it is unlikely that repeated exposure to an aversive sound or texture would lead to reduced stress or anxiety. Therapists can improve their decision making by considering the reason or function of the patient's unwanted behavior. For example, if a patient avoids going to the local grocery store, the interventions will differ greatly if the reason for the avoidance is a sensory sensitivity to the volume of the music being played at the store versus an OCD fear of germs.

If the therapist and patient identify neurodiversity-related differences are driving the patient's problem behaviors, then they can collaboratively decide how best to accommodate the patient's differences while also allowing them to engage in the situation. Going back to the grocery store example, it may be that wearing headphones or ear plugs is most helpful.

Clinical Considerations

Returning to the vignette, in the context of the current clinical recommendations, the social skills training program has the potential to reify deficit-oriented beliefs about Tina's differences. To help prevent this, therapists can focus on normalizing autism-related differences, emphasizing the strengths that come with an autistic profile, and framing the skills training as added learning to increase patient choices, rather than a needed remediation of a deficit. The goal with this frame is to improve motivation, while also promoting a positive self-view and advocacy for accommodation or recognition of autistic differences.

Tina clearly benefited from the program. What stands out, however, is the gains may be better explained by her finding a like-minded peer than an increase in (neurotypical) social skills. This is consistent with research suggesting autistic individuals feel more connected to and understood by other autistic individuals (e.g., Crompton, et al., 2020, Morrison et al., 2020). Clinicians should consider alternate paths to well-being that focus on a sense of inclusion and belonging that do not require the development of neurotypical social skills and behaviors. Similarly, research on minority stress has shown significant mental health benefit in building community with those who share important aspects of their minoritized identities. For AAPI neurodivergent youth who ostensibly are holding at least two minoritized identities, finding shared lived experiences and understanding may enhance any work done in the psychotherapy context.

Summary of Recommendations

Below, in Table 8.3, we provide a summary of our clinical recommendations for common problems that may arise for clinicians working with neurodivergent youth. While these recommendations are specifically targeted to clinicians, these concepts can be applied by professionals, caregivers, or

Table 8.3 Summary of common problems and recommendations.

Common problem	Clinical recommendations
Difficulty responding to direct questions by the therapist	**1.** Assume the patient understands what is being asked. **2.** Reduce the "spotlight effect" on patient and reduce verbal demand **a.** Ask patient to write answers between sessions **b.** Prepare patient with plan for next sessions **c.** Provide language to help explain patient's experiences **3.** Encourage patient to take lead in sharing stories or areas of interest to encourage a verbal "flow state."
Difficulty meeting expected social norms	**1.** Name differences that conflict with existing norms. **2.** Help patient learn how to advocate for differences by explaining them to others and seeking accommodations (when appropriate). **3.** Present patient with choice to develop skills to meet norms.
Difficulty with sensory sensitivities and other restricted, repetitive behaviors or patterns	**1.** Identify the reason (or function) for the patient's problem or interfering behaviors by asking, "Why is this happening? What is the patient trying to do?" **2.** If the reason is autism-related, then assume the reason is unchangeable. **3.** Find another way to meet the need or reason driving the behavior to reduce interference in the person's life.

community members. For example, teachers could reduce the spotlight effect in classrooms by normalizing ways for students to participate beyond traditional verbal participation, such as writing down answers on a whiteboard. Caregivers can teach children how to advocate for themselves by requesting accommodations, from asking their teacher if they can use fidget toys in class to asking their doctor if they can avoid wearing a paper gown they may find itchy. As the neurodiversity framework described earlier highlights the benefits of a more generally inclusive society in which neurodiversity-related differences are considered valuable, ideally all community members should be open to the ways neurodiversity can show up and apply such knowledge when applicable.

The overall themes are for the clinician and other professionals to adjust their own behaviors to support autism and culture-related differences to enhance patient learning. Clinicians are encouraged to use the research on patient-related differences outlined in this and other chapters in this book to help formulate and address barriers to patient learning and identify potential pathways to well-being that may differ from majority norms or existing treatment protocols, but are better aligned with patient differences and values.

References

American Psychiatric Association. (2013). *Diagnostic and Statistical Manual of Mental Disorders* (Fifth Edition). https://doi.org/10.1176/appi.books.9780890425596

Bothra, S. (2021). Parental stress in Asian American and non-Asian American families of children with developmental disabilities during COVID-19 (Senior thesis, Scripps College). Scholarship@ Claremont. https://scholarship.claremont.edu/scripps_theses/1670/

Bury, S. M., Haschek, A., Wenzel, M., Spoor, J. R., & Hedley, D. (2024). Brief report: learning about autism: is the source of autism knowledge associated with differences in autism knowledge, autism identity, and experiences of stigma? *Journal of Autism and Developmental Disorders*, *54*(11), 4346–4353. https://doi.org/10.1007/s10803-022-05823-5

Bury, S. M., Jellett, R., Spoor, J. R., & Hedley, D. (2023). "It defines who I am" or "it's something I have": what language do [autistic] Australian adults [on the autism spectrum] prefer? *Journal of Autism and Developmental Disorders*, *53*(2), 677–687.

Cénat, J. M., Blais-Rochette, C., Morse, C., Vandette, M. P., Noorishad, P. G., Kogan, C., Ndengeyingoma, A., & Labelle, P. R. (2021). Prevalence and risk factors associated with attention-deficit/hyperactivity disorder among US Black individuals: a systematic review and meta-analysis. *JAMA Psychiatry*, *78*(1), 21–28.

Cheng, A. W., Chang, J., O'Brien, J., Budgazad, M. S., & Tsai, J. (2017). Model minority stereotype: influence on perceived mental health needs of Asian Americans. *Journal of Immigrant and Minority Health*, *19*(3), 572–581. https://doi.org/10.1007/s10903-016-0440-0

Cooc, N. (2018). Examining the underrepresentation of Asian Americans in special education: new trends from California school districts. *Exceptionality*, *26*(1), 1–19. https://doi.org/10.1080/09362835.2016.1216847

Coren, S. (1993). *The Left-Hander Syndrome: The Causes and Consequences of Left-Handedness*. Vintage.

Crompton, C. J., Hallett, S., Ropar, D., Flynn, E., & Fletcher-Watson, S. (2020). "I never realised everybody felt as happy as I do when I am around autistic people": a thematic analysis of autistic adults' relationships with autistic and neurotypical friends and family. *Autism*, *24*(6), 1438–1448. https://doi.org/10.1177/1362361320908976

DeLambo, D., Chung, W., & Huang, W. (2011). Stress and age: a comparison of Asian American and non-Asian American parents of children with developmental disabilities. *Journal of Developmental and Physical Disabilities*, *23*(2), 129–141. https://doi.org/10.1007/s10882-010-9211-3

Dere, J., Falk, C. F., & Ryder, A. G. (2012). Unpacking cultural differences in alexithymia: the role of cultural values among Euro-Canadian and Chinese-Canadian students. *Journal of Cross-Cultural Psychology*, *43*(8), 1297–1312. http://dx.doi.org/10.1177/0022022111430254.

Drescher, J. (2002). Sexual conversion ("reparative") therapies: a history and update. In B. E. Jones, & M. J. Hill (Eds.), *Mental Health Issues in Lesbian, Gay, Bisexual, and Transgender Communities* (pp. 71–91). American Psychiatric Association Publishing.

Gallin, Z., Kolevzon, A. M., Reichenberg, A., Hankerson, S. H., & Kolevzon, A. (2025). Racial differences in the prevalence of autism spectrum disorder: a systematic review. *Journal of Autism and Developmental Disorders*, *55*(9), 3364–3377. https://doi.org/10.1007/s10803-024-06403-5

Hall, G. C. N., Berkman, E. T., Zane, N. W., Leong, F. T. L., Hwang, W.-C., Nezu, A. M., ... Huang, E. R. (2021). Reducing mental health disparities by increasing the personal relevance of interventions. *American Psychologist*, *76*(1), 91–103. https://doi.org/10.1037/amp0000616

Kerns, C., Rast, J. E., & Shattuck, P. (2020). Prevalence and correlates of caregiver-reported mental health conditions in youth with autism spectrum disorder in the United States. *The Journal of Clinical Psychiatry*, *82*(1), 11637. https://doi.org/10.4088/jcp.20m13242

Kim, I., Wang, Y., Dababnah, S., & Betz, G. (2021). East Asian American parents of children with autism: a scoping review. *Review Journal of Autism and Developmental Disorders*, *8*(3), 312–320. https://doi.org/10.1007/s40489-020-00221-y

Leadbitter, K., Buckle, K. L., Ellis, C., & Dekker, M. (2021). Autistic self-advocacy and the neurodiversity movement: implications for autism early intervention research and practice. *Frontiers in Psychology*, *12*(12), 635690. https://doi.org/10.3389/fpsyg.2021.635690

Linkous, O., Soon, K., Lee, J. D., Du, A., Shih, W., Bearss, K., Kasari, C., & Locke, J. (2024). Short report: examining race, ethnicity, sex, and gender among autistic youth and their educators who participated in school-based research. *Autism: The International Journal of Research and Practice, 28*(10), 2675–2681. https://doi.org/10.1177/13623613241262144

Morrison, K., DeBrabander, K., Jones, D., Faso, D., Ackerman, R., & Sasson, N. (2020). Outcomes of real world social interaction for autistic adults paired with autistic compared to typically developing partners. *Autism, 24*(5), 1067–1080. https://doi.org/10.1177/1362361319892701

Pham, A. V., & Charles, L. C. (2023). Racial disparities in autism diagnosis, assessment, and intervention among minoritized youth: sociocultural issues, factors, and context. *Current Psychiatry Reports, 25*(5), 201–211. https://doi.org/10.1007/s11920-023-01417-9

Qiu, S., Lu, Y., Li, Y., Shi, J., Cui, H., Gu, Y., & Liang, X. (2020). Prevalence of autism spectrum disorder in Asia: a systematic review and meta-analysis. *Psychiatry Research, 284*, 112522. https://doi.org/10.1016/j.psychres.2019.112522

Shorey, S., Ng, E. D., Haugan, G., & Law, E. (2020). The parenting experiences and needs of Asian primary caregivers of children with autism: a meta-synthesis. *Autism: The International Journal of Research and Practice, 24*(3), 591–604. https://doi.org/10.1177/1362361319886513

Taylor, G. J. (2000). Recent developments in alexithymia theory and research. *Canadian Journal of Psychiatry, 45*(2), 134–142.

Truong, D. M., Barth, A. M., Mire, S. S., Ayala, M. L., Ramclam, A. N., Tan, S. X. L., & McKee, S. L. (2022). Cultural considerations for conducting autism assessment with Asian American and Pacific Islander students. *Psychology in the Schools, 59*(7), 1430–1444. https://doi.org/10.1002/pits.22671

Wang, C., Yang, A.M., & Tsai, J.L. (2026). What cultural differences in ideal affect can teach us about East Asian American youth. In N.H. Liu (Ed.) *For the Next Generation: Mental Health in Asian American, Native Hawaiian, and Pacific Islander Youth*. John Wiley & Sons.

Wilk, P., Maltby, A., & Cooke, M. (2017). Residential schools and the effects on Indigenous health and well-being in Canada—a scoping review. *Public Health Reviews, 38*(1), 8. https://doi.org/10.1186/s40985-017-0055-6

Yan, M., Kim, S., Kang, H., & Wilkerson, K. L. (2017). Perceptions of disability and special education among East Asian parents: U.S. immigrants and non-immigrants. *Journal of International Special Needs Education, 20*(1), 41–55. https://doi.org/10.9782/2159-4341- 20.1.41

Zechella, A. N., & Raval, V. V. (2016). Parenting children with intellectual and developmental disabilities in Asian Indian families in the United States. *Journal of Child and Family Studies, 25*(4), 1295–1309. https://doi.org/10.1007/s10826-015-0285-5

9

Pacific Islander Youth Mental Health in the United States

Tessa Palafu[1], Danielle L. Carreira Ching[1,2], Deborah Goebert[3], Kelsie H. Okamura[1,4], Davis Rehuher[3], Lorinda Riley[3], Anamalia Anusaga Su'esu'e[3], Sione Tafune[5], and Nadia Yoshizumi-Kim[1]

[1]The Baker Center for Children and Families, Boston, MA, USA
[2]Hawai'i Pacific University, Honolulu, HI, USA
[3]University of Hawai'i at Manoa, Honolulu, HI, USA
[4] University of Pennsylvania, Philadelphia, PA, USA
[5]Kahuku Medical Center, Kahuku, HI, USA

Introduction

Pacific Islander youth in the United States face significant challenges in maintaining their mental health and well-being. While their experiences share similarities with those of other Indigenous, migrant, and immigrant communities, they are influenced by unique historical, political, and social contexts surrounding their migration and settlement. The legacies of colonization, militarization, and economic migration have contributed to intergenerational trauma and stressors that impact mental health outcomes. Additionally, Pacific cultures are incredibly resilient, featuring strong family networks, cultural traditions, and collective healing practices that serve as protective factors for youth. US Census data from 2020 highlight the diversity of Pacific Islander groups in the United States, enumerating 31 unique ethnicities. Samoans, Tongans, Tahitians, Māori, and Tokelauans had the highest populations among Polynesians. Among Micronesians, Chamorros, Marshallese, Chuukese, Palauans, and Pohnpeians were the highest. Fijians and Papua New Guineans were the most among Melanesians.

The Indigenous inhabitants of the western-central Pacific Islands, known as Micronesians, are ethnically and culturally varied. Although they only make up a small portion of the US population, Micronesians living there are among the fastest-growing groups, with their numbers growing by two to five times (Palauans to Chuukese; Rico et al., 2023). Behavioral and mental health remain a critically important concern for Micronesians living in the United States, particularly among young Micronesians. Samoans are the Indigenous people of the Samoan Islands located in the South Pacific Ocean. The 2020 US Census showed that Samoans are the second largest Native Hawaiian or Pacific Islander (NHPI) group in the country, behind only Native Hawaiians (Rico et al., 2023). Nearly 400,000 people identified as either Samoan alone or in combination with another race, which is a 39.3% increase from the 2010 census (Rico et al., 2023). This chapter examines the mental health of Micronesian and Samoan youth in the United States by reviewing historical and systemic influences, current mental health trends, and cultural models of well-being. It focuses mainly on Micronesian and Samoan youth due the growing population in the United States, as well as the availability of research.

Disaggregation for Pacific Islander Communities

Historically, Pacific Islanders have been grouped together, initially within the larger Asian category label, later expanded to the Asian American and Pacific Islander category, and finally Native Hawaiian and Other Pacific Islanders category (McCubbin & Marsella, 2009). These practices have their roots beginning as early as the 1970s, as a way to commemorate the contributions of Japanese Americans during the war, with the creation of Asian and Pacific Islander Heritage Month in 1992 (U.S. Library of Congress, 2023; Roth, 2023). The classification of Pacific Islanders in this way has worked to mask distinct histories, experiences, and issues faced by these groups (Kamaka et al., 2021). These practices have also made it difficult to differentiate among the aggregates to gather specific data on individual groups for the purposes of developing treatments and other health promoting resources or programs (Shimkhada et al., 2021).

Just over thirty years ago, efforts began to be made to create separate categories for Native Hawaiians and Other Pacific Islanders beginning with the 1990 census which included the option "Other Asian or Pacific Islander" and the option to write-in specific groups under this category (Asian Pacific Institute on Gender-Based Violence, 2022). Ten years later, in 2000, the census began to include separate boxes for Native Hawaiians along with Samoan and Guamanian or Chamorro options (Asian Pacific Institute on Gender-Based Violence, 2022).

Despite this progress, data collection continues to lag for Pacific Islander populations often due to the diversity of the Pacific Islander category and difficulties in collecting adequate data (Substance Abuse and Mental Health Services Administration, 2021; University of California Irvine, 2021; University of Hawai'i at Mānoa, 2014). For Micronesian youth in particular, data are often limited due to a lack of infrastructure following the Compacts of Free Association (Derauf et al., 2011; Saunders et al., 2010). Therefore, this chapter aims to report on the limited research available for specific Pacific Islander groups.

State of Mental Health

Overall, there is a lack of data on the prevalence of mental disorders (Leckie & Hughes, 2017). Available epidemiological data show elevated rates of depression, anxiety, and suicide in certain Pacific Island countries. Suicide rates in Kiribati (30.6 deaths/100,000 people), the Federated States of Micronesia (29.0/100,000), Vanuatu (21.0/100,000), and Samoa (14.6/100,000) were much higher than the global rate (9.0/100,000) in 2019 (World Health Organization, 2021). A review article found that Pacific Islander youth in the region had a higher prevalence of depression and anxiety compared to other ethnic groups (Tucker-Masters & Tiatia-Seath, 2017). A self-administered depression survey completed by Marshallese teenagers in Arkansas indicated that Marshallese students generally achieved scores higher than those necessary for a clinical evaluation (Fitzpatrick & Willis, 2018; Gavin, 2017). Similarly, Pacific Islander youth were found to be particularly at risk for suicide and suicide attempts (Mathieu et al., 2021). In their 2004 study on Guam's adolescent suicide and same-sex orientation, Pinhey and Millman found that Micronesian and European American girls had fewer suicidal ideations than Asian, Chamorro, Filipino, and Micronesian teens. Suicidal ideation was most prevalent among Micronesian boys.

A recent study conducted by the Asian American Foundation (2024) surveyed Asian American Native Hawaiian and other Pacific Islander (AANHPI) youth across the United States to develop a comprehensive mental health profile of this population. Results showed that 64% of Pacific Islander youth in this study reported moderate to severe depressive symptoms. These rates are notably higher compared to other subgroups in the study, including East Asian, Filipino, Southeast Asian, South Asian, and Native Hawaiian youth, whose reported prevalence of moderate to severe depressive symptoms was in the 40% range. The study also found that among Pacific Islander youth who reported moderate depressive symptoms, 81% had consulted a mental health professional in the past year, representing the highest rate of service use among all subgroups. This suggests that despite particularly elevated rates of depression, Pacific Islander youth in the United States may be more likely to utilize mental health services in comparison to other AANHPI subgroups. The Western region of the Pacific has had one of the highest rates of schizophrenia in the world (Hezel & Wylie, 1992; Waldo, 1999). Compared to Chamorro and Filipino youth, Micronesians reported the greatest percentage of current drinking among Guam's adolescents, especially binge drinking (David & Lapid-Rosadino, 2015; David et al., 2016). Micronesians were more likely than non-Micronesians to have more alcoholic family members (34% vs. 23%, $p = .10$), more drinking friends (82% and 64%, respectively), and higher alcohol consumption at one point (17% and 5%, respectively). Additionally, compared to Chamorros, Chuukese and Palauans reported greater percentages of indulging in various drinking practices (Saleh, 1994). An emerging concern is the co-occurrence of physical and mental health conditions mentioned above. For example, diabetes, heart diseases, cancer, and respiratory diseases are prevalent in the Pacific and may be linked with poor mental health outcomes across the region (Ali et al., 2020). Despite these concerns, there is a notable lack of prevention and intervention research addressing mental health across the region (Mathieu et al., 2021).

Enduring Impacts of Historical Trauma

Historical trauma refers to the "cumulative emotional and psychological wounding over the lifespan and across generations, emanating from massive group trauma" (Brave Heart, 2003, p. 7). Importantly, historical trauma does not simply refer to past trauma but incorporates the systemic issues that these communities continue to face on a daily basis in the present. While the concept of historical trauma originally grew out of the mental and physical impacts that the children of Holocaust survivors were experiencing, Brave Heart adapted these ideas for Native American communities. Since then, the body of literature around historical trauma has expanded to a variety of geographies and cultures that have been negatively impacted by colonization.

For Pacific Islanders, historical trauma is deeply intertwined with militarization, land dispossession, and the broader impacts of colonialism. The history of colonization in the Pacific is complex and varied. In the 16th and 17th centuries, Europeans began a period of exploration partly in an effort to encourage trade. This early contact period brought periodic conflict but was largely focused on trade. Later, as missionaries began to join these exploratory trips, the relationship shifted to focus on settlement and spiritual colonization. As more European settlers came to the Pacific, efforts to colonize became more prominent resulting in wholescale attempts to Christianize and assimilate Pacific Islanders. Conflicts between the Indigenous communities and the settlers occurred more frequently as resources like land became scarcer.

This Age of Imperialism left an indelible scar on these communities. As more Europeans settled in the Pacific, disease priorly unknown to these communities spread and the Indigenous populations began to precipitously decline. The process of assimilation left these communities with less internal resources to draw upon in order to counteract the stresses of colonization. As European interests in imperialism began to wane in the 1960s, Pacific Island nations began to seek and gain independence. However, ongoing structural and historical injustices continue to shape the well-being of Pacific Islander youth today, underscoring the need to focus on healing historical trauma.

The Micronesian Region

The terms Micronesia, Melanesia, and Polynesia were imposed on the Pacific Islands by Western explorers. They do not reflect Pacific Islander epistemology and ignore cultural and linguistic diversity within each region. The Micronesian region comprises five independent countries and two territories. Three of the countries are the Republic of the Marshall Islands (Marshall Islands), the Republic of Palau (Palau), and the Federated States of Micronesia (FSM). Guam and the Commonwealth of the Northern Mariana Islands (CNMI) are US territories. The other two countries are Nauru and Kiribati, which were historically associated with Australia and Great Britain and are omitted here. Decades of colonialism have left the islands highly dependent on the United States, adopting a Western lifestyle and consuming nontraditional diets (Hanlon, 2009), contributing to greater health disparities (Palafox & Hixon, 2011).

The term Micronesia reflects a colonial gaze by categorizing nations based on land mass and thereby minimizing Pacific Island nations. Rather than calling these nations Micronesia or "small islands," Pacific Islander scholars have reframed this region as a vast "sea of islands" connected by the ocean, which acts as a highway. Despite the abundance and resilience of Micronesia, the region is often marginalized or dismissed by larger nation-states who continue to treat these islands as peripheral actors on the global stage.

The Micronesian region has been colonized by numerous countries for almost 500 years (see Table 9.1). Today, several nation-states in Micronesia have gained their independence, while also maintaining close ties to the United States having signed a Compact of Free Association. As a result, the 2020 US Census Bureau estimates that approximately 1.4 million NHPIs (alone or in combination with one or more races) live in the country. Micronesians represent the third-largest group of Pacific Islanders in the United States and approximately 2% of Pacific Islanders in Hawaiʻi where the majority of research on Micronesians takes place (Hixon et al., 2012). The fastest growing NHPI community are the Chuukese, increasing by 296% to 10,500 from 2010 to 2020 with the largest percentage living in Hawaiʻi. Notably, the US NHPI population is young with an average age of 30.

More recent research has focused on the large Marshallese population in northwest Arkansas. Over one-third of the Marshall Islands population has migrated to the United States (McClain et al., 2019). Arkansas and Hawaiʻi are home to the largest Marshallese community in the United States (McElfish et al., 2021). Data are limited on this population due to accessibility issues as well as an overall lack of infrastructure following the colonization, militarization, and destruction of their homelands that led to the Compacts of Free Association (COFA) which provides travel to the United States and the promise of opportunities for economic advancement and access to education, a promise that has fallen short many times (Diaz, 2012). In return, the United States gets sole

Table 9.1 Brief timeline of major geopolitical events in Micronesian region from 1521 to present.

Major colonial power in Micronesian region	Years	Historical colonial examples
Spain in Micronesian region	1521–1898	• Local uprisings met resistance from colonial powers, which resulted in forced geographic migration. • Introduction of novel illnesses (e.g., sickness of the ship) and frequent epidemics resulted in significant population decline.
Guam becomes US territory	1898–present	• US Navy assumes control and converts a sizable portion of land for military use. • Use of Chamorro language outlawed.
Germany in Micronesian region	1899–1914	• Land surveys covertly shifted the meanings of land tenure. • Rebellion led by the Sokeh people due to forced manual labor and poor treatment by the German government. Ended with exile of the Sokeh people.
Japan in Micronesian region	1914–1944	• State Shinto established as the official ideology, while many Indigenous religious practices were outlawed. • Restricted interisland travel and traditional voyaging practices.
United States enters Micronesian region	1944–present	• Establishment of the Trust Territory of the Pacific Islands by the United Nations with the United States as the administering authority. Allowed the United States to maintain military installations in Micronesian region and limited the political autonomy of the local population. • Nuclear testing by the US military that resulted in mass displacement, severe environmental degradation, and physical health impacts.
Northern Mariana Islands becomes US Commonwealth	1978–present	• Residents are US citizens but are unable to vote in Presidential elections and have a nonvoting delegate in the House of Representatives. • Continued and increased military presence as tensions with foreign countries rise.
*Federated States of Micronesia gains independence**	1986–present	• The Compact of Free Association (COFA) is established which allowed residents free entry into the United States and outlined various financial supports that the United States would provide. • Through COFA, the United States has exclusive military access to these regions.
*Republic of the Marshall Islands gains Independence**	1986–present	
*Republic of Palau gains Independence**	1994–present	

* United States acts similar to a protectorate by entering in the Compact of Free Association with these nation-states.

military and strategic rights to the region, including the right to deny any other country military use of the region (Derauf et al., 2011; Saunders et al., 2010).

Samoa

Similar to the Micronesian region, Samoa has a long and complex history with colonial powers (see Table 9.2). Samoa became an independent nation in 1962 (Government of Samoa, n.d.) while American Samoa is an unincorporated territory of the United States (American Samoa Bar

Table 9.2 Brief timeline of major geopolitical events in Samoa.

Major colonial power in Samoa	Years	Historical colonial examples
Germany, Britain, and United States in Samoa	1878–1899	• Germany, Britain, and the United States sign treaties with Samoa and create the Tripartite Convention. This resulted in the creation of the Municipal of Apia which was controlled by the three powers and undermined Samoan sovereignty. • Ongoing civil wars with opposing sides backed by conflicting colonial powers. Resulted in many casualties and erosion of traditional political systems. • Land commission resulted in the distribution of more than one-third of cultivable land to colonial settlers.
Germany annexes Western Samoa	1900–1914	• Trilateral convention divides Samoa, with Germany claiming the West. • Preferable treatment toward German interests in regard to land acquisition to support German-owned plantations.
United States in American (Eastern) Samoa	1900–present	• Trilateral convention divides Samoa, with the Eastern regions, now known as American Samoa, becoming a US territory. • US Navy leadership in the first half of the 1900s causes issues related to trade and political power for Samoans. • American Samoa residents are not granted US citizenship, limiting political power.
New Zealand in Western Samoa	1914–1961	• 1918 Influenza pandemic killed an estimated 22% of the population. • Black Saturday catastrophe where eight Samoan protestors were killed by New Zealand Police Officers at an Independence parade.
Western Samoan gains independence	1962–present	• Western Samoa gains independence from New Zealand on January 1, 1962. • New Zealand Prime Minister visits Western Samoa in 2002 and issues formal apology.

Association, 2012; Office of Insular Affairs, n.d.). Though political distinctions are made between Samoa and American Samoa, the two share a common culture, *Fa'a Samoa* or Samoan way of life (Bond & Soli, 2011). The *Fa'amatai* or *Matai* (chief) system serves as the central social, political system in traditional and contemporary Samoan culture with the village as the main socio-geographic unit on the islands made up of *aiga* or extended family (Bond & Soli, 2011).

American Samoa became an unincorporated territory of the United States in 1900 (Office of Insular Affairs, n.d.). Migration to the United States has been ongoing since, especially to states such as California, Alaska, and Hawai'i, with Samoans arriving in the islands for employment and education as well as religious purposes. American Samoa has a high net emigrant rate—in a 2024 estimate, an excess of persons leaving American Samoa was rated at −24.8 migrant(s) per 1,000 persons. Samoans from American Samoa are considered US Nationals who may reside or work in the United States without a Visa or Green Card and may serve in the US military. Though Samoan life has experienced generations of migration and Western contact, Samoan worldviews and conceptions of self remain primarily relationship-based, (Lilomaiava-Doktor, 2009), as renowned Samoan author, poet, and scholar, Albert Wendt, describes the primacy of interdependence and relationships through the well-known Samoan expression, "'*Ia teu le va*," meaning to care for the relational space or relationships (Wendt, 1996).

Militarization of the Pacific

The United States has had a long-standing military presence in Micronesia and across the Pacific, starting during World War II and continuing to the present day. During World War II, the Micronesian islands saw some of the bloodiest and most damaging fighting (Hanlon, 1998; Poyer 1991). In 1944, the United States attacked the Marshall Islands in the east before moving westward, attacking Palau in the west and Saipan and Guam in the Mariana Islands (Poyer, 1991; Poyer et al., 2000). Despite not being invaded, the islands of Kosrae, Pohnpei, Chuuk, and Yap in central Micronesia were surrounded, cut off from outside resources, and subjected to air and sea bombardment (Hanlon, 1998; Poyer, 1991; Poyer et al., 2000). Micronesians suffered from malnutrition as the war went on and supplies dwindled or were cut off (Poyer, 1991; Poyer et al., 2000). Whether invaded or bombarded, Micronesians throughout the Japanese-held territory endured bodily harm, arduous work, and starvation as conditions deteriorated (Poyer et al., 2000). Micronesians experienced fright, dislocation, famine, and hardship as well as executions toward the conclusion of World War II (Poyer et al., 2000).

In American Samoa, the US military presence began earlier, in the late 1890s, with the US Navy maintaining control of the islands in 1899 followed by becoming a US territory in 1900. Though there are currently no active-duty military bases in American Samoa, the presence of the US military is still strongly felt including the Pele US Army Reserve Center established in 2002 and the US Army Reserve's first Modular Small Arms Range which opened in 2019.

One of the most devastating periods in Micronesian history was the US nuclear testing program in the Marshall Islands from 1946 to 1958, during which 67 nuclear bombs were detonated. These tests exposed local communities to high levels of radiation, resulting in long-term health crises, forced displacement, and intergenerational trauma. Entire islands became uninhabitable, and many Micronesians continue to suffer from cancer, congenital disabilities, and other radiation-related illnesses.

Moreover, the military presence in American Samoa has led to land dispossession and environmental degradation. The conversion of communal lands into military facilities has disrupted traditional Samoan land tenure systems, impacting the connection between youth and their cultural heritage. This, along with the movement of individual troops to different parts of the United States and world, has created a gap in this community.

In addition to the environmental destruction, the United States established military bases throughout the region, including in Guam and the Federated States of Micronesia. The militarization of these islands disrupted traditional governance and economies, making Micronesian nations heavily reliant on US financial aid. The Compact of Free Association (COFA) agreements, signed between the United States and Micronesia, allowed for free migration but left COFA migrants in a precarious legal status. They are permitted to work and reside in the United States but are ineligible for many federal benefits, including Medicaid.

Despite this, Pacific Islanders enroll in the military at some of the highest rates in the United States. For example, American Samoa has one of the highest military enlistment rates per capita of any US territory or state. For many Samoan families, military service is both an economic necessity and a deeply rooted tradition. While enlistment provides stable income and educational benefits, it also comes at a significant cost—many Samoan youths grow up with absent parents who are deployed overseas. The stress of long-term family separation, combined with the expectations placed on young Samoans to continue the tradition of military service, contributes to anxiety, depression, and struggles with identity.

Despite the presence of the US military, most land still remains in the control of American Samoans, a feat related to the unique status of the territory. As mentioned, those born in American Samoa hold the status of US National versus US Citizen, which can lead to complexities regarding legal, political, and even cultural identities. US Nationals may receive certain benefits with their status, such as the ability to move throughout the United States without a Visa or Green Card, but at the same time are restricted from certain rights granted to US citizens, such as voting in federal elections or running for certain public office positions. Efforts to contest this National status and grant US citizenship for American Samoans were addressed in the US Supreme Court Case, *Tuaua v. United States* (2015); however, the Supreme Court refused to hear the case leaving the US National status for American Samoans unchanged, but a remaining question for some as this status is seen to protect the control of lands by American Samoans.

In addition to complex legal and political statuses, other issues remain prominent for American Samoans due to their relationship with the United States, such as military service and mental health. Veterans returning to American Samoa often face challenges such as posttraumatic stress disorder (PTSD) and other service-related mental health issues, which can have lasting effects on their families and communities. Mental health and primary healthcare for Veterans and active-duty members in American Samoa are available through several facilities including the American Samoa Vet Center and Faleomavaega Eni Fa'aua'a Hunkin VA Clinic. Current wait times for services vary, with new patients for primary care at the VA clinic waiting an average of 13 days and new patients for women's Veteran care waiting an average of 66 days as of April 2025 (Faleomavaega Eni Fa'aua'a Hunkin VA Clinic, 2025).

Intergenerational Impact on Mental Health

The long-term effects of colonization and militarization in Micronesian and Samoan communities have contributed to ongoing cycles of trauma. While colonization may be directly tied to the original trauma event, the sustained suppression of traditional practices leads to the reduction of coping mechanisms that existed in past generations leading to youth internalizing these stressors. These combined stresses can lead to depression, anxiety, PTSD, suicidal ideation, alcohol misuse, and more (Onoye et al., 2021). The historical trauma experienced by Pacific Islanders has a distinct origin and impact compared to the trauma endured by Asian groups. For example, much of the discussion surrounding historical trauma in NHPI groups focuses on land dispossession and cultural disconnection because of colonization, which produces wide-scale impacts to well-being (Palafu et al., 2024; Riley et al., 2022). Research on historical trauma in Southeast Asian refugees typically highlight the impact of forced migration and wartime experiences (e.g., torture) on the presentation of chronic psychological concerns, such as PTSD (Lor et al., 2022; Hinton et al., 2009). This highlights the need to disaggregate AANHPI groups in research in order to account for the distinct experiences that shape psychological symptom expression among Indigenous populations, who are too often inappropriately grouped together within this category. The traumatic effects of colonization in Pacific Islander groups have led to the complex, interconnected health disparities seen among NHPIs today. In a 2014 study, Pokhrel and Herzog administered the Historical Loss Scale to NH college students and found that historical trauma was associated with higher levels of perceived discrimination, which in turn correlated with increased substance use. A recent report found that the prevalence of drinking before age 13 in Hawai'i was 30% for NHs and 19% for other Pacific Islanders compared to 14% for Asians, and 13% for Whites. Pacific Islander students were also more likely to engage in binge drinking during the last 30 days than their White peers (18% vs. 11%). Similarly, moderate–heavy use, defined as 6 or more drinks in the past 30 days, was substantially more frequent among NHs (6.7%) and Pacific Islanders (7.1%) than Whites (4.2%). The use of alcohol and substance as emotional anesthesia from the mental health impacts of colonization is ever present among this population.

Research on historical trauma suggests that acknowledging cultural loss is a crucial aspect of mental health interventions. A recent study with NHPI youth experiencing homelessness in Hawai'i found that housed youth reported greater cross-generation experience of historically traumatic events in their family than unhoused youth (Palafu et al., 2024). Other studies have found that disconnection from family through the child welfare system was associated with unhoused status for Indigenous youth later in life (Shaikh & Rawal, 2018; Palafu et al., 2024). Together, this may point to the role that knowledge and awareness of historical events play in reported experience of historical trauma, which aligns with Riley et al. who discussed that not all youth are able to conceptually connect current trauma with past historic events (2022). Additionally, some youth develop resilience and cultural pride to cope (Pokhrel & Herzog, 2014) underscoring the need for mental health interventions that not only acknowledge historical trauma but also foster cultural connection and empowerment.

Similarly, ethnic and racial identity (ERI; i.e., the personal meaning people attach to their race) and ethnic-racial socialization (ERS; i.e., parental messaging surrounding race that informs children's identity) have been identified as key mental health protective factors for other minoritized populations (Neblett, 2023, pp. 363 & 365). A study with American Indian families, a population that faces similar historically traumatic experiences, found that high levels of parental cultural socialization predicted lower levels of youth depression (Yasui et al., 2015). Research on the impacts of ERI and ERS for Pacific Islander populations is limited (Nieri et al., 2024); however, these findings indicate that the transmission of cultural and historical knowledge could curb the impacts of intergenerational trauma. The richness of storytelling traditions in Pacific Islander cultures could be used to help youth connect to their culture through movies (e.g., Whale Rider), documentaries (e.g., Loimata: The Sweetest Tears), books (e.g., Black Marks on the White Page), and more.

Juvenile Justice System

Historically, Native Hawaiians have been overrepresented in the Hawai'i juvenile justice system; however, in recent years, this trend has shifted in part due to an influx of programming targeting the overrepresentation of Native Hawaiian youth. According to Warden Patterson, Micronesians and other Pacific Islanders make up a significant portion of the incarcerated youth population; however, due to incomplete and inconsistent reporting, the official data of Micronesian counts is artificially low, while the race "unknown" category is inflated. In other jurisdictions such as Guam, Chuukese and Chamorro young people were significantly overrepresented in the juvenile justice system between 1987 and 2000 (Rapadas, 2001). One study found that NHPI youth in the juvenile justice system frequently had extensive histories of exposure to violence, mental health diagnoses, family loss, and parental substance use or criminal involvement (Pasko & Mayeda, 2011). These findings suggest that youth with significant histories of trauma are at heightened risk for continued system involvement. Unlike the NH population where the cycle of incarceration is passed down from generation-to-generation, Micronesians families in Hawai'i are less involved with child welfare services and have less rates of parental incarceration and substance, yet are overrepresented in the juvenile justice system with high recidivism rates (Benda & Tollett, 1999; Carreira Ching et al., 2023).

Despite the data issues, it is clear that NHPI are disproportionately impacted by the justice system in Hawai'i. NHPIs represent 39% of the population under age 18 but 54% of adjudicated cases and 64% of incarcerated youth (Hawai'i Department of Human Services, 2022). These disparate rates are similar to other marginalized groups across the United States. For instance, in 2013, African American youth comprised 13% of the total US population, but 35% of the youth detained (Voisin et al., 2016). Because youth who are detained, even temporarily while awaiting trial, are 3 times more likely to be institutionalized in the future, identifying programs that support positive growth among these youth (Holman & Ziedenberg, 2006). In an attempt to redirect youth and reduce disproportionate interaction with the system, a diversion program was implemented in urban Honolulu targeting Chuukese teenagers who are overrepresented (Miao et al., 2022). While a number of diversion services are employed to support youth and families including hospital- or community-based residential programs, family intervention, department of education services, outpatient treatment, out of home placement, and youth programs, prevention research suggests that successful interventions for Indigenous youth should be tailored to their social and cultural context (Carreira Ching et al., 2023; Dixon et al., 2007). Although efficacious interventions exist for American Indian and Alaska Native youth (Donovan et al., 2015), systematic reviews reveal a lack of interventions tailored for NHPI youth (Edwards et al., 2010; Durand et al., 2016).

Incarcerated youth suffer long-term effects that can limit future opportunities. For example, incarcerated youth are less likely to graduate from high school, hold continuous employment, or enjoy upward socioeconomic mobility than their nonincarcerated peers. Moreover, many youths involved in the justice system are also involved in gangs, in order to receive protection and to fill the gap in familial support in this new environment. Gang members comprise 47% of incarcerated youth, have higher rearrest rates, and commit crimes at an earlier age than nonmembers (Huebner et al., 2007; Varano et al., 2011). This has culminated into an environment where this population is denigrated, experience discrimination, suffer economic hardship, and endure unstable housing, all of which contribute to mental and physical health challenges. The lack of access to healthcare further exacerbates their vulnerability, leaving youth and their families with limited options for mental health support.

Acculturation Stress and Systemic Barriers

Pacific Islander youth in the US experience the dual pressures of preserving their cultural heritage while adapting to American society. Many encounter racism, discrimination, and economic hardship, leading to feelings of alienation and stress. Increasing rates of these youth have adopted unhealthy western behaviors related to diet and substance use which exacerbates challenges related to social, cultural, and language barriers, putting them at greater risk of substance use, school dropout, abuse, and neglect (Derauf et al., 2011; Okamoto et al., 2008). Like other Indigenous peoples who have experienced colonization, these groups exhibit health disparities including poor health, lower life expectancy, and higher rates of chronic and infectious diseases (Riklon et al., 2010).

Racism and Stereotyping

Pacific Islander youth frequently face stereotypes that depict them as either hyper-athletic or aggressive, which limit their opportunities and sense of self-worth. These racialized narratives contribute to negative educational experiences, including increased rates of disciplinary action and lowered academic expectations. These stereotypes may become self-fulfilling prophecies, combined with the western capitalist drive to achieve material success, which may lead to illegal activity and police profiling of Pacific Islander youth. Communities are impacted by youth activity as well as police activity, sometimes leading to instances of violence and youth death at police hands creating animosities and further racialization in the public opinion (Hofschneider, 2021).

Micronesian youth have had to contend with a particularly vile racism directed at their communities, who have been labeled as leeches and cockroaches who come to Hawaiʻi only to use government services (Okamura, 2019). Given the stigma Micronesians face for being Micronesian (Rita et al., 2020), it is not surprising that some Micronesians do not disclose experiences of racial discrimination for fear of repercussions (Inada et al., 2019). Micronesian youth experience racism in their schools (Okamoto et al., 2008; Talmy, 2009) and in their communities (Faller et al., 2019).

Racism and stereotyping are also heavily impactful to youth schooling, education, attendance, and attainment (Blair, 2022; Harlow, 2022; Okamura, 2019). These impacts highlight the need for efforts to improve cultural understanding of community and school service providers (Okamoto et al., 2008). Some efforts have been made to bridge this gap, unfortunately these have almost exclusively had to come from the community while governmental efforts to assess and address have lagged for years but some more recent efforts have been made (Hofschneider, 2022; Ordonio, 2024).

Family Pressures and Cultural Expectations

The collectivist nature of Pacific cultures emphasizes the importance of family responsibility and communal support, which can be both a source of strength and a source of stress. Many Pacific youth act as cultural brokers for their families, navigating healthcare systems, legal paperwork, and financial responsibilities. While this role helps foster resilience, it can also lead to burnout, anxiety, and depression. Often youth serve as interpreters for their older family members, with some rates as high as 94% of Micronesian youth (Carreira Ching et al., 2023).

Pacific youth frequently face stereotypes that depict them as either hyperathletic or aggressive, which limit their opportunities and sense of self-worth. These racialized narratives contribute to negative educational experiences, including increased rates of disciplinary action and lowered academic expectations. Many youth experience long gaps in educational attendance due to diversion services and justice system involvement leading to difficulties in reentering education with their same-age peers, and many end up dropping out altogether (Carreira Ching et al., 2023).

Systemic Barriers to Mental Health Care

Pacific Islander youth are increasingly involved in systems including the child welfare, foster, and justice systems. For crossover youth (youth involved in more than one), family support services are less frequently engaged by these families (Carreira Ching et al., 2022). Although rates of parental incarceration and parental substance use history are often much lower compared to their Native Hawaiian peers, Other Pacific Islander Youth seem to exhibit equally high rates of substance use (Carreira Ching et al., 2023). In fact, more than two-thirds of the overall services offered to Micronesian youth and their families in Hawaiʻi across five fiscal years (2018–2022) were to address substance use (Carreira Ching et al., 2023).

While many families are offered services or have the potential to receive services (70%), many decline or lose contact perhaps due to cultural or language barriers (Carreira Ching et al., 2023). Some factors to consider in treatment are cultural factors related to help-seeking, a lack of trust in acceptance of services particularly government services due to the overpromises and failures of the COFA program as well as racism faced in the United States (Carreira Ching et al., 2023).

Recommendations

Recommendations for improving acculturative stress and its many complex issues focus on cultural approaches for providers and organizations. Approaches embodying collectivistic cultural values may be more effective at reducing acculturation barriers to help-seeking behaviors and engagement with care providers (Cassel et al., 2020). There is a great need for the development of culturally relevant programs specifically geared toward prevention and harm-reduction strategies for substance use (Monick et al., 2023). Additionally, cultivating community partnerships and building relationships with cultural experts to address language and cultural barriers may help to directly impact effects as well as assist in implementation of other efforts (Ellis et al., 2011).

Pacific Islander Well-being models

In the face of ongoing challenges, Pacific Islander youth continue to find strength in their cultural heritage, family networks, and traditional healing practices (see Table 9.3). There is limited research available on Pacific Islander well-being models in the United States. The majority of research in this area has been conducted with Pacific Islanders living outside of the United States, in countries such as Aotearoa.

Common Principles Across the Pacific

There are similar principles that can be found across the diverse Pacific Island groups and, with caution, could be used as a starting point to understand the worldview of Pacific Islander youth. A recent literature review by Teariki and Leau (2024) found five recurring values across various

Table 9.3 Pacific principles and models of well-being.

Model/Principle	Group	Overview
Holistic systems	Transpacific	Interconnection between all living and nonliving things that make up the whole
Family	Transpacific	Encompasses present and ancestral connections, as well as the values that govern relationships
Spirituality	Transpacific	Systems of belief and spiritual connection to the world
Connection to the natural world	Transpacific	Reciprocity and care in relation to the world
Theory of space and time	Transpacific	Space that connects and holds things together
Fonofale Model of Health	Samoa, Cook Islands, Tonga	Model of well-being emphasizes the multifaceted nature of health that includes family, culture, physical, spiritual, mental, and other
Fa'afaletui	Samoa	Research method that advocates for the inclusion of multiple perspectives
Relational and Navigational Framework	Micronesia	Emphasizes the importance of relationships, connection, and community

Pacific Island cultures (see Table 9.3). The five values are: (1) holistic systems, (2) family, (3) spirituality, (4) connection to the natural world, and (5) theory of space and time.

A holistic system represents the interconnection between all living and nonliving things that make up the whole. Pacific Islander groups emphasize the importance of these connections and the balance between them to promote well-being. For example, the *Fonofale* model of health describes the connection and balance between three distinct parts of a house. The maintenance of each part of the house is critical in protecting the well-being of an individual. The family, or "collective family," encompasses both present and ancestral connections. It also represents the cultural values that govern the relationship between family members, such as respect and reciprocity. Spirituality refers to systems of belief and spiritual connection to the world. This could mean practice of ancient spirituality or Christianity. Connection to the natural world is a large part of many Pacific Island cultures. Unlike western ideals, this connection to the natural world focuses on reciprocity and care, rather than extraction. Lastly, *Vā, Te Vā, Teu le va, Tā-Vā, Tauhi Va* refer to a theory of space and time that cuts across different Pacific Island cultures. Space, in this context, does not refer to emptiness, but instead space that connects and holds things together. For example, social relationships and connection to land are bound by space.

Fonofale Model of Health

The *Fonofale* model of health (see Figure 9.1) was originally used to promote the well-being of Pacific Islanders in Aotearoa (Suaalii-Sauni et al., 2009). It incorporates values from multiple Pacific Islander groups including Samoa, Cook Islands, and Tonga. This model of health is visually represented by a traditional Samoan *fale*, or house, which depicts three distinct parts: (1) the foundation, (2) the four posts, and (3) the roof. It is the connection between and maintenance of all parts that allow the fale to stand strong.

The foundation of the house represents the family, highlighting the critical importance of this connection in well-being. To be healthy, is to be supported by and connected to one's family. The family also includes considerations of history and genealogy, which can trace important connections to the land, sea, and culture. The four posts represent four different aspects that create a connection between the foundation and the roof: (1) physical, (2) spiritual, (3) mental, and (4) other. The physical speaks to a person's biological or physical well-being. This may include talks about diet, hydration, or other substances that impact a person's physical health. The spiritual post refers to a person's spiritual belief system, whether that be traditional spirituality or religion.

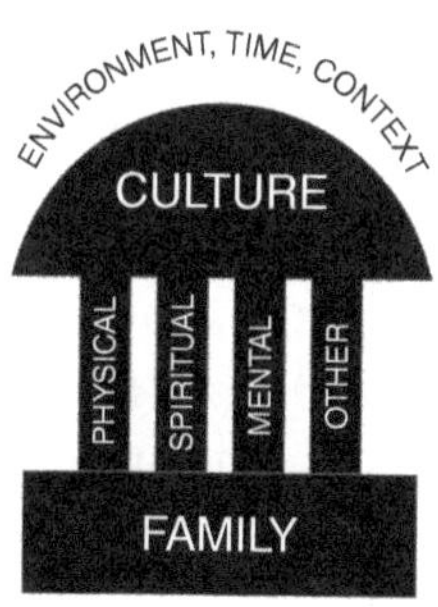

Figure 9.1 *Fonofale* model of health.

The mental post involves considerations of an individual's thoughts, emotions, and behaviors. Other, which is the last post, refers to variables that do not fall within the other domains but can impact an individual's health, including gender, sexuality, and socioeconomic status. The roof of the house represents a person's cultural beliefs or practices, which provides shelter for all parts of the *fale*. This model also calls for the examination of external factors that may impact well-being. This is visually represented as a circle that surrounds the *fale* and includes the environment, time, and context. Every aspect of the *fale* and its surrounding context plays a critical role in an individual's overall well-being and is important to consider when working with Pacific Islander youth.

Samoan Models of Well-being

Frameworks and models for conducting research with Samoan populations in a culturally sensitive way have been developed, such as *Fa'afaletui* (Tamasese et al., 2005). *Fa'afaletui* is defined as weaving together different houses and is a research method that emphasizes the importance of considering and valuing different perspectives when discussing important issues. However, there is limited research on Samoan models of overall well-being.

A groundbreaking study by Dunlop-Bennett et al. (2019) was the first to examine Samoan children's conceptualization of well-being. The children spoke of five broad themes in relation to well-being. First, children described well-being as a "bunch of stuff," such as physical, social, spiritual, and cultural considerations, highlighting their holistic view of health. The other four themes discuss specific variables that are important to maintain well-being. Children expressed the importance of connecting with loved ones, either by hanging out with their friends or spending time with their families. Feeling secure and not having to worry was another variable that the children shared that impacts their well-being. This could be represented by having a person to rely on and trust. The third theme was feeling valued, included, and with a sense of belonging. This sense of belonging may be fostered through the family, religious organizations, sports teams, and more. Lastly, children describe the importance of being a good person by helping others or being respectful. The act of good deeds could help contribute to an overall sense of well-being. This study provides a foundation to future research involving Samoan youth and their conceptualization of well-being.

Micronesian Models of Well-being

Similar to Samoan populations, there is very little research on Micronesian models of well-being and overall conceptualizations of health. We are Oceania (WAO) is a Hawai'i-based nonprofit organization that services the large Micronesian community in the State. WAO CEO, Josie Howard, often describes a relational and navigational framework for Micronesian populations, which references the importance of relationships, connection, and community to Micronesian groups. Specifically, Josie Howard shares that, "When we [Micronesian people] come to a new place, we get to know it, respect it, and become aware of our surroundings," (Hahn, 2023). This understanding of how Micronesians view and interact with the world around them echoes the common principles that cut across different Pacific Islander groups, such as a connection to the natural world and time and space (Teariki & Leau, 2024). It is important to appropriately engage with Micronesian populations to aid in the development of a well-being model.

Clinical Case Study: Culturally Grounded Group Therapy

Dr. Sione Tafuna, a Licensed Clinical Psychologist, shared a powerful case example of creating a therapy group grounded or rooted in Polynesian culture while working at the Hawai'i State Hospital. Dr. Tafuna created and facilitated group therapy for approximately ten adult patients in collaboration with a clinical team that included a Recreational Therapist and two Occupational Therapists. The group was created with the objective of teaching participants emotional regulation and social skills from a Polynesian cultural framework, mainly Hawaiian and Tongan cultures. The theoretical foundation of wellness and how that is achieved was based on a Polynesian cultural framework rather than a Western one. The ethnic composition of the group was mainly participants of Polynesian ancestry (e.g., Hawaiian, Tongan, Samoan). Many of the participants were dual diagnosed, meaning they had one or more mental disorders (e.g., mood disorders, anxiety disorders, personality disorders, schizophrenia, and/or substance use).

The group met in the unit's cafeteria. From the very first group until it ended, the clinical team decorated the tables with *ti* leaves and plumeria flowers. *Mamaki* tea was also made available for the participants. Before the participants went into the cafeteria, they gathered as a group at the front door. Dr. Tafuna welcomed the participants and explained that this group was going on a journey of healing, and the cafeteria would be the *va'a* (canoe). He also explained that the Hawai'i State Hospital was built on sacred land that was meant to be a place of healing for all those who came here. The Recreational Therapist, also a Hawaiian cultural practitioner, then prayed and sanctified the cafeteria as a sanctuary, a place of healing, and a place of growth.

The beginning sessions emphasized and taught participants about Polynesian culture and values. Each participant was given time to talk about the specific place in Hawai'i they were born and raised and what they knew was significant or important about that place. The same was done with participants who were not from Hawai'i. Next, they were introduced to key Polynesian values such as respect, *aloha* (love), maintaining social ties, humility, being *pono*, and community. These values were taught and reinforced through the sharing of cultural stories (e.g., Maui) and discussion facilitation. One of the participants found a small taro plant growing in the yard, dug it up, and proposed to the group that it could be their mascot. The participants named the baby taro, Taro. Throughout the group session, Dr. Tafuna and his team, including the Polynesian guards, modeled and reinforced Polynesian culture and ways of being which set the tone for the entire group. In the later parts of the group, the clinical team facilitated activities that supported emotional regulation, stress tolerance, and social skills development.

This group demonstrated how building a treatment foundation based on Polynesian culture can bring about healing and effective change. The participants began to change as the group went on. They responded with openness and eagerness to learn because of their personal connection to the values that underlaid treatment and guided discussions. The Polynesian participants strongly embraced their cultural identity and integrated cultural values into their daily lives. While this case focused on adults, the same principles hold promise for Polynesian youth. Clinicians working with young people should prioritize opportunities to connect them with their ancestry, place, and cultural values, framing healing through strengths rather than deficits. By weaving cultural practices into therapy, providers can help youth cultivate resilience and deepen their sense of identity.

Conclusion

Youth from the Pacific in the United States encounter distinct mental health challenges that stem from historical trauma, militarization, and systemic barriers. Despite showing significant resilience, it is essential to address their mental health needs through a culturally responsive approach that recognizes intergenerational trauma and promotes identity development. Research and policy development should prioritize the voices and needs of Pacific Islander communities, recognizing their agency and leadership in shaping mental health solutions. By centering the experiences and wisdom of these communities, we can build a more inclusive and responsive mental health landscape that respects and uplifts diverse cultural identities. Investing in initiatives led by Pacific communities, increasing access to mental health care, and incorporating traditional healing practices can help create a future where Micronesian and Samoan youth can have the tools and support they need to navigate their challenges, celebrate their heritage, and envision a hopeful future.

Glossary of terms.

Term	Definition
Aloha	Love
Fale	House
Fonofale	Model of well-being that uses the house as a visual to outline key aspects of health
Fa'afaletui	Weaving together; also name of a research method
Fa'amatai	Samoan political system
Fa'a Samoa	Samoan way of life
La teu le va	Care for the relational space or relationships
Matai	Chief
Va'a	Canoe
Vā, Te Vā, Teu le va, Tā-Vā, Tauhi Va	Theory of space and time

References

Ali, S., Williams, O., Chang, O., Shidhaye, R., Hunter, E., & Charlson, F. (2020). Mental health in the Pacific: urgency and opportunity. *Asia Pacific Viewpoint, 61*(3), 537–550. https://doi.org/10.1111/apv.12286

American Samoa Bar Associations. (2012). Convention of 1899. https://asbar.org/convention-of-1899/

The Asian American Foundation. (2024). Beyond the surface: youth mental health report. https://beyond-the-surface.s3.amazonaws.com/beyond-the-surface-youth- mental-health-report-2024.pdf

Asian Pacific Institute on Gender-Based Violence. (2022). Census Data and API Identities. https://api-gbv.org/resources/census-data-api-identities/

Benda, B. B., & Tollett, C. L. (1999). A study of recidivism of serious and persistent offenders among adolescents. *Journal of Criminal Justice, 27*(2), 111–126. https://doi.org/10.1016/S0047-2352(98)00051-8

Blair, C. (2022). Why Micronesian students struggle in Hawaii. *Honolulu Civil Beat*. https://www.civilbeat.org/2022/05/chad-blair-why-micronesian-students-struggle-in-hawaii/

Bond, J. R., & Soli, F. M. (2011). The Samoans. In J. F. McDermott, & N. N. Andrade (Eds.), *People and Cultures of Hawaii: The Evolution of Culture and Ethnicity*. University of Hawaii Press. https://doi.org/10.1515/9780824860264

Brave Heart, M. Y. H. (2003). The historical trauma response among natives and its relationship with substance abuse: a Lakota illustration. *Journal of Psychoactive Drugs, 35*(1), 7–13. https://doi.org/10.1080/02791072.2003.10399988

Carreira Ching, D. L., Acosta, V. M., Gerson, J., Harris, M., Hiura, A., & Higa, C. (2022). Trauma-related mental health trends and family history factors of Native Hawaiian adolescents at the Hawai'i Youth Correctional Facility. [Poster presentation]. 19th Annual Hawai'i International Summit of the Institute on Violence, Abuse, and Trauma, Honolulu, HI.

Carreira Ching, D. L., Acosta, V. M., Hiura, A., Garcia, P., Logreco, S., Hsu, S., & Higa, C. (2023). Considerations of acculturative stress and trends in background factors of Micronesian youth at Hawai'i Youth Correctional Facility (HYCF) [Poster presented]. *20th Annual Hawai'i International Summit of the Institute on Violence, Abuse, and Trauma*, Honolulu, HI.

Cassel, K., Willingham, M., Lee, H., Somera, L. P., Badowski, G., & Pagano, I. (2020). Acculturation and cancer risk behaviors among pacific islanders in Hawai'i. *Ethnicity & Disease, 30*(4), 593–602. https://doi.org/10.188865/ed.30.4.593

David, A. M., & Lapid Rosadino, M. G. on behalf of the Guam State Epidemiological Outcomes Workgroup (SEOW). (2015). *Guam State Epidemiological Profile 2014 Update*. Hagatna, Guam: Prevention and Training Branch, Guam Behavioral Health and Wellness Center.

David, A. M., Lapid-Rosadino, M. G., & Tydingco, T. on behalf of the Guam State Epidemiological Outcomes Workgroup (SEOW). (2016). *Guam State Epidemiological Profile 2015 Update*. Hagatna, Guam: Prevention and Training Branch, Guam Behavioral Health and Wellness Center.

Derauf, D., Fleishchaker, M., Fujimoto, N. C., Gardner, P., O'Brien, F. T., Reber, D. J., & Geminiani, V. (2011). Broken promises, shattered lives: the case for justice for Micronesians in Hawai'i. Hawai'i Appleseed Center for Law and Economic Justice. Policy Brief: Systemic barriers to self-achievement and economic security for compact of free association migrants in Hawai'i. https://hiappleseed.org/publications/brokenpromises-shattered-lives

Diaz, K. K. (2012). *The Compact of Free Association* (COFA): A history of failures. University of Hawaii at Manoa.

Dixon, A. L., Yabiku, S. T., Okamoto, S. K., Tann, S. S., Marsiglia, F. F., Kulis, S., & Burke, A. M. (2007). The efficacy of a multicultural prevention intervention among urban American Indian youth in the southwest U.S. *The Journal of Primary Prevention, 28*(6), 547–568. https://doi.org/10.1007/s10935-007-0114-8

Donovan, D. M., Rey Thomas, L., Sigo, R. L. W., Price, L., Lonczak, H., Lawrence, N., ... Bagley, L. (2015). Healing of the canoe: preliminary results of a culturally grounded intervention to prevent substance abuse and promote tribal identity for Native youth in two Pacific Northwest tribes. *American Indian & Alaska Native Mental Health Research: The Journal of the National Center, 22*(1), 42–76.

Dunlop-Bennett, E., Bryant-Tokalau, J., & Dowell, A. (2019). When you ask the fish: child wellbeing through the eyes of Samoan children. *International Journal of Wellbeing, 9*(4), 97–120. https://doi.org/10.5502/ijw.v9i4.1005

Durand, Z., Cook, A., Konishi, M., & Nigg, C. (2016). Alcohol and substance use prevention programs for youth in Hawaii and Pacific Islands: a literature review. *Journal of Ethnicity in Substance Abuse, 15*(3), 240–251. https://doi.org/10.1080/15332640.2015.1024811

Edwards, C., Giroux, D., & Okamoto, S. K. (2010). A review of the literature on Native Hawaiian youth and drug use: implications for research and practice. *Journal of Ethnicity in Substance Abuse, 9*(3), 153–172. https://doi.org/10.1080/15332640.2010.500580

Ellis, B. H., Miller, A. B., Baldwin, H., & Abdi, S. (2011). New directions in refugee youth mental health services: overcoming barriers to engagement. *Journal of Child & Adolescent Trauma, 4*, 69–85. https://doi.org/10.1080/19361521.2011.545047

Faleomavaega Eni Fa'aua'a Hunkin VA Clinic. (2025). Veterans Affairs. https://www.va.gov/pacific-islands-health-care/locations/faleomavaega-eni-faauaa-hunkin-va-clinic/

Faller, E. K., Jean-Pierre, G., Inada, M., & Acido, J. M. (2019). Pedals and pedagogy: cycles of hope and health. *Hawai'i Journal of Medicine & Public Health, 78*(6 Suppl 1), 61–64.

Fitzpatrick, K. M., & Willis, D. (2018). Risks, resources, and depressive symptomatology among Marshallese adolescents. *The American Journal of Orthopsychiatry, 88*(2), 189–198. https://doi.org/10.1037/ort0000288

Gavin, L. (2017). Risks, protections, and weight status among Springdale High School students (Publication no. 10278003). [Master's Thesis, University of Arkansas]. ProQuest Dissertations & Theses Global.

Government of Samoa. (n.d.). Samoa. https://www.samoagovt.ws/about-samoa/

Hahn, D. (2023). A conversation with We Are Oceania: navigating good jobs from a Micronesian perspective. Hawai'i Workforce Funders Collaborative. https://www.hawaiiwork.org/resources/a-good-job-on-hawaii-island-z6e2j

Hanlon, D. (2009). The "sea of little lands": examining Micronesia's place in "our sea of islands." *The Contemporary Pacific, 21*(1), 91–110. https://doi.org/10.1353/cp.0.0042

Hanlon, D. L. (1998). *Remaking Micronesia: Discourses over Development in a Pacific Territory, 1944-1982*. United States: University of Hawaii Press.

Harlow, C. (2022). New research highlights racial inequities faced by Micronesian students in Hawai'i schools. *Honolulu Civil Beat.*

Hawai'i Department of Human Services. (2022). *Three-Year Comprehensive Juvenile Justice and Delinquency Prevention State Plan: FY2021–2023 Year 2 Update*. https://humanservices.hawaii.gov/wp-content/uploads/2022/12/FY2022-Hawaii-3-Year-2021-2023-State-Plan-Year-2-update.pdf

Hezel, F. X., & Wylie, M. A. (1992). Schizophrenia and chronic mental illness in Micronesia: an epidemiological survey. *ISLA: A Journal of Micronesian Studies, 1*, 329–354. https://micronesianseminar.org/article/schizophrenia-and-chronic-mental-illness-in-micronesia-an-epidemiological-survey/

Hinton, D. E., Hinton, A. L., Pich, V., Loeum, J. R., & Pollack, M. H. (2009). Nightmares among Cambodian refugees: the breaching of concentric ontological security. *Culture, Medicine, and Psychiatry, 33*(2), 219–265. https://doi.org/10.1007/s11013-009-9131-9

Hixon, L., Hepler, B. B., & Kim, M. O. (2012). *The Native Hawaiian and Other Pacific Islander Population: 2010* (US Census Briefs No. C2010BR-12). United States Census Bureau. https://www.census.gov/content/dam/Census/library/publications/2012/dec /c2010br-12.pdf

Hofschneider, A. (2021). Police killing of Micronesian teen in Hawaii prompts grief and questions. *Honolulu Civil Beat.* https://www.civilbeat.org/2021/04/police-killing-of-micronesian-teen-in-hawaii-prompts-grief-and-questions/#:~:text=In%20the%20absence%20of%20more,consequence%20for%20his%20alleged%20crimes

Hofschneider, A. (2022). Micronesian community group hosts conversation with Honolulu police. *Honolulu Civil Beat.* https://www.civilbeat.org/beat/micronesian-community-group-hosts-conversation-with-honolulu-police/

Holman, B., & Ziedenberg, J. (2006). The dangers of detention: the impact of incarcerating youth in detention and other secure facilities. Justice Policy Institute. https://justicepolicy.org/wp-content/uploads/2022/02/06-11_rep_dangersofdetention_jj.pdf

Huebner, B.M., Varano, S.P., & Bynum, T.S. (2007). Gangs, guns, and drugs: recidivism among serious, young offenders*. *Criminology and Public Policy*, *6*(2), 187–221. https://doi.org/10.1111/j.1745-9133.2007.00429.x

Inada, M. K., Braun, K. L., Mwarike, P., Cassel, K., Compton, R., Yamada, S., & Sentell, T. (2019). Chuukese community experiences of racial discrimination and other barriers to healthcare: perspectives from community members and providers. *Social Medicine (Social Medicine Publication Group), 12*(1), 3–13. https://doi.org/10.71164/socialmedicine.v12i1.2019.994

Kamaka, M.L., Watkins-Victorino, L., Lee, A., Mersberg Freitas, S., Wong Ramsey, K., Quint, J., ... Keawe'aimoku Kaholokula, J. (2021). Addressing Native Hawaiian and Pacific Islander data deficiencies through a community-based collaborative response to the COVID-19 pandemic. *Hawaii Journal of Health and Social Welfare, 80*(10), 36–45.

Leckie, J., & Hughes, F. (2017). Mental health in the smaller Pacific States. In H. Minas, & M. Lewis, (Eds.), *Mental health in Asia and the Pacific: Historical and Cultural Perspectives* (pp. 253–272). Springer US. https://doi.org/10.1007/978-1-4899-7999-5_17

Lilomaiava-Doktor, S. (2009). Beyond "migration": Samoan population movement (malaga) and the geography of social space (Vā). *The Contemporary Pacific, 21*(1), 1–32. http://www.jstor.org/stable/23724742

Lor, M., Yu, Z., Chen, W., Xiong, Y., Yonker, J. A., Brown, R., & Krahn, D. D. (2022). Refugee-related trauma patterns and mental health symptoms across three generations of Hmong Americans. *Journal of Traumatic Stress, 35*(4). https://doi.org/10.1002/jts.22813

Mathieu, S., de Leo, D., Koo, Y. W., Leske, S., Goodfellow, B., & Kõlves, K. (2021). Suicide and suicide attempts in the Pacific Islands: a systematic literature review. *The Lancet Regional Health. Western Pacific, 17*, 100283. https://doi.org/10.1016/j.lanwpc.2021.100283

McClain, S. N., Seru, J., & Lajar, H. (2019). Migration, transition, and livelihoods: a comparative analysis of Marshallese pre- and post-migration to the United States. *Journal of Disaster Research, 14*(9), 1262–1266. https://doi.org/10.20965/jdr.2019.p1262

McCubbin, L. D., & Marsella, A. (2009). Native Hawaiians and psychology: the cultural and historical context of indigenous ways of knowing. *Cultural Diversity and Ethnic Minority Psychology, 15*(4), 374–387. hops://doi.org/10.1037/a0016774

McElfish, P. A., Purvis, R., Willis, D. E., & Riklon, S. (2021). COVID-19 disparities among Marshallese Pacific Islanders. *Preventing Chronic Disease, 18*, E02. https://doi.org/10.5888/pcd18.200407

Miao, T.-A., Hishinuma, E. S., & Umemoto, K. N. (2022). Implications for a system of care in Hawai'i for youth involved in the justice system and substance use. *Hawai'i Journal of Health & Social Welfare, 81*(12 Suppl 3), 27–36.

Monick, B., Rehuher, D., Wilczek, K., & Helm, S. (2023) Eliminating disparities in youth substance use among Native Hawaiian, Micronesian, and sex and gender minorities: a qualitative needs assessment from interviews with public service leaders. *American Psychological Association, 20*(Supp 1), 103–116. https://doi.org/10.1037/ser0000609

Neblett, E. W. (2023). Racial, ethnic, and cultural resilience factors in African American youth mental health. *Annual Review of Clinical Psychology, 19*(1). https://doi.org/10.1146/annurev-clinpsy-072720-015146

Nieri, T., Yoo, M., & Tam, C. (2024). Ethnic-racial socialization in mono-racial Asian American and Pacific Islander families: a 21-year systematic literature review. *Sociology Compass, 18*(2). https://doi.org/10.1111/soc4.13185

Office of Insular Affairs. (n.d.). American Samoa. https://www.doi.gov/oia/islands/american-samoa
Okamoto, S., Mayeda, D., Ushiroda, M., Rehuher, D., & Lauilefue, T. (2008). Risk and protective factors of Micronesian youth in Hawai'i: an exploratory study. *The Journal of Sociology & Social Welfare, 35*(2), 127–147. https://scholarworks.wmich.edu/jssw/vol35/iss2/8
Okamura, J. Y. (2019). What about racial groups and boundaries (and race and racism)? *Anthropological Notebooks, 25*(1), 37–56.
Onoye, J, Miao, T, Goebert, D, Thompson, M., Helm, S., Akamu, C., ... Kuniyoshi, E. (2021). 2019-2020 Hawai'i student Alcohol, Tobacco, and Other Drug (ATOD) survey: statewide report. https://health.hawaii.gov/wp-content/uploads/2022/01/2019-2020-Hawaii-ATOD-Survey-Statewide-Comprehensive-Report.pdf
Ordonio, C. (2024). 'A great first step': Hawai'i Island police undergo Micronesian culture training. *Hawai'i Public Radio*. https://www.hawaiipublicradio.org/hawaii-island-police-micronesian-culture-training
Palafox, N. A., & Hixon, A. L. (2011). Health consequences of disparity: the US affiliated Pacific Islands. *Australasian Psychiatry: Bulletin of the Royal Australian and New Zealand College of Psychiatrists, 19*(1_suppl), S84–S89. https://doi.org/10.3109/10398562.2011.583072
Palafu, T., Carreira Ching, D. L., Acosta, V. M., Okamoto, S. K., & Okamura, K. H. (2024). Native Hawaiian and Pacific Islanders' identity and housing status: the impact on historical trauma and perceived stress. *International Journal of Environmental Research and Public Health, 21*(9), 1249. https://doi.org/10.3390/ijerph21091249
Pasko, L., & Mayeda, D. T. (2011). Pathways and predictors of juvenile justice involvement for Native Hawaiian and Pacific Islander youths: a focus on gender. *Journal of Ethnic & Cultural Diversity in Social Work, 20*(2), 114–130. https://doi.org/10.1080/15313204.2011.570120
Pinhey T. K., & Millman S. R. (2004). Asian/Pacific Islander adolescent sexual orientation and suicide risk in Guam. *American Journal of Public Health, 94*, 1204–1206. https://www.ncbi.nlm.nih.gov/pmc/articles/PMC1448422/pdf/0941204.pdf
Pokhrel, P., & Herzog, T. A. (2014). Historical trauma and substance use among Native Hawaiian college students. *American Journal of Health Behavior, 38*(3), 420–429. https://doi.org/10.5993/AJHB.38.3.11
Poyer, L. (1991). *Micronesian Experiences of the War in the Pacific*. Honolulu, HI: Center for Pacific Islands Studies, School of Hawaiian, Asian, and Pacific Studies, University of Hawai'i at Mānoa.
Poyer, L., Falgout, S., & Carucci, L. M. (2000). *The Typhoon of War: Micronesian Experiences of the Pacific War*. Germany: University of Hawaii Press.
Rapadas, J. (2001). Demographic, clinical, and offense variables among juvenile delinquents in Guam: a longitudinal analysis for the period of 1987-2000 (Publication no. 3005222). [Doctoral Dissertation, University of Hawai'i]. UMI.
Rico, B., Hahn, J. K., Jacobs, P. (2023). *Chuukese and Papua New Guinean populations fastest growing Pacific Islander groups in 2020*. (US Census Bureau Detailed Look at Native Hawaiian and Other Pacific Islander Groups). United States Census Bureau. https://www.census.gov/library/stories/2023/09/2020-census-dhc-a-nhpi-population.htm
Riklon, S., Alik, W., Hixon, A., & Palafox, N. A. (2010). The "compact impact" in Hawai'i: focus on health care. *Hawai'i Medical Journal, 69*(6 Supp 3), 7–12.
Riley, L., Su'esu'e, A., Hulama, K., Neumann, S. K., & Chung-Do, J. (2022). Ke ala i ka Mauliola: Native Hawaiian youth experiences with historical trauma. *International Journal of Environmental Research and Public Health*, 19(19). https://doi.org/10.3390/ijerph191912564

Rita, N., Darrah-Okike, J., Engel, R., & Garboden, P. (2020). Contesting the right to the city under scarcity: the case of Micronesians in Hawai'i's public housing. *Housing and Society 47*(3). https://doi.org/10.1080/08882746.2020.1765667

Roth, M.S. (2023). Asian American and Pacific Islander heritage month. *History, A&E Television Networks.*

Saleh, M. A. (1994). Patterns, problems and attitudes towards alcohol consumption among Micronesian college students. *Journal of Instructional Psychology, 21*(3), 267–273. https://search.proquest.com/openview/0e01b3d6c7f16fcbfb0b8dd157 69a2cf/1?pq-origsite=gscholar&cbl=2029838

Saunders, A., Schiff, T., Rieth, K., Yamada, S., Maskarinec, G. G., & Riklon, S. (2010). Health as a human right: who is eligible? *Hawai'i Medical Journal, 69*(6 Suppl 3), 4–6.

Shaikh, A., & Rawal, H. (2018). Interconnections among homelessness, family separation, and mental health: implications for multi-sectoral social services. *Journal of Social Service Research, 45*(4), 543–557. https://doi.org/10.1080/01488376.2018.1481174

Shimkhada, R. Scheitler, A.J., & Ponce, N. A. (2021). Capturing racial/ethnic diversity in population based surveys: data disaggregation of health data for Asian American, Native Hawaiian and Pacific Islanders (AANHPIs). *Population Research and Policy Review, 40*, 81–102. https://doi.org/10.1007/s11113-020-09634-3

Suaalii-Sauni, T., Wheeler, A., Saafi, E., Robinson, G., Agnew, F., Warren, H., Erick, M., & Hingano, T. (2009). Exploration of Pacific perspectives of Pacific models of mental health service delivery in New Zealand. *Pacific Health Dialog, 15*(1), 18–27. https://www.researchgate.net/publication/26655124

Substance Abuse and Mental Health Services Administration. (2021). One size does not fit all: appreciating the diversity of Asian Americans, Native Hawaiians, and Pacific Islanders (AANHPIs) and the implications for mental health, pp. 1–14.

Talmy, S. (2009). Becoming "Local" in ESL: racism as resource in a Hawai'i public high school. *Journal of Language, Identity, and Education, 9*(1), 36–57. https://doi.org/10.1080/15348450903476840

Tamasese, K., Peteru, C., Waldegrave, C., & Bush, A. (2005). Ole Taeao Afua, the new morning: a qualitative investigation into Samoan perspectives on mental health and culturally appropriate services. *Australian and New Zealand Journal of Psychiatry, 39*(4), 300–309. https://doi.org/10.1111/j.1440-1614.2005.01572.x

Teariki, M. A., & Leau, E. (2024). Understanding Pacific worldviews: principles and connections for research. *Kōtuitui: New Zealand Journal of Social Sciences Online, 19*(2), 132–151. https://doi.org/10.1080/1177083X.2023.2292268

Tucker-Masters, L., & Tiatia-Seath, J. (2017). Reviewing the literature on anxiety and depression in Pacific youth: a fresh perspective. *New Zealand Medical Student Journal, 25*, 24–28.

University of California Irvine. (2021). Data collection, reporting gaps harm Native Hawaiians, Pacific Islander health, UCI-led study says. *University of California Irvine News*, 1–8.

University of Hawai'i at Mānoa. (2014). Health data to be collected on Native Hawaiians and Pacific Islanders. *Kaunana*. https://manoa.hawaii.edu/kaunana/health-data-to-be-collected-on-native-hawaiians-and-pacific-islanders/

Varano, S. P., Huebner, B. M., & Bynum, T. S. (2011). Correlates and consequences of pre-incarceration gang involvement among incarcerated youthful felons. *Journal of Criminal Justice, 39*(1), 30–38. https://doi.org/10.1016/j.jcrimjus.2010.10.001

Voisin, D. R., Kim, D., Takahashi, L., Morotta, P., & Bocanegra, K. (2016). Involvement in the juvenile justice system for African American adolescents: examining associations with behavioral health problems. *Journal of Social Service Research, 43*(1), 129–140. https://doi.org/10.1080/01488376.2016.1239596

Waldo, M. C. (1999). Schizophrenia in Kosrae, Micronesia: prevalence, gender ratios, and clinical symptomatology. *Schizophrenia Research, 35*(2), 175–181. https://doi.org/10.1016/S0920-9964(98)00118-2

Wendt, A. (1996). Tatauing the post-colonial body. New Zealand Electronic Poetry Centre. https://www.nzepc.auckland.ac.nz/authors/wendt/tatauing.asp

World Health Organization. (2021). Suicide worldwide in 2019: global health estimates. https://iris.who.int/bitstream/handle/10665/341728/9789240026643-eng.pdf?sequence=1

Yasui, M., Dishion, T. J., Stormshak, E., & Ball, A. (2015). Socialization of culture and coping with discrimination among American Indian families: examining cultural correlates of youth outcomes. *Journal of the Society for Social Work and Research, 6*(3), 317–341. https://doi.org/10.1086/682575

10

Ho'oulu Na Pua: Supporting Mental Well-being for Kānaka 'ōiwi Youth

Danielle L. Carreira Ching[1,3], Sheri-Ann Daniels[2], Jillian M.N. Freitas[4], Deborah Goebert[4], Melissa Kahili-Heede[2], Samantha Keaulana[2], Kelsie H. Okamura[1,5], Tessa Palafu[1], Lorinda Riley[4], and Nadia Yoshizumi-Kim[1]

[1]The Baker Center for Children and Families, Boston, MA, USA
[2]Papa Ola Lokahi, Honolulu, HI, USA
[3]Hawai'i Pacific University, Honolulu, HI, USA
[4]University of Hawai'i at Manoa, Honolulu, HI, USA
[5]University of Pennsylvania, Philadelphia, PA, USA

Introduction

Mental health is essential to overall well-being. Kānaka 'ōiwi or Native Hawaiian youth encounter unique challenges in this area. These challenges arise from a mix of historical and contemporary factors, including the legacy of colonization, cultural suppression, and systemic inequities. Today in Hawai'i, economic and housing instabilities disproportionately affect Hawaiian families, often leading to stress and anxiety in families.

Native Hawaiian youth are disproportionately involved in systems including foster, child welfare, and corrections. These youth and their families experience high rates of mental health issues including trauma and substance related disorders that have generational impacts (Carreira Ching et al., 2022). In 2020 and 2021, research on Native Hawaiian ($n = 24$) justice-involved youth reported high instances of involvement with child welfare (79.2%), parental incarceration (83.3%), and a history of parental substance use (100%), while all youth sampled (100%) had at least one substance use disorder, and the majority (79.1%) had a trauma-related diagnosis. These reports may account for high rates of youth suicide, drug use, and physical health issues found in Native Hawaiian youth (Hawaii Health Matters, n.d.).

Cultural identity may be paramount to youth resilience and may increase exponentially the impact of various protective factors (Palafu et al., 2024). However, the struggle to maintain cultural identity in an age dominated by social media, ongoing socioeconomic disparities, and environmental stressors exacerbates these issues. To effectively address these challenges, adopting a culturally responsive approach that acknowledges the connection between historical trauma, cultural resilience, and frameworks for well-being is crucial.

This chapter delves into the mental health landscape of Native Hawaiian youth by examining historical and systemic influences, current trends in mental health conditions, and culturally grounded models of well-being. It underscores the critical need for culturally responsive mental health services, highlighting existing programs that support Native Hawaiian youth mental health and offering recommendations for future directions. By integrating cultural knowledge with contemporary mental health frameworks, we can contribute to more holistic and effective approaches that promote healing, resilience, and well-being for Native Hawaiian youth.

Historical Trauma and Colonization

> I think with Native Hawaiians, and some compare with the indigenous people of America, with the displacement of their culture and history, you see a lot of generational trauma, and because of this generational [historical] trauma, having a kind of negative outlook sometimes of what people are good at or good enough for...[To discourage these impacts,] I think a big one is kind of really going back to values of what it means to be Hawaiian. The Hawaiian values really range in the community. Like one is ʻohana, you know. The families. And really bringing back the importance of the family and helping one another, each other out... Helping them to speak up for each other, doing more of the traditional hoʻoponopono (process for setting things right).
>
> *Ian Chun, MD Medical Director, Psychiatrist and Pediatrician*
> *Kīpuka o ke Ola (Rural Health Clinic)*
> *E Ola Mau a Mau, 2019*

Dr. Chun offers his patients and their family's insight into the effects of past trauma and strategies for resilience. The cumulative emotional and psychological wounds caused by severe group trauma that lasts throughout a person's life and across generations is known as historical or cultural trauma (Blaisdell, 1989; Blaisdell & Mokuau, 1991; Brave Heart, 1998, 1999a, 1999b, 2000; Brave Heart & DeBruyn, 1998; Brave Heart-Jordan & DeBruyn, 1995; DeCambra et al., 1998; Mokuau & Matsuoka, 1995; Papa Ola Lōkahi, 2019; Riley et al., 2022; Trask, 1993, 1994). Poor health may be a result of the specific history of colonial exploitation and oppression that Native Hawaiians have endured (Blaisdell & Mokuau, 1991; DeCambra et al., 1998; Kanahele, 1986; Mokuau & Matsuoka, 1995; Trask, 1993, 1994). Historical trauma is akin to kaumaha—profound grief rooted in heavy, oppressive sadness, and hōʻinoʻino—broken spirit (Hwang et al., 2025; Kaholokula, 2007; McCubbin et al., 2007; Rezentes, 1996; Streltzer et al., 1996; Riley et al., 2022).

Native Hawaiian history reflects colonization, land loss, and cultural repression, significantly impacting youth in ways unique from other Indigenous and non-Native communities (Riley et al., 2023). Colonization involves one group asserting dominance over another, impacting individuals through systems and structures that discriminate against and disenfranchise Indigenous peoples (Akamu & Ravida, 2025). The late 18th century brought disease, foreign legal systems, and a decline in traditional governance, leading to the loss of political sovereignty by the late 1800s. The overthrow of the Hawaiian Kingdom in 1893 and annexation in 1898 resulted in social and economic inequalities, displacing Native Hawaiians from their traditional lifestyles and pushing many into low-wage labor, creating ongoing stressors.

The loss of land disrupted traditional practices and governance, contributing to issues like poverty, homelessness, and food insecurity. Additionally, cultural suppression, such as the ban on the Hawaiian language in schools, severed connections to ancestry and identity, leading to declines in mental well-being. Consequently, Native Hawaiian youth faced higher rates of depression, anxiety, and suicide (Goebert et al., 2018). Additionally, insufficient representation of their experiences in schools can cause identity confusion and lowered self-worth, worsening mood disorders and anxiety. An initial study measuring the impact of historical trauma among Native Hawaiians (Pokhrel & Herzog, 2014) found that the vast majority of ($N = 128$) community college student participants reported thinking about the following losses at least annually or on special occasions: culture (89%), ancestral land (81%), language (87%), traditional spiritual ways (83%), respect by children for both traditional ways (83%) and for elders (79%). Nearly one-third of participants reflected upon such losses on a daily basis and the majority also thought about the likelihood of early death (80%) for Native Hawaiians (Pokhrel & Herzog, 2014). In examining the relationship with substance use, the authors found that historical trauma was linked indirectly to higher substance use through higher perceived discrimination. However, it was also linked directly to lower substance use.

Thoughts, knowledge, or experiences associated with historical trauma that increase substance use behavior via increased perceived discrimination may also, paradoxically, promote resilience. One possible explanation for this seemingly contradictory finding is that the historical trauma component that is separated out by the correlation with perceived discrimination may be a proxy or measure of cultural identification or ethnic pride. More research in this area is needed given the limitations of this study (e.g., cross-sectional design, different measures of substance use that appeared to be differentially associated with historical trauma, and definition of overall substance use). Understanding these historical and structural factors is crucial for developing effective mental health interventions that promote cultural healing and resilience. Identification and socialization are issues faced by Native Hawaiian youth; however, these issues are under researched, and thus, specific risks and protective factors of ethnic and racial identity (ERI) and ethnic-racial socialization (ERS) are yet to be documented. Understanding ERI and ERS among Native Hawaiian youth demands a consideration of how the ongoing impacts of settler colonialism continues to perpetuate risk factors like collective historical trauma. Conversely, there is a need to document the protective factors experienced by beneficiaries of Hawaiian cultural renaissance efforts which have led to cultural reclamation, pride, and resilience, following historical events and policies that sought to ban Hawaiian language and culture.

Alameda (2005) proposed a process model for Native Hawaiian healing that (1) synthesizes the historical events that occurred during the last 200 years and how they shaped—and continue to influence—the evolution of the Native Hawaiian ethnocultural identity and (2) provides a cultural paradigm for healing an ethnic group from the effects of generational trauma at the individual and group levels. He posited that ancestral memory and awareness of cultural values, beliefs, and practices lead to self-validation and self-worth. Furthermore, he posited that new behaviors, combined with positive reinforcement and community recognition, lead to a change in self-perception of behavior, which is necessary to increase resilience. These are considerations for ERI and ERS impacts due to the competing positive and negative impacts of socialization and identity formation for Native Hawaiian youth.

Resilience refers to the process of adapting well despite adversity or trauma, and the ability to increase capacity for dealing with future adverse events (Carlton et al., 2006; Masten, 2007). Given the value of promoting resilience in response to historical trauma, integrating cultural values into interventions is critical. Interventions must focus on the whole person as a cultural being connected to their ʻohana (family and extended family). For interventions to be successful, they must target resilience, family relationships, social and interpersonal stressors, cohesion, and functioning (Beardslee & Knitzer, 2004). This approach is essential for prevention and intervention programs. Programs that integrate cultural processes and encourage participation in meaningful cultural activities such as 'āina (land) based learning, stewardship, and traditional dance or arts can improve mental health and wellness for Native Hawaiians (Trinidad, 2009). Greater identification with Native Hawaiian culture is considered to be protective against risky behaviors such as substance use (Po'a-Kekuawela et al., 2009). Prevention and treatment interventions that build on cultural strengths, such as resilience in the face of multiple challenges and adaptive coping methods (e.g., connecting with extended family, strengthening kinship ties, spirituality, and creating positive meaning), can reduce symptoms.

Culture is reflected in help-seeking patterns, coping styles, social networks and support systems, the role of stigma, and treatment engagement (Satcher, 2001). To achieve cultural competence, the whole person must be observed and understood as a cultural being. To this end, resilience, family relationships, social and interpersonal stressors, and cohesion and functioning around family and community needs must be assessed. Furthermore, building cultural strengths reduces symptom dysfunction. This enhancing strength entails cultivating resilience in the face of multiple challenges and developing coping strategies that enhance kinship ties and spirituality to create positive meaning. Programs integrating cultural processes enhance participation, improvement of self-concept, connectedness, health, and wellness (Carlton et al., 2011; Hill, 2006; Liddell & Burnette, 2017).

Additionally, enhancing cultural strengths lessens problematic symptoms through resilience building in the face of various difficulties and the creation of coping mechanisms that strengthen spirituality, familial bonds, and the production of constructive meaning. Participation is increased in programs that incorporate cultural practices, which improve well-being, health, connectivity, and self-concept (Carlton et al., 2011; Hill, 2006; Liddell & Burnette, 2017). Harry Kūnihi Mitchell (1977), a leader, advocate, educator, and organizer, who has been instrumental in the revival of the island of Kaho'olawe, conveys this idea in the lyrics and melody of *Mele O Kaho'olawe*. The last verse of this song gives hope for future generations:

Hanohano nā pua o Hawai'i nei No ke kaua kauholo me ka aupuni
Pa'a pu ka mana'o o no ka pono o ka 'aina Imua nā pua
Lanakila Kaho'olawe
Popular are the young people of Hawai'i nei
For the civil strife they cause against the Government
Together in one thought to bring prosperity to the land
Forward, young people and bring
Salvation to Kaho'olawe

Current Rates of Mental Illness Among Native Hawaiian Youth

Mental health disparities among Native Hawaiian youth are well-documented, with research indicating elevated rates of depression, anxiety, and suicidality compared to their non-Native peers (Andrade et al., 2006; Goebert & Sugimoto-Matsuda, 2017; Okamura et al., 2016). According to studies conducted in Hawai'i, Native Hawaiian youth report higher levels of psychological distress, with some surveys suggesting that they experience depression at nearly twice the rate of other ethnic groups in the state. Suicide rates among Indigenous peoples have been rising for over a century, particularly affecting youth and devastating local communities (Else et al., 2007; Goebert, 2014). In recent decades, there has been a significant increase in suicide rates in Hawai'i and the United States, especially among Indigenous populations, including Native Hawaiian youth

(Curtin et al., 2016; D. Galanis, presentation to Prevent Suicide Hawaiʻi Task Force, February 20, 2025). Native Hawaiian adolescents exhibit high levels of suicide-related behaviors, including depression, suicidal thoughts, planning, attempts, and attempts that require medical intervention (Matsu et al., 2013; Subica & Wu, 2018; Wong et al., 2012). In 1999, Native Hawaiians were 1.8 times more likely to attempt suicide than their White counterparts, increasing to 3.1 times by 2009, and 1.4 times by 2019 (Center for Behavioral Health Statistics and Quality, 2023; Ehlman et al., 2022). Recent reductions in these rates can be attributed to local efforts focusing on Native Hawaiian communities (Goebert et al., 2018). These statistics point to significant challenges that require culturally responsive interventions.

Several risk factors contribute to these elevated rates of mental illness. Socioeconomic disparities play a significant role, as Native Hawaiian families are more likely to experience poverty, housing instability, and limited access to health care. Many Native Hawaiian youth attend underfunded schools and face systemic barriers in the education system, including disproportionately high suspension and expulsion rates. These experiences of marginalization contribute to chronic stress and a sense of disenfranchisement (Riley et al., 2022). Additionally, Native Hawaiian youth often experience discrimination and racial stereotyping, which can negatively impact self-esteem and identity development.

Environmental and community factors also influence mental health outcomes. The ongoing displacement of Native Hawaiians from their ancestral lands due to tourism-driven development and rising housing costs creates stress and instability within families (Riley et al., 2021). Disconnection from land and cultural practices can erode a sense of belonging and contribute to feelings of alienation. Furthermore, intergenerational trauma—passed down from the historical injustices of colonization—continues to manifest in cycles of family hardship, substance use, and mental health struggles (Keaulana et al., 2024; Riley et al., 2022). While these risk factors present significant challenges, protective factors such as cultural resilience, strong community networks, and culturally based programs can play a vital role in improving mental health outcomes for Native Hawaiian youth.

Risk factors linked to Native Hawaiian youth suicide encompass previous attempts, identification as a sexual minority, symptoms of anxiety and depression, substance use, incarceration, experiences in foster care, the death of a parent, exposure to violence, and historical trauma (Augustin et al., 2021; Goebert & Sugimoto-Matsuda, 2017). Native Hawaiian youth face a higher number of risks compared to their non-Native peers; however, most young people do not develop suicidal tendencies or other behavioral issues (Carlton et al., 2006; Goebert & Sugimoto-Matsuda, 2017; Hishinuma et al., 2018). More importantly, Native Hawaiian youth exhibit resilience, along with a strong sense of community and hope for the future. Initiatives to identify protective factors and adopt a strength-based approach to prevention and intervention are on the rise. Several protective factors have been recognized as crucial in preventing suicidality, including connections with family and community (Antonio et al., 2020; Else et al., 2007; Goebert et al., 2018; Medeiros & Tibbetts, 2008; Yahata & Kaninau, 2009). Furthermore, schools can create a positive environment that enhances the community's overall sense of connection and care (Goebert et al., 2012).

Hawaiian Models of Health and Well-being

Native Hawaiian models of health and well-being guide and care for the individual, family, community, and lāhui (nation). Traditional Hawaiian models of health and well-being emphasize the interconnectedness of mind, body, spirit, and environment. Contrary to traditionally taught Western biomedical approaches that separate mental, physical, and spiritual health, Native

Hawaiian perspectives view well-being holistically. The Ahupua'a Model is a framework for mauli ola (optimal health) illustrating the interconnectedness and reciprocity in the health of 'ohana (family), kaiāulu (community), 'āina (land), and akua/mana (spirituality) (Daniels et al., 2022).

Native Hawaiian models of well-being build upon and reinforce this understanding (Handy & Pukui, 1998; Pukui et al., 1972; Wong-Wilson, 2016). Concepts such as lōkahi, harmony and balance; pono, righteousness and alignment; and mana, spiritual energy or power are central to maintaining individual and collective health. These beliefs suggest that mental distress is not merely a medical condition but is often the result of an imbalance within oneself, one's family, or one's relationship with the environment. When these relationships are disrupted—whether due to personal struggles, family conflict, or systemic barriers—mental and emotional suffering can arise. Although the necessity of a holistic approach to Native Hawaiian well-being is emphasized in all models, this approach is not yet standardized. The current initiative is to increase the impact of systems, place, and resilience on Native Hawaiian well-being among youth.

For Native Hawaiian youth, reconnection with cultural identity through language, land-based practices, and traditional knowledge and practices can serve as a powerful protective factor against mental health challenges. Studies suggest that youth who engage in cultural lifestyles and activities, such as mo'olelo (intergenerational storytelling), mālama 'āina (caring for the land), and attending Kula Kaiapuni (Hawaiian immersion schools), exhibit greater resilience and a stronger sense of purpose (Goodyear-Ka'opua, 2013; Hishinuma et al., 2009; Kana'iaupuni et al., 2017). Cultural connection has been linked to lower rates of substance use, depression, and suicidal ideation among Indigenous populations (Gray & Cote, 2019).

Ho'oponopono, a process of reconciliation and forgiveness, is used within families to resolve conflicts and restore harmony. The practice involves open discussions guided by a trained practitioner, emphasizing values of pono (righteousness) and pilina (relationships), in addition to accountability, emotional healing, spirituality and making things right. In recent years, ho'oponopono has been used in schools and youth programs; however, respectful and appropriate implementation remains an ongoing cultural concern for many (Paglinawan et al., 2020). Programs that incorporate these traditional Hawaiian values and practices into mental health support systems offer an alternative to Western psychiatric models which may not always align with Indigenous worldviews. Additionally, implementation of culturally grounded community-based participatory interventions may provide ethical attempts to create highly customized interventions for youth (Okamoto et al., 2020).

Recognizing and implementing these culturally based models within mental health care can help bridge the gap between conventional treatment and Indigenous healing practices, making services more effective and accessible for Native Hawaiian youth. However, as with ho'oponopono, inclusion of culture in conventional treatment requires the involvement of recognized Native Hawaiian traditional healers, practitioners and individuals (e.g., experts in voyaging or navigation, healing of various forms, dance, storytelling, traditional practice, language, health/well-being) to determine the appropriateness of integration to maintain ethical and cultural sensitivity, and most importantly the sacredness of Hawaiian cultural practices.

Key Barriers to Mental Health Care Access

Hawai'i faces significant geographic barriers and economic limitations impacting access to mental health care. Access to mental health care in Hawai'i is complicated by geography; Hawai'i is comprised of multiple different islands of varying sizes, seven of which are inhabited. O'ahu being the most populated, Hawai'i, Maui, Moloka'i, Lana'i, Kaua'i, and Ni'ihau are considered rural with more limited access to health care. Much of the island state is designated as a mental health professional shortage area as defined by the Health Resources and Services Administration (n.d.). Nationally, the demand for mental health services outweighs capacity, with nearly 40% of psychologists reporting having a waitlist, and Native Hawaiians and Pacific Islanders representing the largest ethnic or racial group waiting to receive services (Stamm et al., 2023b). Even when Native Hawaiians are able to access mental health services, clinicians report that they are ill-equipped with the skills and knowledge to provide culturally responsive care for this population more than for any other cultural group (Stamm et al., 2023a). In 2022, Native Hawaiians and Pacific Islanders had the lowest representation in psychology degrees awarded (bachelor or masters: 0.2%, doctorate 0.1%) than any other group (Stamm et al., 2024), which highlights not only the need for more workforce development pathways, but also the importance of increasing culturally safe and responsive training for non-Native Hawaiian clinicians serving our communities. Stigma and mistrust in health services: Historically, a disconnect in the Kānaka ʻōiwi world view of holistic health to the current Western perception of "mental health," combined with a lack of representation in service providers, discrimination, stigmatization, and other cultural stressors has led to mistrust and underutilization of Western health services (Kaholokula et al., 2020; White & Landis, 1982; Young, 2016).

Education reform is another critical area for improving mental health outcomes. Schools play a central role in shaping the well-being of youth. However, many Native Hawaiian students face discrimination, inadequate support systems, and Eurocentric curricula that overlook Indigenous histories, perspectives, and learning styles. Implementing culturally relevant education, including Hawaiian language immersion programs, cultural practices, and land-based learning opportunities, can foster a greater sense of identity and belonging among Native Hawaiian youth. Additionally, incorporating mental health education into school curricula can help destigmatize mental health issues and encourage youth to seek support when needed.

Education reform among mental health professionals is equally as important. As mentioned, there is a strong need to incorporate Native Hawaiian values in conventional care. However, authentically understanding and promoting such values requires a Native Hawaiian approach to learning that goes beyond cultural competency. To incorporate Native Hawaiian values in practice is to know them by experience. Therefore, prioritizing culture and Indigenous ways of knowing in mental health curricula is urgently needed. The Myron B. Thompson School of Social of Social Work, now the Thompson School of Social Work and Public Health, previously offered the Hawaiian Learning Program which trained Native Hawaiian social workers in Native Hawaiian values and practices to provide culturally grounded care among Native Hawaiians. Currently, the school's Department of Social Work offers Ke A'o Mau, a course that trains students on approaches to healing through interdisciplinary education informed by Native Hawaiian values, practices, and principles (Krief et al., 2018; Mokuau et al., 2023). Some efforts have been made to increase cultural influences in public and charter schools including the Nā Hopena A'o (HĀ) framework mandated by Hawai'i revised statues (Hawai'i State Department of Education, n.d.).

There also a number of funding opportunities for Native Hawaiians through a variety of organizations including Papa Ola Lōkahi, The Office of Hawaiian Affairs, The University of Hawai'i at Mānoa, Alu Like, Inc., Ho'omau Foundation, and Kamehameha Schools. Programs and courses should be uplifted and promoted to truly address Native Hawaiian mental health disparities. Alongside the cultural stigma surrounding mental health in Native Hawaiian communities and generational mistrust of Western medical systems is the lack of qualified mental health providers within the islands.

Native Hawaiian Mental Health Programs in Hawai'i

Recognizing the unique mental health challenges faced by Native Hawaiian youth, several community-driven programs have emerged to provide culturally grounded support (see Table 10.1). These initiatives integrate Native Hawaiian values, traditional healing practices, and modern psychological approaches to create holistic mental health interventions. One such program is The Pono Curriculum, an interactive and culture-specific prevention program, first introduced in schools, that incorporates essential Native Hawaiian values (Kim et al., 2007). This program promotes the practice and embodiment of 21 cultural and spiritual principles, which in turn enhances cultural identity and self-esteem, improves family and social communication skills, and raises awareness about the risks of substance use. Evaluation findings revealed that the curriculum had a significant positive impact on students' self-worth and commitment to school, while also reducing favorable views of harmful drugs and lowering drug use rates. Additionally, the curriculum laid the groundwork for a culturally relevant residential substance abuse intervention aimed at youth involved with drugs (Withy et al., 2007). Consequently, the Pono Curriculum serves as a model for community- and Native Hawaiian-led, culture-based initiatives that are contextually appropriate for both prevention and intervention strategies (Rehuher et al., 2008).

The Queen's Medical Center's Family Treatment Center in Hawai'i supports adolescent health through evidence-based strategies, including individual therapies, family strengthening, and promoting physical well-being (Bell et al., 2010; Carlton et al., 2011; The Queen's Medical Center, n.d.). The inpatient residential program emphasized Native Hawaiian values, fostering community and relationships. Adolescents learn values such as āpono and ho'āpono (acceptance), loli and ho'ololi (change), kuleana (responsibility), ahonui (patience), mana'o'i'o (faith), and kala and ho'okala (forgiveness), which aid their treatment and healing. This cultural integration in education curriculum and group therapy helped youth develop holistically and enhanced therapists' understanding of their perspectives. The program also included a collaborative healing through art project, featuring murals that reflect Native Hawaiian mo'olelo (stories), reinforcing these values. Renewed interest from other disciplines to improve the values program for the acute setting led

Table 10.1 Native Hawaiian mental health programs in Hawai'i.

Program	Summary
The Pono Curriculum	An interactive and culture-specific prevention program incorporating Native Hawaiian values by promoting the practice and embodiment of 21 cultural and spiritual principles.
The Queen's Medical Center—Family Treatment Center	An inpatient residential program supporting adolescents through a culturally integrated curriculum inclusive of evidence-based strategies, including individual therapies, family strengthening, and promoting physical well-being.
Ho'ola Nā Pua	A trauma-informed program aimed at preventing sex-trafficking among at-risk youth through mental health counseling, mentorship, and education that honors Native Hawaiian cultural perspectives.
Kawailoa Youth and Family Wellness Center	An 'āina-based program to support youth through indigenous knowledge, values, and practices alongside leadership training.
Hawai'i's Caring Communities Initiative for Youth Suicide Prevention	A project out of the University of Hawai'i partnered with community organizations aimed at integration of evidence-based practices into youth-led community awareness activities grounded in that community's strengths and needs.

to the new program integrating the Hawaiian lunar calendar (Silva, 2017) and moʻolelo (Malo, & Emerson, 2021) with Western treatments.

Another program, Hoʻōla Nā Pua (2025), focuses on trauma-informed care and the prevention of sex trafficking among at-risk youth, primarily Native Hawaiians (64%). The program provides mental health counseling, mentorship, and education in ways that honor Native Hawaiian cultural perspectives.

Another key initiative is Kawailoa Youth and Family Wellness Center (2025), a program to support youth through Indigenous knowledge, values, and practices alongside leadership training. Participants strengthen their sense of cultural identity and community connection by engaging in activities such as moʻolelo (storytelling) and mālama ʻāina (caring for the land).

Research has shown that fostering a strong cultural identity provides a protective factor against mental health challenges, reducing rates of depression and substance abuse among Indigenous youth. Programs like these demonstrate the importance of grounding mental health interventions in Hawaiian cultural knowledge. Expanding and sustaining these programs will be essential to addressing the mental health needs of Native Hawaiian youth in ways that resonate with their cultural values and lived experiences.

Hawaiʻi's Caring Communities Initiative (HCCI) for Youth Suicide Prevention, a University of Hawaiʻi project, partnered with six community organizations primarily serving Native Hawaiian youth in rural communities across the State of Hawaiʻi. This project evolved to include more communities and greater emphasis on youth leadership. The goal was to integrate evidence-based practices into youth-led community awareness activities that were grounded in each community's strengths and needs (Chung-Do et al., 2014, 2015, 2016a, 2016b; Goebert et al., 2018). This resulted in improved integration and social networking.

Other community-based programs that holistically address well-being exist. School-based programs may face unique implementation issues due to the necessary protective factors around the public education system and its students. However, a number of educational recommendations exist across the literature in the form of culturally relevant adaptations, advocacy and systemic change, reconnection to culture, and reconnection to resources (Carreira Ching, 2024). At the same time, the ongoing development and implementation of culturally grounded substance abuse prevention programs in and for Hawaiʻi school-aged youth spans nearly a decade and multiple substances with its most recent segway into electronic vape devices (Okamoto et al., 2016; 2018; 2019; 2020, Okamura et al., 2022).

To improve mental health outcomes for Native Hawaiian youth, a multifaceted approach that includes policy changes, increased funding for community- and school-based programs, and greater access to culturally competent care is needed. One of the most pressing needs is expanding mental health services incorporating Native Hawaiian cultural values. Currently, many mental health programs in Hawaiʻi operate under Western models that may not fully align with Indigenous worldviews. Investing in training Native Hawaiian mental health professionals and integrating traditional healing practices into mainstream health care would go a long way toward bridging this gap.

Case Studies and Examples

Case Study: Sources of Strength—A Universal Approach to Suicide Prevention

Comprehensive and integrated strategies have proven to be more effective in tackling youth suicide prevention with Native Hawaiian youth. One of the few evaluated strengths-based programs is Sources of Strength (SoS), a universal approach to suicide prevention that enhances well-being by building on protective factors (Wyman et al., 2010). This multidimensional program incorporates evidence-based suicide prevention techniques that leverage the protective influences of peers and supportive adults while integrating cultural and community activities. The program identifies eight strengths or protective factors to foster resilience in young people, equipping them to handle life's natural ups and downs (LoMurray, 2005; Sources of Strength, 2025). Youth are trained to become peer leaders, connecting them with adult advisors and community supporters. Advisors collaborate with youth leaders to create and implement well-defined messaging activities that recognize and enhance individual and community strengths, increase connectedness, and promote help-seeking behaviors. Building strengths and inspiring hope through SoS builds on these gatekeeper strategies, focusing on the strengths of Native Hawaiian youth and their communities (Agustin et al., 2021).

> *To me, that's the biggest impact that we've made—that people know we're here and that we're willing to help and that we care. That's big—I feel like that's one thing that could save a life—just knowing that people care.*
>
> *Youth Leader*

Youth feedback identified a central theme of strength for the SoS program (Trinh & Goebert, 2020). Participants either referenced the wheel of strengths, a tool employed in SoS, or expressed the importance of recognizing their own strengths, acting as a source of support for others, and seeking strength from those around them. In feedback from SoS program participants, 68% of youth and 33% of supportive adults commented on the need to focus on strengths. One youth expressed, "Strengths are everywhere. Sharing your sources of strength and support is crucial for a person's well-being." A supportive adult remarked, "We should dedicate more time to highlighting strengths."

Past participants in the SoS program have noted the power of youth voice within the theme of strength, with 86% of young participants and 100% of supportive adults agreeing that youth can take charge and be empowered to prevent suicide within their communities (Trinh & Goebert, 2020). One young person remarked, "We can actually make a difference in our school and community." Another added, "Suicide prevention is everyone's responsibility. I can be there for someone feeling suicidal."

Additionally, another youth mentioned, "I know how to respond better to certain situations, how to teach this information, and how to offer support." Supportive adults echoed this sentiment, stating, "Youth can do this. We need to allow them to lead," and "We should create opportunities for youth to promote this program on [my island]."

Clinical Case Study: Hawaiʻi Youth Correctional Facility

Many Native Hawaiian youth struggling with mental health issues end up involved in the justice system. According to Mark Patterson, former warden of the Hawaiʻi Youth Correctional Facility (HYCF), mental health is the key to not only youth wellness, but also carceral reform (Patterson, 2025). During Patterson's tenure, HYCF transformed from a youth correctional facility into a puʻuhonua or place of refuge, renamed Kawailoa Youth and Family Wellness Center (Patterson, 2025; Patterson et al., 2020). Here, troubled youth could get the support they needed before returning to their home community. Integration of mālama ʻāina (caring for the land) supported youth who needed time to do self-work. One youth shared how the ʻāina fed his soul by sharing his "first time being in a lo'i patch. [ ] It was beautiful. [ ] It's like really dirty though . . . so we went over there, and we cleaned up . . . and I was lovin' it! I was lovin' it cuz" (Riley et al., 2022). Kawailoa, recognizing that not all youth have stability once released, also provides a continuum of care, including a youth shelter, school, and several job training programs.

Incarcerated Native Hawaiian youth recognize the situation that they are in. Despite their young age, many are able to connect colonization with the ever-presence of systems and institutions in their lives. Many youth shared statements like "this [facility] shouldn't even be a place," and if "Hawaiians still governed, [they] probably wouldn't have lock down facilities like this" (Riley et al., 2022). These statements shed light on the belief that incarcerating youth does not align with Hawaiian values. Instead, developing a culturally responsive, local, trauma-informed curriculum that also works to "heal historical trauma" should be the ultimate goal. Drawing from the collective pride that youth feel about their culture, programs should take strides to integrate culture into their mental health services.

Clinical Case Example: Native Hawaiian Justice-involved Youth with a History of Suicidal Ideation and Intent

Providing a safe base for which to explore identity in a culturally responsive environment is meaningful for Native Hawaiian youth facing crisis. For example, a teenage boy frequently endorsing suicidal ideation and intent in a youth correctional setting had been sentenced to a brief incarceration in the hope that this would influence his life-threatening substance use and aggressive behaviors. Despite numerous attempts to examine his ruminations and self-harming behaviors, he continued to experience intermittent sobbing episodes, recurrent suicidal intent, and aggressive outbursts. Many of the programs he attended had a Native Hawaiian cultural emphasis, something that was complicating to his identity due to experiences of childhood trauma at the hands of his biological parents. Allowing this youth to explore his own identity, responsively, without cultural prescription, provided the safe base from which he could process precipitating factors to his suicidal ruminations and self-harming behaviors.

Future Directions and Recommendations

On a policy level, advocacy efforts should focus on securing long-term funding for Native Hawaiian-led mental health initiatives from prevention to intervention. Policymakers must recognize the importance of Indigenous self-determination in shaping mental health solutions. This includes support of legislation prioritizing land rights, economic equity, and access to culturally competent health care. Community-driven solutions, such as strengthening mentorship programs, increasing access to traditional healing resources, and fostering intergenerational knowledge exchange, can also help create a more supportive environment for Native Hawaiian youth. By centering Native Hawaiian voices and perspectives in mental health policymaking, Hawai'i can move toward a more just and effective care system.

A historical understanding and context should be included in any work, research, treatment, program development, adaptation, or inclusion of Native Hawaiian individuals, families, and populations. The consideration of historical trauma and its impacts should be factors for work in community sectors of health care (i.e., physical and mental/behavioral), education, government (i.e., executive, legislative, and judicial), business, religion, and banking. Cultural identity should be prioritized and targeted as it can provide protection to a number of adverse outcomes for youth (Riley et al., 2022).

Given the dearth of Native Hawaiian mental health providers, it is critical that legislation support pathways to education and loan repayment to increase the workforce and retain clinicians in the islands. Additionally, advocacy should include training of all clinicians, those who identify as Native Hawaiian and non-Native Hawaiian, in basic understanding of Hawaiian history, culture and worldview to better serve our communities. There are multiple potential avenues for dissemination of cultural humility and cultural safety trainings, such as through licensure boards, professional organizations, schools, clinics and medical settings. Future research should consider evaluating the impact of such cultural humility training programs on therapeutic rapport and mental health outcomes. Other research considerations may include investigating the role of youth peer mediators in bolstering mental health and well-being, and effective, culturally grounded interventions for reducing mental health stigma.

Research should be conducted independent of other groups to assure the appropriate development of any concepts, programs, and treatments for Native Hawaiians when Native Hawaiians are the treatment target group. Aggregation of research (e.g., Native Hawaiian and Other Pacific Islanders, Asian American and Pacific Islanders) can contribute to further oppression of communities and individuals impacting youth and families and confuse cultural elements. Still, a number of research gaps exist. More work may be needed in order to have a documented academic understanding of land connection and Native Hawaiian culture, the impacts of disconnection through colonization (e.g., land loss, diaspora) as well as the extent to which land reconnection may mitigate these impacts. Quantitative research may be needed to build on the vast and illuminating body of qualitative research on Native Hawaiians with inclusions of considerations for cultural identity and intersectional differences (e.g., sexuality, gender identity, lifespan/generational) particularly for youth which may improve outcomes in education and physical/mental health (Carreira Ching, 2024).

Conclusion

The mental health challenges faced by Native Hawaiian youth are deeply rooted in historical trauma, socioeconomic disparities, and ongoing cultural disconnection. However, the strength and resilience of Native Hawaiian communities offer pathways for healing. By integrating traditional Hawaiian models of well-being with modern mental health frameworks, we can create more effective and culturally relevant solutions. Programs emphasizing cultural identity, community support, and traditional healing practices have successfully promoted mental well-being among Native Hawaiian youth.

Looking ahead, addressing the mental health needs of Native Hawaiian youth requires sustained commitment from policymakers, educators, health care providers, and community leaders. Expanding access to culturally competent care, reforming education systems to be more inclusive of Hawaiian perspectives, and supporting Native Hawaiian-led initiatives are crucial steps in creating lasting change. Through advocacy, policy reform, and culturally grounded interventions, it is possible to build a future where Native Hawaiian youth thrive mentally, emotionally, and spiritually.

Ultimately, improving Native Hawaiian youth mental health is not just about addressing individual conditions—it is about restoring collective well-being, fostering cultural pride, and ensuring that future generations have the support and resources they need to flourish. By prioritizing culturally rooted solutions, we honor the resilience of Native Hawaiian youth and pass life forward.

Glossary of terms.

Term	Definition
Ahonui	patience
ʻāina	land
akua/mana	spirituality
āpono/hoʻāpono	acceptance
hōʻinoʻino	broken spirit
hoʻoponopono	a process of reconciliation and forgiveness
Kaiāulu	community
Kānaka ʻōiwi	Native Hawaiian
Kaumaha	profound grief rooted in heavy, oppressive sadness
Kuleana	responsibility
Lāhui	nation
Lōkahi	harmony and balance
loli/hoʻololi	change
kala/hoʻokala	forgiveness
kula kaiapuni	Hawaiian immersion school
mālama ʻāina	caring for the land
Mana	spiritual energy or power
manaʻoʻiʻo	faith
mauli ola	optimal health
moʻolelo	stories, intergenerational storytelling
ʻohana	family and extended family
pilina	relationships
pono	righteousness and alignment

References

Agustin, M., Garcia, B. K., Goebert, D., Lyman, J., Mah, S., Kackley, R. P., & Oh, Y. (2021). Inspiring hope through sources of strength among predominantly Pacific Islander communities. *Journal of Indigenous Social Development*, *10*(2), 54–79.

Akamu, C., & Ravida, M. (2025). Colonization. In D. G. Friedman-Wheeler, & A. Wenzel (Eds.), *The Sage Encyclopedia of Mood and Anxiety Disorders* (Vol. 3) (pp. 270–272). SAGE Publications, Inc. https://doi.org/10.4135/9781071886229

Alameda, C. K. (2005). Cultural competency for nursing, sociology, and psychiatry students. Presentation to the John A. Burns School of Medicine, University of Hawai'i at Mānoa, Honolulu, HI.

Andrade, N. N., Hishinuma, E. S., McDermott, Jr., J. F., Johnson, R. C., Goebert, D. A., Makini, Jr., G. K., ... Waldron, J. A. (2006). The National Center on Indigenous Hawaiian Behavioral Health study of prevalence of psychiatric disorders in Native Hawaiian adolescents. *Journal of the American Academy of Child and Adolescent Psychiatry*, *45*(1), 26–36. https://doi.org/10.1097/01.chi.0000184933.71917.f4

Antonio, M. C. K., Chung-Do, J. J., Goebert, D. A., Bifulco, K., & Alvarez, A. R. G. (2020). A qualitative evaluation of the impacts of a strength-based and youth-driven approach to suicide prevention in rural and minority communities in Hawai'i. *Hawai'i Journal of Health & Social Welfare*, *79*(5 Suppl 1), 96–100.

Agustin, M., Garcia, B.K., Goebert, D., Lyman, J., Mah, S., Kackley, R.P., & Oh, Y. (2021). Inspiring hope through sources of strength among predominantly Pacific Islander communities. *Journal of Indigenous Social Development, 10*(2), 54–79.

Beardslee, W. R., & Knitzer, J. (2004). Strengths-based family mental health services: a family systems approach. In K. Maton, C. Schellenbach, B. Leadbeater, & A. Solarz (Eds.), *Investing in Children, Youth, Families, and Communities: Strengths- Based Research and Policy* (pp. 157–171). American Psychological Association. https://doi.org/10.1037/10660-009

Bell, C. K., Guerrero, A., Matsu, C., Takeshita, J., Haning, W., & Schultz, R. N. (2010). Circular adaptations in inpatient child psychiatry for the 21st century: The flexner model revisited. *Academic Psychiatry, 34*, 195–202.

Blaisdell, K. (1989). Historical and cultural aspects of Native Hawaiian health. *Social Process in Hawai'i, 32*, 1–21.

Blaisdell, K., & Mokuau, N. (1991). Kānaka Maoli: indigenous Hawaiians. In N. Mokuau (Ed.), *Handbook of Social Services for Asian and Pacific Islanders* (pp. 131–154). Greenwood Press.

Brave Heart, M. (1998). The return to the sacred path: healing the historical trauma and historical unresolved grief response among the Lakota through a psychoeducational group intervention. *Smith College Studies in Social Work, 68*(3), 287–305. https://doi.org/10.1080/00377319809517532

Brave Heart, M. (1999a). Gender differences in the historical grief response among the Lakota. *Journal of Health & Social Policy, 10*(4), 1–21. https://doi.org/10.1300/J045v10n04_01

Brave Heart, M. (1999b). Oyate Ptayela: rebuilding the Lakota Nation through addressing historical trauma among Lakota parents. *Journal of Human Behavior in the Social Environment, 2*(1–2), 109–126. https://doi.org/10.1300/J137v02n01_08

Brave Heart, M., & DeBruyn, L. (1998). The American Indian holocaust: healing historical unresolved grief. *American Indian & Alaska Native Mental Health Research, 8*(2), 56–78.

Brave Heart, M. Y. H. (2000). Wakiksuyapi: carrying the historical trauma of the Lakota. *Tulane Studies in Social Welfare, 21–22*, 245–266.

Brave Heart-Jordan, M., & DeBruyn, L. (1995). So she may walk in balance: integrating the impact of historical trauma in the treatment of Native American Indian women. In J. Adleman, & G. Enquidanos (Eds.), *Racism in the Lives of Women: Testimony, Theory, and Guides to Antiracist Practice* (pp. 345–368). Haworth Press.

Carlton, B., Goebert, D., Bell, C. K., Horton, M., Else, I., Marcinowski, M., & Yamada, L. (2011). Integrating cultural values into mental health treatment. *Multidisciplinary Research on Hawaiian Well Being, 7*, 159–184.

Carlton, B. S., Goebert, D. A., Miyamoto, R. H., Andrade, N. N., Hishinuma, E. S., Makini, G. K., ... Nishimura, S. T. (2006). Resilience, family adversity, and well-being among Hawaiian and Non-Hawaiian adolescents. *International Journal of Social Psychiatry*, *52*(4), 291–308. https://doi.org/10.1177/0020764006065136

Carreira Ching, D. L. (2024). *Understanding the Historical Trauma Impact of Colonization on Native Hawaiian Health and Well-Being: A Scoping Review*. ProQuest Dissertations & Theses.

Carreira Ching, D. L., Acosta, V. M., Gerson, J., Harris, M., Hiura, A., & Higa, C. (2022). Trauma-related mental health trends and family history factors of Native Hawaiian adolescents at the Hawai'i Youth Correctional Facility [Poster presentation]. *19th Annual Hawai'i International Summit of the Institute on Violence, Abuse, and Trauma*, Honolulu, HI.

Center for Behavioral Health Statistics and Quality. (2023). 2021 National survey on Drug Use and Health: detailed tables. Substance Abuse and Mental Health Services Administration.

Chung-Do, J., Goebert, D., Bifulco, K., Tydingco, T., Wilcox, S., Aea, D., ... Alvarez, A. (2015). Mobilizing communities at-risk to prevent youth suicides. *Journal of Health Disparities Research and Practice*, *8*(4), 108–123.

Chung-Do, J. J., Bifulco, K., Antonio, M., Tydingco, T., Helm, S., & Goebert, D. A. (2016a). A cultural analysis of the NAMI-NH Connect Suicide Prevention Program by rural community leaders in Hawai'i. *Journal of Rural Mental Health*, *40*(2), 87.

Chung-Do, J. J., Goebert, D. A., Bifulco, K., Sugimoto-Matsuda, J., Balberde-Kamali'i, J., Ka'ae, D., ... Walter, L. (2016b). Insights in public health: safe messaging for youth-led suicide prevention awareness: examples from Hawai'i. *Hawai'i Journal of Medicine & Public Health*, *75*(5), 144.

Chung-Do, J. J., Napoli, S. B., Hooper, K., Tydingco, T., Bifulco, K., & Goebert, D. (2014). Youth-led suicide prevention in an indigenous rural community. *Psychiatric Times*. http://www.psychiatrictimes.com/cultural- psychiatry/youth-led-suicide-prevention-indigenous-rural-community. Accessed 08/12/2014

Curtin, S. C., Warner, M., & Hedegaard, H. Increase in suicide in the United States, 1999–2014. Hyattsville, MD: National Center for Health Statistics; 2016. (NCHS data brief No. 241). https://stacks.cdc.gov/view/cdc/39008/cdc_39008_DS1.pdf

Daniels, S. A. P., Kauahikaua, L., Kaio, C., Casson-Fisher, J. N., & Ku, T. (2022). Conceptualizing a new system of care in Hawai'i for Native Hawaiians and substance use. *Hawai'i Journal of Health & Social Welfare*, *81*(12 Suppl 3), 43.

DeCambra, H., Marshall, W. E., & Ono, M. (1998). Ho'omau ke Ola: "to perpetuate life as it was meant to be." In N. Mokuau, L. G. Epstein, G. Pacheco, & J. W. Quinlan (Eds.), *Responding to Pacific Islanders: Culturally Competent Perspectives for Substance Abuse Prevention* (pp. 73–96). Washington, DC: Substance Abuse and Mental Health Services Administration, U.S. Department of Health and Human Services. https://files.eric.ed.gov/fulltext/ED449290.pdf

Ehlman, D. C., Yard, E., Stone, D. M., Jones, C. M., & Mack, K. A. Changes in Suicide Rates — United States, 2019 and 2020. MMWR Morb Mortal Wkly Rep 2022;71:306–312. http://dx.doi.org/10.15585/mmwr.mm7108a5

Else, I. R., Andrade, N. N., & Nahulu, L. B. (2007). Suicide and suicidal-related behaviors among indigenous Pacific Islanders in the United States. *Death Studies*, *31*(5), 479–501. https://doi.org/10.1080/07481180701244595

Goebert, D. (2014). Chapter 19: Indigenous/native populations. In S. H. Koslow, P. Ruiz, & C. B. Nemeroff (Eds.), *A Concise Guide to Understanding Suicide: Epidemiology, Pathophysiology, and Prevention* (pp. 159–165). Cambridge University Press. https://doi.org/10.1017/CBO9781139519502.021

Goebert, D., Alvarez, A., Andrade, N. N., Balberde-Kamalii, J., Carlton, B. S., Chock, S., ... Kaulukukui, G. (2018). Hope, help, and healing: culturally embedded approaches to suicide prevention, intervention and postvention services with Native Hawaiian youth. *Psychological Services, 15*(3), 332.

Goebert, D., Chang, J. Y., Chung-Do, J., Else, R., Hamagami, F., Helm, S., Kinkade, K., & Sugimoto-Matsuda, J. J. (2012). Social ecological determinants of youth violence among ethnically diverse Asian and Pacific Islander students. *Maternal and Child Health Journal, 16*(1), 188–196. https://doi.org/10.1007/s10995-010-0726-0

Goebert, D., & Sugimoto-Matsuda, J. (2017). Medical school hotline: advancing suicide prevention in Hawai'i. *Hawai'i Journal of Medicine & Public Health: A Journal of Asia Pacific Medicine & Public Health, 76*(11), 310–313.

Goodyear-Ka'opua, N. (2013). *The Seeds We Planted: Portraits of a Native Hawaiian Charter School.* University of Minnesota Press.

Gray, A. P., & Cote, W. (2019). Cultural connectedness protects mental health against effect of historical trauma among Anishinabe young adults. *Public Health, 176*, 77–81. https://doi.org/10.1016/j.puhe.2018.12.003

Handy, E. S. C., & Pukui, M. K. (1998). *The Polynesian Family System in Ka-'U, Hawai'i.* Honolulu, HI: Mutual Publishing.

Hawai'i State Department of Education. (n.d.). *Nā hopena a'o (HĀ).* Retrieved from https://hawaiipublicschools.org/about/na-hopena-a%CA%BBo-ha/

Hawaii Health Matters. (n.d.). Health/adolescent health. Conduent Health Communities Institute.

Health Resources & Services Administration. (n.d.). *HRSA Data Warehouse.* https://data.hrsa.gov/about/aboutus

Hill, D. L. (2006). Sense of belonging as connectedness, American Indian worldview, and mental health. *Archives of Psychiatric Nursing, 20*(5), 210–216.

Hishinuma, E. S., Chang, J. Y., Sy, A., Greaney, M. F., Morris, K. A., Scronce, A. C., ... Nishimura, S. T. (2009). HUI Mālama O Ke Kai: a positive prevention-based youth development program based on Native Hawaiian values and activities. *Journal of Community Psychology, 37*(8), 987–1007.

Hishinuma, E. S., Smith, M. D., McCarthy, K., Lee, M., Goebert, D. A., Sugimoto-Matsuda, J. J., ... Andrade, J. K. L. (2018). Longitudinal prediction of suicide attempts for a diverse adolescent sample of Native Hawaiians, Pacific Peoples, and Asian Americans. *Archives of Suicide Research: Official Journal of the International Academy for Suicide Research, 22*(1), 67–90. https://doi.org/10.1080/13811118.2016.1275992

Ho`ola Nā Pua. (2025). Ho'ōla Nā Pua: new life for our children. https://hoolanapua.org/

Hwang, P., Keaulana-Scott, S., & Akamu, C. (2025). Historical trauma. In D. G. Friedman-Wheeler, & A. Wenzel (Eds.), *The Sage Encyclopedia of Mood and Anxiety Disorders* (Vol. 3) (pp. 606–610). SAGE Publications, Inc., https://doi.org/10.4135/9781071886229

Kaholokula, J. K. (2007). Colonialism, acculturation, and depression among Kānaka Maoli of Hawai'i. In P. Culbertson, M. N. Agee, & C. O. Makasiale (Eds.), *Penina Uliuli: Confronting Challenges in Mental Health for Pacific Peoples* (pp. 180–195). Honolulu, HI: University of Hawai'i Press.

Kaholokula, J. K., Miyamoto, R. E. S., Hermosura, A. H., Inada, M., Benuto, L. T., Masuda, A., O'Donohue, W., & Duckworth, M. P. (2020). Prejudice, stigma, and oppression on the behavioral health of Native Hawaiians and Pacific Islanders. In L. Benuto, M. Duckworth, A. Masuda, & W. O'Donohue (Eds.), *Prejudice, Stigma, Privilege, and Oppression* (pp. 107–134). Springer. https://doi.org/10.1007/978-3-030-35517-3_7

Kana'iaupuni, S. M., Ledward, B., & Malone, N. (2017). Mohala i ka wai: cultural advantage as a framework for Indigenous culture-based education and student outcomes. *American Educational Research Journal, 54*(1_suppl), 311S–339S.

Kanahele, G. (1986). *Kū kanaka/Stand Tall: A Search for Hawaiian Values*. Honolulu, HI: University of Hawaiʻi Press.

Kawailoa. (2025). Kawailoa, ending youth incarceration in Hawai'i. https://wearekawailoa.org/

Keaulana, S., Keli'iholokai, L., Lee, R., Coleman, P., Kipapa, M. L., Ho-Lastimosa, I., & Chung-Do, J. J. (2024). Revealing ʻeha: a qualitative project on historical trauma experiences among wāhine. *Behavioral Science (Basel)*, *14*(12), 1238. https://doi.org/10.3390/bs14121238

Kim, R., Withy, K., Jackson, D., & Sekaguchi, L. (2007). Initial assessment of a culturally tailored substance abuse prevention program and applicability of the risk and protective model for adolescents of Hawaii. *Hawaii Medical Journal*, *66*, 118–123.

Kreif, T. M., Yoshimoto, S. K., & Mokuau, N. (2018). Insights in public health: Ke A'o Mau: Strengthening cultural competency in interdisciplinary education. *Hawai'i Journal of Medicine & Public Health: A Journal of Asia Pacific Medicine & Public Health*, *77*(12), 333–336.

Liddell, J., & Burnette, C. E. (2017). Culturally-informed interventions for substance abuse among indigenous youth in the United States: a review. *Journal of Evidence-Informed Social Work*, *14*(5), 329–359.

LoMurray, M. (2005). *Sources of Strength Facilitators Guide: suicide Prevention Peer Gatekeeper Training*. Bismarck, ND: The North Dakota Suicide Prevention Project.

Malo, D., & Emerson, N. B. (2021). *Hawaiian Antiquities: Moʻolelo Hawaiʻi*. Mint Editions.

Masten, A. S. (2007). Resilience in developing systems: progress and promise as the fourth wave rises. *Development & Psychopathology*, *19*(3), 921–930. https://doi.org/10.1017/S0954579407000442

Matsu, C. R., Goebert, D., Chung-Do, J. J., Carlton, B., Sugimoto-Matsuda, J., & Nishimura, S. (2013). Disparities in psychiatric emergency department visits among youth in Hawai'i, 2000-2010. *The Journal of Pediatrics*, *162*(3), 618–623. https://doi.org/10.1016/j.jpeds.2012.09.006

McCubbin, L. D., Ishisaka, M. E., & McCubbin, H. I. (2007). The Kanaka Maoli: Native Hawaiians and their testimony of trauma and resilience. In A. J. Marsella, J. L. Johnson, P. Watson, & J. Gryczynski (Eds.), *Ethnocultural Perspectives on Disaster and Trauma: Foundations, Issues, and Applications* (pp. 271–298). Springer. https://doi.org/10.1007/978-0-387-73285-5_9

Medeiros, S. M., & Tibbetts, K. A. (2008). *Hoʻomau i nā ʻŌpio: Findings from the 2008 Pilot Test of the Nā ʻŌpio: Youth Development and Assets Survey*. Honolulu: Kamehameha Schools Research & Evaluation.

Mitchell, H. K. (1977). Mele o Kahoʻolawe. [Recorded by Olomana.] On And so we are [Vinyl LP]. Seabird Sound – 1002.

Mokuau, N., & Matsuoka, J. (1995). Turbulence among a native people: social work practice with Hawaiians. *Social Work*, *40*(4), 465–472. https://doi.org/10.1093/sw/40.4.465

Mokuau, N. K., Yoshimoto, S. K., & Braun, K. L. (2023). *Ka Māno Wai: The Source of Life*. University of Hawaii Press. https://doi.org/10.1515/9780824894405

Okamoto, S. K., Helm, S., Chin, S. K., Hata, J., Hata, E., & Okamura, K. H. (2020). The implementation of a culturally grounded, school-based, drug prevention curriculum in rural Hawai'i. *Journal of Community Psychology*, *48*(4), 1085–1099. https://doi.org/10.1002/jcop.22222

Okamoto, S. K., Helm, S., Ostrowski, L. K., & Flood, L. (2018). The validation of a school-based, culturally grounded drug prevention curriculum for rural Hawaiian youth. *Health Promotion Practice*, *19*(3), 369–376. https://doi.org/10.1177/1524839917704210

Okamoto, S. K., Kulis, S., Helm, S., Lauricella, M., & Valdez, J. K. (2016). An evaluation of the ho'ouna pono curriculum: a pilot study of culturally grounded substance abuse prevention for rural Hawaiian youth. *Journal of Health Care for the Poor and Underserved*, *27*(2), 815–833. https://doi.org/10.1353/hpu.2016.0061

Okamoto, S. K., Kulis, S. S., Helm, S., Chin, S. K., Hata, J., Hata, E., & Lee, A. (2019). An efficacy trial of the ho'ouna pono drug prevention curriculum: an evaluation of a culturally grounded substance abuse prevention program in rural Hawai'i. *Asian American Journal of Psychology, 10*(3), 239–248. https://doi.org/10.1037/aap0000164

Okamura, K. H., Ebesutani, C., Bloom, R., Higa-McMillan, C. K., Nakamura, B. J., & Chorpita B. F. (2016). Differences in internalizing symptoms across specific ethnic minority groups: an analysis across Chinese American, Filipino American, Japanese American, Native Hawaiian, and White youth. *Journal of Child and Family Studies 25*, 3353–3366. https://doi.org/10.1007/s10826-016-0488-4

Okamura, K. H., Okamoto, S. K., Marshall, S. M., Chin, S. K., Garcia P. M., Stern, K. A., Becker, S. J., & Mandell, D. S. (2022). Ho'onau pono implementation: applying concept mapping to a culturally grounded substance use prevention curriculum in rural Hawai'i schools. *Implementation Science Communications, 3*(1), 111. https://doi.org/10.1186/s43058-022-00359-2

Paglinawan, L. K., Paglinawan, R. L., Kauahi, D., Kanuha, V. K., & Kalahele, I. (2020). *Nānā i ke kumu: Helu 'ekolu*. Liliuokalani Trust.

Palafu, T., Carreira Ching, D. L., Acosta, V. M., Okamoto, S. K., & Okamura, K. H. (2024). Native Hawaiian and Pacific Islanders' identity and housing status: the impact on historical trauma and perceived stress. *International Journal of Environmental Research and Public Health, 21*, 1249. https://doi.org/10.3390/ijerph21091249

Papa Ola Lōkahi. (2019). E Ola Mau a Mau. https://www.papaolalokahi.org/program/e-ola-mau-a-mau

Patterson, M. (2025). Mental health key to youths' wellness. *Star Advertiser*. https://www.staradvertiser.com/2025/01/26/editorial/island-voices/column-mental-health-key-to-youths-wellness/

Patterson, M., Uchigakuichi, P., & Bissen, T. (2020). Can prison be a place of healing? The trauma-informed care initiative at the women's community correctional center. *Hulili, 19*(11), 305–338.

Po'a-Kekuawela, K., Okamoto, S. K., Nebre, L. R. H., Helm, S., & Chin, C. I. (2009). 'A'ole drugs! Cultural practices and drug resistance of rural Hawaiian youths. *Journal of Ethnic & Cultural Diversity in Social Work, 18*, 242–258. https://doi.org/10.1080/15313200903070981

Pokhrel, P., & Herzog, T. A. (2014). Historical trauma and substance use among Native Hawaiian college students. *American Journal of Health Behavior, 38*(3), 420–429. https://doi.org/10.5993/AJHB.38.3.11

Pukui, M. K., Haertig, E. W., & Lee, C. A. (1972). *Nana i ke kumu (Look to the Source)* (Vols. 1 & 2). Honolulu, HI: Queen Lili'uokalani Children's Center.

Rehuher, D., Hiramatsu, T., & Helm, S. (2008). Evidence-based youth drug prevention: a critique with implications for practice-based contextually relevant prevention in Hawai'i. *Hawai'i Journal of Public Health, 1*(1), 52–61.

Rezentes III, W. C. (1996). *Ka lama kukui: Hawaiian Psychology: An Introduction*. Honolulu, HI: 'A'ali'i Books.

Riley, L., Dorios, S., Hostetter, C., Kehahio, W., Lee, P., Pantumsinchai, P., ... Watkins-Victorino, L. (2021). Much needed medicine: a qualitative study of Hawai'i resident views during COVID-19. *Hawai'i Journal of Health and Social Welfare, 80*(10 Suppl 2), 18–24.

Riley, L., Su'esu'e, A., Hulama, K., Neumann, S. K., & Chung-Do, J. (2022). Ke ala i ka Mauliola: Native Hawaiian youth experiences with historical trauma. *International Journal of Environmental Research and Public Health, 19*(19), 12564. https://doi.org/10.3390/ijerph191912564

Riley, L., Su'esu'e, A., & Ravida, M. (2023). Unsilencing the echoes of historical trauma: a comparative analysis. *Trauma Care, 3*(2), 66–81. https://doi.org/10.3390/traumacare3020008

Satcher, D. (2001). Mental health: culture, race, and ethnicity—a supplement to mental health: a report of the surgeon general. U.S. Department of Health and Human Services.

Schaefer-McDaniel, N. J. (2004). Conceptualizing social capital among young people: towards a new theory. *Children Youth and Environments, 14*(1), 153–172.

Silva, W. (2017). *'Ano lani; 'Ano honua: A Heavenly Nature; an Earthly Nature: A Spiritual Guide to the Hawaiian Lunar Calendar.* Hawai'i Cultural Services.

Sources of Strength (2025). Discover sources of strength. https://sourcesofstrength.org/discover/

Stamm, K., Assefa, M., & Lin, L. (2023a). Psychologists need more experience working with Indigenous populations. *Monitor on Psychology, 54*(7). https://www.apa.org/monitor/2023/10/gaps-treating-race-ethnicity-populations

Stamm, K., Assefa, M., & Page, C. (2023b). Nearly 40% of psychologists have a waitlist. *Monitor on Psychology, 54*(6). https://www.apa.org/monitor/2023/09/many-psychologists-have-waitlist

Stamm, K., Page, C. A. M., & Ward, K. (2024). Progress in psychology degrees earned by underrepresented racial identities. *Monitor on Psychology, 55*(8). https://www.apa.org/monitor/2024/11/datapoint-psychology-degrees-racial-diversity

Streltzer, J., Rezentes III, W. C., & Arakaki, M. (1996). Does acculturation influence psychosocial adaptation and well-being in Native Hawaiians? *International Journal of Social Psychiatry, 42*(1), 28–37. https://doi.org/10.1177/002076409604200104

Subica, A. M., & Wu, L. T. (2018). Substance use and suicide in Pacific Islander, American Indian, and multiracial youth. *American Journal of Preventive Medicine, 54*(6), 795–805. https://doi.org/10.1016/j.amepre.2018.02.003

Trask, H. (1993). *From a Native Daughter: Colonialism and Sovereignty in Hawai'i.* Honolulu, HI: University of Hawai'i Press.

Trask, H. K. (1994). Kupa'a 'aina: Native Hawaiian nationalism in Hawai'i. In U. Hasager, & J. Friedman (Eds.), *Hawai'i: Return to Nationhood* (pp. 15–32). Copenhagen, Denmark: International Work Group for Indigenous Affairs.

Trinh, T., & Goebert, D. (2020). Youth voice in suicide prevention in Hawai'i. *Hawai'i Journal of Health & Social Welfare, 79*(5 Suppl 1), 71–75.

Trinidad, A. M. O. (2009). Toward kuleana (responsibility): a case study of a contextually grounded intervention for Native Hawaiian youth and young adults. *Aggression & Violent Behavior, 14,* 488–498. https://doi.org/10.1016/j.avb.2009.07.008

White, A. N., & Landis, M. (1982). The mental health of Native Hawaiians: a report. Alu Like.

Withy, K. M., Lee, W., & Renger, R. F. (2007). A practical framework for evaluating a culturally tailored adolescent substance abuse treatment program in Molokai, Hawai'i. *Ethnicity and Health, 12*(5), 483–496. https://doi.org/10.1080/13557850701616920

Wong, S. S., Sugimoto-Matsuda, J. J., Chang, J. Y., & Hishinuma, E. S. (2012). Ethnic differences in risk factors for suicide among American high school students, 2009: the vulnerability of multiracial and Pacific Islander adolescents. *Archives of Suicide Research, 16*(2), 159–173.

Wong-Wilson, M. N. N. (2016). Native Hawaiian well-being at Hawai'i community college: an initiative for academic success. [Unpublished dissertation, University of Waikato, New Zealand].

Wyman, P. A., Brown, C. H., LoMurray, M., Schmeelk-Cone, K., Petrova, M., Yu, Q., ... Wang, W. (2010). An outcome evaluation of the Sources of Strength suicide prevention program delivered by adolescent peer leaders in high schools. *American Journal of Public Health, 100*(9), 1653–1661. https://doi.org/10.2105/AJPH.2009.190025

Yahata, D., & Kaninau, P. (2009). *Native Hawaiian Youth Violence, Bullying, and Suicide Needs Assessment Report.* Honolulu, HI: Papa Ola Lōkahi.

Young, B. (2016). Early physicians of Hawai'i and reflections on the emergence of Hawaiian doctors. *Hūlili: Multidisciplinary Research on Hawaiian Well-Being, 10,* 35–82.

11

Critical Consciousness: Mental Health Benefits of Young Persons Taking Action Against Anti-Asian Hate[1]

Russell Jeung[1], Boaz Tang[1], Annie Bae[2], Alyssa Yeh[1], Caleb Hui[3], Julie Heejung Kim[4], Maria Zhang[5], and Abigail Sedlar-Yamada[1]

[1] *SF State, Asian American Studies, San Francisco, CA, USA*
[2] *UC Angeles, UCLA School of Education and Information Studies, Los Angeles, CA, USA*
[3] *UC Berkeley, Political Economy, Berkeley, CA, USA*
[4] *California Pacific Medical Center, Psychiatry, San Francisco, CA, USA*
[5] *Pomona College, Pomona, CA, USA*

Introduction

The rise in anti-Asian hate during the COVID-19 pandemic galvanized a new generation of leaders to take action. Priya, a dynamic South Asian organizer and rising junior from Malvern, Pennsylvania, became shocked and alarmed at the surge in xenophobia and violence targeting Asian communities in 2020. Priya recalled the defeat she felt:

> When I first learned about the rise of anti-Asian hate and people were just blaming the whole pandemic on Asians as a whole, it felt demoralizing and kind of demeaning...I was surprised because I didn't know this kind of hate existed.[2]

Priya's emotions reflected the fears and heightened concerns that Asian American youth across the nation experienced. They were witnessing, perhaps for the first time in their lives, virulent anti-Asian violence against their own families and communities. The traumatizing impact of racism "demoralized" and "demeaned" Asians, as elected leaders and others scapegoated them for the COVID-19 pandemic.

The anti-Asian hate took its toll on the mental health of Asian American and Pacific Islander (AAPI) youth. The growing hostility she witnessed in her community deeply alarmed and distressed Priya as she expressed,

> I felt unsafe...I just felt sad that this [anti-Asian hate] was happening and the fact that not many people were talking about it discouraged me more, I thought people were belittling this issue.

---

1 The SF State Asian American Research Institute is directed by Dr. Russell Jeung. Steven Quach. Joyce Mok, Stella Kim, Mina Fedor, and Ryan Idemoto provided research assistance.

2 Names have been changed to protect the anonymity and confidentiality of the participants of this oral history of AYR. They include a sample of 12 leaders from across the United States.

Recognizing the erasure of Asian Americans' pain and her school's neglect of Asian American history and narratives, Priya saw "ignorance" as a critical factor contributing to the anti-Asian hate. She then discovered AAPI Youth Rising (AYR) through their website and immediately became involved. "After I saw...how the organization was doing so much to raise awareness about the issue, I just knew I wanted to join," Priya enthused.

AYR is a youth-led organization with 180+ chapters across 35 states and counting. AYR's mission is to take small actions to make positive changes in our communities.[3] It believes in the power of collective action—one student, one lesson, and one day at a time. The organization first came together in March 2021 when its founders organized a 1,200+ person rally to bring awareness to the increase in xenophobia against Asians in America. Since then, their 180 chapters continue to teach the histories of Asian Americans nationwide. Through collaborations, AYR has implemented its programs in more than 52,000 middle and high schools across the United States. They unite against hate through civic engagement, advocate for diverse curricula in schools, and celebrate AAPI youth creativity. Their platform provides youth with many ways of getting involved through taking legislative action, participating in art activism, public speaking, and teaching in classrooms.[4]

To join AYR, chapter student leaders sign up on the organization's website and must pledge to bring their "One Day of AAPI History" lesson into their classroom or student organization. They also must: (1) join at least one AYR event during the year (virtual or in person); (2) attend at least one AYR organizational meeting; and (3) sign up for an AYR action, including blogging, writing an op-ed, or creating art.

Through AYR, Priya and her peers got involved to combat stereotypes, inform others about anti-Asian racism, and promote mental health among Asian American youth. She concluded that rather than assimilating into American society in order to avoid racism, Asian Americans need to come together:

> I feel a lot more people need to not lose sight of who you are as a person because of all this hate. It's easy to think that we have to change ourselves and [fit in by erasing] our heritage. But I feel like through AYR, I've learned that's not necessary, and you just need to unite, and that in itself, is enough.

With the support of her peers at AYR and her activism within her school, Priya gained newfound resilience and hope during a very troubling period.

Priya and her AYR counterparts shared three themes that reflect the development of their critical consciousness and the mental health benefits of taking action. Psychologist Sapna Chopra defines the components of critical consciousness:

> For Asian Americans, critical consciousness involves the following: (a) becoming aware of messages that have been internalized (e.g., colorism, model minority myth, white supremacy, anti-Black racism) and the sociopolitical context of oppression and (b) taking steps individually and/or collectively to combat oppression. (2021: 507)

---

3 AYR's website: https://aapiyouthrising.org/

4 In 2023, the California Civil Rights Department named AYR as a community partner to develop and launch California's first nonemergency hate reporting hotline. AYR has provided testimony about youth mental health to the President's Advisory Commission on Asian Americans, Native Hawaiians and Pacific Islanders, the California Commission on Hate, the Los Angeles Commission on the Status of Women, and many others. AYR has successfully advocated for legislation including California's ethnic studies mandate and Asian American history mandates nationwide.

Similarly, AYR members first developed not only an awareness of anti-Asian hate, but also an analysis of its systemic sources. They then took action to address these institutionalized root causes of racism. Furthermore, Priya and her peers noted that her AYR involvement alleviated their fears, anxieties, and demoralization related to anti-Asian hate. For Priya, her role as a social media manager with AYR replaced pandemic-related isolation and helplessness with a like-minded community and a sense of agency. In so doing, Priya, like other AYR leaders, said that her participation brought about change in her local communities and in her own mental health.

This chapter includes three sections. First, it reviews the negative psychological impact of COVID-19 racism on AAPI adolescents and emerging adults, as well as the coping mechanisms found to be helpful in alleviating their anxiety, depression, and posttraumatic stress symptoms. In particular, the chapter examines research on how critical consciousness is an effective coping mechanism for the AAPI community. Second, it provides a case study of AYR and its members. Through profiles of its leaders, the chapter describes the development of their critical consciousness and how activism offered them social support, meaning, and hope. Finally, it concludes with recommendations for how this model might be adopted by other AAPI communities, both young and old.

The Collective Racial Trauma of COVID-19

The Asian American Research Initiative at San Francisco State University identified seventy peer-reviewed research articles published between June 2020 and June 2024 that documented the significant correlation between COVID-19 racism and its negative impacts on AAPI mental health. Of these, 21 reported that both direct and indirect racism (discrimination experienced vicariously) led to greater psychological distress among AAPI adolescents and emerging adults (18–30 year olds). These issues include anxiety, depression, posttraumatic stress symptoms, and other negative health measures. Of these articles, 12 identified the coping mechanisms found to improve AAPI well-being, with the most reviewed mechanisms being social support, racial socialization, and ethnic identity.

Each of these mechanisms address the development and use of a critical consciousness. First, social support is the emotional comfort provided by one's interpersonal relationships, such as family, friends, or community members (American Psychological Association, 2018). It ranges from acts of intangible support, like listening and validating their experiences, to direct and tangible acts like offering a ride or sharing a meal. These acts of comfort help create a sense of belonging and security. Social support can help youths cope with experiences of direct racism by reinforcing a sense of being cared for, understood and valued in their communities. It can also provide them with guidance and advice from people who have had similar experiences with racial discrimination. Not only does social support enhance ethnic pride and belonging, but it also furthers opportunities for young people to take action in their networks (Cheng et al., 2022).

Second, racial socialization, defined as caregivers teaching their children to feel proud of their culture and to prepare for racialized experiences, is an effective buffer against discriminatory experiences during youth (Eboigbe et al., 2023; Wing and Park-Taylor, 2022; Zhang et al., 2022). Asian American parents instruct young persons to become racially literate and critically reflective, "by sharing stories of racism, pointing out sociopolitical and historical causes, and naming systems of oppression" (Tsong et al., 2022: 388).

Third, ethnic identity commitment is described as a sense of belonging and strongly identifying within that ethnic group (Phinney, 1992). It was found to mitigate the effects of racism on generalized anxiety symptoms (Cheng et al., 2022). To summarize, Asian American young persons can cope by becoming critically aware of sources of racism and getting engaged to confront it. AAPI Youth Rising is one such coalition that established a space for adolescents to do so.

Clinical Case Study

AAPI Youth Rising

This section highlights AYR's three leaders who reflect the main reasons why students joined AYR. The anti-Asian hate during the pandemic raised their critical consciousness to the institutionalized, oppressive nature of racism: to systemic racism, to pervasive stereotypes, and to the erasure of their community.

Anti-Asian Hate and Systematic Racism

Like Priya in the introduction, Owen became alarmed by anti-Asian hate and its traumatizing impact and so joined AYR with hopes to educate others and prevent further hate against the Asian community. Owen is a precocious 12-year-old Korean American from Pasadena, California, who is interested in biochemistry. At the start of the pandemic, he heard about the increased hate and violence against Asians in America from his parents and on the news:

> I was a little bit scared, because at the time I wasn't that old. So I was always thinking, what if they are trying to get me? Obviously, I was also scared for my grandparents.

He noticed that the elderly were targets and felt especially anxious for his grandparents. Motivated by this fear for his family and himself, which he could not stop thinking about, he took action.

As he dealt with the fear and anxiety stemming from anti-Asian hate, Owen recognized that inaccurate narratives blamed Asians for the spread of COVID-19, noting, "I was also mad because I knew that everything that was being said was not exactly true." Beyond the falsehoods spread by elected officials, Owen became angered and upset by their use of mocking terms such as "kung flu," which disparaged his community. As he paid attention to the news, he became aware that American politicians fomented interpersonal violence directed at elders. His critical consciousness began to form as he began to recognize the sources of racism.

Owen joined AYR because he saw it as a way to alleviate his anger and anxiety, and to find a sense of community. He also saw his participation as a tangible action step toward raising awareness and educating people about racism and Asian American history. He explained:

> I have my own grandparents, and I don't want them to get injured. I want to try to do anything to prevent that from ever happening. [Being in AYR] helped me, because I was doing something, even if it was just a little bit, I was still doing something, and that helped.

AYR provided Owen means to address his anxiety regarding his family's safety. To address racism at a broader level, Owen presented to other students in Los Angeles about Asian American history and preventing anti-Asian hate. He also fundraised for AYR and wrote for the AYR newsletter.

Anti-Asian Hate and Stereotypes

While Priya and Owen were driven to activism by anti-Asian hate incidents and racial scapegoating, Robin developed their collective consciousness by dealing with another form of racial oppression: stereotypes, particularly the model minority myth. An 18-year-old transracial adoptee from Taiwan with a no-nonsense attitude, Robin resides in a rural town in Ohio with a very small Asian American population. As a neurodivergent individual, Robin recalled how they grew up trying to live up to the model minority stereotype and faced constant pressure to perform academically. They added how their adopted father, a Vietnamese war refugee, "always had high expectations and would push his anxieties onto them." While they couldn't pinpoint when they were first exposed to the model minority myth, they shared that a combination of the stereotype, their neurodivergence, and generational trauma harmed their mental health.

Consequently, Robin struggled to socialize and was "ostracized in school, judged for just being Asian, and called racial slurs," according to them. Furthermore, Robin experienced burnout from the pressures of the model minority myth: "It started going downhill, and my expectations of living up to that standard of getting into Ivy League schools [became] ridiculous to me."

While enduring persistent racial microaggressions and academic pressure, Robin often felt angry and depressed, which they channeled into action and leadership. Refusing to live "the experience of being the silent minority," they sought ways to challenge this stereotype and anti-Asian racism by reaching out to AYR to get involved. In one of their advocacy efforts, Robin gave out books with BIPOC representation to young kids so that they could see themselves reflected in the media. Robin summarized why they, not she took action around racist stereotypes:

> To debunk these expectations and to let kids see themselves—I know that would have helped me as a child. Being able to do that for the next generation is just amazing.

While they mentioned that it can be challenging to be engaged from the Midwest, they've continued to actively engage with AYR by managing its social media pages and attending rallies and events.

Anti-Asian Hate and Erasure of the Community

Just as Priya mentioned the erasure of Asian Americans in her school's curriculum, the lack of representation for Asian Americans motivated Lily to join AYR. Being a first-generation Indian American growing up in a predominantly white part of Maryland, she struggled to find friends who understood her. The lack of role models in the media and in education who looked like her exacerbated her, not this feeling of marginalization. Wanting to belong, she desired to be white and described her emotions as:

> The feeling of being lost and misguided, but then also this resentment that's built up towards your community, because you feel like, What's so good about being Asian American if there's no Asian Americans that I see in the media or in education that are really making a difference?

The gradual realization about Asian Americans' erasure motivated Lily to find a community with whom she could relate. She found AYR through Instagram and felt inspired and understood by the organization, driving her to take action.

In her own words, Lily sought to "advance the amount of representation in society that Asian Americans have" through AYR. Subsequently, she prepared and presented on Asian American history for classrooms and corporate diversity day events.

Critical Consciousness and Improved Mental Health

Not only has AYR been a space to develop critical consciousness, but it also has been a site to heal and grow for Asian American youth like Priya, Owen, Robin, and Lily. First, they found an organization of like-minded people and social support. While the mental health benefits vary, AYR serves as a space for Asian American youth to gain a sense of belonging, as well as ethnic pride, which has validated their experiences. Second, it instilled a sense of purpose within Asian American youth as it empowered them to take active steps to liberate themselves, their families, and communities from xenophobia and violence. Third, it provided hope and a sense of efficacy by equipping them with the capabilities to spark the change they desired. This next section continues the stories of Lily, Owen, and Robin to demonstrate these mental health benefits of involvement with AYR.

AYR has connected Lily with different Asian Americans from across the country who share similar experiences and have validated her feelings of ostracization. As a result, this social support helped her to realize she is not alone and has improved her sense of self and ethnic pride:

> My perspective definitely has changed in terms of understanding that members of my community have had an impact on history and on like American history in general, and I think that the way that that's affected me is it's made me feel more proud of being who I am and being part of the community that I'm in. And again, that pride brings a benefit to my mental health.

Through finding a close-knit Asian American youth community and teaching Asian American history, Lily has felt more acknowledged and seen in her everyday life. Additionally, her anxieties about her future have eased because she knows about more Asian American role models with whom she can model herself.

Indeed, Lily described the organization as a community of advocacy and healing for her:

> [AYR is] an organization where not only could I make a difference and help other people who are struggling with their mental health or struggling with being Asian American, but I could address my own challenges with my identity, and find people who are similar to me.

Lily thus highlights the benefits of critical consciousness: taking action empowers individuals to effect change and working in solidarity promotes ethnic pride.

Owen also experienced a strong sense of community through AYR, which provided the second mental health benefit: purpose and meaningful action, which alleviated his feelings of powerlessness and persistent fear. Previous to joining, Owen constantly worried about his safety and the safety of his grandparents, as he had heard about the rise in anti-Asian hate during the pandemic. He also felt angry that people were blaming Asian Americans for the COVID-19 virus. Owen felt empowered and more at ease as a result of taking action with AAPI Youth Rising.

Finally, Robin's mental health improved as they went from feeling burnt out to gaining hope and agency. They explained: "I'm a lot happier [after getting involved]. I think it was because rather than expecting others to give hope, I was trying to give myself hope." Through their activism, Robin felt "liberated" from trying to fit the model minority stereotype and instead found a sense of belonging that significantly boosted their confidence: "I felt very energized...like I finally fit in." While they acknowledged experiencing occasional burnout from not seeing the change they hoped for, activism ultimately served as a gateway for Robin to truly explore their passions instead of prescribing to the model minority stereotype.

Conclusion and Recommendations

The critical consciousness that developed among these AYR members helped them to address the alienation, fear, and anxiety produced during the COVID-19 pandemic and the anti-Asian hate that ensued. Through AYR, they developed a community and network that offered social support around their concerns as Asian American youth. They became more committed to their ethnic identity and to their communities, as they organized around their common racial issues. And by taking action, they developed a sense of efficacy that they could make some change at their schools and communities. While these members were remarkable in their leadership and outspokenness, research confirms the helpful benefits of a critical consciousness.

As described, AYR members take action by presenting Asian American Studies curriculum that addresses stereotypes and provides positive role models, as well as by creating art to express their Asian American or Pacific Islander identities. According to Mina Fedor, founder of AYR, these varied platforms provide options for students, both those who enjoy making presentations and those who prefer to express themselves through other media. Fedor and Maxwell Wong, another AYR board member, identified three barriers confronting the coalition and its ability to teach Asian American history.

First, Wong noted that in cases where AYR members did not have a faculty classroom sponsor but had to teach sessions in student organizations spaces, the members had to do outreach on their own. How could they draw in other, non-Asian American classmates to their history lessons? He responded that AYR members became adept at using social media to publicize their lessons and their importance. "Young people really have the power of social media," he explained. "That's a powerful tool that young people have to push forward—this new wave of like online activism."

Second, Wong observed a decline in student engagement since the 2024 election. He observes:

> I live in like a relatively safe state to do this kind of work, but I think that many students across the country, particularly in more Republican-leaning environments, have a harder time being public about their activism work right now because it can come with like retaliation or backlash. There's very fierce resistance from a lot of people who really didn't want Asian American studies taught at the high school level.

He believes that most students starting chapters with AYR are in more "safe" environments, where they would not face as much backlash for their activism.

In the current political context, when schools may risk losing federal funding if they engage in Diversity, Equity and Inclusion activities, AYR primarily focuses on student-initiated programs or on schools that invite them. They also plan to offer virtual presentations so that students may participate on their own. Further, Fedor noted that AYR curriculum is not divisive nor threatening; instead she notes that it offers historically accurate content:

> Our curriculum covers some of the main stereotypes that Asian Americans have historically faced, the model minority myth and the perpetual foreigner myth. And then we talk about

those stereotypes in a greater historical context by going over different main events in AAPI history that we think are significant.

The sessions end positively by providing role models who have challenged these stereotypes and fought for change.

The final issue facing the AYR students is burnout. Following the elections, the AYR leaders expressed disappointment that the public opinion had shifted in ways that did not align with the goals of their organizations. They took some "time to rest and reset," Fedor mentioned, and now they are trying to maintain their mission and core values, especially with regards to inclusive history. Fedor stated that "it is even more important to teach Asian American history, during a time where diverse narratives are being directly targeted by our government." AYR members are feeling even greater urgency and more motivation to fight for Asian American youth, despite some of their fears. They continue to teach their Asian American history lesson in schools across the country.

The following recommendations include resources and examples for young persons themselves who want to become engaged in racial justice, for parents and caregivers wanting to guide and prepare their Asian American young persons for racial issues, and for schools seeking to promote positive school climates for racial unity and equity (see Table 11.1).

Table 11.1 Recommendations to promote critical consciousness.

Target group	Recommendation	Resources
Young Persons	Explore and learn from texts, media, and resources that promote ethnic pride and teach about issues of systemic racism.	*Asian Americans* five-episode docuseries created for PBS. https://www.pbs.org/weta/asian-americans/ AAPI Youth Rising https://aapiyouthrising.org/
	Establish Asian American, Native Hawaiian, and Pacific Islander student affinity organizations that not only promote ethnic and cultural pride, but also actively address issues of race relations and racism.	The Education Coalition for Asian American Representation. Example of student-run high school cultural and advocacy organization https://theasianamericanstory.weebly.com/ How to start an affinity group (K-12) Learning for Justice https://www.learningforjustice.org/magazine/summer-2015/making-space How to start an affinity group (College) https://www.thecrimson.com/article/2019/5/15/asian-affinity-groups/
	Build multiracial coalitions with other student groups and cosponsor school events and activities in order to promote racial solidarity.	
	Act as upstanders: those who intervene in incidents of bullying, harassment, and microaggressions.	Virtual workshops on bystander training cosponsored by Asian Americans Advancing Justice Southern California and Right To Be. https://ajsocal.org/bystander-intervention-trainings/

Target group	Recommendation	Resources
Caregivers	Listen empathetically and validate students' experiences of bullying because of ethnicity, gender, race and other forms.	Communication tips for Asian American caregivers on decisions youth make https://ajsocal.org/bystander-intervention-trainings/
	Hold open conversations about ethnic and racial identity, race relations and racism, and mental health and resilience. Foster pride in their own heritage and race.	Example to foster positive parent–student conversations. The Boba Project https://www.thebobaproject.com/
	Share family stories and histories, especially those dealing with overcoming adversity and discrimination, working collectively with coethnics and across race, and civic/political engagement.	Key terms in discussing racial issues https://parentsarehuman.com/
	Introduce youth to Asian American narratives—books, movies, dolls, and toys.	Selection of Multicultural & Social Justice Books, sponsored by Teaching for Change (South Asian, Chinese, Japanese) https://socialjusticebooks.org/booklists/asian-americans/ Filipino Books from Bayani
Schools	Offer Asian American Studies curriculum from kindergarten through 12th grade which is developmentally appropriate, culturally open, and critical in analysis.	
	Provide training and curriculum development opportunities on Ethnic Studies for faculty and staff.	AA Education Project: workshops for professional development https://asianamericanedu.org/
	Host more Asian American, Native Hawaiian, and Pacific Islander resources at schools year-round, such as library books, guest speakers, diverse role models.	
	Organize multicultural events celebrating cultural pride and improving race relations.	Example of Boston University multicultural rice dish-based potluck event https://www.instagram.com/p/CcGQWw2uVDH/?igsh=MzRlODBiNWFlZA%3D%3D Example of Cherry Hill East Multicultural Day: CHE Multi Cultural Day https://www.facebook.com/eastsidenewspaper/posts/cherry-hill-easts-annual-multicultural-day-mcd-celebration-was-held-on-thursday-/1170123794293941/ Example of city AAPI Heritage Month Festival: Asian American Alliance in South Jersey Heritage Month Festival https://frontrunnernewjersey.com/2024/05/10/cherry-hill-high-school-west-celebrates-4th-annual-aapi-heritage-month-festival/

(*Continued*)

Table 11.1 (Continued)

Target group	Recommendation	Resources
	Increase staff diversity	
	Provide culturally responsive mental health services.	Directory of providers, support groups, and mental health resources (Asian Community Mental Health Collective) https://www.asianmhc.org/ Mental health resources and workshops for immigrants from Brown Girl Therapy https://sahajkaurkohli.com/brown-girl-therapy Train and host student-led mental health programs https://www.naapimha.org/friends-do-make-a-difference

References

American Psychological Association. (2018). Social support - Dictionary of psychology. https://dictionary.apa.org/social-support

Cheng, H.-L., Wong, Y. J., Li, P. F. J., & McDermott, R. C. (2022). COVID-19 racism, anxiety, and racial/ethnic attitudes among Asian American college students. *Counseling Psychology Quarterly*, *35*(4), 897–920. https://doi.org/10.1080/09515070.2021.1988514

Eboigbe, L. I., Simon, C. B., Wang, Y. S., & Tyrell, F. A. (2023). The compounded effect of the dual pandemic on ethnic-racial minority adolescents' mental health and psychosocial well-being. *Current Opinion in Psychology*, *52*, 101626. https://doi.org/10.1016/j.copsyc.2023.101626

Phinney, J. S. (1992). The multigroup ethnic identity measure: a new scale for use with diverse groups. *Journal of Adolescent Research*, *7*(2), 156–176.

Tsong, Y., Chopra, S. B., & Cheng, H.-L. (2022). Racial healing during the COVID-19 and anti-Asian pandemics through critical consciousness informed antiracist parenting practices (CCIARP). *Asian American Journal of Psychology*, *13*(4), 325–337. https://doi.org/10.1037/aap0000143

Wing, H. M., & Park-Taylor, J. (2022). From model minority to racial threat: Chinese transracial adoptees' experience navigating the COVID-19 pandemic. *Asian American Journal of Psychology*, *13*(2), 234–247.

Zhang, E., Hyun, S., Yip, T., Hahm, H. C., & Liu, C. H. (2022). Learning about discrimination during childhood: implications for racial trauma among Asians and Asian Americans during the pandemic. *Asian Journal of Psychiatry*, *77*, 103250. https://doi.org/10.1016/j.ajp.2022.103250

12

Adaptation of an Evidence-based, Online Stress Management Intervention for Young Vietnamese Americans in the Gulf South

Mai P. Do[1], PhuongThao D. Le[2], Savannah Badt[1], Lawrence H. Yang[3], Emily Goldmann[2], Jannette Diep[4], Anne Li[5], Hang Ngo[6], and David Abramson[6]

[1]*Tulane University Celia Scott Weatherhead School of Public Health and Tropical Medicine, New Orleans, LA, USA*
[2]*Boston University School of Public Health, Boston, MA, USA*
[3]*Duke School of Nursing, Duke University; Department of Population Health Sciences, Duke University; Affiliate, Duke Global Health Institute, Duke University, Durham, NC, USA*
[4]*BPSOS/Houston, Houston, TX, USA*
[5]*Boston University Chobanian and Avedisian School of Medicine, Boston, MA, USA*
[6]*New York University School of Global Public Health, New York, NY, USA*

Introduction

Ethnic minority groups living in the Gulf Coast region often bear disproportional impacts from weather-related events. In addition, social vulnerabilities and cultural beliefs and nuances indicate that interventions aimed to mitigate such impacts among these population groups need to be culturally appropriate, relevant, and feasible. In this chapter, we describe the process of adapting an evidence-based mental health intervention, Self-Help Plus, to young Vietnamese Americans in the Gulf Coast, who have culturally influenced views of mental health. The intervention, developed by the World Health Organization (WHO), is aimed at reducing psychological distress in individuals affected by adversities. Our team conducted a community engaging, preimplementation assessment process that included input from representatives of the participant group (i.e., audience members) and adaptations to the intervention content and delivery to ensure that it was feasible, acceptable, and understood by the audience, while maintaining the integrity of an evidence-based intervention. We highlight important lessons learned from the codesign process between the research team and the target audience, including working with members of the team who served as cultural brokers—from designing the formative process to recruiting participants and facilitating discussions. Our two-prong approach—a research team and cultural brokers with established community relationships, combined with a codesign process with members of the target audience—proved critical in the adaptation of the intervention. This approach can be generalized to adapt and deliver mental health interventions digitally to other Asian American groups. It is especially helpful in making mental health intervention delivery to the broader Asian American community possible when face-to-face intervention delivery is potentially stigmatizing or not possible in a postdisaster or pandemic context.

People living along the Gulf Coast have experienced many collective traumas, most notably hurricanes Katrina and Rita (2005), Harvey (2017), Laura and Zeta (2020), and Ida (2021) as major hurricanes of Category 3 or higher, and most recently the health and economic disruptions of the COVID-19 pandemic. There has been evidence of disproportionate impacts of extreme weather events (EWEs) on Vietnamese Americans (VA) and other ethnic minorities (Choi et al., 2022; Fong et al., 2022), as well as those of the pandemic on Asian Americans (Smith et al., 2023; Tiwari & Zhang, 2022; Wang et al., 2020).

In addition to the geographical vulnerabilities to EWEs, VAs in the Gulf Coast have unique social vulnerability often shaped by their socio-economic status, culture, relatively restricted social networks, and access to political power, resources, and information (Cho et al., 2021; Covert et al., 2020; Lightfoot et al., 2020; Mayfield-Johnson et al., 2020). VA young adults have additional struggles, as they often need to navigate between an English-speaking society and non-English speaking, less acculturated parents and grandparents at home (Do et al., 2020). While mental health distress remains prevalent among VA communities, it often goes unrecognized and un-managed (Do et al., 2020). Previous research with VAs in the New Orleans area highlighted not only poor understanding of mental health conditions and severe stigma toward mental illness, but also significant generational differences in the understanding of mental health and stigma among VAs (e.g., Do et al., 2014, 2020). Yet, in addition to several socio-cultural barriers to accessing health care among VAs (Kaji, 2017), a number of additional barriers exist among this generation, including the need to balance two different cultures and obligations to uphold family values (Do et al., 2020; Nguyen et al., 2021; Nguyen, 2019). Consequently, young people tend to seek support from their personal networks outside the home, or look up information themselves, instead of seeking professional help (Do et al., 2020; Kim-Mozeleski et al., 2018). Our research has also shown diverse and inconsistent experiences in recovery after an EWE, as well as mental health and care seeking among VAs in cities along the Gulf Coast (Do et al., 2023; Kaji et al., 2021; Pham et al., 2023). Such diversities in the experiences of VAs underscore the needs for tailored interventions that address mental health challenges among this population.

Obtaining input from the target audience (i.e., representatives of the potential participant group) is critical to ensure that a public health intervention is acceptable, feasible, and understood (Health Compass, 2023). This step is even more important when the target audience is a culturally and linguistically diverse group, like the VAs. In this paper, we describe a process in which input from the target audience was obtained and incorporated into adapting the intervention and lessons learned.

Project Background

Calm After the Storm Project

The Calm After the Storm (CATS) project is a collaboration between New York University (NYU), Tulane University, and BPSOS-Houston (Boat People SOS-Houston)—a national Vietnamese community-based organization with a branch office in Houston. The project aimed to test the feasibility of an online version of the stress management intervention (Self-Help Plus or SH+) for disaster exposed VA young adults aged 18–30 years living in the Gulf Coast region.

Young VAs present as a key target group for several reasons. First, young adults in New Orleans and Houston have experienced multiple catastrophic hazards as children, in addition to the more recent exposure as young adults to COVID-19. Mental health consequences are likely, yet stigma is still prevalent among this group, although there is evidence that VAs aged 18–35 years have a better understanding of mental illness, and value mental health services more, compared to their older counterparts (Do et al., 2020). They are also critical in providing support and care for older adults, which puts additional stress on them during disasters as well as the pandemic. Additionally, this generation is likely digitally savvy and receptive to online services (Lee et al., 2022, 2023), which is important to testing an online intervention.

The aim of the CATS project is to test the fit and feasibility of adapting and employing an online version of an evidence-based mental health intervention, Self-Help Plus, among VA young adults living in the Gulf Coast region. The project's long-term goal is to address mental health needs of this community through accessible, culturally appropriate interventions and strategies, which could provide a roadmap to reaching other high-need, Asian American groups.

Self-Help Plus (SH+) Intervention

SH+ is an evidence-based mental health intervention developed by the World Health Organization (WHO) aimed at reducing psychological distress in individuals affected by adversities, including humanitarian crises, potentially traumatic events and chronic poverty (Epping-Jordan et al., 2016). SH+ consists of five prerecorded audio lessons (approximately 90 minutes each) delivered weekly to a group of 20–30 people by minimally trained lay facilitators. The facilitators play the audio recordings, showing the accompanying pictures and pausing the recordings to facilitate practice exercises and pair discussions when prompted.

SH+ is based on Acceptance and Commitment Therapy (ACT), a form of cognitive and behavioral therapy (CBT) that focuses on identifying personal values and strategies to live in accordance with those values despite hardships. ACT promotes acceptance of emotions and provides skills for individuals to engage in mindfulness activities that emphasize the three pillars of ACT: (1) be present (nonjudgmentally), (2) opening up, and (3) doing what matters (Hayes et al., 2006). The five core SH+ skills include: (1) "Grounding," which normalizes and validates strong emotions and guides participants to practice being present; (2) "Unhooking," which directs participants to notice and name their difficult sensations, thoughts, and feelings in order to "unhook" from them; (3) "Acting on Your Values," which encourages participants to identify their personal, communal, and cultural values for which they would like to guide their actions; (4) "Being Kind," which promotes awareness and encouragement of prosocial behaviors; and (5) "Making Room," in which participants are guided to accommodate difficult thoughts and feelings rather than trying to get rid of them.

SH+ can also include an illustrated self-help book, "Doing What Matters in Times of Stress," that participants can read for further information and additional exercises for each session topic (World Health Organization (WHO), 2020). While SH+ has yet to be evaluated within VA communities, ACT's mindfulness approach is congruent with Vietnamese culture, which is heavily influenced by Buddhist philosophies and practices, including the widespread promotion of meditation to achieve self-realization.

Two separate trials have identified benefits of the SH+ intervention with diverse refugee populations in Turkey and various European settings who have experienced a wide range of traumas, including war-related experiences, violence, and stressors associated with migration and social integration into their new residences (Purgato et al., 2019). Efforts are underway to scale up the intervention to other populations (Tol et al., 2020). SH+ is well suited for our identified Vietnamese young adult population because it is intended to be easily culturally adaptable and is nonspecific to the type of trauma or mental health condition. There have also been calls by the WHO to test the online delivery of SH+ (World Health Organization (WHO), 2021). While SH+ has yet to be adapted to an online format, the nature of the intervention lends itself well to an online format, and group conferencing technologies such as Zoom can help facilitate virtual group meetings. The ability to provide this intervention virtually signifies a substantial advance and is critical in postdisaster contexts, when individuals may have been displaced from their homes and facilities where individuals might meet to participate in a group intervention are not available. An online adaptation of SH+ may also produce a more feasible and acceptable intervention for the VA youth population, as they are more digitally connected, compared to older generations. Finally, if this new, online version of SH+ is found to be acceptable, appropriate, and feasible among Vietnamese young adults, it could also be expanded to address the mental health needs of the broader Asian American community (e.g., anti-COVID racism and discrimination).

Acute collective stressors such as natural hazards and technological disasters have historically led to enduring mental health issues among affected populations (Kaji et al., 2021; Norris et al., 2009; VanLandingham et al., 2022; VanLandingham & VanLandingham, 2017; Vu & VanLandingham, 2012). In addition to the need to assess disaster-exposed communities for mental health distress, there is a corresponding need to identify appropriate evidence-based mental health interventions (Goldmann & Galea, 2014). Furthermore, initial feelings of stress and distress, if untreated, may lead to more significant mental health illness and delayed disaster recovery (VanLandingham et al., 2022; VanLandingham & VanLandingham, 2017). Postdisaster settings are chaotic, and health service systems are often disrupted. This proposed SH+, delivered online, is particularly well-suited as a disaster mental health intervention. It can be rapidly scalable, may be delivered to displaced populations (assuming Internet connectivity), and can be delivered by facilitators distant from the disaster setting.

Getting Input from the Audience

SH+ was developed based on extensive field testing and continues to be deployed or tested in different settings and populations (Fietta et al., 2024; Purgato et al., 2025; Riello et al., 2021), including women in Viet Nam (Le, 2021–2026). Our team was faced with several challenges during the preimplementation assessment of the acceptability and feasibility of SH+ among VA young adults in the Gulf Coast. First, VA young adults are a diverse group living across the Gulf Coast region, likely having different lived experiences with and resilience in the face of EWEs. Second, they are an audience group for whom there has not been evidence of successful interventions for stress management. Third, SH+ has not been used in an online platform before. Thus, two key questions arose: (1) how would VA youth perceive SH+ in a group setting? and (2) how appropriate is an online platform for this intervention for the VA group and what, if any, changes are needed?

Three focus group discussions (FGDs) were implemented in April 2024 with a total of 17 male and female VAs aged 18–30 years who had lived in the Gulf Coast region for at least a year. These young VAs were recruited through publicly posted flyers and outreach activities by BPSOS-Houston, our community-based partner. We intentionally assigned research team members who are also VAs of the same age group to facilitate the discussions to minimize potential cultural and age-related barriers. Three FGDs took place via Zoom, in English, and were audio and video recorded. Ethical approval for this activity was obtained from the New York University's and Tulane University's Institutional Review Boards. Verbal consent was sought from every participant during recruitment and repeated at the beginning of each FGD. Each participant received a $50 Amazon gift card at the end of the FGD.

A discussion guide (Appendix 1) was developed by the research team, with input from members who were peer VAs to make the discussion guide more relevant and appropriate. While the guide included questions on social and emotional needs and services, its focus was on the SH+ intervention. After a brief introduction of the intervention, during which participants were shown examples of slides and audio narration of the training, questions were asked about participants' overall impression of the intervention, its structure, and how to best publicize the intervention and engage young adults in the community. Participants were probed about the extent to which such an intervention might help address the social and emotional needs of young VAs living in areas affected by natural disasters and cultural considerations for its adaptation. Participants were also asked follow-up questions about the delivery of the intervention in an online format. Each FGD lasted approximately an hour.

We employed a rapid qualitative data analysis approach to analyzing the transcripts. First, transcripts were independently reviewed (MD, SB, PTL) to gain familiarity with the data. Second, the main findings and excerpts from each transcript were summarized in columns in a table whereby rows included the different intervention components and elements (e.g., SH+ skills and concepts, illustrations, voice actors, online format, length of sessions). In the section below, we discussed how input from the young VA participants was incorporated into the adaptation of the SH+ intervention.

Intervention Adaptation

The need for a stress management intervention, like SH+, for young VAs was underscored by our participants, who expressed feelings of isolation both within and outside of the home. At home, common stressors for young VAs often came from pressures to live up to parental and cultural expectations of being the "model minority" and the stereotype of successful Asian Americans. Many participants also discussed intergenerational traumas—traumatic experiences that their parents and grandparents carried through the Vietnam War and immigration to the United States and then vicariously passed down to them. At the same time, language barriers due to limited English proficiency among older adults often restricted open communication between generations. Outside the home, participants also did not feel well represented in existing intervention programs for stress and mental health challenges related to natural disasters in general. Differences in cultural values compared to other racial and ethnic groups made them feel that available interventions were neither culturally relevant nor appealing.

While appreciating SH+ as a stress management intervention for young VAs, stigma related to mental illnesses was mentioned as a potential barrier. At the same time, FGD participants practiced one of the key SH+ exercises—grounding—together on Zoom. Consequently, "community building" and "connecting with others," who might have had similar potentially traumatic experiences, were seen as possible benefits of the SH+ intervention being delivered in group settings that could be appealing to their peers. As a result, our recruitment materials were adapted to emphasize individual stress reduction skills and community connection enhancements as benefits of the CATS project (see Figure 12.1). The photo in the flyer was also selected to reflect the "calming" element after a tropical storm. The flyer was tested by BPSOS staff during their initial outreach activities with communities.

1. **SH+ content**

   The original SH+ intervention is structured into five weekly sessions, each focusing on one of the five core skills, or "pillars." The content of each session and skill was briefly introduced in the FGDs. Participants overwhelmingly welcomed trainings on these skills; they also stated

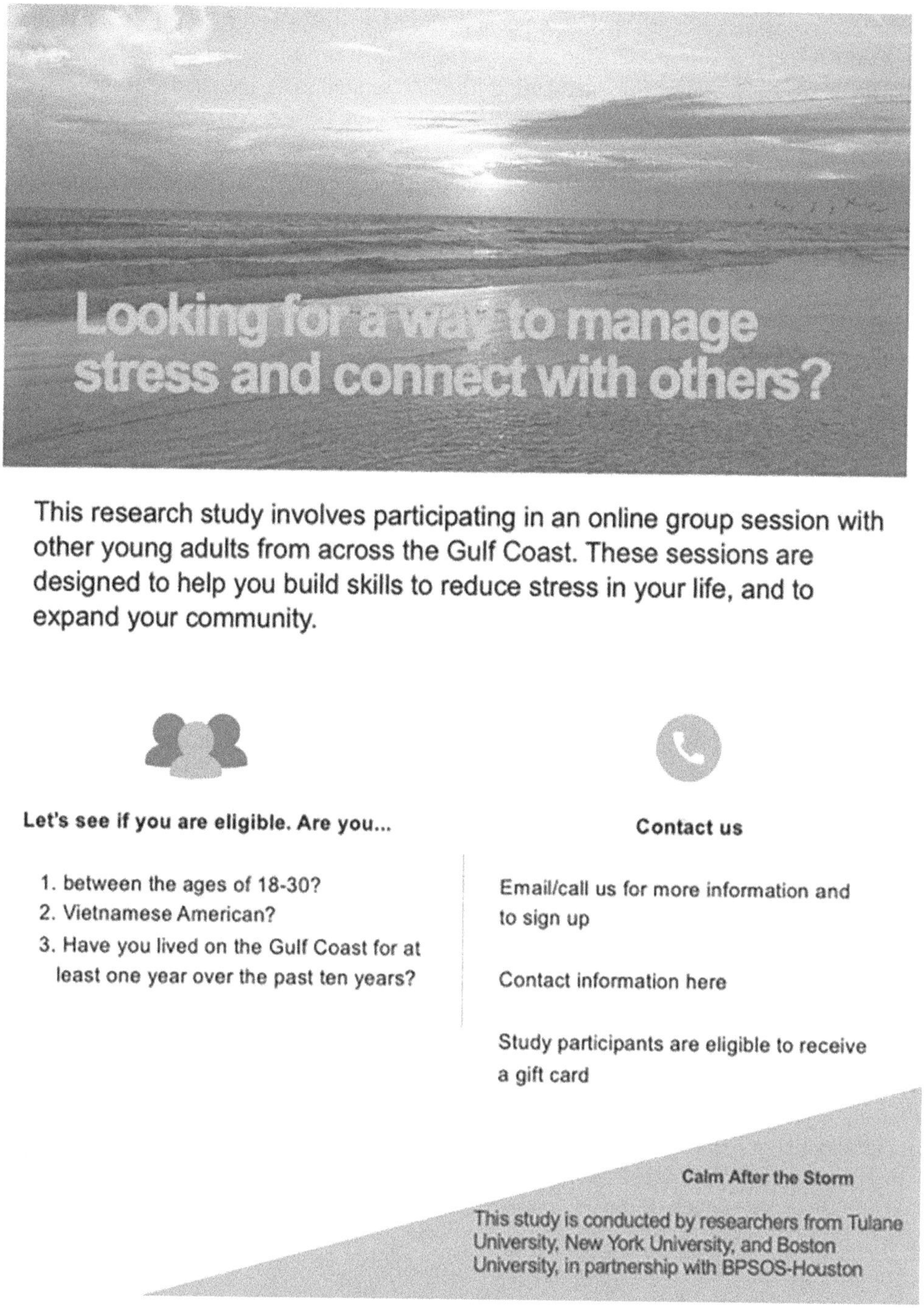

Figure 12.1 Recruitment flyer. *Source:* MaineCoast / Pixabay / CC BY 0.

that these skills were consistent with Vietnamese cultural values. A participant stated that taken altogether, the SH+ skills underscore the Vietnamese ethos of "*cố gắng lên*" (i.e., try your best to do well/better; being resilient). This suggested cultural acceptability for the SH+ core concepts; thus, the five skill sets remained the five pillars of this intervention.

While it has proven to work well in in-person settings, participants expressed concerns about both the number of sessions and the session length, which could deter busy young people from participating. In response, the intervention was restructured to be delivered in three sessions, each for approximately two hours, while maintaining the key content of the five pillars. We combined sessions 1 ("Grounding") and 2 ("Unhooking") to one, sessions 3 ("Values") and 4 ("Being Kind") to another, and kept session 5 ("Making Room") as its own. While doing so, we also reduced the amount of time needed at the beginning and the end of each session to discuss ground rules, Zoom etiquette, and reflections. By having session 5 by itself (now, session 3), we anticipate having adequate time during this last session for participants to review and reflect on the training—e.g., what may have worked or not.

Several specific content areas of the sessions were modified to be more appropriate and interactive for our target audience, most of whom were likely born in the United States and had finished at least high school, thus are likely to have a higher education level than older VA immigrants. For example, instead of narrating what stress is, we revised this section by having the facilitator encourage participants to share their own perceptions of stress, emphasizing that stress could take many shapes and forms.

2. **SH+ delivery**
   To make SH+ more conducive to online delivery, we also converted SH+ materials from audio recordings with paper copies of images to slides with embedded pictures and audio clips. We also modified the narration and slides to be less wordy, as well as made key exercises more engaging and appropriate for an online group setting. For example, for the two exercises below in "Unhooking" and "Acting on Your Values," the modifications were relatively simple by employing breakout rooms and the white board in Zoom; however, this required some additional training for facilitators to manage online work groups. In the "Unhooking" exercise (Figure 12.2a), participants were asked to circle figures or write down words that described their thoughts and feelings when they were stressed, so that they could learn to "unhook," while in the "Values" exercise (Figure 12.2b), participants were asked to share their values.

Another modification was related to the composition of the participants in each session. During the FGDs, several participants expressed concerns about privacy and confidentiality of participants, especially with discussions related to mental health challenges, stigma, and how individuals might have coped with them. In response, two modifications were made. First, we plan to include a mix of young VAs from Texas, Louisiana, and Florida in each cohort to minimize the likelihood that participants may know each other and hence, do not feel comfortable being in the same group. By having a mix of participants from different locations, we anticipate minimizing the chance that participants in the same cohort are somehow connected. Second, while not ideal from both research and community engagement perspectives, we will also not record the sessions, nor will we require participants to have their camera on, although it is still encouraged. Not requiring the camera on would also help eliminate accessing barriers as some participants were concerned that they might be in a setting not appropriate to be on camera.

Finally, a very important modification was the narration of the prerecorded audios. The original lessons were narrated by a voice that sounded male and spoke at a slower pace. Some participants thought that the slow pace might be calming, while others felt a faster pace would make the lesson somewhat more engaging. All participants, however, expressed strong preferences of a test audio clip, where we recorded the voice of a young VA female narrating part of a lesson introduction. Although she recorded it at her normal pace of talking, it was also much faster than the original soundtrack which could help condense the original sessions from five to three total. As a result, the revised lessons were renarrated also by a young VA.

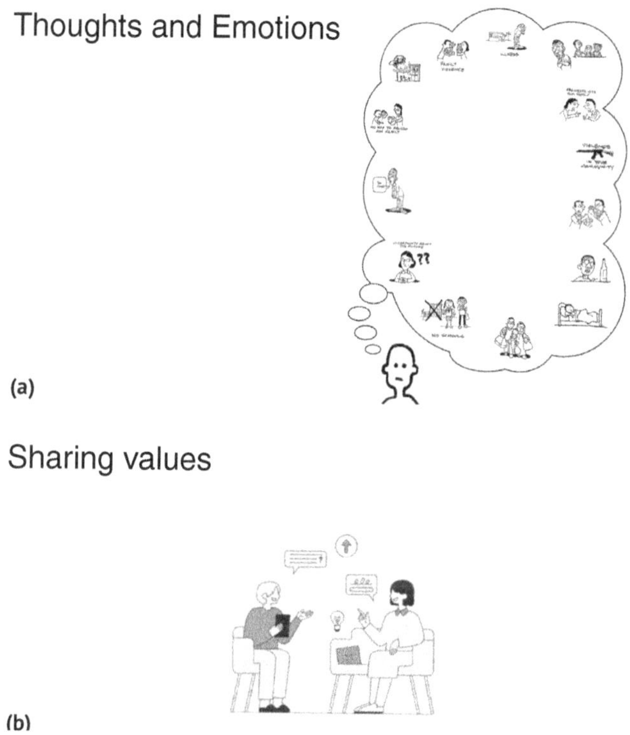

Figure 12.2 (a) Identify thoughts and feelings when stressed. (b) Sharing values.

Table 12.1 below summarizes some of the key modifications for the sessions to be relevant to our young audience and appropriate for the online format.

Lessons Learned

Once adapted, the SH+ intervention will be piloted in a randomized controlled trial where participants will be randomly assigned into one of two groups: (1) the intervention group where they will receive three weekly sessions of the intervention, and (2) the control group where they will receive an hour virtual session on natural disaster related stress and management, with no SH+ specific information. Everyone will receive assessments of stressful event experience; perceived stress; general self-efficacy; mental health symptoms (e.g., depression, anxiety, nonspecific psychological distress); and access to, use of, and stigma related to mental health services at baseline and endline (immediate after the intervention period) to evaluate the potential effectiveness of the adapted intervention to reduce stress and distress. At the end of the pilot, participants will also be asked to reflect on the intervention and its delivery for further refinement prior to implementation in a randomized clinical trial.

In this chapter, we have described a process in which members of the target audience provided inputs to the adaptation of a standardized intervention to fit their health and cultural needs. Feedback was incorporated into the revision of the structure, content, as well as the delivery of the SH+ intervention, while retaining the five key stress management skills, thus maintaining

Table 12.1 Summary of key modifications to the SH+ intervention.

Section	Modification
Section 1: Introduction, Grounding, and Unhooking	
Facilitator introduction	Instead of facilitators being community leaders or community health workers, we intentionally recruit those who are lay community members, and some are peers with young VAs. The introduction will reflect this connection to help establish rapports in an online forum.
Video recording	In the original version, video recording in introduced as a way for quality control, to provide assessments of the facilitators and the training sessions. Since our audience expressed some concerns about sharing private information and stories with others who may be from the same community, which could contribute to stigma, we make two modifications: (1) we intentionally have participants from different communities in the same sessions, and (2) for each session, we do not record the session or require participants' cameras to be on, although it is encouraged.
Participant introduction	In the original version for in-person training, this part comes after privacy and confidentiality principles are discussed. In the online version, we move this part up to right after facilitators' introduction to help establish open and equal rapports between facilitators and participants, one of the concerns from both our team and participants.
Definition of stress	We revise it so that instead of the facilitators' listing symptoms of stress, we ask participants to share their stories and/or symptoms, creating an open-ended conversation and a more participatory process with young people
Drinking exercise and discussion	Instead of the facilitators' handing out water and leading the discussion afterward in a big group, we revise the exercise for the online format when all are not in the same room. We also create breakout room exercises to make it easier for participants to share their thoughts in a smaller group.
Section 2: Values and Being Kind	
Definition of values, personal values, and discussion	Instead of having the narration on what values and personal values are, we modify the content and have questions to make them open-ended so participants can share their thoughts and perceptions, recognizing that everyone can view values differently and have different personal values.
Identify one's personal values	Similarly, instead of having a list of pre-prescribed values, we ask participants to come up with their own values using a format relevant for online exercises, e.g., Menti format to create a word cloud.
Sharing personal values	In the original version, the exercise is designed for participants to share with the person next to them what their personal values are. We revise it for the online format when all are not in the same room and create breakout room exercises to make it easier for participants to share their thoughts in a smaller group.
Section 3: Making Room	
Paper pushing exercise	Instead of the facilitators handing out pieces of papers and narrating through the exercise in the big group, we also revise it for the online format and create breakout room exercises to make it easier for participants to focus on the exercise and share their thoughts in a smaller group.
Additional slide	In addition to a brief evaluation after every session, we add a final slide on participants' reflection: how participants see these skills fit into their stress management mechanisms, and if there is anything they would change in the training?

its integrity as an evidence-based practice. Some of the adaptations of the WHO-approved intervention could be considered substantial, e.g., the modification from five to three weekly sessions, given a new type of audience and a new delivery format that have not been tested before. Pretesting of the revised materials is advisable and will be implemented in the next project phase. That the adapted intervention will be delivered online makes it less vulnerable to interruptions (assuming uninterrupted internet service), such as natural disasters or infectious disease outbreaks (e.g., COVID-19), when in-person gatherings may not be possible.

An important lesson learned from this process is the necessity of undertaking the codesign process between the research team and the target audience. Besides researchers who are experts on the topical areas and have worked with the Vietnamese communities for nearly two decades, half of our team are members of the community, primarily peers of our target audience. Key staff members of BPSOS-Houston served not only as researchers but also cultural brokers (Benoit et al., 2011; Brar-Josan & Yohani, 2019), which enabled understanding and communicating cultural nuances to improve public health programs and interventions for ethnic minority groups. BPSOS-Houston staff provided input throughout the process on what might or might not work regarding engagement, recruitment, messaging, and implementing focus groups. Previous work by several team members has also underlined the role of cultural brokers between the research team and the VA community (VanLandingham et al., 2023). In addition, peer research team members also provided input on the design of recruitment materials. More importantly, they served as facilitators of group discussions, which helped establishing rapport and trust with the target audience. After the FGDs, the same team members conducted qualitative data analysis and interpretation, followed by SH+ intervention modifications, including re-recording the sessions. The entire research team frequently met to provide suggestions and support to young team members along the way. By doing so, we were confident that we incorporated key and relevant cultural nuances as much as possible into intervention adaptation.

Our two-prong approach—a research team and cultural brokers with an established relationship with the community, combined with a codesign process with members of the target audience—was successfully employed by several members of the team during the COVID-19 pandemic (Meekers et al., 2024). While the approach to "move from audience testing to community co-design to build trust" (Quinn et al., 2023) was recommended for public health emergencies, our exercise showed that it has broader utility for programs and interventions. A limitation is that at the time of the publication, the pilot of the adapted intervention was still underway, and further modifications may ensue following actual implementation. There is still a need for actual evaluation data to assess the acceptability and potential effectiveness of the SH+ intervention in a pilot with young VAs. Nevertheless, we believe that the process and lessons describe here are widely applicable for public health programs targeting ethnic minorities and vulnerable groups, and have applicability to expanding in particular an evidence-based, online intervention to address mental health needs of diverse Asian American groups. This approach is especially important in making mental health intervention delivery possible when face-to-face intervention delivery is potentially stigmatizing or not possible in a postdisaster or pandemic context. An illustration of how the core SH+ skills can guide clinical practice with a Vietnamese American young adult is presented in Table 12.2 below.

Many VA youth in the US Gulf Coast navigate not only the stress of climate-related disruptions but also the challenges of adolescence, bicultural identity, and intergenerational expectations, as do young immigrants elsewhere. When presented in culturally responsive and developmentally appropriate ways, SH+ can provide youth with accessible tools to manage distress, enhance

Table 12.2 Clinical case illustration: application of core SH+ skills to VA young adults.

SH+ core skills	Description	Application to VN young adults
Grounding	Focusing on the present moment to reduce overwhelming feelings. Simple techniques (e.g., focusing on breathing, bodily sensations, or present surroundings) to manage overwhelming emotions.	Guide VA youth through short grounding exercises during hurricane season or storm drills. For example, invite them to name five things they can see, four they can touch, three they can hear, two they can smell, and one they can taste. Linking this to familiar sensory anchors, such as the smell of Vietnamese cooking or the sound of ocean waves, may enhance comfort and connection.
Unhooking	Noticing and naming painful thoughts or memories; refocusing on the present moment.	Help clients "unhook" from distressing memories of property loss or displacement by practicing noticing and naming the emotions or thoughts. Clinicians can use metaphors rooted in Vietnamese culture (e.g., "thoughts are like passing clouds after a storm"). Support clients in recognizing stress signals (e.g., insomnia, hypervigilance) triggered by storm warnings. Clinicians can frame this skill as mindful awareness that aligns with Buddhist or Catholic contemplative practices common among Vietnamese Americans.
Acting on your values	Identifying values that are in accordance to cultural and community values, and can guide personal actions, even when distressed.	Guide clients to reconnect with core values (e.g., family harmony, community resilience) when rebuilding after storms. Clinicians can encourage youth to identify culturally salient values like filial piety, family harmony, and community solidarity as motivators for adaptive action. For instance, a youth who values family might help pack emergency supplies before hurricane season, reinforcing a sense of purpose and agency.
Being kind	Practicing compassion toward oneself and others in the face of hardship.	Encourage self-kindness when clients feel guilt or shame about needing assistance after hurricanes. Clinicians can introduce short self-kindness practices such as writing themselves a supportive note in Vietnamese or English, or sharing encouraging words within peer groups. Normalize help-seeking, connecting kindness to cultural values of collective care—mutual aid, temple or church support networks—can make this skill more acceptable and powerful.
Making room	Accepting the presence of difficult emotions rather than suppressing them.	Use metaphors from Vietnamese culture: "Like water in a river—it flows, but it doesn't stop you from crossing."

resilience, and strengthen family and community ties. In practice, these skills can be introduced in clinical settings, schools, community centers, and faith-based organizations. When adapted with attention to language, metaphors, and cultural values, SH+ provides a structured yet flexible and culturally relevant approach to addressing the compounded stressors of both adolescence and climate-related adversity in VA youth. This alignment of evidence-based skills with cultural strengths underscores the potential of SH+ as a valuable resource for practitioners, researchers, and community leaders seeking to enhance youth mental health in the context of environmental and social challenges.

Appendix 1: Focus Group Discussion Guide

In this project, we seek to understand the emotional stresses that Vietnamese American young adults may experience and to adapt and test a group-based stress management program—Self-Help Plus (SH+)—to reduce the psychological distress among young adult Vietnamese Americans on the Gulf Coast.

This focus group will likely last about 60 minutes.

Section 1: Social, Emotional Needs of Young Adult Vietnamese Americans

1. From your experience, what are some common social and emotional issues/problems that young Vietnamese Americans in your communities experience? (explicitly about young adults and Vietnamese Americans)
2. What about specific stressors for different types of disasters?
   i. Immediate versus longer-term stressors
   ii. Do the needs vary by disaster type—natural, manmade, biological
   iii. Think about how to distinguish pre, peri, and postdisaster
   iv. Distinguish broadly the issues that young VAs have, before focusing on disaster-related

Section 2: Self-Help+ Intervention

We will now ask your opinions about a proposed program to help young adult Vietnamese Americans cope with their stress. The program is called Self-Help Plus, which was developed by the World Health Organization.

[FACILITATOR: SHOW SLIDE 1]

Self-Help Plus is a stress management audio course that is designed to be delivered in a group setting; the group can have about 20 to 30 participants. The course may feel to some like a class on guided meditation, or yoga for the mind. Participants listen to a series of audio recordings and do some exercises in the group setting, under the guidance of a facilitator. The exercises are typically on an individual basis, or being paired up briefly with another person in the group to briefly share your thoughts and experiences. The group meets weekly for about 1 1/2 to 2 hours for 5 consecutive weeks.

1. We have recorded three different potential narrators for the course. [FACILITATOR: PLAY AUDIO CLIP 1] What do you think of each one?
   a. Pacing
   b. Accent
   c. Do you find one more inspirational or more accessible than the others?

[FACILITATOR: SHOW SLIDE 2]

The five weekly sessions will discuss the following themes/skills: (1) grounding, (2) unhooking, (3) values, (4) being kind, and (5) making room. These lesson topics are based on a type of therapy called Acceptance and Commitment Therapy, which is a form of cognitive behavioral therapy, or CBT. These five skills are meant to provide practical exercises to anyone who has experienced stress so that they can manage their stress better.

There is also an illustrated self-help book called "Do what matters in times of stress." This book can be used in addition to the audio lesson, but is not required. It can also be used by itself.

2. These are brief descriptions of the five skills in SH+. What do you think about these skills?
   a. The course will go into more detail about these skills, but based on your current understanding of them, how do you think young VAs will receive them?

[FACILITATOR: SHOW SLIDE 3]

3. Here are some illustrations that will be used in SH+. Could you tell me what think about these illustrations?
   a. How well do you think they illustrate the concepts/skills?
   b. To what extent are they relevant and appealing to you?
4. Let's try one of the exercises in SH+ together. [FACILITATOR: PLAY AUDIO CLIP 2—GROUNDING EXERCISE] What is your impression of this type of exercise?
   a. How receptive do you think young VAs are with this type of exercise?
   b. How willing would they be to do this exercise during the weekly online session? How about them doing it at home on their own, like a homework, before the next session?

For our study, we are adapting the course to be delivered as an online program, and we are customizing it for young adult Vietnamese Americans, who may have experienced stress from exposure to disasters, such as hurricanes or the Deepwater Horizon oil spill, or the COVID-19 pandemic.

5. How do you think YA will receive a program such as this—will they welcome it? What needs to be done to make it more attractive or appealing to them?
6. What are your *overall impressions* of this program?
   a. To what extent will this meet the social and emotional needs of Vietnamese Americans living in areas affected by natural disasters such as hurricanes?
   b. Cultural considerations: cultural concepts of stress and resilience
      What needs to be done to allow older generations to accept and support such MH programs for YAs?
7. What do you think about the *structure of the program*? Should anything be changed to make it more acceptable, appropriate, and feasible for Vietnamese YA?
   a. Audio lessons
   b. Weekly sessions
   c. Duration
      i. What is best timing—right now we are thinking about delivering the program as a weekly 60-minute intervention over a five-week period ...
   d. Facilitators
      i. Who should be the facilitators (e.g., a distinguished community leader, a peer (fellow young VA)?
8. For this project, we are planning to implement the program with the online format. What are your thoughts on this format when it comes to the Vietnamese YA population?
   a. What are some potential challenges with this format?
9. The program includes exercises where individuals reflect on their own experiences, and they may or may not share them to the group. These exercises are conducted in the group setting, but not necessarily as group exercises.
   a. What do you think about this format?
   b. To what extent do you think young people like you would be willing to share experiences in a group setting like this focus group?
10. *LASTLY, what is the best way to market* this to the community of YAs, how to make it accessible and acceptable more broadly within the community?

References

Benoit, C., Casey, L., Jansson, M., Phillips, R., & Burns, D. (2011). Developing knowledge transfer with non-profit organizations serving vulnerable populations. In A. Marshall, B. Leadbeater, & E. M. Banister (Eds.), *Knowledge Translation in Context: Indigenous, Policy, and Community Settings* (pp. 15–34). University of Toronto Press.

Brar-Josan, N., & Yohani, S. C. (2019). Cultural brokers' role in facilitating informal and formal mental health supports for refugee youth in school and community context: a Canadian case study. *British Journal of Guidance & Counselling, 47*(4), 512–523.

Cho, Y. J., Lee, W. J., Oh, H., Lee, J. O., Kim, B.-K. E., & Jang, Y. (2021). Perceived racial discrimination and mental health in diverse groups of Asian Americans: the differing impacts by age, education, and ethnicity. *Journal of Immigrant and Minority Health, 24*, 1–7.

Choi, S., Powell, T. M., Muller, J. M., & Lux, E. A. (2022). Exploring the disproportionate impact of disasters: social service providers' perceptions of factors increasing vulnerability among hurricane survivors. *Families in Society, 103*(3), 314–327.

Covert, H. H., Sherman, M., Le, D., & Lichtveld, M. Y. (2020). Environmental health risk relationships, responsibility, and sources of information among Vietnamese Americans in coastal Mississippi. *Health, Risk & Society, 22*(5–6), 362–376.

Do, M., Diep, J., & Pham, N. K. (2023). Vietnamese Americans' experiences with Hurricane Harvey: diversities and unequal challenges with recovery. *International Journal of Disaster Response and Emergency Management (IJDREM), 6*(1), 1–14.

Do, M., McCleary, J., Nguyen, D., & Winfrey, K. (2020). Mental illness public stigma and generational differences among Vietnamese Americans. *Community Mental Health Journal, 56*, 1–15.

Do, M., Pham, N. N. K., Wallick, S., & Nastasi, B. K. (2014). Perceptions of mental illness and related stigma among Vietnamese populations: findings from a mixed method study. *Journal of Immigrant and Minority Health, 16*(6), 1294–1298.

Epping-Jordan, J. E., Harris, R., Brown, F. L., Carswell, K., Foley, C., García-Moreno, C., Kogan, C., & van Ommeren, M. (2016). Self-Help Plus (SH+): a new WHO stress management package. *World Psychiatry, 15*(3), 295.

Fietta, V., Rizzi, S., De Luca, C., Gios, L., Pavesi, M. C., Gabrielli, S., Monaro, M., & Forti, S. (2024). A chatbot-based version of the World Health Organization–validated Self-Help Plus intervention for stress management: co-design and usability testing. *JMIR Human Factors, 11*, e64614.

Fong, K. C., Heo, S., Lim, C. C., Kim, H., Chan, A., Lee, W., ... Bell, M. L. (2022). The intersection of immigrant and environmental health: a scoping review of observational population exposure and epidemiologic studies. *Environmental Health Perspectives, 130*(9), 096001.

Goldmann, E., & Galea, S. (2014). Mental health consequences of disasters. *Annual Review of Public Health, 35*(1), 169–183.

Hayes, S. C., Luoma, J. B., Bond, F. W., Masuda, A., & Lillis, J. (2006). Acceptance and commitment therapy: model, processes and outcomes. *Behaviour Research and Therapy, 44*(1), 1–25.

Health Compass. (2023). How to conduct a pretest. https://thecompassforsbc.org/how-to-guide/how-conduct-pretest

Kaji, A. (2017). *Health Needs Assessment for Vietnamese Americans in New Orleans*. Working Paper No. 2017-01. Center for Studies of Displaced Populations, Tulane University. New Orleans, LA.

Kaji, A., VanLandingham, M., Do, M., & Anglewicz, P. (2021). Trajectories of post-disaster recovery in healthcare access for a major refugee enclave: Vietnamese Americans in post-Katrina New Orleans. *Journal of Refugee Studies, 34*, 3985–4009.

Kim-Mozeleski, J. E., Tsoh, J. Y., Gildengorin, G., Cao, L. H., Ho, T., Kohli, S., ... McPhee, S. J. (2018). Preferences for depression help-seeking among Vietnamese American adults. *Community Mental Health Journal*, *54*(6), 748–756. https://link.springer.com/content/pdf/10.1007%2Fs10597-017-0199-3.pdf

Le, P. D. (2021–2026). Adaptation and pilot of a peer-facilitated Self-Help Plus stress management intervention for breast cancer patients in Viet Nam [Grant]. Vietnam. https://www.fic.nih.gov/Grants/Search/Pages/irsda-k01tw012174.aspx

Lee, G., Chang, A., Pal, A., Tran, T.-A., Cui, X., & Quach, T. (2022). Understanding and addressing the digital health literacy needs of low-income limited English proficient Asian American patients. *Health Equity*, *6*(1), 494–499.

Lee, G., Tran, T.-A., Cui, X., & Quach, T. (2023). Assessing digital literacy and willingness to communicate with providers using digital technology among underserved Asian American patients at a Federally Qualified Health Center: a cross-sectional study. *Preprint*.

Lightfoot, E. S., Lesen, A. E., & Ferreira, R. J. (2020). Gender and resilience in Gulf Coast communities: risk and protective factors following a technological disaster. *International Journal of Disaster Risk Reduction*, *50*, 101716.

Mayfield-Johnson, S., Fastring, D., Le, D., & Nguyen, J. (2020). Addressing the social vulnerability of Mississippi Gulf Coast Vietnamese community through the development of community health advisors. *Sustainability*, *12*(9), 3892.

Meekers, D., Pham, N. K., Tran, C.-T., VanLandingham, M. J., & Do, M. (2024). Rapidly developing communications materials during public health emergencies: the Âu Cơ campaign in the USA. *Health Promotion International*, *39*(1), daad198.

Nguyen, T., Cho, Y. J., & Jang, Y. (2021). Perceived discrimination, psychosocial resources, and mental distress in Vietnamese Americans. *Journal of Migration and Health*, *3*, 100039.

Nguyen, T.-N. (2019). Mental health perceptions in a Vietnamese American college student population. [Master of Arts Thesis, August 2019, University of Houston, TX].

Norris, F. H., Vanlandingham, M. J., & Vu, L. (2009). PTSD in Vietnamese Americans following Hurricane Katrina: prevalence, patterns, and predictors [Research Support, N.I.H., Extramural]. *Journal of Traumatic Stress*, *22*(2), 91–101. https://doi.org/10.1002/jts.20389

Pham, N. K., Do, M., & Diep, J. (2023). Social support and community embeddedness protect against post-disaster depression among immigrants: a Vietnamese American case study. *Frontiers in Psychiatry*, *14*, 1075678. https://pmc.ncbi.nlm.nih.gov/articles/PMC10501809/

Purgato, M., Carswell, K., Acarturk, C., Au, T., Akbai, S., Anttila, M., ... Bird, M. (2019). Effectiveness and cost-effectiveness of Self-Help Plus (SH+) for preventing mental disorders in refugees and asylum seekers in Europe and Turkey: study protocols for two randomised controlled trials. *BMJ Open*, *9*(5), e030259.

Purgato, M., Tedeschi, F., Riello, M., Zaccoletti, D., Mediavilla, R., Ayuso-Mateos, J. L., ... Rusconi, E. (2025). Effectiveness of Self-Help Plus in its digital version in reducing anxiety and post-traumatic symptomatology among nursing home workers during the COVID-19 pandemic: secondary analysis of randomised controlled trial data. *BMJ Mental Health*, *28*(1), e301379.

Quinn, A., White, A., Abbatangelo-Gray, J., McCarron, S., Schub, T., & Ratzan, S. C. (2023). COVID-19 communication campaigns for vaccination: an assessment with perspectives for future equity-centered public health efforts. *Journal of Health Communication*, *28*(sup1), 54–66. https://www.tandfonline.com/doi/pdf/10.1080/10810730.2023.2208529

Riello, M., Purgato, M., Bove, C., Tedeschi, F., MacTaggart, D., Barbui, C., & Rusconi, E. (2021). Effectiveness of Self-Help Plus (SH+) in reducing anxiety and post-traumatic symptomatology among care home workers during the COVID-19 pandemic: a randomized controlled trial. *Royal Society Open Science*, *8*(11), 210219.

Smith, M. K., Ehresmann, K. R., Knowlton, G. S., LaFrance, A. B., Benitez, G. V., Quadri, N. S., ... Stauffer, W. M. (2023). Understanding COVID-19 health disparities with birth country and language data. *American Journal of Preventive Medicine*, *65*(6), 993–1002.

Tiwari, B. B., & Zhang, D. S. (2022). Differences in mental health status among Asian Americans during the COVID-19 pandemic: findings from the Health, Ethnicity, and Pandemic Study. *Health Equity*, *6*(1), 448–453.

Tol, W. A., Leku, M. R., Lakin, D. P., Carswell, K., Augustinavicius, J., Adaku, A., ... Garcia-Moreno, C. (2020). Guided self-help to reduce psychological distress in South Sudanese female refugees in Uganda: a cluster randomised trial. *The Lancet Global Health*, *8*(2), e254–e263.

VanLandingham, M., Bui, B., Abramson, D., Friedman, S., & Cisneros, R. (2022). Health and mortality consequences of natural disasters. In *International Handbook of Population and Environment* (pp. 331–345). Springer. https://link.springer.com/chapter/10.1007/978-3-030-76433-3_16

VanLandingham, M. J., Nguyen, T., Tran, C.-T., Pham, N. K., Bui, B., & Anglewicz, P. (2023). Building bridges and mending fences: cultural conflict and cultural brokering between academic and immigrant communities. *Journal of Applied Social Science*, *17*(3), 324–337.

VanLandingham, M. J. (2017). *Weathering Katrina: Culture and Recovery Among Vietnamese Americans*. Russell Sage Foundation.

Vu, L., & VanLandingham, M. J. (2012). Physical and mental health consequences of Katrina on Vietnamese immigrants in New Orleans: a pre-and post-disaster assessment. *Journal of Immigrant and Minority Health*, *14*(3), 386–394.

Wang, D., Gee, G. C., Bahiru, E., Yang, E. H., & Hsu, J. J. (2020). Asian-Americans and Pacific Islanders in COVID-19: emerging disparities amid discrimination. *Journal of General Internal Medicine*, *35*(12), 3685–3688.

World Health Organization (WHO). (2020). *Doing What Matters in Times of Stress: An Illustrated Guide*. Geneva, Switzerland: WHO.

World Health Organization (WHO). (2021). *Self Help Plus (SH+): a group-based stress management course for adults. Generic field-trial version 1.0*. (Series on low-intensity psychological interventions, No.5. Licence: CC BY-NC-SA 3.0 IGO). Geneva, Switzerland: WHO.

13

Empathy Across Time and Space: Negotiating Hybrid Identities Through Reading and Writing About Modern Chinese Stories

Eileen J. Cheng

Department of Asian Languages and Literatures, Pomona College, Claremont, CA, USA

Issues of identity and mental health struggles may be difficult for young adults to process, let alone discuss with others. Reading, discussing, and writing in community about the stories of young protagonists grappling with similar challenges can provide a "benign entry point" (Liu & Chen, 2025, in press) for reflecting on mental health and identity issues affecting the Asian diaspora and Asian Americans. While the focus is on modern Chinese literature and the Chinese and Chinese-American experience, clinicians, educators, and policymakers might similarly consider the use of literature, popular media, history, and other nontraditional sources as a way to explore and deepen conversations about identity and mental health in general.

Storytelling is a fundamental part of being human. It is how we make sense of the people and world around us and our place in the world. What stories do we tell about others? What stories do we tell about ourselves? Can reading, thinking, and writing about the stories of others affect how we see the world and the stories we tell about ourselves?

I have been teaching courses on modern Chinese literature in translation at a private liberal arts college in Southern California now for well over two decades. The goals for the course include introducing students to Chinese history and culture through reading literature. Students acquire "objective" knowledge and learn to situate stories in the context of another space and time.

Reading stories "out of context"—relating them to the readers' own time and space—can also provide a meaningful space to discuss issues of identity and mental health that are directly relevant to the students' lives. The discussions about race, class, gender and sexuality at the height of Western imperialism in 20th century China resonate with the experiences of many of the Asian American Pacific Islander (AAPI) students. Reflecting on the stories—predominantly of youths navigating their identity and place in a world—often becomes entry points for students to share their own personal experiences. Having a space to voice one's own experiences, have them heard, validated, and responded to may be especially important for AAPIs and others who live in communities where there is little diversity. The sharing of stories and experiences often fosters feelings of empathy and community and has generative effects, prompting students to self-reflect about the stories they read and the stories they tell.

Students' inclination to connect the stories we read to their own lives and intense yearning to express themselves became glaringly apparent in the first literature course I taught in person post-Covid. The discussions for the Friday afternoon seminar, which meets for almost 3 hours, often went over time. Students organically linked and shared their own personal experiences regarding topics that arose from reading the stories and responded to each other with enthusiasm. This led me to modify the subsequent courses I taught to include more opportunities for students to engage with the stories individually and communally and in more creative and personally meaningful ways.

The class size is typically around 15 students, and the composition of the class has been diverse, from different colleges in our consortium, a wide of majors and disciplines—more students from STEM (Science, Technology, Engineering, and Mathematics) in recent years—at different stages in their college careers and with varying familiarity with the material. Throughout the years, there has been one constant: the class composition has predominantly been AAPI women, many identifying as Chinese, Chinese-American, and/or mixed-race with Chinese descent. In recent years, the class has had more international students or students who immigrated to the United States as young adults, predominantly from mainland China. Some expressed feeling dislocated and wanting to gain a deeper understanding of their culture by reading—and in some cases rereading—Chinese literature through another lens; for many, the class was a way to maintain a connection to their native culture and Chinese identity while studying abroad. Their personal identity aside, all students shared a common motivation for taking the course: to learn about and be more in touch with Chinese culture.

The course went beyond discussions about Chinese culture to the meaning of "Chineseness" and the formation of identity and culture itself. Among the questions we explored through reading, reflecting, and discussing modern Chinese stories include:

- How can a hybrid identity be reframed, not as a lack or site of marginalization and rejection, but an empowering space from which the constructed nature of identity itself is questioned?
- How can questioning one's "belonging" (or not belonging) allow one to be empathetic to others' stories of navigating multiple identities and cultural expectations?
- How can these stories provide lessons that might be relevant to readers navigating their own conflicting identities and social expectations and enable empathy for the struggles of others?

"Chineseness" as Hybridity: Between East and West, Tradition, and Modernity

> "Chinese-Americans, when you try to understand what things in you are Chinese, how do you separate what is peculiar to childhood, to poverty, insanities, one family, your mother who marked your growing with stories, from what is Chinese?"
>
> *Kingston (1989), Woman Warrior (1976)*

Maxine Hong Kingston's (1940–) imaginative memoir *Woman Warrior* (1989) draws upon Chinese mythology, stories told by her mother, and stories she invents to weave a powerful, imaginative, and complex narrative of identity formation. The confusion that comes with the search for personal identity, however, is not unique to those with hyphenated identities. The terms "Asian," "Chinese," and "American" assume fixed and stable identities which are immediately called to question by modern writers in early 20th century China, who were themselves in the process of constructing a new culture and asking the question: What does being "Chinese" mean in the modern world?

After the collapse of the Qing (1644–1911), the last imperial dynasty, and the institution of the Republic in 1912, Chinese intellectuals called for a cultural revaluation. "New Culture" or "May Fourth" intellectuals congregated around the journal Xin Qingnian/*La Jeunesse* (*New Youth)* published in 1916 and promoted the advent of a new culture. Conscious of the depictions of China as "backward" and in need of "civilizing" by Western imperial powers, the "new youths" sought to rejuvenate the nation and its citizenry by rejecting what they viewed as an oppressive Confucian tradition defined by strict hierarchies and outdated rituals. In their stead, they embraced Western ideals built on democracy, science, and individualism, among others. Many youths were inspired to redefine their culture to ensure the future of a revitalized China in the global world.

Note. Photograph of Chen Duxiu (1879–1942) and Hu Shih (1891–1962), founders of *Youth* journal, later renamed *New Youth*, Wikimedia Commons (Chen Duxiu/wikimedia Commons/Public Domain/https://en.wikipedia.org/wiki/Hu_Xiansu#/media/File:Hu_Hsen_Hsun_and_Hu_Shi.jpg/Public Domain/Last accessed on January 05, 2026).

In a culture that has venerated the elderly, the terms of "Chineseness" were, at the turn of 20th century China, being defined by youths who sought to free themselves from the shackles of what they deemed an "oppressive" tradition. Many intellectuals promoting a new culture were themselves steeped in the very traditions they sought to overthrow. How does one reject a culture or tradition that has defined one's identity and that of one's parents and ancestors? Can one simply discard it and appropriate the cultural ideals of another? What are the costs and effects of such a process?

Students enrolled in the class to learn more about China and, for some, to become closer to an "authentic" Chinese identity. The works they read in translation for the first half of the course were about the experience of Chinese youths who were rejecting Chinese traditions and defining "Chineseness" by appropriating Western ideals and ideas. The quest to learn more about "China" and for some, to become closer to one's heritage by taking a course on modern Chinese literature took a circuitous turn, inspiring questions about authenticity, hybridity, and how culture and identity are formed and understood to begin with.

The Limits of Subjectivity and the Power of Representation

The course incorporates a wide range of Western historical and theoretical texts and Chinese fictional works and media translated into English. We begin with an introduction to the history of China from the conditions that led to the first Opium War in 1840. A central topic is the effects of what Edward Said has termed "orientalism" (1978) and "cultural imperialism" (1994) as it relates to China at this time. Western Orientalist narratives of "Chineseness"—including stereotypes of exotic, submissive women and effeminate, impotent Chinese men—were widely disseminated globally and introduced to China. Those stereotypes had highly detrimental psychological effects on the Chinese who internalized them and continue to impact public perceptions of Asians and Asian Americans in the United States today. Many students expressed astonishment and anger at the overtly racist and sexist stereotypes. More so, many felt appalled by the prevalence of these stock depictions and how they continue to be perpetuated in more subtle ways in contemporary cultural imaginations.

Major themes of the course include the limits of subjectivity and the power of representations. Questions we ask early on include: Who gets to represent, who and what gets represented, how are they represented and why? Representations are not pure objective reflections of the "real." They can be subjective, interpretive, creative, with agendas that are sometimes stated but also latent, concealed, contradictory, etc. and some or all of the above at once. Representations themselves, for good or for ill, have the capacity to affect perceptions and the experience of reality itself. In that same vein, we interrogate the production of knowledge about Asia in more contemporary times and what it means to be taking a course about modern Chinese literature in translation in an American academy curated by a particular instructor. We read critically, beneath the surface, and in between the lines, to understand that representation, like interpretation, is always already mediated, and to unravel the terms and effects of that mediation.

Reading Beyond Dualities: Self-dissection as Self-discovery

> "It is true that I often dissect others, but I dissect myself even more mercilessly."
>
> *Lu Xun (2017), "Afterword to Graves" (1926)*

The very fraught predicament of being caught between two cultures and conflicting expectations is a common theme of the stories we read. In the search for individuality and an identity apart from the dictates of family and tradition, modern Chinese writers experimented with autobiographical fiction and the fictional diary form. First-person narratives allow for the articulation of a distinct personal voice and give readers a glimpse into the inner world of the young protagonists. In contrast to the protagonists' projection of a coherent identity, their thoughts are often confused, contradictory, and marked by self-doubt, raising thorny questions about personal identity: who is this "I"? How does one begin to separate and excavate the "I" from prescribed and proscribed roles delineated by one's family, culture, tradition, and education?

The notion that this "I" is always already indelibly inscribed by one's family, tradition, culture, and education is well delineated in Lu Xun's (1881–1936) "Diary of a Madman (1985a)," published in 1918 and now widely credited as the first modern Chinese short story written in the vernacular. A formal preface declares the diary that follows it as a medical case study of an insane man suffering from "persecution complex." In keeping with the narrative of "madness," the diary contains seemingly random and confused musings about animals, history, and cannibalism interspersed with the diarist's careful observations of his society and critical reading of historical texts. Reading the Confucian Classics intently, he sees two words emerge in between the lines: "Eat people." This leads to the diarist's first revelation: the four thousand years of Chinese civilization he has inherited is cannibalistic and its practices are threatening to put its very culture and people into extinction.

Through a process of retrospection and observation, the diary writer arrives at another revelation: that his brother and the villagers are all cannibals, in the process of "fattening him up" to consume more of his flesh. Further retrospection and introspection lead him to an epiphany: that he, himself, may have unwittingly eaten the flesh of his younger sister. Space and time collapse, as the dichotomies of cannibal and the cannibalized, the victimizer and the victim, the observer and the observed disintegrate in this moment of revelation: "I, myself, am cannibal."

In line with the New Culture's rejection of traditional culture, "Diary of a Madman" is commonly read as a searing indictment of Confucian culture. The story itself, however, is also a lesson in reading critically. "Diary of a Madman" is marked by ambiguity and resists any one simple interpretation. Two different narrators offering competing narratives—the preface writer claims the diary is a "medical case study" of its insane subject while the diary writer proclaims that his culture and society are made up of cannibals about to consume him. Two different linguistic registers coexist in the piece—the preface is written in classical Chinese and the diary entries are in the vernacular. It is not fully clear if the madman is possibly insane or one of the few that are truly awakened. The diary entries are also filled with double entendres and ambiguous imagery—notably, the moon as a symbol of enlightenment and lunacy. The reality of the world of the text is interpretative, caught between dualities that no longer hold.

Lu Xun's "Diary of a Madman," then, can also be read as a performative lesson in reading and storytelling. The diarist himself is a critical reader, reading in and out of context, reading not just the lines, but also in between them. As a critical reader, he examines how texts are framed, decodes their ostensible and hidden messages, and finds how the insights derived are applicable to his own time and space. The diarist reads, reflects, and writes to navigate his own place in the world. He discovers that this "I" is not an autonomous identity, but a relational one, and that his self-understanding is partial, fractured, and incomplete.

This revelation shatters the diarist's sense of self as an autonomous agent as he is forced to confront his limited understanding of himself and the world. That moment when one's prior understanding of oneself and the world suddenly becomes unintelligible can lead to disorientation, confusion, and a complete breakdown, akin to an episode of insanity.

Yet, this moment of rupture also brings clarity, as one's ties to prevailing norms and the world as we have been taught to see it are severed. That suspension of belief, the dissolution of binaries that order one's world, when one become fully "unhinged" from society itself, enables a new way of seeing and being in the world that can lead one to recognize the precarity of our shared human condition.

"Diary of a Madman," then, can also be read as a performative re-enactment of identity formation and self-understanding. The diarist's revelation leads us to consider how we are all implicated in our cultures in ways that we may not know and may not be able to extricate ourselves from. As the diarist comes to understand the limits of his own perspective and subjectivity, we too confront our own limits as readers of the text and as individuals in our own journey to understand ourselves and our place in the world.

Identity Formation: Conflict, Contradiction, Reconciliation

> A reader who really understood would know the diary revealed only
> a fraction of me and could then help me see my limitations and misery.
> How could I hope for understanding from a reader, when all I give him
> is a diary carefully crafted to convey meaning solely through writing?
>
> *Ding Ling (1995), "Miss Sophia's Diary" (1927)*

For Lu Xun and other writers, the fictionalized confessional form was conducive to exploring questions of personal and cultural identity and the conditions for their formation. "The Diary of a Madman" provides an entryway into talking and thinking about our own identities and the role that critical self-reflection and self-writing can play in the evolution of one's identity as a reader, writer, and individual. At the same time, many of the modern Chinese writers were aware of the therapeutic impact of writing and experimented with Western psychoanalytic theories in their stories. Fictional diaries provided a mediated space for discussing an array of topics that would ordinarily be considered too personal, sensitive, shameful, and/or taboo.

The stories' protagonists are mostly young adults from different backgrounds and diverse life experiences. Self-writing is used in a variety of ways, including but not limited to: recording memories, self-reflection, self-denial, self-discovery, as a therapeutic outlet, etc. The experiences of the characters, however diverse, reveal the contradictions and challenges of navigating identities when caught between two or more cultures, traditions, and value systems. Also revealed is the fraught process of identity formation as protagonists come to terms (or not) with themselves and their place in society. Some examples of stories and topics we discussed in the first half of the course:

- Lu Xun's "Diary of a Madman" (1918/1985a): deals with the effects of social ostracism and discrimination; scapegoating; mental illness; modern psychiatry as a form of discipline and punish.
- Lu Xun's "Regret for the Past: Juansheng's notes" (1925/1985b): a young man's account about his elopement and failed relationship, ultimately leading to the death of the female protagonist. Intergenerational conflict, gender discrimination, cognitive dissonance, defense mechanisms, narcissism, and projection.
- Yu Dafu's "Sinking" (1921/1996): confessional narrative of a student who studies abroad in Japan dealing with racism and repressed sexual desires. Racial discrimination, loneliness

and isolation; stereotypes of the "effeminate Chinese man," sexual repression and addiction, obsessive compulsive behavior, misogyny, self-hatred, and suicide.
- Ding Ling's "Ms. Sophia's Diary" (1927/1995): a young woman's frank account of emotional yearning and sexual desire while navigating illness and life away from her family and hometown. Illness and disability; loneliness and isolation; sexual obsession; same sex-desires; male gaze; self-objectification; cognitive dissonance; self-hatred.
- Xiao Hong's "Hands" (1936/1995): a young adolescent's account of discrimination she witnesses in the modern girls' school. Rural and urban divide; class prejudice; peer pressure; schools as reproduction of elite privilege and racial, gender, and class biases; the cost of academic success

Intergenerational conflict, the contradictions between self and society, racial and gender discrimination, feelings of shame, rejection, self-hate, experiences of exclusion and ostracism and a host of other issues brought up in the stories resonate with many that AAPI youth face today. More often than not, the stories became entry points for thinking about and discussing otherwise difficult topics in an organic manner, as students shared their own personal experiences in their weekly reflection posts, in class discussion, and/or in their final projects.

Reading Between Disciplines and Beyond the Text

The literature courses I teach are writing intensive. Partly in response to student interest and the advent of AI, I have accentuated some of the more "human," personal, and communal components of the course. The seating is arranged so that students are facing one another. I give short lectures at the start of class. Students take turns doing oral presentations introducing the main themes of the week. Prior to presenting, the students, individually or in pairs, meet me outside of class to talk about the readings ahead of time. The rest of the class is conducted discussion style, often with small group work first, followed by whole class discussion.

I assign writing assignments of different lengths and styles. Students write short weekly reflections on one or more of the readings. I provide some questions for guidance, but students are encouraged to freely engage with the pieces and write on any aspect of the texts that they find personally meaningful, be it a quote, a character, or a theme. Students post and read each other's reflections before class, and are asked to respond with short comments to two reflections that resonate with them.

For the first paper, students turn in either a literary analysis of one or more of our readings or submit a creative piece, such as writing one of diaries from another character's point of view or writing an alternative ending. The end of the semester course reflection project is designed to be more creative and open-ended and written in a personal style. The requirement is that the project engages with at least two themes or works we discussed throughout the semester and how they resonated with the student personally. (Final project description and one student's final project appended.)

The students enjoyed reading, writing, and responding to the weekly personal reflections. By the time the class met, the students already have the opportunity to synthesize a variety of perspectives. Many expressed that their understanding of the texts were vastly expanded after reading other students' reflections. The most engaging and generative discussions were often prompted by readings which elicited polarized views—and more often than not were related to issues that came closest to the students' own experiences.

In a course I taught recently, one of the most animated discussions revolved around the memoir *Bound Feet and Western Dress* (1996), written in English by the Asian American author Pang-Mei Natasha Chang. The book might strike some as an odd choice for a class on modern Chinese literature. Nonetheless, the inclusion of this piece of self-writing provided a unique opportunity to discuss disciplinary boundaries, knowledge production, the gap between Asian American Studies and Asian Studies, how biases can be reproduced by disciplines and the possibilities for bridging them through interdisciplinarity. Going beyond disciplinary boundaries enables students to think about institutionalized knowledge production itself as something that is mediated which in turn informs notions of culture and personal identity.

Given that the course theme was gender and sexuality, the memoir about a mostly forgotten woman filled a gap and brought up questions about the field of "modern Chinese literature" as a whole. Whose stories are written and by whom? Whose voices are heard and submerged? The responses highlighted the overtly elite male voices that defined the "new culture" of that time. Our understanding of literature and history itself is constantly being revised as more voices come to be heard in and through translation and representation, sometimes through unexpected channels.

Bound Feet and Western Dress contains two intertwining first-person narratives that cross space and time. One is the recreation of the voice of Zhang Yu-i (1900–1989), a Chinese woman born in the early 20th century who reflects upon her path navigating conflicting worlds of East and West and tradition and modernity at a time of cultural transformation. She is also the ex-wife Xu Zhimo (1897–1931), arguably China's most famous modern poet. Xu Zhimo studied at Columbia University and Cambridge and is, to this day, associated with the values of individualism and free love. The story of Zhang Yu-i, whom Xu married and divorced, became a footnote buried in the lore of "China's Shelley."

Bound Feet and Western Dress recounts Zhang Yu-i's childhood, marriage, divorce, and later life as she becomes a successful banker, business woman, wife, and mother who ends up immigrating to and living a quiet life in New York. This narrative is told in the first person, as imagined and recreated by the author, based on personal research, observations, and conversations with Zhang Yu-i, who happens to be the author's great-aunt. The second narrative is about the author Natasha herself. Natasha recounts her experience growing up in the suburbs of Connecticut grappling with her hybrid identity as a Chinese-American. As a child, she wanted to assimilate to American culture and felt ashamed of her Chinese identity, even as aspects of it defined her childhood in meaningful ways. As a college student, she majored in East Asian Studies to learn more about China. What she studied didn't resonate with her, and she found herself judged for not being "Chinese" enough by both Chinese and non-Chinese alike.

The intergenerational narratives are interspersed, told in a way that parallel, intersect, and at times blend into one another. By the end of the novel, concluding with the death of Zhang Yu-i and the author's reflection of how her great aunt's choices as a woman caught between two cultures inspired her own, the author comes to embrace her own hybrid identity, not as a source of shame or conflict but one of pride and acceptance.

Bound Feet and Western Dress, written by a then unknown Asian American student hoping to connect with her "roots," was subsequently translated into Chinese in the same year it was published. Zhang Yu-i, once a mere footnote to her famous ex-husband, was reintroduced to Chinese-reading communities as a veritable subject in her own right through the memoir written in English by her great niece. Of the first-person narratives we read, *Bound Feet and Western Dress* generated the most extreme reactions—from students who loved it to some who were infuriated by it. On the one hand, some students from mainland China expressed being bothered by the stereotypical title and disliked the portrayal of Zhang Yu-i as a self-sacrificing model of womanhood. Some students expressed concern that the book was reinscribing stereotypical images of the oppressed Chinese woman to be consumed by a Western audience. On the other hand, some students, Asian-American and non-Asian, identified with the feelings of shame, rejection, and unbelonging that the author felt growing up as a minority in a predominantly White neighborhood. Some found the entwined and parallel narrative that gave voice to Yu-i and Natasha in their search for identity inspiring and moving. Almost all students were surprised to read and hear about the polarized reactions to the book.

Our discussion on Wei Hui's fictionalized biography *Shanghai Baby* (2002) also elicited strong reactions. Set in the 1990's, the novel chronicles a young woman's exploration of her sexuality and search for identity while navigating a society with conflicting expectations for women. Set in Shanghai, it is filled with references to Western popular and material culture. Some students noted that characters, settings, and experiences were ones they could readily identify and connect with. Some found the frank portrayal of female sexuality liberating and the plot relatable and interesting. On the other extreme, some students disliked the novel and the protagonist intensely. Some took particular issue with the author's self-promotion and overt celebration of materialism, consumerism, and Western culture. To some, the love triangle—of a woman caught between her impotent Chinese boyfriend and her virile German lover—reinforced troubling racist and sexist stereotypes tracing back to the late 19th century.

These polarized discussions prompted students to reflect on the reasons for their own reactions and that of others, recalling a conversation we had on the first day of class on "why we read." I found it surprising that the question did not, at first, generate much discussion. The most frequent answer given was "to get information." A larger variety of responses was generated when students were given time to come up with as many responses as they could in small group discussions. Among them: for pleasure, adventure and escape, as means of solace, to feel less alone, alleviate boredom, for emotional connection, to learn more about the world and others, etc.

I offered a thought about reading as community that first day: Reading a story is a way that individuals from diverse backgrounds and life experiences can come together to experience a common world. Reading and hearing so many diverse thoughts and reflections in written responses and class discussions made this point evident to students. Particularly with the polarizing reactions to *Bound Feet and Western Dress* and *Shanghai Baby*, it became apparent that the responses had less to do with the text themselves and more to do with each reader's personal experiences that led them to engage with the world of the text uniquely.

Reading in Community, Reading as Community

> The making of Asian American culture includes practices that are partly inherited, partly modified as well as partly invented.
>
> *Lisa Lowe (2000), "Heterogeneity, Hybridity, Multiplicity: Marking Asian American Differences"*

Questions about cultural and personal identity that the modern Chinese intellectuals were navigating a century ago continue to resonate with AAPI students today. The complex and fraught process of negotiating multiple identities and contradictory expectations experienced by the protagonists in the stories—most of whom were young adults of a similar age—led students to reflect upon the nature of identity formation itself and for some, a rethinking of their own identity.

Students enrolled in the class to learn more about and maintain ties to an "authentic" China found their preconceptions of "Chineseness" dispelled as their reading of modern Chinese stories took an unexpected turn. Some AAPI students were struck by an irony: modern Chinese intellectuals were trying to define their identity by rejecting traditional Chinese culture and embracing Western culture, a process that some Chinese-American students who grew up in predominantly White communities were all too familiar with. And now as some students were trying to define their own identity by "going back to their roots," they were reading about youths who attempted to shape a new generation by shedding their ties to traditional Chinese culture. Similarly, some students who identified as Chinese also came to question the meaning of "Chineseness" and to rethink the meaning of identity itself.

Reading modern Chinese stories together for our class took on a new meaning beyond the time and space of texts, as they touched on issues much closer to home and to the heart of self-identity itself. At the end of the course, students of diverse backgrounds came to a similar conclusion: Like "Asian-American," "Asian," "American," "Chinese" and other racial and ethnic identifications are not static and encompass a wide and diverse range of unique individual experiences which, as Lisa Lowe writes, "includes practices that are partly inherited, partly modified as well as partly invented." Sharing personal reflections in writing and discussion also fostered empathy and a sense of community.

At the end of the semester, a Chinese-American student expressed particular appreciation for the reflections of the international students, which differed so much from their own. A Chinese student commented that the discussions enabled them to better understand the experience of their Asian American classmates. Another Chinese student expressed that some discussions left them frustrated as they recognized that others would not understand the significance that a particular text held for them. That same student noted that through reading and hearing others' reflections, they also came to realize that while everyone's paths diverged, they are all on parallel journeys, each reconciling their past with their future destinations. A non-Asian student, who was initially nervous about fitting in a course consisting predominantly of Asian and AAPI students, expressed appreciation for the diversity of opinions and experiences they were exposed to and the strong sense of community the course fostered. Many students commented that they felt the course made them more empathetic. While reading and writing individually about their unique reflections about the common world of the texts and sharing them communally, students also felt in community.

In Table 13.1, sample activities are provided based on short stories on p. 7 and 2 novels, *Bound Feet and Western Dress* and *Shanghai Baby*. They provide a good starting point for potential assignments and discussion prompts. Although used in a college classroom setting, they can be adapted for a high school class, young adult book club, and/or self-study as part of individual therapy. Sample questions are provided below as potential reflection or discussion prompts.

Table 13.1 Sample class activities.

Debates	Have students discuss a question related to the readings in small group and divide the class in two for a debate. Sample questions: Does the protagonist deserve our sympathy? Why or why not Pros and cons of arranged marriages vs. modern marriage Pros and cons of nuclear family vs. living together with extended family Pros and cons of living in the rural village vs. the modern city
Group work	Work in small groups and representative from each group sharing with the class. Sample activities: Write on the board as many reasons as you can come up with for why you read/why writers write Discuss whether you like or don't like the ending of the story and why. Come up with an alternate ending and share with the class Come up with a list of 10 pieces of advice you would give to the protagonists that might have helped them better navigate the challenges they faced Draw an image of the setting of the story and introduce us to the most salient aspects of this hometown/community Pretend you are characters in the story and come up with reasons for why we should join your community
Small group general discussion questions	What was your life like when you were the same age of the protagonist? What were the challenges you encountered? How do they compare to the challenges faced by the protagonists? How do you feel about the way the protagonist handled the challenges they faced? What did they do well and not? What advice would you give them? How would you have handled the challenges the protagonist of the story is going through?
Written assignments	**Weekly reading response**: (2 paragraphs, about 250–300 words): Submit weekly reading reflections on class discussion board by 8 pm the night before class. Please make time to read all reflections and provide a short response to two student reflections (several sentences will do) before class. Sample prompts are given for each story, but students are free to write about any aspect of the text that resonates with them personally.
Final course reflection	This open-ended assignment (4–5 pages double spaced) is designed for you to reflect on the course both intellectually and personally. Please look back at the syllabus and your notes as you craft your response. Do not answer the questions below point by point, rather, use the questions that are most relevant to help you shape your essay into a coherent personal narrative. Feel free to mix and match any of the questions and/ or come up with your own. You can add a title, incorporate images, poems, or write creatively as it suits you. Please include at least two themes/ issues/ works that had an impact on you intellectually and personally in your response. You may incorporate and analyze particular quotes, characters, and scenes that resonated with you. You are welcome to choose a creative assignment inspired by the course, but please speak with me first. (Past projects include: a photo essay about one's family history; reflections with the incorporation of poems inspired by some of the themes discussed.)

(*Continued*)

Table 13.1 (Continued)

	What were your expectations when you took this course? Did this course deviate from your expectations or surprise you in any way? What questions, themes, or ideas of the course had the most impact on you/did you find intellectually and personally meaningful and why? For example, did the course give you new insights to the world around you? Give you insights into human nature, culture, or psychology? Enhance or change your own thinking about your own culture, family, relationships, or identity?
	Did the course contribute to your personal development and if so how? Did you develop any new ways of thinking, interests, skills, habits, as a result? Is there anything you learned that you feel will be helpful to you for the future in terms of your academic or personal goals? Did it contribute to your worldview, personal well-being, self-understanding, etc.?

Conclusions

Issues of identity and mental health struggles may be difficult for young adults to process, let alone discuss with others. Reading, discussing, and writing in community about the stories of young protagonists grappling with similar challenges can provide a space of solace and potentially encourage reflections that enhance one's understanding of, and empathy for, the self and other. Projects that encourage self-writing and creative self-expression in conjunction with reading and writing about stories of others can also have therapeutic effects as readers become active agents reflecting and writing about their own lives in ways they might not have otherwise (See Figure 13.1).

May 9, 2025

Between Worlds: Fragments of an Asian-American Life

Zoe Adams

Growing up, I lived across three cities in China and then crossed the ocean to start again in the U.S. I was adopted, raised in Mandarin-speaking communities, and spent my childhood switching between homes, languages, and expectations. My life was a constant negotiation between cultures, balancing the traditions of my Chinese heritage with the realities of my new life in America. But over time, the language faded, and with it, parts of my connection to the place and people that once defined me.

Reading stories like *Bound Feet and Western Dress*, I recognized the feeling of duality, the sensation of wanting to belong in both places but never fully being accepted by either. It's a liminal space where you are both inside and outside of each world, a space that can be both painful and liberating. Through the lens of language, customs, and identity, I began to see that the process of translation wasn't just about words; it was about navigating and reinterpreting my place in the world.

This photo essay captures the fragments of a life lived in translation, focusing on the in-between moments that reflect my journey from the identity I inherited to the one I grew into. It's a journey marked by loss and adaptation, by the things that were left behind and the new things I embraced along the way. Yet, in all of this, I found that identity is not a fixed thing, but something that evolves with time, shaped by both where we come from and where we choose to go.

As you explore this collection, I hope you see not just the story of a girl caught between two cultures, but the resilience of someone who, through the tension of these contrasts, learned how to hold both worlds in her heart.

I don't remember the orphanage, but I know it's where my story started. It's where my Chinese name, *Lei Jin Jie*, came from, a name that carried the sound of home long before I knew what home meant. The name Lei Jin Jie is more than just a label; it's a connection to my Chinese heritage and a constant reminder of my roots. As someone who is Chinese, this name carries a profound sense of identity, grounding me in a history and culture that span far beyond my own experiences. It is through this name that I feel connected to a part of me that I might never have known otherwise, the traditions, the values, and the deep sense of belonging to a place and people that shaped who I am today. Even in the face of not remembering the orphanage or the life before my adoption, my name holds the weight of my heritage, linking me to a past I never experienced but will always carry within me.

Figure 13.1 "Adams, Z. (2025). Between Worlds: Fragments of an Asian-American Life" submitted for a seminar on gender and sexuality in modern Chinese literature and culture taught at Pomona College.

(Continued)

Me, my sister, and our Ayi.

Looking back, Beijing was where I felt most in touch with my cultural roots. I was surrounded by a language I could speak without thinking, and an environment that felt instinctively familiar. My world was warm and familiar: I had an Ayi who cared for me, neighbors who knew me, and friends who played with me until the sun went down. I built a community there, one rooted in language, routine, and a deep sense of belonging. Mandarin flowed through everything we did. It filled every game, every snack shared after school, every shout across the courtyard. We celebrated Chinese traditions together, from lighting firecrackers during Lunar New Year to eating mooncakes in the fall. I didn't think about being Chinese. I simply was.

Harrow school days with friends.

That sense of certainty began to shift when I moved to Shenzhen and later enrolled in a British international school in Hong Kong. Suddenly, the cultural instincts I once took for granted were placed in contrast with new ones I was expected to understand. Lisa Lowe, a professor of American Studies at Yale University, shares an example of a story in which two Chinese American women of the same generation refrain from talking about their identities, each fearing that the other might perceive them as insufficiently "Chinese." In the end, they ease their feelings of not being "Chinese" enough by discovering a sense of belonging through each other's experiences within their communities. I saw a similar dynamic unfold during my time at school in Hong Kong, where I connected with other bilingual students, who, like me, were living in China but being educated through a British curriculum. Surrounded by classmates from diverse backgrounds, I formed friendships built on our shared experience of studying in a culture that differs from the one we were raised in.

When I was nine, I moved to Woodside, California, a place that felt entirely unfamiliar. The school felt unfamiliar, and I didn't know how to fit in. I stopped speaking Chinese, not because I wanted to forget, but because there was no space for it. The other kids already knew each other, shared inside jokes, and understood customs I hadn't yet learned. I had to start from scratch, learning not just their names, but how they talked, what they cared about, how they played. Everything felt foreign, including the simplest parts of daily life.

As a child, Notasha Chang in *Bound Feet and Western Dress*, grapples with W.E.B. Du Bois' concept of double consciousness, particularly as she navigates life in a primarily white neighborhood. At home with her amah Xu Ma and her parents, she feels a sense of pride in her Chinese identity. However, this confidence begins to diminish at her mostly white school, where she starts to wish she were not Chinese. One early example of this internal conflict arises when she proudly wears clothing sewn by Xu Ma, only to be mocked by classmates who say her pants look "too Chinese." When her handmade pants are mocked for looking "too Chinese," she decides to keep her culture hidden at school, performing her identity differently depending on her surroundings.

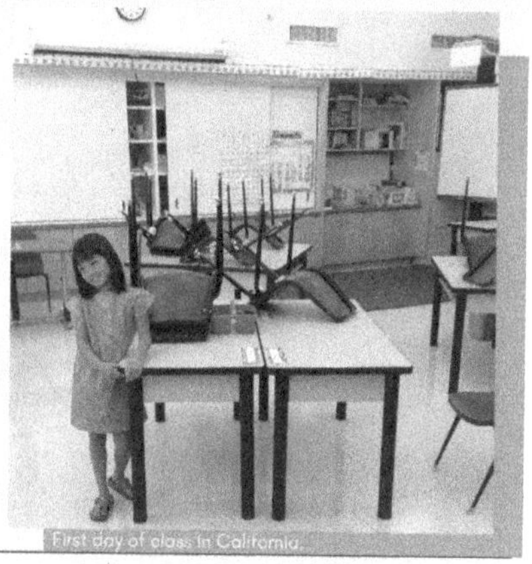
First day of class in California.

1 1. W. E. B. Du Bois, *The Souls of Black Folk* (Chicago: University of Chicago Press, 1903), 10.

Figure 13.1 (Continued)

I remember experiencing a similar sense of displacement, particularly through food. In elementary school, we were required to bring our own lunches, which was very different from my experience attending school in China. My dad often packed traditional Chinese dishes such as dumplings, noodles, or fried rice. While I loved these meals at home, I felt hesitant to eat them in front of my peers. Surrounded by classmates with sandwiches, wraps, or pizza, I became self-conscious about how different my lunches looked. Although I often felt like an outsider in those moments, my appreciation for these foods never faded. I frequently asked my parents to make them, and I cherished the times we shared them together as a family or when we ate at Chinese restaurants.

May Day magic, my first American tradition at school

A snapshot of home.

Even as I struggled to find where I belonged at school, home was different. If the classroom made me feel like I had to choose between cultures, our kitchen reminded me I didn't have to. In *Bound Feet and Western Dress*, several moments in Pang-Mei/Natasha's relationship with Yu-I reminded me of my childhood, especially the way their bond formed early on: "As we cooked, she talked to me, half in English, half in Chinese… When Yu-I spoke to me, there was never any recrimination in her voice that I was too American or could not possibly understand the China about which she spoke" (Chang 4). This experience reflects the quiet comfort of being accepted across cultural lines and seen as whole, even when straddling two worlds. For Pang-Mei/Natasha, Yu-I doesn't criticize or question her American upbringing or her distance from Chinese traditions. Instead, she welcomes her into the conversation, blending languages, bridging generations, and honoring connection over perfection.

When I reached 7th grade, I re-enrolled in Chinese. In class, instead of building on what I already knew, I had to relearn what had once come naturally. Mandarin became a subject, something to study, not something that was part of me. I found myself memorizing vocabulary I had once spoken without thinking.

That's how I felt at home. My dad spoke to me in both English and Chinese, often switching between the two without thinking. I always understood him, and that's the part of why my understanding of Chinese stayed, even as I stopped speaking it as much. When I was home, hearing Chinese didn't feel foreign or forced. It felt natural, familiar. It made home feel like a place where both parts of me could exist at once.

Reading Pang-Mei/Natasha's memory in *Bound Feet and Western Dress*, of her white friends reacting with surprise that her parents "don't seem Chinese" or "don't have an accent" (Chang 17) resonated with me deeply. What seemed like a compliment back then now reveals how much effort goes into adapting and reshaping oneself to be accepted. Her experience reminded me of my own complicated relationship with language. As someone who grew up speaking Mandarin but gradually lost fluency, I have felt that shift in my own voice. Now, when I try to speak Chinese, my accent sounds off, hesitant, unauthentic, like a foreigner fumbling through the words. It no longer feels natural on my tongue; that loss carries a quiet shame. I am embarrassed sometimes to speak it in front of others, especially native speakers, afraid they will hear how far I have drifted from something that once felt like an integral part of who I am.

2. Pang-Mei Natasha Chang, *Bound Feet & Western Dress: A Memoir* (New York: Anchor Books, 1999).

Figure 13.1 (Continued)

Before choosing to attend a boarding high school, I was searching for something I had not yet found yet, diversity. My middle school lacked this. It was a space where I was often the only Asian student in the room, and that difference, both visible and unspoken, began to shape how I saw myself. I wanted to be around people who looked like me, who shared aspects of my culture or at least understood what it meant to live between identities. I believed a more diverse environment would bring clarity, but what I discovered instead was a deeper understanding of who I was.

It was not about the cultural differences but also about navigating the complexities of identity. Attending a high school boarding school significantly shifted my sense of identity. It became clear that I was not fully Chinese, as I struggled to connect with and communicate with students from China. Their experiences, cultural references, and even the way they expressed themselves felt distant from mine. At the same time, I did not fully fit in with the American students either, as their world seemed unfamiliar, shaped by norms and values I had not grown up with. I often found myself caught in the middle, trying to understand my place in a space where I did not quite fit into either group. Yet, despite these differences, I recognized that I belonged to both worlds in my own way, existing somewhere between them, neither fully one nor the other.

Us residential prefects from all over the world, brought together in one dorm.

Similar to Natasha Chang, whose understanding of her identity was influenced by her peers, parents, and Amah, I also began to recognize that my own sense of self was shaped by a blend of cultural influences. Each of these influences taught her various aspects of what it meant to be Chinese American. Likewise, I came to understand that my identity could not be confined to a single label; instead, it was defined by my ability to navigate between cultures, with each one contributing to and enriching the other.

Creating this photo essay taught me to see identity not as a static label, but as something continually shaped by place, people, and memory. As I selected and reflected on each image, I began understanding how deeply my daily life involves navigating between cultures, languages, and expectations. Growing up Chinese, attending a British international school, and living in Hong Kong have often complicated my sense of self. Still, through this process, I have come to see that complexity is a source of richness, not confusion. The in-betweenness I once saw as disorienting now feels like a space of possibility. These moments between worlds, never entirely inside one, yet never fully outside either, have helped me realize that identity is not something to be solved but explored, layered, and lived.

This evolving sense echoes the ideas of professors like Lisa Lowe, who frames Asian American identity as inherently fluid and relational. Lowe's exploration of Asian American identity emphasizes its fluidity, presenting this always-changing nature as both liberating and uniting. By introducing the concept of the horizontal method, Lowe argues that the Asian American experience is not simply passed down through generations. Instead, it is continuously shaped through peer interactions and engagement with various communities. This framework challenges the idea of a singular, uniform Asian American identity, advocating instead for recognizing its complexity and diversity. Lowe encourages using this dynamic nature of identity as a tool for challenging and transforming existing power structures. Like many characters we met this semester, I am still figuring out how to exist entirely, not in pieces, but in layers. Maybe there isn't a clean resolution. Maybe the beauty is in the blend.

3. Lisa Lowe, "Heterogeneity, Hybridity, Multiplicity: Marking Asian American Differences," Diaspora: A Journal of Transnational Studies 1, no. 1 (1991): 24–44.

Figure 13.1 (Continued)

References

Adams, Z. (2025). *Between Worlds: Fragments of an Asian-*[Unpublished manuscript]. Pomona College.

Chang, P.-M. N. (1996). *Bound Feet and Western Dress*. Doubleday.

Ding, L. (1995). Miss Sophia's diary (T. Barlow, Trans.). In T. Barlow (Ed.), *I Myself Am A Woman: Selected Writings of Ding Ling* (pp. 50–81). Beacon Press.

Kingston, M. H. (1989). *The Woman Warrior: Memoirs of a Girlhood Among Ghosts*. Vintage International.

Liu, N. H., & Chen, S. (2025, in press). Expanding psychotherapeutic intervention frameworks for Asian American & Pacific Islander mental health: qualitative synthesis of multidisciplinary perspectives. *Clinical Psychological Science*.

Lowe, L. (2000). Heterogeneity, hybridity, multiplicity: marking Asian American differences. In J. Wu & M. Song (Eds.), *Asian American Studies: A Reader* (pp. 423–431). Rutgers University Press.

Lu, X. (1985a). Diary of a madman (Y. Hsien-yi & G. Yang, Trans.). In *Lu Xun: Selected Works* (Vol. 1) (pp. 39–51). Foreign Languages Press.

Lu, X. (1985b). Regret for the past (Y. Hsien-yi & G. Yang, Trans.). In *Lu Xun: Selected Works* (Vol. 2) (pp. 249–271). Foreign Languages Press.

Lu, X. (2017). Afterword to graves (T. Huters, Trans.). In E. J. Cheng & K. A. Denton (Eds.), *Jottings Under Lamplight* (pp. 30–36). Harvard University Press.

Said, E. W. (1978). *Orientalism*. Pantheon Books.

Said, E. W. (1994). *Culture and Imperialism*. Vintage Books.

Wei, H. (2002). *Shanghai Baby* (B. Humes, Trans.). Washington Square Press.

Xiao, H. (1995). Hands (H. Goldblatt, Trans.) In *Columbia Anthology of Modern Chinese Literature* (pp. 174–187). Columbia University Press.

Yu, D. (1995). Sinking (J. S. M. Lau & C. T. Hsia, Trans.). In J. S. M. Lau & H. Goldblatt (Eds.), *The Columbia Anthology of Modern Chinese Literature* (pp. 125–141). Columbia University Press.

Index

Note: Page numbers in *italics* and **bold** refers to figures and tables respectively.